Azure
FinOps Essentials

Cost management and optimization strategies

Parag Bhardwaj

Arun Kumar Samayam

bpb

www.bpbonline.com

First Edition 2025

To View Complete
BPB Publications Catalogue
Scan the QR Code:

Dedicated to

The entire technology community for advancing the cloud technology and financial operations for inspiring us to write this book.

Foreword

The co-authors, Arun Kumar Samayam and Parag Bhardwaj, have provided comprehensive, soup-to-nuts coverage of topics related to Microsoft Azure, with a particular focus on the FinOps framework.

I have had the privilege of knowing both the technical reviewers, Y V Ravi Kumar and Velu Natarajan, for many years as highly regarded technical speakers and mentors in the field of multi-cloud technologies.

As cloud computing continues to transform how organizations operate, manage, and scale their infrastructures, it has become clear that managing cloud costs is not merely a technical challenge—it is a fundamental business imperative. Companies worldwide are embracing cloud platforms like Microsoft Azure for their potential to unlock unprecedented flexibility and scalability. However, alongside this potential comes a new complexity: keeping cloud costs under control while ensuring that cloud investments align with business objectives.

The discipline of FinOps, or Cloud Financial Operations, has emerged as the critical bridge between technology and finance, uniting IT, engineering, finance, and business teams under a common goal—optimizing cloud costs without sacrificing performance or innovation. Azure FinOps is more than just a framework for tracking expenses; it is a methodology that emphasizes real-time visibility, collaboration, and strategic decision-making to maximize the value derived from cloud investments.

I am delighted to introduce this book on Azure FinOps, a comprehensive guide that brings clarity and structure to a challenging, often misunderstood aspect of cloud computing. The author has successfully navigated the intricate landscape of Azure cost management, providing readers with practical insights, strategies, and tools to tackle cost inefficiencies head-on.

The future of cloud computing is not just about technical advancements—it is about mastering the balance between innovation and financial discipline. This book serves as an essential guide for any organization looking to navigate the complexities of cloud cost management and governance while fostering a collaborative culture of financial efficiency.

I strongly believe that readers of this book will come away with a profound understanding of how to optimize cloud costs in Microsoft Azure and, more importantly, how to build a FinOps culture that will serve as the foundation for long-term success in the cloud.

– Swamy Kiran
Senior IT Officer, Data & Information Management
ITS Treasury Portfolio
World Bank Group, United States of America

About the Authors

- **Parag Bhardwaj** is the principal cloud solutions architect for a global airline's cloud and engineering platform. He specializes in deploying optimized, cost-efficient cloud solutions and implementing FinOps practices. Proficient in infrastructure technologies, including Windows/Linux IaaS, security, and networking, Parag ensures sound financial management to maximize business value across various cloud services using DevOps tools like App Services, Containers, and Kubernetes.

  Parag architects collaborate with business development to create complex end-to-end enterprise systems on Azure. His expertise includes Azure Landing Zones, Architectural Design Sessions (ADCs), and setting up Azure Policy configurations for security and compliance.

  Parag is a Cloud Center of Excellence (CCoE) member and influences his organization's cloud transformation. We benefit from his experience with cloud governance and cost optimization to enable better cloud integration into our workflow while controlling costs. Parag also provides helpful speaker sessions on optimizing resources in massive cloud landscapes at FinOps X. Parag also offered great speaker sessions on traditions of how to manage resources at scale in massive cloud landscapes.

- **Arun Kumar Samayam** is a renowned technology architect and author with a focus on cost optimization. As a Principal Cloud Solutions Architect for a leading global airline, he excels in creating efficient, cost-effective cloud solutions and managing databases.

  Arun's career started as a Product Technical Leader for Enterprise Database Services, where he mastered various platforms, including Oracle, MySQL, PostgreSQL, SQL Server, and MongoDB, achieving significant cost savings through performance optimization.

  In his current role with the Cloud Center of Excellence (CCoE), Arun guides cloud transformation initiatives, leveraging his expertise in cloud governance and cost control.

He is a recognized industry expert, having presented at events like Oracle OpenWorld and the MySQL Heatwave Summit. As an author, Arun co-wrote "Mastering MySQL Administration" and reviewed technical content for the Oracle Cloud Infrastructure (OCI) GoldenGate book.

Arun Kumar Samayam remains a leading figure in technology, committed to advancing cost-effective practices and sharing his knowledge with others.

About the Reviewers

❖ **Y V Ravi Kumar** is an Oracle Certified Master (OCM) with 26+ years of experience in the banking, financial services, and insurance (BFSI) verticals. He is an Oracle Certified Professional (OCP) from Oracle 8i to 19c and also an Oracle Certified Expert (OCE) in Oracle GoldenGate, RAC, Performance Tuning, Oracle Cloud Infrastructure, Terraform, and Oracle Engineered Systems (Exadata, ZDLRA, and ODA), as well as Oracle Security and Maximum Availability Architecture (MAA) certified.

He has published over 100+ Oracle technology articles, including on Oracle Technology Network (OTN), OraWorld Magazine, UKOUG, Otech Magazine, and Redgate. He has spoken four times at Oracle Open/Cloud World (OOW), San Francisco/Las Vegas, United States. He has designed, architected, and implemented the core banking system (CBS) database for the central banks of two countries – India and Mahé, Seychelles. He completed Multi-Cloud Certified Architect in Oracle Cloud Infrastructure Architect Professional, AWS Certified Solutions Architect Professional, and Google Cloud Architect Professional (GCP).

He has co-authored the book, "Oracle GoldenGate with Microservices" with BPB Publications and also co-authored several books for other publications. He has also participated in the three technical reviews for BPB Publications' books, 'Oracle 19c AutoUpgrades Best Practices', "End-to-End Observability with Grafana" and "Maximum Availability Architecture (MAA) with Oracle GoldenGate MicroServices in HUB Architecture" and also participated as the technical reviewer for several books for other publications. He has received the EB-1A Extraordinary Ability green card, colloquially known as the 'Einstein visa' from the United States of America (USA). He is also a Senior Member of IEEE (Advancing Technology for Humanity), showcasing his commitment to advancing technology for the betterment of society.

Ravi Kumar is Certified in "FinOps Certified Practitioner" and "Snowflake Pro".

❖ **Velu Natarajan** is a seasoned professional with over 18 years of expertise in delivering scalable analytics solutions across diverse platforms. His passion lies in the relentless pursuit of modernizing data platforms, ensuring they are not only efficient and high-performing but also scalable and durable to meet the evolving needs of the industry. As an industry trailblazer, Velu has been an early advocate for Cloud FinOps frameworks, leveraging them to both elevate business success and achieve notable cost savings.

As a leader in the Database Cloud Center of Excellence (CCoE), Velu plays a crucial role in driving his organization's cloud transformation journey. His deep knowledge of database practices enables him to lead initiatives that ensure seamless migrations, business continuity, and operational efficiency.

Velu's pioneering work with Cloud FinOps frameworks has led to significant business success and cost savings. His application of FinOps framework to control cost to cloud-based data warehouses was recognized with the Discover President Award in 2024. Through effective collaboration with cross-functional teams to understand database usage, optimize performance, manage costs, and establish best practices, Velu developed self-service tools and processes to optimize usage, identified potential issues, and created cost management plans. Additionally, Velu has shared his expertise at prestigious events such as Snowflake Summit 2024, where he discussed strategies for optimizing performance and cost on Snowflake, maximizing business value, reducing budget risk, and improving the user experience with the data tool.

Certified as a "FinOps Certified Practitioner," "Snowflake Pro," and "Snowflake Architect," Velu is renowned for his insights into database products and his commitment to excellence. Outside of work, he enjoys playing soccer and watching epic movies.

Acknowledgements

○ To my parents **RS Sharma** and **Daya Sharma** who are always there for me. Thanks from the bottom of my heart to all those who supported and believed in me, starting with my family. I could never truly thank everyone who has contributed to this book.

To my soulmate and wife, **Anshu Bhardwaj**, our daughter, **Nehal Bhardwaj**, and our son, **Pranshu Bhardwaj**, whose unwavering love and constant support have always been my source of strength. Your belief in me has motivated me to strive for excellence in all I do.

I would like to thank **Y V Ravi Kumar** and **Velu Natarajan** for their valuable guidance on this project. Their expertise and encouragement are important to the work presented here. I appreciate their commitments and the time they spent helping us ensure that our research is of superior quality.

It is also a privilege to have **Arun Samayam** as a co-author of this book. His knowledge and collaborative nature have been crucial in developing the content and guiding the direction of our project.

Many individuals and organizations supported this study. We are forever grateful to the dedicated team at *BPB Publications* for their continuous motivation and support while publishing the research.

I appreciate everyone for playing an important role in this amazing journey.

— *Parag Bhardwaj*

○ I am forever grateful for the love and support of those who have shaped my life's journey and made this book possible.

To my parents, **Ram Kumar** and **Lakshmi Sarada**, for nurturing me with unwavering love, kindness, and the freedom to pursue my passions. Your encouragement and support have fueled my determination to chase my dreams.

To my beloved wife, **Ramya**, and our daughter, **Iraa**, whose boundless love, and unwavering support have been the bedrock of strength in my life. Your belief in me has propelled me forward, urging me to strive for excellence in all endeavors.

To my mentor, **Y V Ravi Kumar**, for recognizing my potential, guiding me through challenges and opening doors to new opportunities. Your wisdom, dedication, and noble pursuit of knowledge have been a constant source of inspiration.

To my co-author, **Parag Bharadwaj**, and technical reviewers **Y V Ravi Kumar** and **Velu Natarajan**, your technical knowledge, dedication, collaboration, and unwavering support throughout the writing process have enriched this book and made it truly special.

To my publisher, *BPB Publications* and team - thank you for entrusting me with the opportunity to share our experience on FinOps. With your support, this book will serve as a guide for many aspiring FinOps enthusiasts and inspire and motivate them, making a significant impact in their FinOps journey.

Thank you all for being an integral part of this incredible journey.

— *Arun Kumar Samayam*

Preface

This book on Azure FinOps explores into strategies and best practices for optimizing your cloud costs within the technical framework of Microsoft Azure. It explores financial operations in cloud environments with an in-depth look at cost management, monitoring, and governance in Azure. Key aspects of FinOps, such as tagging, budgeting, and alert configuration, are covered to help readers implement effective cost controls and maximize their cloud investments.

This Book includes practical insights on cost optimization through real-world examples and industry best practices, guiding you through Azure FinOps Essentials. It discusses advanced principles like right-sizing, RI coverage, and serverless optimization, facilitating comparisons of different architectures. The program also addresses governance and compliance by guiding and enforcing policies and controls to ensure financial accountability and adherence to guidelines.

The book comprises **12 chapters**, beginning with the basics of cost management in Azure and concluding with sophisticated, real-world FinOps methods explained through detailed case studies. You will gain a comprehensive understanding of developing a FinOps culture, creating dashboards for financial visibility, and identifying future trends in Azure FinOps. Individual chapters provide in-depth guidance on running cloud operations efficiently with CCoE and optimizing Azure spending. The chapters are outlined as follows:

Chapter 1: Introduction to Azure FinOps- In this chapter, readers will learn that FinOps is a financial operations practice essential for modern cloud environments, bridging the gap between finance and tech teams to manage cloud costs effectively. Implementing FinOps in Azure environments offers benefits like enhanced cost visibility, optimized resource utilization, and better financial collaboration across teams. Azure FinOps aids in reducing cloud expenses by providing real-time cost monitoring and aligning business insights to optimize resources efficiently.

Chapter 2: Azure Fundamentals for FinOps- In this chapter, you will learn about Azure services like virtual machines, databases, and storage are crucial components in FinOps practices for managing costs. Organizing these resources into resource groups and using tagging techniques helps streamline cost management, providing better insights and control over spending. Azure Cost Management further supports this by enabling cost tracking, setting budgets, and identifying savings opportunities through its various phases.

Chapter 3: Azure Cost Management and Billing- This Chapter explains how to access the Azure Cost Management and Billing portal to learn about the different ways of navigating financial information, viewing invoices, and accessing financial savings. How to optimize Cost Analysis to get more details on spending ways, create budgets, and monitor them to avoid overruns. Understand the concepts behind the best ways to create and manage Azure subscriptions, considering proper resource segregation and the need to monitor financial data. Learn how to set up alerts and financial notifications to inform users of financial irregularities and flag them whenever budgets are about to be overrun.

Chapter 4: Cost Optimization Strategies- In this chapter, you will learn about the Key considerations for right-sizing resources such as VMs to meet demand and prevent over-provisioning, which results in waste costs. Offers pricing discounts via Azure Reserved Instances and Same Region Capacity Price Offers for well-understood workloads, enabling meaningful savings opportunities over time. This section highlights the cost-saving advantage of utilizing existing on-premises licenses for Windows and SQL on Microsoft Azure through the Azure Hybrid Benefit. A lower-cost approach using unused capacity for non-critical workloads. These options help save money but may experience interruptions.

Chapter 5: Azure Monitoring- This chapter will provide an introduction to using Azure Monitor tools to track the performance of your applications and resource metrics, enabling early detection of inefficiencies for real-time cost optimization. Introduction to the Compelling and Cloud Performance & Cost Management Tools. These tools enable users to analyze data across resources and create rich, interactive reports. This part instructs users on building personalized dashboards for cost oversight, presenting crucial cost metrics in a transparent and accessible layout. This section discusses the various reporting capabilities within Cost Explorer that business units will find particularly useful for showcasing costs with great visuals.

Chapter 6: Cost Allocation and Chargebacks- Implementing and Managing resource tagging to achieve detailed cost allocation by mapping it to departments, teams, or projects. Validates how to leverage cost management APIs and automation services to control expenses, gain insights into all spending, and prevent unexpected charges on cloud resources. Guide on establishing RBAC to regulate permissions regarding cost management, ensuring security and compliance.

Chapter 7: Governance and Compliance- This chapter explains how to utilize Azure Policy to implement cost control strategies, ensuring all resources adhere to the organization's cost optimization guidelines.

This section focuses on leveraging ACS improvements to manage costs effectively while maintaining security during regular operations. This chapter explains how FinOps practices need to meet compliance requirements, such as GDPR laws or industry-related rulings. Considerations for managing costs and maintaining data protection/privacy while remaining compliant with regulatory Standards.

Chapter 8: Advanced Azure FinOps Techniques- This chapter explores how IaC tools like ARM templates and Terraform enable cost savings by automating optimal resource provisioning and usage. It describes how Azure functions using Python can adjust resource allocation based on usage patterns to help optimize costs. Understand serverless architecture with no constant costs, charging users only for actual usage, requiring no fixed compute resources, resulting in highly scalable and efficient operations. Integrate FinOps with DevOps methodologies to ensure that cost optimization remains a focal point throughout the entire software development lifecycle.

Chapter 9: Azure FinOps Best Practices- This chapter outlines existing cloud cost optimization frameworks at a high level, helping teams to align their strategies with established best practices for managing expenses. This chapter outlines how to establish an environment where cloud spending is controlled by the teams utilizing the resources. This highlights the cultural shift needed for finance, engineering, and business units to work together towards a shared FinOps objective.

Chapter 10: Azure Case Studies and Real-world Examples- A detailed case study of how a web application was optimized for cost, including techniques and results. Discuss how a large enterprise implemented effective cost allocation and chargeback models to enhance financial accountability. Showcases how DevOps and FinOps teams can collaborate effectively to optimize operational efficiency and costs.

Chapter 11: Future Trends and Innovations in Azure FinOps- This chapter talks about how managing cloud costs is changing, including the role of AI and machine learning in making things cheaper and more efficient. It discusses the specific challenges and opportunities related to optimizing costs for AI and machine learning workloads in Azure environments.

Chapter 12: Final Thoughts and Next Steps- Summarizes the key takeaways from the book and reinforces the importance of adopting a FinOps mindset. It encourages continuous learning and iteration in optimizing cloud costs and highlights how adopting FinOps practices can lead to long-term financial and operational success in cloud environments.

Code Bundle and Coloured Images

Please follow the link to download the
Code Bundle and the *Coloured Images* of the book:

https://rebrand.ly/m1ekl0i

The code bundle for the book is also hosted on GitHub at
https://github.com/bpbpublications/Azure-FinOps-Essentials.
In case there's an update to the code, it will be updated on the existing GitHub repository.

We have code bundles from our rich catalogue of books and videos available at
https://github.com/bpbpublications. Check them out!

Errata

We take immense pride in our work at BPB Publications and follow best practices to ensure the accuracy of our content to provide with an indulging reading experience to our subscribers. Our readers are our mirrors, and we use their inputs to reflect and improve upon human errors, if any, that may have occurred during the publishing processes involved. To let us maintain the quality and help us reach out to any readers who might be having difficulties due to any unforeseen errors, please write to us at :

errata@bpbonline.com

Your support, suggestions and feedbacks are highly appreciated by the BPB Publications' Family.

Piracy

If you come across any illegal copies of our works in any form on the internet, we would be grateful if you would provide us with the location address or website name. Please contact us at **business@bpbonline.com** with a link to the material.

If you are interested in becoming an author

If there is a topic that you have expertise in, and you are interested in either writing or contributing to a book, please visit **www.bpbonline.com**. We have worked with thousands of developers and tech professionals, just like you, to help them share their insights with the global tech community. You can make a general application, apply for a specific hot topic that we are recruiting an author for, or submit your own idea.

Reviews

Please leave a review. Once you have read and used this book, why not leave a review on the site that you purchased it from? Potential readers can then see and use your unbiased opinion to make purchase decisions. We at BPB can understand what you think about our products, and our authors can see your feedback on their book. Thank you!

For more information about BPB, please visit **www.bpbonline.com**.

Join our book's Discord space

Join the book's Discord Workspace for Latest updates, Offers, Tech happenings around the world, New Release and Sessions with the Authors:

https://discord.bpbonline.com

Table of Contents

CHAPTER 1
Introduction to Azure FinOps

Introduction

FinOps is a domain for cloud financial and operation management. It enables organizations to extract the highest possible business value by encouraging collaboration between engineering, finance, IT, and business teams. The goal is to effectively leverage the cloud platform's flexible and scalable cost structure.

FinOps is the practice that brings a finance accountability culture to the team. FinOps recommends a variable spend model of the cloud by enabling distributed engineering and business teams. Also, the business team decides their cloud architecture and investment decisions by trading cost, speed, and quality.

Cloud spending can be driven through more customer base growth and revenue, enabling product and feature releases. It is all about removing the huddles, empowering the engineering team to deliver new features, apps, and migrations faster, and enabling a cross-functional conversation about where to invest and when.

In simpler terms, FinOps helps companies make the most out of cloud services like *Azure* by bringing different teams together. This collaboration allows them to optimize costs and maximize the benefits of using cloud resources. By working together, engineering teams can make informed decisions about resource usage. Finance teams can allocate costs efficiently, IT teams can ensure compliance, and business teams can align cloud spending with goals.

The following figure outlines the FinOps framework developed to optimize an organization's financial processes. It highlights components of the FinOps lifecycle, including cost analysis, resource allocation, optimization, and ongoing monitoring. This framework enables businesses to manage cloud and IT expenses efficiently, control costs, and make informed financial decisions.

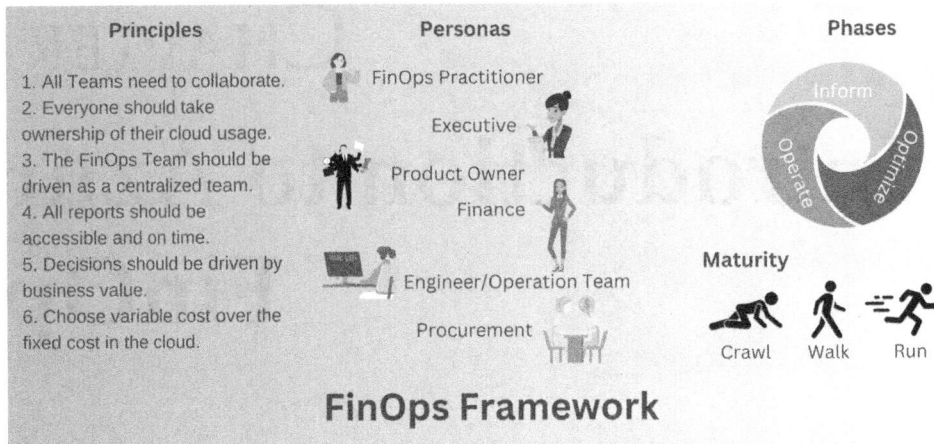

Figure 1.1: *FinOps framework*

Structure

In this chapter, we will learn the following topics:

- Key points for the Azure cloud
- Understanding FinOps
- Benefits of Azure FinOps
- Azure FinOps manage cloud cost

Objectives

The scope's objective is to educate the reader about the principles and critical points linked to FinOps and how it is applied in cloud management, especially in Azure. After going through this chapter, the reader will learn the principles of FinOps, the benefits of implementing FinOps, understanding FinOps culture, cross-functional collaboration, FinOps framework, performance monitoring and optimization, adaptability, and continuous learning. In summary, this content aims to educate the reader about the principles and practices of FinOps and how they can be applied in the context of cloud management, including Azure. The critical points for Azure relate to specific Azure features and services that can support FinOps practices.

Key points for the Azure cloud

FinOps is built upon three fundamental principles:

- Accountability is one of the crucial principles where we need to encourage a culture where teams take ownership of cloud costs and understand the impact of their decisions on finances.
- Transparency encourages the visibility of cloud costs and usage data, enabling teams to monitor and analyze spending patterns.
- Optimize cloud resources and costs by impacting the right-sizing, reserved instances, and automation strategies.

Implementing FinOps practices can bring several benefits to organizations, including:

- Cost optimization analyzes usage patterns, identifies inefficiencies, and implements cost-saving measures; the company can optimize its cloud spend and reduce unrequired expenses.
- Collaboration and alignment encourage cross-functional cooperation between engineering, finance, IT, and business teams, fostering alignment and enabling better decision-making.
- Increased business agility variable cost model of the cloud allows organizations to scale resources based on demand, providing flexibility and agility to meet changing business needs.

Understanding FinOps

FinOps is a culture that involves progressive discipline culture in cloud financial management, which facilitates organizations in achieving business value through collaboration among engineering, finance, IT, and business teams. FinOps first principle is that every couple needs to collaborate.

FinOps = Finance + DevOps

FinOps is a combination words of 'Finance' and '*DevOps*'. As the name shows, this is based on communications and collaboration between multiple teams, such as Business and engineering.

FinOps culture

The importance of FinOps lies in its culture. It represents a mindset that encourages teams to proactively control their cloud expenditures, enabling a sense of ownership among all stakeholders. This collective responsibility is complemented by a centralized best-practices group, providing guidance and support to optimize cloud usage.

Cross-functional

Coordinated teams comprising various fields, such as engineering, finance, product, and more, join forces to facilitate efficient product development. This collective effort expedites the delivery process and enhances financial oversight and predictability.

FinOps framework

The FinOps framework is a methodical approach to driving cloud costs within an organization. It consists of several vital components and practices to optimize cloud spending while preserving functional efficiency.

Here is a description of the FinOps framework:

- FinOps involves setting budgets and creating projections for cloud spending. This helps organizations plan and allocate resources effectively, allowing better financial management and predictability. Budgeting and forecasting also encourage proactive cost management and support teams to identify and address variations in the intended spending.

- The FinOps framework promotes the adoption of diverse cost optimization techniques. This may include leveraging spot models or low-cost regions, optimizing storage solutions, implementing caching tools, and exploring alternative pricing models cloud providers offer. Organizations are encouraged to identify and implement the most suitable approaches based on their needs and workloads.

- A vital element of the FinOps framework is educating and training teams on cloud cost management best practices. This includes providing resources, teaching workshops, and promoting a learning culture where individuals can enhance their understanding of cloud economics, cost optimization methods, and the tools available to help FinOps practices.

- Organizations establish governance and policy frameworks to provide the valuable performance of FinOps practices. These frameworks describe procedures, benchmarks, and strategies for cloud usage, cost management, and decision-making. They help implement accountability, support compliance, and align FinOps practices with organizational objectives.

- FinOps enables collaboration among diverse stakeholders, including engineering teams, finance teams, product managers, and executives. Organizations can gain various outlooks, align preferences, and drive collaborative ownership of cloud costs by applying all appropriate details in cost management discussions and decision-making processes.

In addition to cost management, the FinOps framework also focuses on performance monitoring and optimization. It enables organizations to follow and analyze cloud implementation metrics, identify jams, and optimize resource configurations to improve overall system efficiency and cost-effectiveness.

The FinOps framework acknowledges that cloud environments and business requirements are involved. It highlights the significance of constant learning, transformation, and growth of FinOps practices to remain aligned with changing technology trends, organizational needs, and evolving cloud provider offerings.

By executing the FinOps framework, organizations can effectively manage their cloud costs, achieve financial visibility, optimize resource utilization, and foster a culture of accountability and collaboration. This framework provides a structured approach to aligning financial and operational objectives, enabling organizations to make informed decisions and drive cost-efficiency in their cloud environments.

FinOps principles

The FinOps framework is created on core principles that guide organizations in effectively handling their cloud costs. These principles provide a foundation for implementing and driving successful FinOps practices:

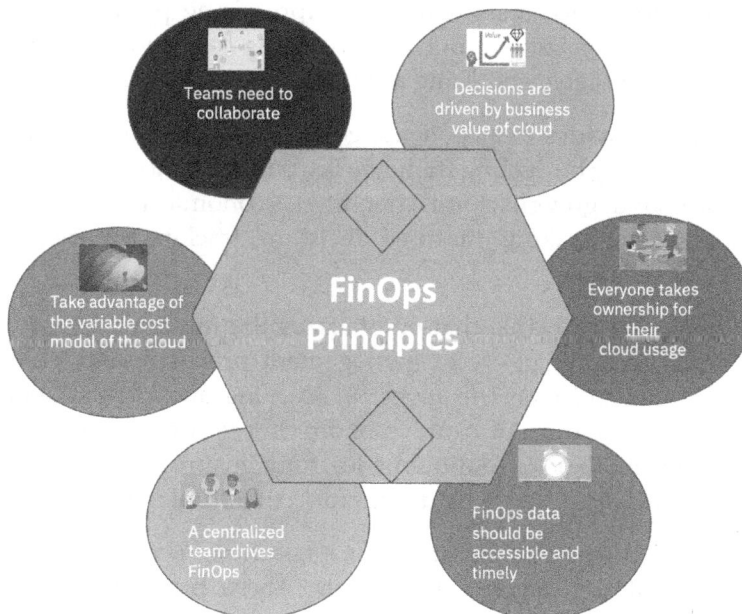

Figure 1.2: FinOps principles

The principle of accountability highlights the need for individuals and teams to take ownership of their cloud usage and associated costs. It promotes a culture of responsibility, where everyone involved understands the impact of their actions on the financial aspects of cloud operations. Accountability ensures that cost optimization is a shared responsibility across the organization.

Collaboration is an essential principle of FinOps, highlighting the importance of cross-functional teamwork. It enables collaboration among engineering, finance, and operations teams to align goals, share knowledge, and collectively work toward optimizing cloud costs.

Transparency refers to the clear visibility of cloud costs and usage data throughout the organization. It concerns providing available and legible cost information to appropriate stakeholders. Transparency ensures teams have the necessary information to make informed decisions, fosters trust and encourages accountability in managing cloud expenses.

The focus on efficiency concentrates on optimizing cloud resource utilization and eliminating waste. It involves continuously considering and improving the efficiency of cloud deployments, such as rightsizing resources, identifying and eliminating idle or underutilized resources, and leveraging automation. Efficiency-driven practices help maximize the value of cloud investments while minimizing unnecessary costs.

Optimization contains the ongoing effort to improve cost-effectiveness and performance. It involves analyzing usage patterns, identifying opportunities for optimization, and implementing plans to reduce costs without compromising performance. Optimization strategies may include rightsizing resources, leveraging cost-saving options like reserved or spot instances, Saving Plans, and using automation for cost-management tasks.

Financial governance provides clear policies, guidelines, and processes to manage cloud costs. It involves specifying budgeting frameworks, cost allocation processes, and financial controls to monitor and govern cloud spending. Economic governance provides the design and guidelines for making informed decisions, tracking expenses, and enforcing compliance.

Continuous learning is a principle that emphasizes the importance of staying updated with evolving cloud technologies, cost management practices, and industry trends. It encourages individuals and teams to invest in learning and professional development to enhance their understanding of cloud economics, cost optimization techniques, and relevant tools and technologies. Continuous learning ensures that organizations remain adaptable and can leverage new opportunities for cost optimization.

With these principles, organizations can foster a culture of accountability, collaboration, and transparency while optimizing cloud costs. These principles provide a strategic direction for managing cloud expenses, enabling organizations to achieve better financial control, maximize resource utilization, and drive cost efficiency.

FinOps phases

FinOps collects and optimizes your cloud spending by teaming across different teams and using data-driven decisions. It is a practice that helps organizations handle and optimize their cloud spending.

FinOps includes three phases, refer to the following figure:

- Inform
- Operate
- Optimize

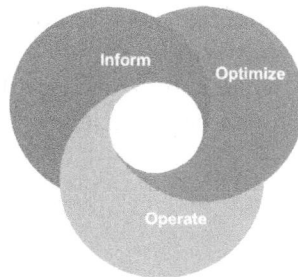

Figure 1.3: *FinOps phases*

Inform

This is the first phase in FinOps, authorizing organizations and teams with visibility, allotment, benchmarking, budgeting, and forecast. The on-demand and flexible nature of the cloud, along with customized pricing and discounts, makes it necessary for correct and timely visibility for wise decisions. Proper distribution of cloud spending based on tags, accounts, or business mappings allows real chargeback and show back. Business and financial stakeholders also want to confirm that they drive ROI while remaining within budget and accurately forecasting spending, avoiding shocks. Benchmarking as a partner and against teams gives organizations the critical metrics to design a more efficient unit.

Optimize

Once organizations and teams are certified, they must optimize their cloud footmark. Cloud providers offer numerous levers to optimize. On-demand capacity is the most costly. To encourage progressive reservation planning and increased obligation, cloud providers offer discounts for commitments, which typically involves complicated calculations for making reservations (**Reserved Instances (RI)** / Committed Use Discounts. In addition, teams and organizations can optimize the conditions by rightsizing and automating, turning off any wasteful use of resources.

Operate

Organizations start to assess business purposes continually, the metrics they follow against those goals, and how they are trending. They calculate business alignment specified on speed, quality, and cost. Any organizational success is only feasible if the organization builds a culture of FinOps, which affects a Cloud Cost Center of Excellence made around business, financial, and operational stakeholders who also determine the right governance policies and standards.

Benefits of Azure FinOps

The adoption of cloud computing has processed how organizations drive their IT infrastructure. However, as cloud environments rise in complexity and scale, so do the challenges associated with operating and controlling cloud costs. This is where FinOps comes into space. FinOps, quick for financial operations, is a procedure that connects financial administration principles with cloud operations to optimize cloud spending and gain more useful financial management. By executing FinOps practices, organizations can open a range of benefits that push cost efficiency, financial visibility, and collective decision-making.

Cost optimization

A vital factor of the FinOps framework is its priority on cost optimization. Organizations can leverage FinOps principles and methods for substantial cost savings in their cloud environment. Here are some typical strategies typically used in FinOps for cost optimization:

Rightsizing resources

FinOps enables organizations to right-size their cloud resources. This applies considering the actual resource conditions of applications and workloads and assigning the proper instance types and sizes accordingly. By deleting over-provisioned resources, organizations can lower costs while retaining optimal performance.

Spot instances

FinOps promotes using spot instances, which are known at remarkably lower prices than on-demand instances. Spot instances permit organizations to use unused cloud capacity, delivering cost savings for non-critical data. By leveraging spot instances, organizations can perform considerable cost reductions.

Reserved instances and savings plans

FinOps enables organizations to use reserved instances or savings plans proposed by cloud providers. These options permit organizations to use typical resources for a defined period, delivering substantial discounts compared to on-demand.

Auto-scaling and auto-shutdown

FinOps highlights using auto-scaling and auto-shutdown to optimize resource utilization. Auto-scaling dynamically changes the number of instances based on demand, providing resources are provisioned only when required. Auto-shutdown schedules instances to shut down automatically during low or no activity. These practices help eliminate wasteful spending on idle resources.

Resource tagging and cost allocation

FinOps enables the implementation of resource tagging and cost allocation methods. Organizations gain visibility into cost distribution by tagging resources with suitable metadata and costs to specific teams, projects, or businesses.

Continuous monitoring and optimization

FinOps enables constant monitoring of cloud costs and performance metrics. By leveraging cloud cost management tools and executing entire monitoring techniques, organizations can determine cost anomalies, optimize spending ways, and make data-driven conclusions for additional cost optimization.

Financial visibility and control

FinOps highlights the extent of visibility into cloud costs and usage across the organization. FinOps provides teams and people with a clear knowledge of their cloud costs by performing vital cost monitoring and reporting. This clarity enables stakeholders to follow and explore their cloud usage patterns, determine cost drivers, and understand the financial result of their findings.

With visibility into their cloud usage, groups, and individuals can take the privilege of their costs and encourage a culture of accountability. When individuals are familiar with their actions' financial implications, they are more likely to make educated judgments that align with cost optimization objectives. This promotes a sense of responsibility and enables stakeholders to organize and manage their cloud expenses actively.

Moreover, visibility into cloud costs permits organizations to determine areas of excessive spending, ineffective resource utilization, or possible cost-saving opportunities. With this knowledge, teams can collaborate to design strategies for cost optimization and guide continuous improvement. They can make data-driven findings, prioritize assets, and implement actions to control costs effectively.

The responsibility enabled by FinOps enables a collective environment where teams across departments optimize costs. It enables cross-functional discussion and facts sharing, directing to more reasonable cost management practices and discovering creative ways to maximize cloud spending.

FinOps ensures that cost management is collaborative throughout the organization by promoting visibility and responsibility. It authorizes individuals with the information they need to create cost-conscious decisions and enables teams to proactively monitor, control, and optimize cloud costs. Ultimately, combining visibility and accountability in FinOps results in more effective cost management and improved financial control.

Accountability and ownership

FinOps highlights promoting a culture of responsibility and ownership within organizations. It enables teams and individuals to take the blame for their cloud usage and associated costs, acknowledging that cost management is a shared commitment across the organization.

One of the critical ways FinOps enables accountability is by implementing cost allocation. This means attributing cloud costs to typical teams, projects, or business units. By allocating costs accurately, FinOps provides transparency and visibility into the financial impact of findings made at various levels of the organization. Stakeholders become mindful of how their actions and choices affect the organization's general cloud expenses.

This transparency and visibility enable a sense of ownership in cost management. When groups and individuals notice the direct correlation between cloud usage and the associated costs, they are additionally likely to take visionary steps to optimize their usage and management costs. They become responsible for their cloud spending and are encouraged to make informed decisions that align with cost optimization purposes.

FinOps enables partnership and cross-functional discussion, further supporting responsibility and ownership. Teams from different departments, such as engineering, finance, and operations, work together to determine cost-saving possibilities, share knowledge and best practices, and collectively drive cost-optimization efforts. This integrated approach provides that cost management is not only the responsibility of a single team or individual but rather a joint effort.

FinOps assigns teams and individuals to actively participate in cost management and optimization by enabling a culture of accountability and ownership. It makes sense to share responsibility for cloud costs and allows stakeholders to proactively determine areas for progress, implement cost-saving strategies, and constantly scan and optimize their cloud usage.

Ultimately, by enabling accountability and ownership, FinOps shows a culture where individuals understand the financial impact of their decisions and are inspired to make cost-conscious choices.

Collaboration and alignment

FinOps enables cross-functional collaboration between technical teams, finance, and other business units, realizing that effective cost management requires joint effort and various expertise. This partnership allows for better communication, knowledge sharing, and alignment of purposes, leading to improved cost optimization and efficiency across the organization.

By conveying together technical teams, finance experts, and other stakeholders, FinOps enables the exchange of insights and outlooks. This environment allows for a deeper understanding of cloud costs, usage patterns, and the result of technical decisions on financial outcomes. It enables teams to leverage their joint ability to identify cost-optimization possibilities and execute effective systems.

Cross-functional teamwork in FinOps enables better communication channels between teams. Technical teams gain visibility into the financial importance of their actions, while finance experts better understand the technical characteristics of cloud infrastructure. This joint understanding allows for more effective communication and decision-making, decreasing misconceptions and facilitating the implementation of cost-optimization measures.

Moreover, partnership in FinOps promotes knowledge sharing and best practices across teams and departments. Through joint discussions and sharing of experiences, organizations can recognize and share cost-saving techniques, tools, and processes. This knowledge-sharing helps teams leverage the expertise of others and execute established strategies for cost optimization.

The alignment of objectives is another meaningful benefit of collaboration in FinOps. By working together, teams can align their goals and preferences to gain cost efficiency and financial control. Specialized teams understand the cost importance of their decisions, letting them prioritize cost optimization alongside technological performance. Finance experts gain insights into technical needs, enabling them to support the needs of technical teams while ensuring cost-effective products.

Through joint efforts, teams can identify cost optimization possibilities that may be encountered when working in isolation. They can consider different options, weigh trade-offs, and make educated decisions based on a thorough understanding of the financial and technical aspects. This alignment and teamwork help organizations drive cost efficiency and achieve better economic outcomes.

Agility and innovation

One of the essential benefits of executing FinOps practices is the ability to move skill and creation within an organization. By optimizing cloud costs, organizations can release valuable help that can be assigned to other key initiatives, such as creation projects or business development. This enables organizations to be more agile and responsive to demand changes, enhancing competitiveness and development opportunities.

When organizations optimize their cloud costs via FinOps, they commit essential cost savings. These cost savings can be reinvested into strategic tasks that drive innovation. By allocating resources to innovation projects, organizations can foster a culture of constant improvement, explore new ideas, and develop solutions to meet growing customer needs.

Also, the cost savings obtained through FinOps allow organizations to answer more effectively to market changes. In dynamic business environments, the ability to adjust fast is essential. Organizations can allocate resources more flexibly by optimizing cloud costs, permitting them to scale up or down as needed, respond to market demands, and seize opportunities promptly.

The skill provided by FinOps authorizes organizations to test, repeat, and innovate faster. It allows them to allocate resources efficiently, test new ideas, and bring products or services to market more rapidly. This agility enables organizations to stay ahead of the contest and capitalize on arising directions and opportunities.

Also, the cost savings gained through FinOps provide financial flexibility for business expansion. Organizations can assign resources to enter new markets, expand operations, or invest in strategic initiatives that drive change. This financial freedom allows organizations to seek new roads and invest in their future success.

Organizations optimize cloud costs through FinOps and create a promising innovation, agility, and maturing environment. They can allocate resources to innovation projects and follow strategic initiatives that fuel business growth. Cost optimization and resource allocation combination enhance the organization's ability to innovate, adapt to market dynamics, and achieve long-term success.

FinOps certifies organizations to manage their cloud costs effectively, achieve financial visibility, drive collaboration, and promote a culture of accountability and ownership. By implementing FinOps practices, organizations can optimize their cloud spending, make data-driven findings, and achieve better financial control, ultimately leading to enhanced cost efficiency and business success.

Cost management is a vital part of running a thriving cloud environment. With FinOps, organizations gain the tools and processes to optimize their cloud costs across the entire organization. By leveraging FinOps practices, organizations can identify cost optimization possibilities, eliminate wasteful spending, and allocate resources more efficiently. This shows improved cost efficiency and better utilization of cloud resources.

FinOps obtains financial visibility into cloud costs. It provides organizations with the necessary knowledge and analytics to understand their cloud spending patterns, identify cost drivers, and track the financial result of their findings. This clarity enables organizations to make educated decisions based on accurate cost data, prioritize investments, and allocate resources.

FinOps also forces collaboration and cross-functional alignment. By involving technical teams, finance professionals, and other stakeholders, organizations can break down silos and promote a joint environment. This partnership facilitates better communication, knowledge sharing, and alignment of goals. Through cross-functional collaboration, teams can identify cost optimization possibilities, share best practices, and collectively drive cost efficiency across the organization.

A core element of FinOps is accountability and ownership. Organizations attribute cloud costs to specific teams, projects, or business units by executing cost allocation mechanisms, creating a sense of right and responsibility. When individuals and groups are aware of the financial impact of their decisions, they are motivated to take proactive steps to optimize their cloud usage and control costs. This culture of accountability ensures that cost management evolves as a transferred responsibility throughout the organization.

Executing FinOps practices also enables organizations to make data-driven decisions. By leveraging cost data, usage metrics, and implementation indicators, organizations can analyze trends, identify opportunities for optimization, and drive cost-saving strategies. This data-driven approach improves decision-making and enables organizations to align their cloud spending with business goals and priorities.

Azure FinOps manage cloud cost

Azure FinOps, also understood as Azure financial operations or Azure cloud financial management, directs to the collection of techniques and tools used to manage and optimize cloud costs in the Microsoft Azure environment. It integrates financial and operational elements to help organizations acquire visibility into their cloud spending, enhance cost control, and make decisions to maximize the value and efficiency of their Azure deployments.

The role of Azure FinOps in cloud cost management concerns several key factors:

Cost visibility

Azure FinOps delivers detailed visibility into Azure resource consumption and associated costs. It helps organizations understand how their cloud resources are utilized and how much they spend across different Azure services, subscriptions, departments, or projects. This visibility is essential for accurately identifying cost drivers, detecting anomalies, and allocating costs.

Following are the key factors for cost visibility:

- Azure resource consumption
- Cost breakdown
- Cost attribution
- Anomaly detection
- Cost optimization opportunities
- Reporting and analysis

Cost optimization

Azure FinOps helps organizations optimize their cloud costs by recognizing cost-saving possibilities and executing strategies to lower undeserved spending. It delivers understandings into underutilized resources, idle instances, and inefficient configurations, allowing organizations to right-size their deployments, scale resources efficiently, and leverage cost-effective such as reserved instances or spot instances.

Following are key factors for cost optimization:
- Identifying underutilized resources
- Managing idle instances
- Optimizing configuration and performance
- Right-sizing deployments
- Leveraging cost-effective alternatives
- Continuous cost monitoring and optimization

Budgeting and forecasting

Azure FinOps allows organizations to set budgets and forecasts for cloud spending. It assists in establishing cost thresholds and alerts to proactively observe and manage cost overruns. By leveraging documented cost data and usage patterns, organizations can project prospective costs and plan accordingly, ensuring they remain within their budgetary limitations.

Following are the critical factors for budgeting and forecasting.
- Setting budgets
- Cost thresholds and alerts
- Historical cost data and usage patterns
- Forecasting future costs
- Planning and optimization
- Cost control and governance

Cost allocation and show back/Chargeback

Azure FinOps enables allocating cloud costs to other business units, projects, or departments within an organization. It allows organizations to implement show back or chargeback, where the costs incurred by different stakeholders are transparently documented and attributed. This provides accountability, promotes cost awareness, and supports decision-making processes related to resource allocation.

Following are the critical factors for cost allocation.
- Cost allocation
- Transparent cost reporting
- Show back
- Chargeback
- Cost awareness and optimization
- Decision-making support

Reporting and analytics

Azure FinOps delivers extensive reporting and analytics capacities to track, analyze, and visualize cloud costs and usage practices. It provides pre-built dashboards, cost reports, and customizable data views that help stakeholders understand cost trends, identify cost drivers, and make data-driven findings. These insights enable organizations to optimize resource usage, deal with better pricing agreements, and drive constant cost improvement.

Following are the critical factors for reporting and analytics:

- Comprehensive reporting
- Cost trend analysis
- Cost driver identification
- Customizable data views
- Data-driven decision making
- Continuous cost improvement

Governance and policy enforcement

Azure FinOps helps the implementation of governance and policy frameworks to implement cost control efforts and align cloud spending with organizational policies and guidelines. It allows organizations to determine and enforce cost management policies, set spending limits, select resource tagging standards, and automate cost allocation and chargeback processes.

Following are the critical factors for governance and policy enforcement:

- Cost management policies
- Spending limits and budget controls
- Resource tagging standards
- Automated cost allocation and chargeback
- Policy enforcement and compliance
- Audit and reporting

Conclusion

Azure FinOps, also known as Azure Financial Operations or Azure Cloud Financial Management, is a practice that focuses on working and optimizing cloud costs in the Microsoft Azure environment. It integrates financial and operational aspects to give organizations enhanced visibility into their cloud spending, strengthen cost control, and make decisions to maximize the efficiency and importance of their Azure deployments.

Critical elements of Azure FinOps in cloud cost management include cost visibility, optimization, budgeting and forecasting, cost allocation and show back/chargeback, reporting and analytics, and governance and policy enforcement. Azure FinOps allows organizations to acquire detailed insights into their Azure resource consumption and associated costs, specify cost-saving opportunities, set budgets and forecasts to control costs proactively, assign costs to different stakeholders transparently, analyze cost trends and drivers, and enforce policies and governance frameworks to align cloud spending with organizational guidelines.

Azure FinOps is vital in enabling organizations to manage, optimize, and control their cloud costs in the Azure environment. It allows stakeholders to make informed decisions, promotes cost accountability, and ensures efficient utilization of cloud resources.

In the next chapter, we will learn the Azure fundamentals for FinOps.

In an Azure services overview, you can gain insights into the diverse range of Azure services and how they can be leveraged to optimize costs effectively. Furthermore, by delving into resource groups and tagging, you can uncover strategies for managing and tracking your Azure resources and allocating costs to different departments or specific tasks. Additionally, Azure Cost Management and Billing tools provide the means to monitor and manage Azure expenses, enabling the implementation of show-back and chargeback models to enhance cost accountability and control.

In summary, Azure fundamentals for FinOps will teach the basics of optimizing Azure costs and tracking usage. This understanding can help you save money on your Azure bill and better allocate your Azure resources. In the next chapter, we will learn about essentials of Azure FinOps.

Point to remember

When considering FinOps fundamentals and framework, regardless of the cloud provider, there are some vital points to keep in mind:

- Promote a culture of cost awareness within your organization. Ensure that everyone understands the financial implications of their actions in the cloud.
- To optimize costs, engage stakeholders from various departments, including finance, IT, and business units.
- Define roles and responsibilities for cost management. Assign ownership of cost-related tasks to specific individuals or teams.
- Establish budgets and regularly forecast your cloud spending to align it with business goals and objectives.
- Continuously seek possibilities to optimize costs by recognizing and eliminating waste, resizing resources, and leveraging cloud provider features for savings.
- Implement tools and processes for real-time monitoring of cloud spending.
- Invest in training and educating your team members about FinOps principles and practices to empower them to make cost-conscious decisions.
- Periodically review and adjust your FinOps framework to adjust to changing business needs and cloud service offerings.
- Leverage cloud cost management tools provided by your cloud service provider and third-party solutions to automate and streamline cost optimization efforts.
- Stay informed about industry best practices and benchmark your cost management efforts against industry standards to identify areas for improvement.

CHAPTER 2
Azure Fundamentals for FinOps

Introduction

Azure Fundamentals Financial Operations (FinOps) means a complete set of best practices and strategies to improve the financial management of resources within the Microsoft Azure cloud platform. At its nature, FinOps, brief for *financial operations*, is a holistic approach that combines financial accountability with cloud operational excellence, enabling communities to efficiently govern their cloud costs while extracting maximum value from their assets.

In the context of Azure, the essential principles of FinOps rotate around cost visibility, cost optimization, and cost control. These principles authorize businesses to make data-driven decisions and take necessary actions to align cloud spending with their budget goals and operational requirements.

By attaching to Azure Fundamentals for FinOps, Teams can create a culture of financial commitment and accountability within their cloud operations. This process enables teams to proactively manage costs, assign resources efficiently, and focus on delivering value to customers without overspending on cloud services. As businesses adopt the cloud as a critical element of their IT infrastructure, mastering Azure Fundamentals for FinOps becomes necessary for optimizing cloud investments and achieving long-term success.

As businesses increasingly adopt cloud computing as a fundamental pillar of their IT infrastructure, optimizing cloud costs has become a critical aspect of overall financial management. Azure Fundamentals for FinOps offers a comprehensive framework that addresses this vital need. As the cloud landscape develops, organizations strike a balance between innovation, scalability, and cost-efficiency, making effective FinOps practices an essential component of their cloud strategy, refer to the following figure:

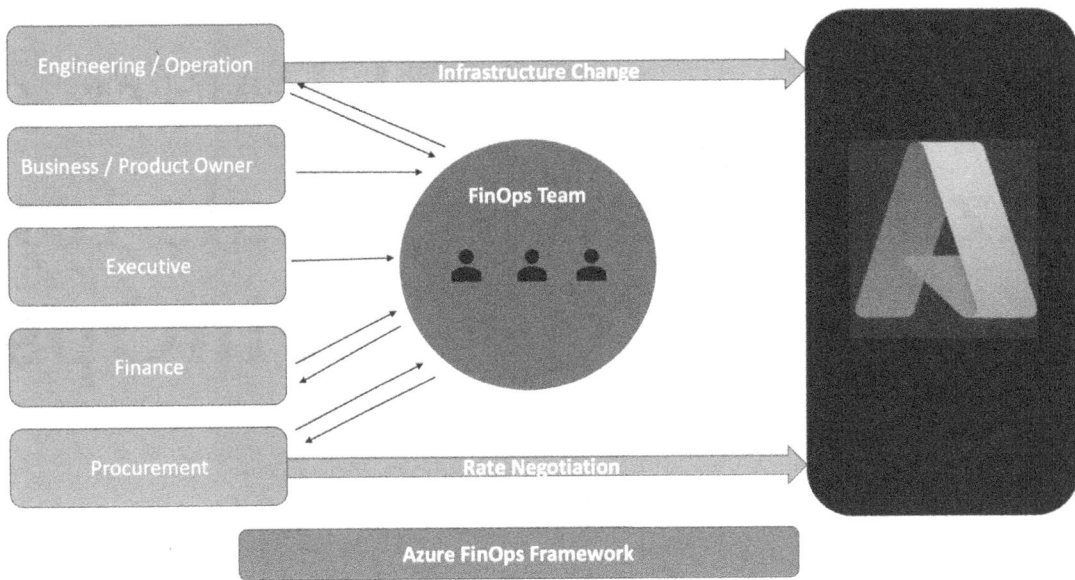

Figure 2.1: *Azure FinOps Framework*

Structure

In this chapter, we will go through the following topics:

- Azure services overview
- Resource group and tagging
- Azure cost management and billing

Objectives

Azure Services for Operational Efficiency and Cost Management This course aims to provide a solid understanding of Azure services, their functionalities, and the pricing model that needs to be considered. In this chapter, we will discuss effective methods for recurring service usage and most importantly, how to manage your resources using tags for cost tracking. Additionally, it covers maintaining procurement standards. The course also instructs on how to monitor, optimize, and budget costs using Azure cost management tools, which will help establish a 'cost-aware' culture and maximize investments in solutions deployed on Azure.

Financial and cloud operational converge

Azure Fundamentals for FinOps connects the principles of financial accountability with cloud operational excellence, creating a method that certifies organizations to make the most of their cloud investments. Financial accountability encourages a sense of ownership and responsibility among teams for their cloud spending. It enables a visionary mindset where stakeholders are mindful of resource utilization and collaborate to optimize costs.

At the same time, cloud operational excellence highlights adopting the best methods in cloud operations. Organizations can streamline resource provisioning, deployment, and management by leveraging automation, infrastructure as code, and DevOps processes. This approach enhances efficiency and aligns cloud resources with actual demand, reducing unnecessary expenses and stopping resource waste.

Empowering data-driven decisions

In the world of cloud computing, data is valuable. Azure Fundamentals for FinOps highlights the importance of data-driven decisions. By leveraging Azure's suite of cost management tools and services, organizations gain deep insights into cloud usage and spending patterns. Detailed reports, customizable dashboards, and granular cost allocation through tagging enable stakeholders to track costs across different projects, teams, or individual resources.

Data-driven visibility, businesses can identify cost drivers, analyze trends, and identify areas where optimization efforts can deliver the most significant impact.

Azure services overview

The five pillars of Azure fundamentals for FinOps:

- Financial accountability
- Cloud operational excellence
- Cost visibility
- Cost optimization
- Cost control

Financial accountability

Financial accountability with Azure means making sure you know where your money is going when you use Azure's cloud services. It is like keeping a close eye on your budget and making sure you are only spending on things that help your business grow. You have to understand how Azure charges for its services, so you can plan your budget and not get any surprises.

Think of it like this: when you are using Azure, you need tools that act like a spending tracker, so you can see what you are using and how much it costs. And just like you would not keep the lights on in an empty room, you make rules for when to turn off Azure services that you're not using to avoid wasting money.

You also want to make sure that you are organizing your Azure services in a way that makes it clear who is using what. This helps everyone understand the costs they are responsible for and ensures that your money is being spent wisely. In the end, being financially accountable with Azure is all about making the most of the cloud without spending more than you need to.

Cultivating a culture of financial responsibility

Financial accountability is a crucial pillar within Azure Fundamentals for FinOps, underpinning the successful optimization of cloud spending. At its core, this principle shows clear ownership and responsibility for cloud spending within the organization. By enabling a culture of financial obligation, organizations can help a collaborative and cost-conscious mindset among teams, allowing them to experience optimizing costs and making mindful financial decisions actively.

Key points for financial accountability

Following are the key points for financial accountability:

- **Establishing ownership and responsibility**: Azure Fundamentals for FinOps highlights the need for clearly defined ownership and responsibility for cloud resources and spending. Organizations create a sense of ownership that drives careful resource usage by assigning specific individuals or teams accountable for managing cloud costs. These responsible stakeholders collaborate with other departments, project teams, and cloud users to ensure that cloud resources are utilized efficiently and cost-effectively.

- **Promoting a culture of financial responsibility**: Financial responsibility is not a solitary task but a collective effort. Azure Fundamentals for FinOps enables organizations to promote a culture of financial responsibility throughout their cloud operations. Educate employees about the cost and importance of their actions and decisions in the cloud environment. Teams become more mindful of their resource consumption and can make choices that align with the organization's financial goals.

- **Show-back and chargeback mechanisms**: To support financial accountability, organizations can implement show-back or chargeback mechanisms. Show-back involves providing teams and stakeholders with detailed reports showcasing the cost of cloud resources they are using. This enables transparency and helps individuals understand the financial impact of their cloud activities, promoting greater accountability.

Chargeback takes the concept of show-back one step further by distributing actual cloud costs among relevant teams or business units. Stakeholders can optimize resource usage and embrace cost-effective practices by assigning actual costs to specific projects or departments. Chargeback can also act as a financial governance mechanism, enabling departments to align their cloud usage with budget constraints and organizational priorities.

- **Collaborative cost optimization**: Financial accountability in Azure Fundamentals for FinOps goes beyond simply tracking expenses. It enables collaboration and communication among different teams. By involving various departments and project owners in the cost optimization process, organizations can leverage multiple perspectives and expertise to identify innovative ways to reduce cloud costs without compromising performance.

- **Continuous improvement and cost awareness**: Financial accountability is not a one-time task but a continuous improvement and cost awareness process. Azure Fundamentals for FinOps encourages regular reviews of cloud spending, cost trends, and optimization efforts. By regularly analyzing cost data and making data-driven decisions, organizations can adapt quickly to changing needs, adjust resource allocation as necessary, and aim to achieve greater cost efficiency.

- **Cloud operational excellence**: Cloud operational excellence is a foundational principle within Azure Fundamentals for FinOps, vital for optimal cloud financial management. It highlights the need for seamless integration of financial practices with cloud operations to drive efficiency and cost-effectiveness. This principle enables teams to adopt the best resource provisioning, deployment, and scaling practices, creating a vital foundation for effective financial management.

Key points for cloud operational excellence

Following are the key points for the cloud operational excellence:

- **Best practices for resource provisioning**: Organizations must adopt well-defined best practices for resource provisioning to achieve cloud operational excellence. This involves accurately estimating the resource requirements of applications and services before deployment. Using historical data and performance metrics, teams can right size cloud resources, ensuring they align exactly with workload demands. Avoiding overprovisioning not only stops unnecessary costs but also optimizes resource utilization, maximizing the value derived from cloud investments.

- **Streamlined resource deployment**: Azure Fundamentals for FinOps highlights the importance of streamlined resource deployment. Organizations can formalize and automate resource provisioning by leveraging automation and **Infrastructure as Code (IaC)** processes. This approach reduces the risk of misconfigurations and human errors, promoting resource efficiency.

- **Dynamic resource scaling**: Dynamic resource scaling is a critical aspect of cloud operational excellence. Azure enables organizations to implement automatic scaling mechanisms that adjust resource capacity in response to fluctuating demand. For instance, autoscaling can automatically add or remove models based on predefined thresholds, providing that resources are efficiently allocated as the market fluctuates. This elasticity optimizes cloud usage by avoiding overprovisioning during times of low need and scaling up seamlessly during peak usage, resulting in significant cost savings.

- **Lifecycle management and resource optimization**: Azure Fundamentals for FinOps highlights the importance of effective lifecycle management and resource optimization. Throughout the lifecycle of cloud resources, it is vital to monitor and evaluate their usage and cost-effectiveness continually. Regularly reviewing resource utilization allows teams to identify underutilized or idle resources, which can be rightsized or decommissioned to reduce costs. This proactive approach to resource management ensures that cloud assets remain efficient and relevant to business needs.

- **Minimizing waste and maximizing resource utilization**: Cloud operational excellence organizations minimize resource waste and maximize resource utilization. Automation and IaC enable rapid resource provisioning and de-provisioning, ensuring that resources are only active when needed. This *just-in-time* approach to resource management reduces costs and eliminates unnecessary spending on idle or unused resources.

- **Cost visibility**: Decision-making and optimal resource allocation: Cost visibility is a foundation principle within Azure Fundamentals for FinOps, serving as a critical driver for efficient cloud financial management. This principle involves understanding cloud usage and spending patterns to give organizations actionable cost optimization and strategic decision-making insights.

Key points for cost visibility

Following are the key points for the cost visibility:

- **Azure cost management and billing**: Azure offers a suite of tools and services, Azure cost management and billing, which forms of achieving cost visibility. This complete platform provides real-time and granular insights into resource consumption and cost allocation across Azure subscriptions. By leveraging Azure Cost Management and Billing, businesses can view detailed reports, create customizable dashboards, and perform deep analyses of their cloud spending.

- **Detailed cost reports**: Detailed cost reports offer a complete breakdown of cloud expenses, clearly showing where and how resources are utilized. Organizations can access cost reports categorized by services, regions, and periods. This level of granularity allows Businesses to identify specific cost drivers and allocate resources more effectively.

- **Customizable dashboards**: Azure Cost Management and Billing enables organizations to build customizable dashboards for their needs and priorities.

These dashboards can be designed to display critical cost metrics and trends in real time. By visualizing data through interactive graphs and charts, teams gain valuable insights that facilitate better cost monitoring and decision-making.

- **Resource tagging**: One of the key features that contribute to cost visibility is resource tagging. Azure allows organizations to apply custom metadata labels (tags) to cloud resources like virtual machines, databases, or storage accounts. Businesses can attribute costs to specific departments, projects, or teams by tagging resources. This level of cost allocation enables responsibility and enables more accurate financial planning.

- **Insights across departments and projects**: Cost visibility further expands individual resources, enabling organizations to track costs across different departments and projects. Spending patterns help stakeholders understand the financial impact of various initiatives and make data-driven decisions when allocating resources.

- **Identifying cost drivers**: By analyzing cost data with the help of Azure Cost Management and Billing, organizations can identify the key cost drivers within their cloud infrastructure. These cost drivers could be specific services, regions, or usage patterns contributing significantly to cloud expenses. Businesses can devise targeted cost optimization strategies to address areas of significant spending.

- **Informed decision-making**: Cost visibility is a fundamental component of informed decision-making in cloud financial management. With real-time data and insights, organizations can make proactive and well-informed choices to optimize cloud resources, streamline operations, and align cloud spending with their budget goals.

- **Maximizing value while minimizing cloud expenditure**: Cost optimization is a central and critical element of Azure Fundamentals for FinOps, the perfect balance between cost-efficiency and performance within the cloud environment. Organizations can continuously review and refine their cloud infrastructure to ensure their cloud spending aligns with business objectives without compromising operational excellence.

Key points for cost optimization

Following are the key points for the cost optimization:

- **Leveraging Azure's cost-saving features**: Azure offers various cost-saving features designed to help organizations optimize their cloud spending. One of the key strategies is leveraging **reserved instances (RIs)**, which allow businesses to commit to using specific virtual machine instances over a predetermined period. By making this commitment, organizations can unlock substantial discounts compared to pay-as-you-go pricing, resulting in significant cost savings for long-term and stable workloads.

- **Spot instances and Spot virtual machines**: Another cost-saving option is Azure Spot Instances or Spot **virtual machines** (**VMs**). These are spare compute capacity instances offered at a considerable discount. Organizations can achieve significant cost reductions by using Spot Instances for workloads.

- **Dynamic resource scaling with autoscaling**: Azure Fundamentals for FinOps the importance of dynamic resource scaling through autoscaling. Autoscaling enables organizations to adjust the number of resources (for example, VM instances) based on real-time demand. Autoscaling also helps avoid overprovisioning during low-traffic periods, preventing unnecessary expenses.

- **Serverless architectures and managed services**: Serverless architectures managed services is another cost optimization strategy. Serverless computing, such as Azure Functions or Logic Apps, allows businesses to execute code or tasks without managing underlying servers. With serverless, users are only billed for the actual execution time, reducing costs for applications with sporadic usage.

Similarly, exploring managed services such as Azure SQL Database or Cosmos DB eliminates the need for organizations to maintain and manage the infrastructure for databases and other services.

- **Right-sizing resources**: The right-sizing resource is a fundamental part of cost optimization. Organizations should continuously assess their resource requirements and adjust the size and type of cloud instances accordingly. By provisioning resources that match workload demands, businesses can avoid overprovisioning and ensure optimal resource utilization, reducing unnecessary costs.

- **Cost optimization and continuous improvement**: Azure Fundamentals for FinOps enables organizations to continuously review and optimize their cloud resources, applications, and services by analyzing usage patterns, performance metrics, and cost data and implementing targeted cost optimization strategies to align cloud spending with budgetary goals effectively.

- **Enforcing budget and governance policies**: Cost control is a critical principle within Azure Fundamentals for FinOps, aimed at providing that cloud spending remains aligned with budget constraints and organizational policies. Organizations can proactively manage their cloud resources by implementing cost control measures, avoiding unexpected cost overruns, and maintaining financial stability within the cloud environment.

Key points for cost control

Following are the key points for the cost control:

- **Establishing budgetary constraints**: A crucial part of cost control is the establishment of budget constraints. Azure Fundamentals for FinOps enables organizations to set clear and realistic budgets for their cloud operations.

Businesses can gain greater control over cloud spending by defining budget limits for different departments or resource groups.

- **Implementing Azure Policy**: Azure Policy is a powerful tool that enables organizations to enforce governance policies. Organizations can define policies to ensure compliance with security and operational requirements. Azure Policy can enforce specific cost-related guidelines, such as stopping using certain expensive VM sizes or services that do not match cost-efficiency goals.

- **Role-Based Access Control (RBAC)**: RBAC is a vital part of cost control. Organizations can control access to cloud resources and services by assigning proper roles to users and groups. RBAC ensures that only authorized users can create, modify, or delete resources.

- **Budget alerts and thresholds**: Azure allows setting up budget alerts. Organizations can configure these alerts to notify Businesses when cloud spending exceeds thresholds. Budget alerts can be sent via email or SMS. By receiving these alerts, Businesses can instantly identify overspending and address costs.

- **Budget forecasting and variance analysis**: Cost control involves constant monitoring and analysis of budget forecasts and actual spending. Azure Cost Management enables organizations to protect their cloud spending based on documented data. By approximating budget forecasts with actual costs, organizations can perform variance analysis to understand variations and take corrective actions.

- **Continuous improvement and iterative cost control**: Cost control is a process. Azure Fundamentals for FinOps enables organizations to review and optimize cost control measures constantly. Through regular audits and performance evaluations, businesses can analyze their cost control and improve their financial management in the cloud environment.

Resource groups and tagging

Azure resource group *is a logical container that relates resources for an application or a specific workload*. It helps manage, organize, and monitor resources.

Logical grouping is a vital part of resource group functionality in Azure. It authorizes organizations to create a hierarchical design that reflects their business requirements, making operating, monitoring, and locating resources within their Azure environment more comfortable.

The below figure explains how the company organizes all its cloud services in Azure. It uses a management group to keep everything in order and separate spaces (subscriptions) for testing and actual products, each with its own set of tools and storage.

At the top, you have the **Azure Management Group**, like the head of the family. This is where the big decisions that affect everyone below are made.

Then, you have two branches: one is for **Dev Subscription** and the other for **Prod Subscription**. These are like the main children of the family. The **Dev Subscription** is where the company tests new ideas, like a playground for apps. It has its tools, like a **Virtual Machine**, like a computer living in the cloud, and **Storage Accounts**, like closets where you keep all your digital stuff.

The **Prod Subscription** is more serious, where the company's real products live. This branch has two main apps, **Prod App1** and **Prod App2**. Each of these apps also has its own set of tools — virtual machines for doing the heavy lifting and storage accounts for keeping all the critical data safe and sound.

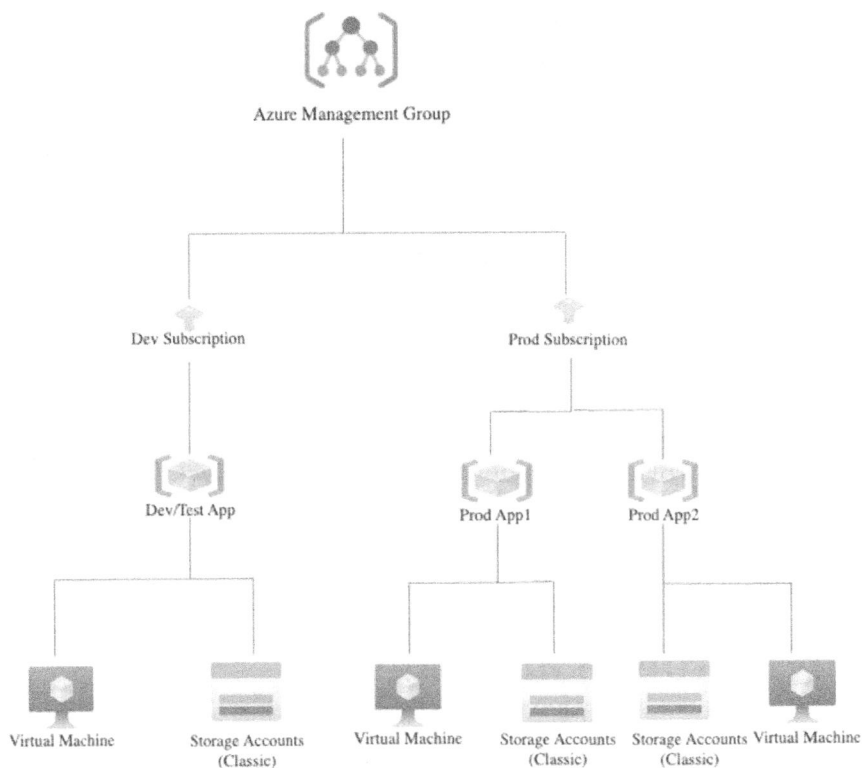

Figure 2.2: Organize Resources using Management Group

Resource groups promote the organization of resources based on their relevance to the organization's business operations. This alignment provides that resources are grouped to align the different projects, departments, or teams, simplifying management and ensuring a clear understanding of resource ownership and duties.

In many cases, resources are associated with typical applications or workloads. By creating resource groups based on applications, organizations can keep related resources together, making it easier to Provision, monitor, and update those applications as a unit.

Resource groups permit the breakup of resources based on different environments, such as development, testing, staging, and production. This separation is essential for maintaining clear limitations between various application lifecycle stages and reducing the risk of forced changes.

Logical grouping can be developed through resource tagging to include project names or other information. Tags serve as metadata, providing additional context to resource group resources, allowing better cost allocation and more accessible tracking costs associated with detailed projects, teams, or cost centers.

Resource groups play an essential role in defining the scope of RBAC assignments. Organizations can ensure that individuals or groups have appropriate responsibilities by associating access permissions with resource groups.

Resource groups allow more efficient monitoring and reporting by providing a high-level view of resource health and performance within detailed logical groupings. Monitoring metrics, logs, and alerts can be managed and filtered by resource groups, making it easier to specify potential issues and take immediate action.

Logical grouping assists in implementing governance and compliance policies. Organizations can enforce exact policies at the resource group level to ensure even configurations, naming conventions, and safety standards across all resources.

Complex applications usually consist of multiple resources with interdependencies. Logical grouping within resource groups enables the management of these dependencies, allowing you to visualize and understand how different resources connect.

Resource groups can be vital in disaster recovery and high availability systems. Organizations can ensure a more efficient and controlled recovery process by organizing resources involved in replication and failover into separate resource groups.

Establishing naming patterns and standardization for resource groups further improves logical grouping. Consistent naming patterns make it easy to determine the purpose and contents of a resource group, promoting a more organized Azure environment.

Azure Policy is an effective service that allows organizations to specify and execute specific rules and compliance essentials across their Azure resources. While policies can be used at different levels, including the subscription and resource levels, resource group-level approaches offer several advantages.

Applying resource group-level policies delivers a centralized method for implementing governance and compliance across resources. This provides constant application of policies within the content of a resource group. Resource group policies allow organizations to apply rules that collectively all resources within a resource group. This approach facilitates control and reduces the risk of misconfigurations within the group.

Azure Policy proposes a wide range of built-in and custom policy definitions that can meet an organization's requirements. Policies can execute various elements, such as resource naming conventions, tagging standards, and access control rules. Azure Policy provides monitoring abilities that allow organizations to set policy compliance across resource groups. Administrators can receive alerts and notifications if any resource within a group breaks a policy, allowing them to take suitable actions to remediate the non-compliant resources.

Resource group policies can be utilized to implement security best practices, such as requiring detailed security configurations for resources. This helps protect resources from possible security breaches and unauthorized access.

Resource group naming and guidelines

Naming resource groups is vital to organizing and managing resources in Azure. Organizations can enhance resource discovery, reduce naming conflicts, and improve overall resource management by observing a well-defined naming convention to best practices.

Following are some basic guidelines for naming resource groups:

- **Clear and meaningful names**: Resource group names should be defined, and the resource group purpose should be. Bypass using generic or unclear names that do not provide sufficient context.

- **Consistent naming patterns**: Consistent naming practice across all resource groups helps users quickly determine their function or category. Consider incorporating a variety of project codes, environment indicators, and other relevant information into the naming convention and random number.

  For example: `[Vertical Name]-[Environment]-[App Name]` (for example, `HR-D-WebApp`)

- **Avoid special characters and spaces**: Resource group names should only contain alphanumeric characters and hyphens ("-"). Avoid using spaces, underscores, or other special characters, as they might cause issues with Azure web services and APIs.

- **Unique within the subscription**: Resource group names must be unique within an Azure subscription. To ensure identity, additional identifiers, such as a date stamp or a sequential number, in cases where multiple resource groups serve similar purposes.

- **Reflect order or relationships**: If there is a hierarchical connection between resource groups or they serve different stages of a task, consider including that information in the naming convention. This system can provide insights into how other resource groups connect.

- **Avoid hardcoding environment names**: Common environment indicators (for example, `Dev`, `Prod`) in resource group names; avoid hardcoding specific environment names. Instead, consider setting the environment using variables or tags within your infrastructure templates.

- **Frequent review and maintenance**: Review and update the naming conventions, if necessary, as the organization's Azure environment develops. This ensures that the patterns remain appropriate, align with changing requirements, and resume to facilitate efficient resource management.

- **Automation and validation**: Automation tools and scripts to validate resource group names against the naming convention before deploying new resources. This practice helps detect naming inconsistencies early during provisioning and encourages using standards.

Azure managing resources in resource groups

Resource groups in Azure act as a suitable hub for managing and administering all the resources. The Azure portal, PowerShell, Azure CLI, or Rest API provides user-friendly options to perform various management tasks within resource groups, offering significant benefits for resources, refer to the following figure:

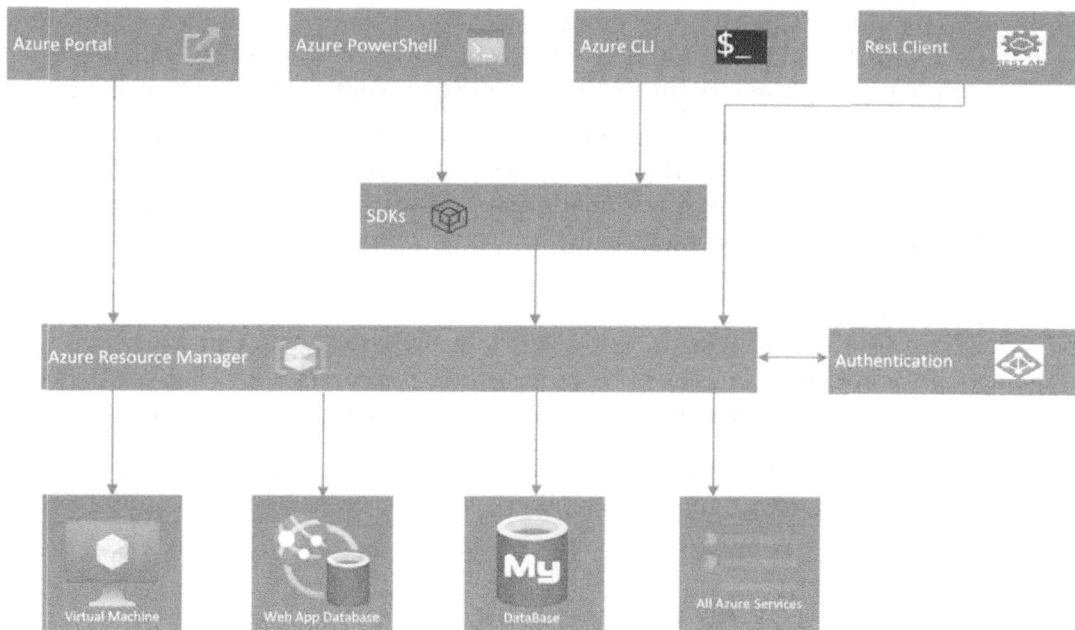

Figure 2.3: *Azure Resource Manager Data Flow-Chart*

Single management interface

The Team can access and manage all associated resources through the interface by organizing related resources within a resource group. This simplifies the management process and eliminates the need to navigate multiple sections.

- **Centralized control**: Resource groups allow for centralized command over multiple resources. The team can apply changes, updates, and configurations across all resources within the group, providing constant settings and reducing the risk of configuration discrepancies.

- **Bulk operations**: The ability to perform bulk operations on resources within a resource group simplifies duplicative tasks, such as starting or stopping multiple virtual machines or applying updates to various web apps. This mainly reduces the time and effort required for administrative tasks.

- **Access control and role-based access control**: Resource groups provide a limit for applying RBAC policies. The Team can contribute specific permissions to users or groups at the resource group level.

- **Resource group templates**: **Azure Resource Manager** (**ARM**) templates can specify and deploy resource groups and their resources. These templates allow for repeatable and even resource provisioning, which is especially valuable when creating multiple environments, such as development, staging, and production.

- **Resource lifecycle management**: Resource groups promote better resource lifecycle management. When a project or workload is complete, the Team can quickly delete the entire resource group, ensuring all associated resources are removed, controlled, and efficiently.

Azure tagging

Tagging *is a feature that permits you to associate Key-value pairs called tags.* Tags are data that provide additional information about resources and manage them effectively.

If you are working on the project, there should be some tagging solution to organize your Azure resources, resource groups, subscriptions, and management groups or for filtering and monitoring.

Best practices for Azure tagging

To make the most of tags in Azure, it is vital to follow best practices to ensure they are effective:

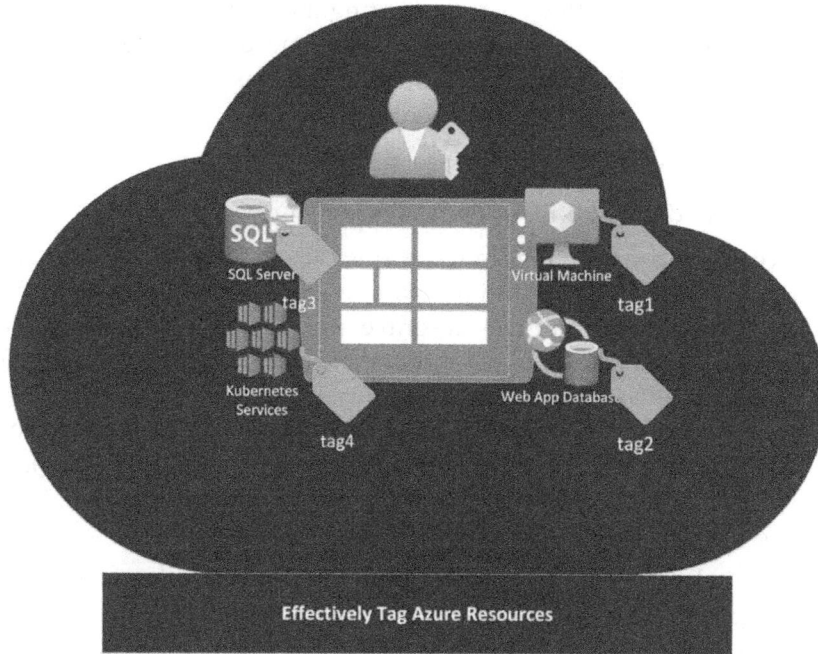

Figure 2.4: *Azure Resource Tag Flow*

1. **Define a tagging strategy**: Verify a transparent tagging technique summarizing per tag's purpose and use cases. Choose traditional tag names that align with your organization's business prerequisites and resource control objectives.

2. **Uniform tag naming patterns**: Implement constant tag naming patterns across all resources. This ensures that labels are easily understood and analyzed by all teams. Avoid unclear or too generic tag keys.

3. **Avoid over-tagging**: While tags are helpful for categorization, avoid over-tagging resources with unneeded tags. Focus on utilizing tags that provide significant information and contribute to your typical resource management requirements.

4. **Use tags at resource provisioning**: Tag resources as they are provisioned. This confirms that all resources are always tagged from the start and prevents the need to tag existing resources.

5. **Educate and train users**: Ensure that all relevant stakeholders, including administrators, developers, and finance teams, understand the importance of tagging and follow the established guidelines. Provide training and documentation on tag usage to promote consistency.

6. **Execute tag compliance**: Execute policies to implement tagging compliance. Azure Policy can be used to require the existence of detailed tags on resources and confirm your tagging standards.

7. **Update tags regularly**: Review your tagging method and tags to ensure they stay appropriate and aligned with varying business needs. Update tags as necessary to adapt to new provisions or organizational adaptions.

Why do we need tags?

In this section, we will discuss why we need tags in Azure.

-   **Resource categorization**: Tags in Azure offer an effective tool to organize and label resources, providing organizations with control over their cloud environment. The tagging method improves resource management, cost optimization, and overall governance. The team can understand resource usage in-depth, determine directions, and allocate costs with tags. For example, by tagging resources based on groups or business units, financial teams can track cloud expenses for each unit and optimize the budget. Additionally, compliance measures are maintained as resources can be tagged to show keeping to detailed regulatory conditions or data categories.

    Tags are vital in resource grouping and key control, allowing teams to apply policies, govern permissions, and execute measurement processes on resources with shared tags. Tags provide a flexible method to organize resources into logical groupings, allowing better resource tracking and dependence management. Teams can also use tags to indicate the status of resources, such as *testing* or *archived*, to facilitate resource lifecycle management.

    A well-defined and always-applied tagging strategy is foundational to the success of FinOps. It authorizes financial teams to accurately allocate costs, monitor resource usage, and ensure financial accountability. By adopting proper resource categorization through tagging, teams can optimize cloud spending, improve partnerships between IT and finance teams, and drive constant progress in cost management within their Azure environment.

-   **Cost allocation and optimization**: Tags are key in cost allocation and optimization within Azure. Cost-related tags with resources, teams acquire valuable understandings of cloud spending practices and can accurately allocate costs to typical projects, departments, or business units. This level of cost attribution allows financial teams to understand the distribution of cloud expenses across the organization and educated budget decisions.

    By tagged resources, organizations can determine areas of possible cost optimization. By investigating resource usage practices and costs associated with different tags, teams can identify opportunities to right-size instances. They can enforce strategies to optimize resource allocation, reduce unnecessary spending, and maximize the value of their cloud investments.

    Altogether, Tags for cost allocation and optimization are vital FinOps practices. It assigns teams to maintain financial accountability, align cloud spending with business importance, and continuously optimize cloud resources for cost efficiency. In their cost management strategy, teams can drive better financial governance, enhance decision-making, and achieve more significant control over their spending.

- **Governance and compliance**: Tags are a powerful tool for implementing governance and compliance policies within the Azure environment. Teams can enforce resource group policies and access management that align with their specific standards and security requirements by utilizing tags to classify resources based on various points.

Tags allow for acceptable policies tailored to different resource categories or business units. For instance, resources tagged with *PCI Data* can have stricter access controls and encryption conditions. On the other hand, resources tagged as *Front Facing* may require additional security measures to protect against external threats.

By integrating tags with Azure Policy, Teams can define rules that automatically apply to resources running specific tags. These policies can contain various measures, including resource naming conventions, virtual machine designs, network access rules, etc. As a result, any resources created or existing within the scope of a specific tag must be to the defined policies, promoting consistent configurations and enhanced security throughout the Azure environment.

Tags enable the team to conduct thorough audits and reporting. Teams can generate detailed reports on compliance status, resource usage, and security posture by tracking and categorizing resources based on relevant tags.

Tags to implement governance and compliance within Azure is a proactive approach to managing cloud resources effectively. By combining tags with policy enforcement agents, teams can ensure that resources always meet specified standards, and minimize security risks, to industry best practices and regulatory obligations. Tags are vital in governance and compliance efforts, protecting data, and investing trust.

Reporting and monitoring

Tags enable efficient monitoring and reporting within Azure. By associating tags with resources, teams can easily organize and tag resources based on various features, allowing them to filter, group, and analyze resource data.

Using tags as an ideal for filtering and group resources allows teams to quickly collect insights on resource usage and performance across different projects, departments, or environments. For instance, by filtering resources with specific tags, such as *Production* or *Development*, teams can quickly assess resource performance and cost implications in different development lifecycle stages.

Tags provide a suitable way to follow spending and resource utilization for specific initiatives or business units. Financial teams can use tags to generate reports of cloud expenses by department, or cost center, assigning them to make data-driven decisions when allocating budgets and optimizing cloud spending.

Analyzing resource data based on tag values helps teams recognize cost-saving possibilities and optimize resource allocation. By comparing resource utilization patterns across different tags, administrators can detect underutilized or idle resources and take appropriate actions, such as resizing or deallocating, to optimize cost efficiency.

Tags facilitate effective resource performance monitoring. By grouping resources with similar attributes, such as operating systems, regions, or service tiers, administrators can track and analyze performance metrics for specific resource categories. This allows for targeted performance optimization and proactive troubleshooting.

Tags also enable organizations to set up custom monitoring and alerts based on specific resource attributes. For example, *Critical* resources can have more stringent monitoring and alert thresholds to ensure prompt notification and swift response to critical incidents.

Tags for reporting and monitoring improve visibility and transparency across the Azure environment. Tags enable organizations to develop meaningful reports, gain valuable insights into resource utilization and performance, and implement practical cost-optimization methods. Using tags to improve reporting and monitoring capabilities, Teams can maintain control over their cloud resources, optimize resource utilization, and ensure that their Azure environment aligns with business objectives.

In FinOps context, tagging is central to optimizing cloud spending and cost management systems. By associating tags with resources, Teams can acquire an understanding of cloud expenses, letting them attribute costs accurately to detailed projects, teams, or cost centers. This group of cost attribution improves financial accountability and transparency, authorizing businesses to follow and allocate cloud expenses.

Tags also enable FinOps teams to conduct detailed cost analysis by categorizing resources based on different attributes. By grouping resources with identical tags, teams can set spending practices across various resource categories, determine areas of overspending, and execute targeted cost-saving measures. This data-driven system allows businesses to optimize their cloud resources, maximize cost efficiency, and align cloud spending with their purposes.

Tags enable data-driven decision-making within the FinOps framework. With the ability to filter, group, and research resource data based on tag values, teams can achieve a helpful understanding of the financial impact of different resource groups, applications, or departments. This helpful information helps FinOps teams make informed decisions, prioritize resource allocation, and optimize cloud spending for optimal cost-effectiveness.

Executing tagging best practices ensures consistency and accuracy in cost allocation, making it easier to track and manage cloud expenses effectively. With well-defined tagging standards, teams can understand resource ownership, facilitate collaboration between IT and finance teams, and improve financial governance within their Azure environment.

Tagging is a vital element of successful FinOps practices. It authorizes teams to understand, assign, and optimize cloud spending in detail. Tags for cost allocation, analysis, and decision-making businesses can achieve better financial control, drive continuous progress in cost management, and align their Azure environment with their business objectives and financial goals.

Azure cost management and billing

Azure Cost Management and Billing is a complete and centralized platform developed to handle cloud spending in the Azure environment. As teams adopt cloud services, understanding and managing cloud costs become critical to their overall design. Cost Management and Billing deliver tools and features that enable businesses to access their cloud costs and implement effective cost-saving measures accurately.

Azure Cost Management is a toolset that can help teams monitor, assign, and optimize the cost of their Azure resources. Cost Management is open to anyone accessing billing or resource management content. The availability contains anyone from the finance team with access to the billing charge. DevOps teams operate their resources and subscriptions.

Azure billing is where you can handle your accounts, invoices, and expenses. Azure Billing is open to anyone accessing a billing account or other billing scope. The team leaders are typically included in the billing scope.

Following figure will explain how the different Azure Management service connecting to cost management. This will help to manage cost reporting from cost management at any granular level.

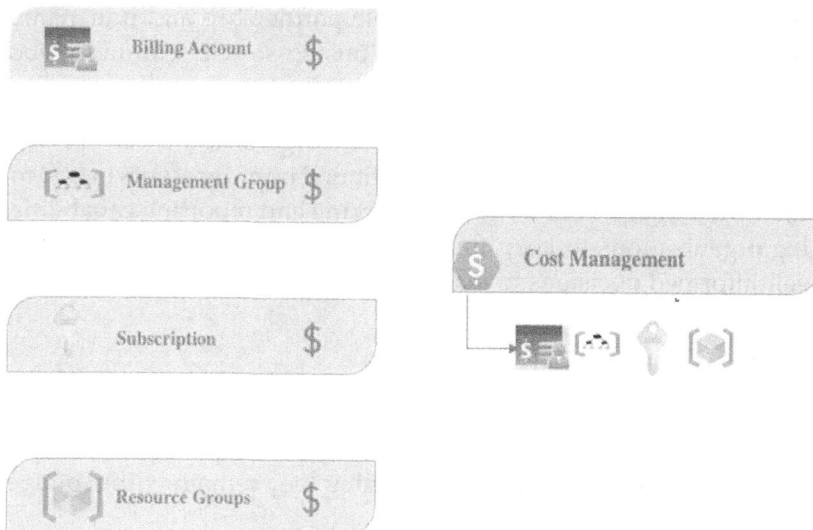

Figure 2.5: *Azure Cost Management*

Key features and capabilities

The following section cover the key features and capabilities.

Cost tracking and reporting

Cost Management proposes an effective platform for complete cost tracking and documenting in the cloud environment, with the ability to develop custom information based on different dimensions, such as resource groups, subscriptions, tags, departments, and services. Reports deliver helpful insights into cost trends, designs, and drivers, allowing FinOps teams and decision-makers to make data-driven findings about resource utilization and optimization.

Cost-tracking features in Azure Cost Management enable teams to keep spending levels. Users can view resource costs, understand how other services contribute to the overall cloud expenses, and determine areas where resource usage may lead to unexpected costs.

Reporting abilities deliver a view of cloud spending across the organization. The reports can be created to specific user needs, presenting data in a way that aligns with various business requirements. Whether investigating costs for a particular project or considering the financial effect of other resource types, Azure Cost Management provides the flexibility and understanding required to support various cost management needs.

In addition to cost data, the platform allows organizations to predict future spending based on data trends. Businesses can effectively plan and assign resources by fixing budgets and forecasting cloud spend.

Cost Management's reporting capabilities enable partnership and transparency between IT and finance teams. With clear cost reports, businesses can commit cloud costs with actual costs and optimize resource allocation across the cloud space.

Data provided by cost-tracking and reporting parts organizations can specify cost-saving options, optimize resource usage, and drive continued improvements in cost management. Overall, Azure Cost Management's vital cost tracking and reporting capabilities are critical in authorizing organizations to keep financial control, align cloud spending with goals, and make well-informed decisions to maximize the value of their cloud investments.

Budgeting and forecasting

Cost Management and Billing provide teams with practical tools for setting budgets and creating forecasts for their cloud spending. This proactive approach allows businesses to prepare and allocate resources efficiently, providing they remain within budget limits and avoid unplanned overspending.

With budgeting, users can explain spending thresholds for other aspects of their cloud environment, such as subscriptions and resource groups. Developing budgets certifies teams to verify clear financial plans and maintain better management over their cloud costs. When actual spending processes exceed the budget limits, Cost Management can send alerts and information to relevant stakeholders, allowing for timely corrective actions and proactive cost management.

Azure Cost Management enables teams to create predictions for future cloud costs based on data and trends. Businesses can make educated forecasts about their future cloud costs by studying past spending designs, enabling more proper resource planning and allocation. Predictions are crucial in decision-making and help teams align cloud spending with overall budget goals.

The combination of budget and forecasting certifies teams to make data-driven decisions about their cloud buys. By clearly understanding their predicted cloud costs and a proactive budgeting plan, businesses can confidently support cloud resources, optimize their cloud usage, and avoid financial shocks.

Azure Cost Management's budgeting and forecasting stuff ultimately help teams optimize their cloud cost, improve financial responsibility, and align cloud resources with their goals. By proactively planning and managing cloud expenses, businesses can achieve greater cost-effectiveness, make informed investment decisions, and maximize the value of their cloud investments.

Cost allocation and chargeback

Azure Cost Management and Billing provide vital support for cost allocation and chargeback, enabling businesses to accurately cloud costs to teams or cost centers. This cost level enhances financial responsibility and transparency, allowing teams to manage cloud spending and allocate costs accurately.

Cost-share methods are tags and resource categorization. By applying tags to cloud resources, businesses can categorize them based on various details, such as team names, verticals, or cost centers. These tags act as useful metadata, enabling the cloud expenses with specific organizations.

With this level of cost allocation performed through tagging, teams can implement show-back or chargeback models. Show back provides internal teams with cloud costs associated with their teams, enabling them to understand the financial impact of their cloud use. This approach promotes a culture of financial responsibility and encourages teams to optimize their cloud spending based on actual costs.

On the other hand, chargeback involves transparent cloud expenses to internal or external clients based on resource usage. Teams perform as service providers or shared services, where business units utilize cloud resources. Chargeback enables the proper allocation of cloud costs to each customer, supporting billing processes and providing that cloud costs are distributed among various teams.

Ultimately, with Cost Management's cost allocation and chargeback support, organizations can improve financial transparency and enhance collaboration between IT and teams. This level of responsibility and transparency enables teams to make data-driven decisions and optimize their cloud cost across the organization.

Resource optimization

Azure Cost Management and Billing provides teams with insights into their resources, enabling them to optimize their cloud spending and ensure cost-effectiveness. The platform's resource optimization capabilities assign FinOps teams to determine and address underutilized or idle resources to drive cost savings without compromising performance.

Azure Cost Management's resource optimization, teams gain visibility into resource usage patterns, including CPU, memory, and network utilization. This data-driven approach allows teams to identify resources not fully utilized for right-sizing.

Azure Cost Management gives insight into idle or unused resources to help teams identify and remove these assets to save cost. Azure Cost Management also provides information into orphaned resources no longer connected to active apps or resources, enabling teams to clean up their cloud environment and eliminate unnecessary expenses.

Azure Cost Management's resource optimization features assign FinOps teams to make informed decisions about resource usage, right-size virtual machines, remove idle resources, and apply cost-effective pricing models. It ensures that teams maintain the performance and reliability of their cloud services.

Azure Advisor

Azure Advisor is an intelligent tool that combines with Azure Cost Management and enables teams to optimize their resources to increase efficiency. Azure Advisor helps teams make informed findings aligned with best practices by giving recommendations.

Azure Advisor focuses on data analytics and machine learning. The platform explores historical usage, resource configurations, and pricing options to suggest cost-saving efforts. Recommendations include rightsizing virtual machines, using Reserved Instances, or using Azure Hybrid Benefit for cost-effective OS (Windows) licenses.

Moreover, Azure Advisor enhances implementation and reliability by identifying bottlenecks and areas for optimization. It considers resource utilization, network throughput, and application response times.

Security is another vital element addressed by Azure Advisor. It considers security configurations and identifies vulnerabilities or misconfigurations, providing recommendations to improve the security posture of cloud resources with industry standards.

Azure Advisor suggests high availability and reliability. Identify resource redundancy and disaster recovery capabilities to help teams improve their applications' resiliency and reduce downtime.

Integrating with Azure Cost Management benefits FinOps teams, providing a complete view of performance and cost efficiency. This approach assigns data-driven findings on resource allocation, cost savings, and performance improvement.

Azure Advisor is valuable, supporting teams in gaining functional excellence and cost optimization in the Azure cloud. With recommendations covering performance, cost, security, and high availability, organizations can align their cloud resources with best practices and business goals.

Conclusion

Azure Cost Management and Billing is a crucial component of FinOps practices, offering businesses the tools and insights needed to optimize cloud spending, achieve financial control, and enhance resource utilization. The platform enables efficient tagging strategies, facilitating accurate cost allocation and transparent spending tracking. By setting budgets, businesses proactively manage cloud expenses, aligning spending with budgetary limits and strategic goals.

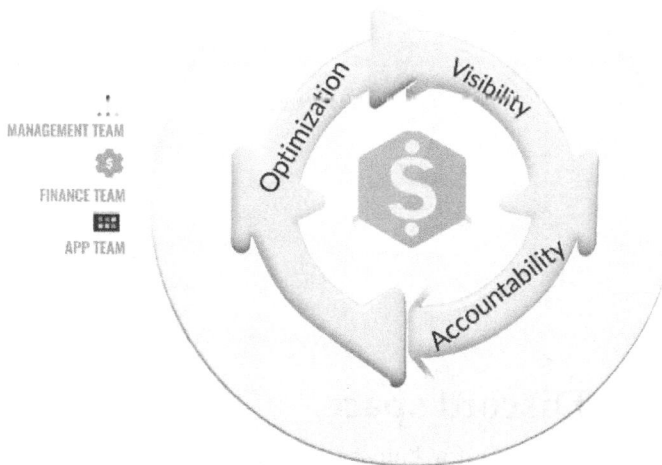

Figure 2.6: Outline of a cost-conscious process

Organizations gain in-depth insights into cloud spending trends and drivers through robust cost analysis capabilities, identifying cost-saving opportunities and optimizing resource usage. Azure Cost Management and Billing fosters collaboration between FinOps teams and business stakeholders, ensuring cloud resources are aligned with business needs and supporting informed decision-making.

Businesses optimize resource allocation by identifying underutilized resources and implementing corrective actions, reducing cloud costs without compromising performance. In summary, Azure Cost Management and Billing empower businesses to make data-driven decisions, collaborate effectively, and drive cloud cost efficiency to achieve their strategic objectives and maximize the value of cloud investments.

In the next chapter, we will learn more about setting up cost management, budgeting, and subscriptions.

Setting up Azure Cost Management and Billing is like establishing a central command center for all your Azure-related expenses. This portal is the go-to place to keep an eye on what you're spending and make sure it's within your budget. It's packed with tools that help you analyze costs and figure out where you might be able to cut back or need to increase your budget. Think of Azure subscriptions like your different bank accounts, each one with its own purpose for managing different Azure services. You can set these up and tweak them right from the Azure portal. Plus, you get alerts and notifications that are like timely reminders or updates about your spending, so you're always in the know if your costs start to change and can react quickly.

Join our book's Discord space

Join the book's Discord Workspace for Latest updates, Offers, Tech happenings around the world, New Release and Sessions with the Authors:

https://discord.bpbonline.com

CHAPTER 3

Azure Cost Management and Billing

Introduction

Azure Cost Management and Billing is a comprehensive set of tools designed to manage, allocate, and optimize Azure cloud expenses efficiently. It provides necessary features to track, examine, and enhance Azure spending for small and large businesses. Additionally, it simplifies billing account management tasks, ensuring a smooth and transparent financial administration experience.

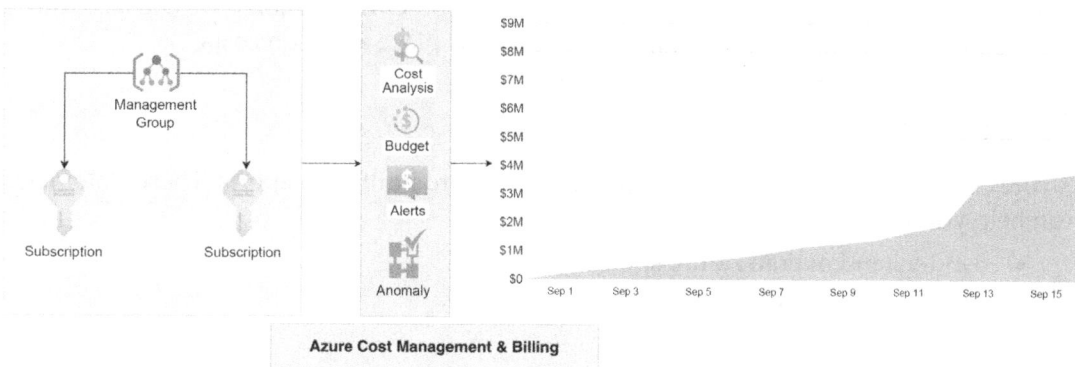

Figure 3.1: *Azure Cost Management and Billing*

Structure

In this chapter, we will go through the following topics:

- Azure Cost Management
- Azure Cost Management and Billing portal
- Enabling cost analysis and budgeting
- Resource groups and tagging
- Azure Cost Management and Billing

Objectives

By the end of this chapter, the reader should be able to navigate and utilize the Azure Cost Management and Billing portal effectively. They will learn how to enable and conduct cost analysis and set up budgeting to monitor and control Azure spending. The chapter will also provide insights into organizing resources through groups and implementing tagging strategies for better cost allocation and reporting within Azure Cost Management and Billing.

Azure Cost Management

Following is the detailed analysis to the creation of custom reports and the strategic budgeting and forecasting aspect of managing costs within Azure, along with the optimization measures like recommendations and alerts.

Cost analysis

Cost analysis is a tool that delivers a high-level overview of Azure costs. It lets you view your costs over time by resource group, service, and other dimensions. We can also utilize cost analysis to develop and manage budgets and to place alerts on costs.

Cost reports

Azure Cost Management delivers a combination of pre-built cost reports. These statements can help you to:

- Understand overall Azure spending.
- Determine the costliest resources and services.
- Track spending over time
- Compare spending across different subscriptions or resource groups.
- Identify trends and areas for refinement.

Cost visualizations

Azure Cost Management also delivers a variety of cost visualizations. These visualizations can help you to:

- Quickly notice where money is going.
- Identify trends and patterns in spending.
- Compare spending to other organizations.
- Understand the impact of cost optimization efforts.

Custom reports

In addition to the pre-built information and visualizations, Azure Cost Management allows the creation of custom reports. This gives the flexibility to get the identical insights that are needed.

Exporting data

We can also export Azure Cost Management data to CSV or JSON format. This allows data analysis in other tools, such as Excel or Power BI.

Optimizing costs with Azure reports and visualizations

Here are samples of how can use Azure Cost Management reports and visualizations to analyze costs:

- **Identify your most expensive resources and services**: We can use the cost analysis to consider costs by resource type and service. This can help identify the resources and services that cost the most money.

- **Track your spending over time**: We can use the cost analysis tool to view costs over time. This can support identifying spending trends and seeing how consumption changes over time.

- **Compare your spending across different subscriptions or resource groups**: We can utilize the cost analysis tool to compare spending across additional subscriptions or resource groups. This will identify areas where we can control spending.

- **Identify trends and areas for improvement**: We can utilize the cost analysis tool and the cost visualizations to determine trends and patterns in spending.

- **Understand the impact of your cost optimization efforts**: We can utilize the cost analysis tool and the cost visualizations to follow the effect of cost optimization efforts. This can support to see how the steps are reducing your costs.

Budgeting and forecasting

Cost Management + Billing allows us to create and manage budgets for your Azure costs. We can also utilize forecasting tools to forecast future spending. This can help to remain on track with budget and avoid overspending.

Recommendations

Cost Management + Billing guides how to optimize your Azure costs. These recommendations are established based on historical use data and best practices.

Alerts

Cost Management + Billing allows alerts to notify users when the costs exceed budget, when there is a sudden change in spending, or when an Azure resource is underutilized.

It also shows a combination of features that can help users manage their billing accounts and pay the invoices:

- **Create and manage multiple billing accounts**: This can be useful if users have additional teams or departments using Azure for other purposes.
- **Configure payment options**: Users can pay their Azure invoices by credit card, debit card, or bank transfer. Users can also select recurring payments, so users do not have to worry about forgetting to settle their bills.
- **Manage your billing information**: Users can manage your billing information, such as your legal entity, tax information, and agreements.

Here are some examples of how the user can use Azure Cost Management + Billing to save money:

- It can help you determine unused resources, such as virtual machines turned on but unused. Users can then depend on these resources to save money.
- It can support users in optimizing their resource usage by suggesting the right size and type of resources for their workloads. For example, users can save money using smaller virtual machines or spot instances.
- It can help users negotiate better pricing with Microsoft by providing insights into Azure usage patterns. For example, if users use a lot of Azure resources in a particular region, you can negotiate a lower price for those resources.

Azure Cost Management and Billing portal

Microsoft Cost Management is a tool that allows one to monitor, allocate, and optimize the cost of Microsoft Cloud workloads. Cost Management is known to anyone with a billing or resource scope. The availability contains anyone from the cloud finance team with a key to the billing account. Assign DevOps groups to subscription, resource group, and resources.

Billing is where we can control accounts, invoices, and payments. Billing is known to anyone accessing a billing account or other billing scope, like billing profiles and invoice sections. The cloud finance team and organizational leaders are commonly included.

Cost Management and Billing are gates to the Microsoft commerce system available to anyone throughout the journey, from the start with signing up and managing billing accounts, to purchasing and handling Microsoft and third-party marketplace offerings, all the way to implementing **financial operations (FinOps)** tools.

A few examples of what we can accomplish in Cost Management and Billing include:

- Report on and research costs in the Azure portal or externally by exporting data.
- Monitor costs along with budget, anomaly, and scheduled alerts.
- Split costs with cost allocation rules.
- Create and organize subscriptions to customize invoices.
- Configure payment choices and pay invoices.
- Manage billing information, such as lawful entity, tax information, and agreements.

How Cost Management and Billing work, we should understand the Finance system. At its core, Microsoft is a data channel that underpins all consumer or commercial transactions. There are multiple information and links to the pipeline. It contains the sign-up and marketplace buy experiences. However, we will concentrate on the elements of a cloud billing account and how charges are processed within the system.

Usage data collection

Azure services gather usage data for all Azure resources that are running, including:

- Compute resources, such as VM, cloud services, and App Service plans
- Storage resources, such as Blob Storage, Disk storage, and File storage
- Networking resources, such as virtual networks, load balancers, and VPN gateways
- Database resources, such as SQL Database, Azure Database for PostgreSQL, and Azure Database for MySQL
- Other resources, such as Azure Active Directory, Azure Monitor, and Azure Kubernetes Service

The usage data is gathered at various intervals, counting on the service. For example, storage usage data is gathered every hour, while compute usage data is collected every minute.

Usage data aggregation

The usage data is aggregated into information by subscription, resource group, and service. This data provides insights into Azure spending and helps determine areas where we can optimize costs.

For example, we can use the Azure Cost Management cost analysis tool to consider their costs by resource type and service. This allows us to determine the resources and services that cost the most. We can also use Azure Cost Management to follow their spending over time and to reach their spending across other subscriptions or resource groups.

Charge calculation

The usage data calculates amounts based on the Azure pricing model for each service. The Azure pricing model changes depending on the service. For example, some services are metered by the charge of time they are running, while others are metered by the cost of resources they consume.

For example, Azure Virtual Machines are metered by their running length. The hourly rate for a virtual machine relies on the size and type of virtual machine.

Discount application

If we have any Azure discounts, they are used to their charges. Azure discounts can be applied at the subscription, resource group, or service level.

For example, we may have a discount for utilizing Azure Reserved Instances. Azure Reserved Instances are a type of Azure commitment that allows you to save money on your Azure Virtual Machines and SQL Database costs.

Invoice generation

Invoices are developed for each billing period, including all billed charges and applicable taxes. Invoices are known in the Azure portal and can be downloaded as PDF files.

The invoice is developed at the end of each billing period and contains all charges incurred. We can view the invoice in the Azure portal and download it as a PDF file.

Additional resources

Azure delivers a combination of resources to assist in understanding and managing Azure charges:

- **Azure cost management**: Azure Cost Management is a collection of tools and services that allow us to understand and manage Azure costs. We can utilize Azure Cost Management to consider charges over time by resource group, service, and other dimensions. We can also use Azure Cost Management to develop and manage budgets and set cost alerts.

- **Azure pricing calculator**: The Azure Pricing Calculator is a tool that helps estimate the cost of running applications on Azure. We can utilize the Azure Pricing Calculator to calculate the cost of computing, storage, networking, and other Azure resources.

- **Azure billing documentation**: The Azure Billing Documentation delivers precise information on how Azure charges are processed and how to manage Azure invoices.

Microsoft Commerce system

To know how Cost Management and Billing work? We need to know about the **Microsoft Commerce system**. It is a data pipeline that helps all Microsoft transactions, whether for consumers or businesses. The channel has many inputs and connections, including sign-up and Marketplace purchase experiences. However, we will focus on the components of your cloud billing account and how charges are processed within the system.

Azure, Microsoft 365, Dynamics 365, and Power Platform benefits push data into the Commerce data pipeline on the left side of the diagram. Each service publishes data at various intervals. The rating system uses discounts to the data as it streams through the pipeline and generates rated usage, which contains the price and quantity for each cost record. This is the basis for what you see in Cost Management. Credits are applied before the invoice is developed, and the process starts 72 hours after your billing period ends, generally the last day of the calendar month for most accounts.

After discounts are applied, cost details flow into Cost Management, where different actions are accepted, including identifying anomalies, splitting shared costs, drawing AWS cost and usage reports, and sending out cost alerts. The Billing experience allows you to manage your billing relationship with Microsoft, including reviewing credits, handling billing address and payment methods, and paying invoices.

Azure Cost Analysis insights

Within the billing experience, we can manage our products, subscriptions, and recurring purchases, view and pay invoices, and check credits and commitments. Invoices can be accessed online or as PDFs and contain all the charges and taxes. When invoices are developed, any applicable credits are used for the total invoice amount. It is worth mentioning that Cost Management data processing runs alongside the invoicing process, but does not include credits, taxes, and some purchases (such as support charges in non-Microsoft Customer Agreement accounts). At present, Cost Management does not help classic **Cloud Solution Provider (CSP)** and support subscriptions, but these will be helped once they transition to **Microsoft Customer Agreement (MCA)**.

Managing Azure Billing Accounts

Microsoft offers various billing accounts, each with customized support for individual factors. To find out more, check out the Billing Accounts and Scopes section. With billing account control tasks, we can complete various actions such as viewing invoices and making payments, configuring billing address and PO numbers, organizing subscriptions into departments, or billing profiles, continuing, or canceling purchased products, allowing access to cost management, reservations, and marketplace offers, and checking agreements, credits, and commitments. However, due to their different billing structures, management for classic CSP and classic sponsorship subscriptions is not available in billing or cost management experiences. Take care of billing accounts and keep track of invoices.

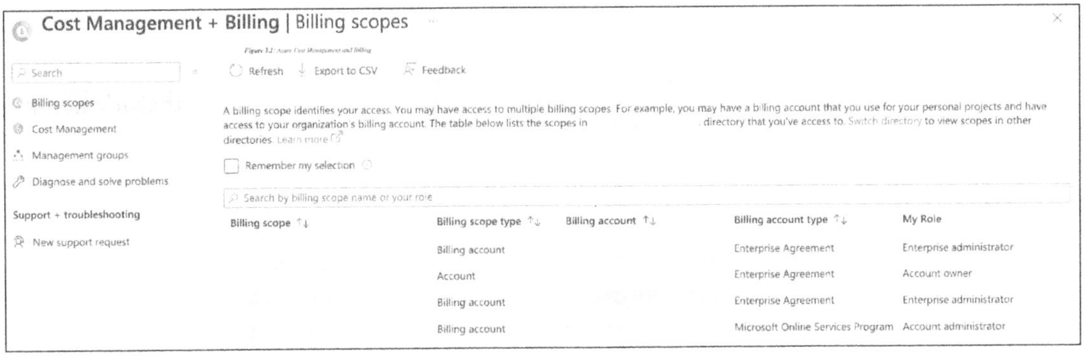

Figure 3.2: Azure Billing Scopes

Expense impact analysis

Microsoft Cloud and AWS show several tools for cost management and billing. We can use cost analysis for answers and lightweight insights into costs and Power BI for more comprehensive dashboards and complicated reports. Additionally, we can export cost details and combine them into external systems or business processes. The credits page shows a general credit or prepaid commitment balance, but it needs to be contained in the cost analysis. The invoices page lists all yet invoiced charges and their payment status. With connectors for AWS, we can ingest AWS cost details into Azure for managing Azure and AWS costs together and even set up budgets and scheduled alerts.

Arrange and distribute expenses

It is essential to correctly sort and distribute expenses to confirm that invoices are sent to the proper departments and can be separated for internal billing purposes. To help with this, Cost Management and Billing provide a combination of options for organizing resources and subscriptions.

MCA billing profiles and invoice sections are used to categorize subscriptions into invoices. With each billing profile describing a distinct invoice that can be billed to another business unit, invoice sections are segmented within those invoices. Additionally, you can view costs by billing profile or invoice section in costs analysis.

- Groups of subscriptions in **Enterprise Agreement (EA)** departments and enrollment accounts have a similar concept to invoice sections, but they are not displayed in the invoice PDF. Instead, they are contained in the support cost details of each invoice. If we want to view costs by department or enrollment account, we can do so in the costs analysis section.

- Another option for grouping subscriptions is through Management groups, which have some distinct advantages. Unlike department or enrollment account groups, management group access is automatically inherited by all subscriptions and resources within that group. Additionally, Management groups can be nested multiple levels deep, and subscriptions can be placed at any level. However, it is important to note that Management groups do not appear in cost details. Instead, all historical costs are aggregated based on the subscriptions within the Management group hierarchy. If a subscription is moved, all historical costs will also move. Lastly, Management groups can be used with Azure Policy to automate compliance reporting for cost governance strategy.

- Cloud solutions can be organized at the subscription and resource group level. Subscriptions are used to manage products at Microsoft and are typically used for business units or separating dev/test from production. Resource groups are used to manage products within subscriptions but can complicate cost management because owners need a way to control costs across groups. It is important to note that not all charges come from resources, and some are not associated with resource groups or subscriptions. This also changes when moving to MCA billing accounts.

- Resource tags are the only option to add your business context to cost details. They show a great deal of flexibility when it comes to mapping resources to different applications, business units, environments, owners, and so on.

Monitor Expenses with alerts

With Cost Management and Billing, we will have the key to different email notifications and alerts that keep us informed about accounts and expenses. These tools can assist us in staying on top of costs and managing your account proactively:

- Anomaly alerts feature, we can set up notifications for any unusual changes in your daily usage. This feature can detect spikes or dips in use and is exclusively available for subscriptions. We can easily access this information by checking out the cost analysis smart view. To configure the rephrased anomaly alerts, head to the cost alerts page.

- Recipients can receive regular alerts about the latest expenses daily, weekly, or monthly by utilizing saved cost views. The notification emails showcase a chart representation of the view and can include a CSV file if desired. It is important to note that even if recipients cannot access cost analysis, they can still view the email, chart, and linked CSV.

- Whenever the EA commitment balance reaches 90% or 100% usage, automatic alerts are sent to the configured notification contacts. For **Microsoft Customer Agreement (MCA)** billing profiles and **Microsoft Online Subscription Program (MOSP)** subscriptions, invoice alerts can be set up as well.

Enabling cost analysis and budgeting

If we have an Azure Enterprise agreement, the access level to cost management data is determined by a combination of permissions granted in the Azure portal. For those with different types of Azure accounts, accessing cost management data is easier with **Azure role-based access control (Azure RBAC)**.

This will show you the method of giving access to cost management data. Once the permissions are given, the user's access scope and the scope they select in the Azure portal choose the data they can consider in cost management. It is essential to mention that users do not multi-select scopes but instead select a larger scope that child scopes roll up to and filter down to consider the desired data. Data consolidation is also necessary, as some users may need access to a parent scope that child scopes roll up to.

To ensure appropriate access within the department, the department admins must have the **Direct Agreement (DA)** view charges choice turned on. This can be configured in the Azure portal. For all other scopes, the Account owners must have the **Account Owner (AO)** view charges option turned on. This will ensure everyone can view charges and keep everything running smoothly.

Azure Cost Data Access Permissions

The DA view charges option must be turned on to ensure the department scope is configured correctly. This can be done in either the Azure portal or the EA portal. For all other areas, the AO view charges option must be enabled.

To activate a feature in the Azure portal:

1. To activate a feature in the Azure portal, first sign in with your enterprise administrator account.
2. From there, navigate to the **Cost Management + Billing** menu.
3. Select billing scopes to see a list of billing accounts and scopes.
4. Choose your desired billing account from the list and then navigate to the policies menu under **Settings** to configure your settings.

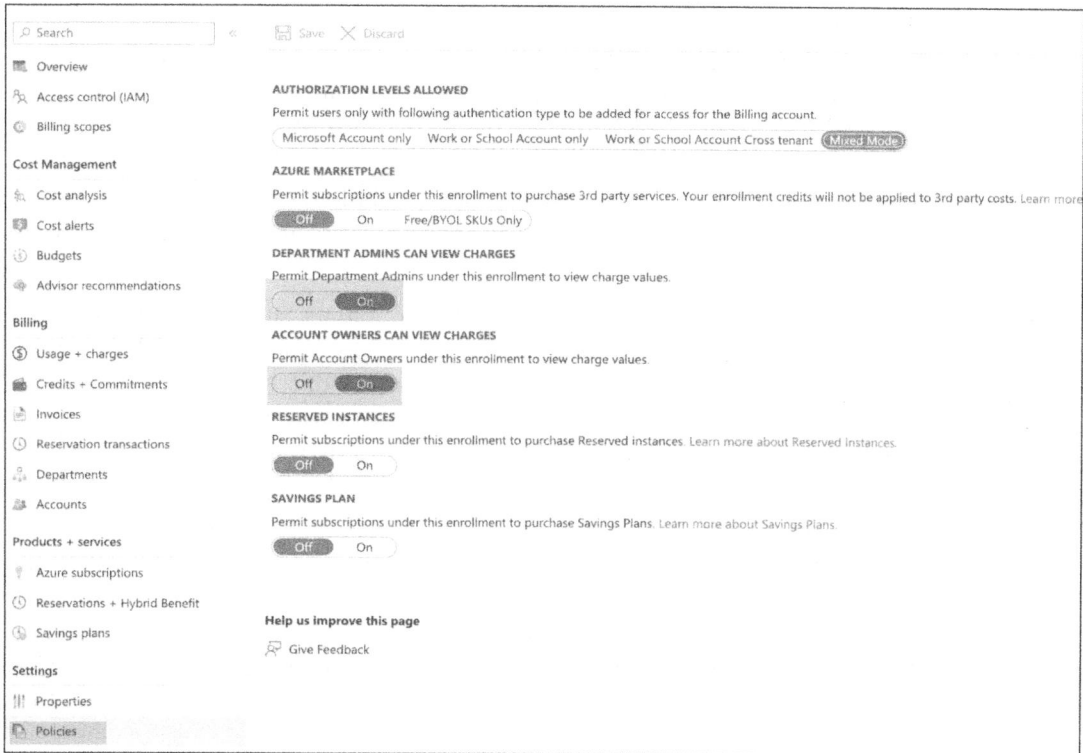

Figure 3.3: *Azure Cost Management and Billing department admin*

Once the view charge options are activated, many scopes will also necessitate the configuration of Azure RBAC permissions through the Azure portal. The five pillars of Azure fundamentals for FinOps

- Financial accountability
- Cloud operational excellence
- Cost visibility
- Cost optimization
- Cost control

Financial accountability

Cultivating a culture of financial responsibility: Financial accountability is a crucial pillar within Azure Fundamentals for FinOps, underpinning the successful optimization of cloud spending. At its core, this principle shows clear ownership and responsibility for cloud spending within the organization. By enabling a culture of financial obligation, organizations can help a collaborative and cost-conscious mindset among teams, allowing them to experience optimizing costs and making mindful financial decisions actively.

Following are the key points for the financial accountability:

- **Establishing ownership and responsibility**: Azure Fundamentals for FinOps highlights the need for clearly defined ownership and responsibility for cloud resources and spending. Organizations create a sense of ownership that drives careful resource usage by assigning specific individuals or teams accountable for managing cloud costs. These responsible stakeholders collaborate with other departments, project teams, and cloud users to ensure that cloud resources are utilized efficiently and cost-effectively.

- **Promoting a culture of financial responsibility**: Financial responsibility is not a solitary task but a collective effort. Azure Fundamentals for FinOps enables organizations to promote a culture of financial responsibility throughout their cloud operations. Educate employees about the cost and importance of their actions and decisions in the cloud environment. Teams become more mindful of their resource consumption and can make choices that align with the organization's financial goals.

- **Show-back and chargeback mechanisms**: To support financial accountability, organizations can implement show-back or chargeback mechanisms. Show-back involves providing teams and stakeholders with detailed reports showcasing the cost of cloud resources they are using. This enables transparency and helps individuals understand the financial impact of their cloud activities, promoting greater accountability.

  Chargeback takes the concept of show-back one step further by distributing actual cloud costs among relevant teams or business units. Stakeholders can optimize resource usage and embrace cost-effective practices by assigning actual costs to specific projects or departments. Chargeback can also act as a financial governance mechanism, enabling departments to align their cloud usage with budget constraints and organizational priorities.

- **Collaborative cost optimization**: Financial accountability in Azure Fundamentals for FinOps goes beyond simply tracking expenses. It enables collaboration and communication among different teams. By involving various departments and project owners in the cost optimization process, organizations can leverage multiple perspectives and expertise to identify innovative ways to reduce cloud costs without compromising performance.

- **Continuous improvement and cost awareness**: Financial accountability is not a one-time task but a continuous improvement and cost awareness process. Azure Fundamentals for FinOps encourages regular reviews of cloud spending, cost trends, and optimization efforts. By regularly analyzing cost data and making data-driven decisions, organizations can adapt quickly to changing needs, adjust resource allocation as necessary, and aim to achieve greater cost efficiency.

Cloud operational excellence

Seamlessly integrating financial management with cloud operations. Cloud operational excellence is a foundational principle within Azure Fundamentals for FinOps, vital for optimal cloud financial management. It highlights the need for seamless integration of financial practices with cloud operations to drive efficiency and cost-effectiveness. This principle enables teams to adopt the best resource provisioning, deployment, and scaling practices, creating a vital foundation for effective financial management.

Following are the key points for the cloud operational excellence:

- **Best practices for resource provisioning**: Organizations must adopt well-defined best practices for resource provisioning to achieve cloud operational excellence. This involves accurately estimating the resource requirements of applications and services before deployment. Using historical data and performance metrics, teams can right size cloud resources, ensuring they align exactly with workload demands. Avoiding overprovisioning not only stops unnecessary costs but also optimizes resource utilization, maximizing the value derived from cloud investments.

- **Streamlined resource deployment**: Azure Fundamentals for FinOps highlights the importance of streamlined resource deployment. Organizations can formalize and automate resource provisioning by leveraging automation and **Infrastructure as Code (IaC)** processes. This approach reduces the risk of misconfigurations and human errors, promoting resource efficiency.

- **Dynamic resource scaling**: It is a critical aspect of cloud operational excellence. Azure enables organizations to implement automatic scaling mechanisms that adjust resource capacity in response to fluctuating demand. For instance, autoscaling can automatically add or remove models based on predefined thresholds, providing that resources are efficiently allocated as the market fluctuates. This elasticity optimizes cloud usage by avoiding overprovisioning during times of low need and scaling up seamlessly during peak usage, resulting in significant cost savings.

- **Lifecycle management and resource optimization**: Azure Fundamentals for FinOps highlights the importance of effective lifecycle management and resource optimization. Throughout the lifecycle of cloud resources, it is vital to monitor and evaluate their usage and cost-effectiveness continually. Regularly reviewing resource utilization allows teams to identify underutilized or idle resources, which can be rightsized or decommissioned to reduce costs. This proactive approach to resource management ensures that cloud assets remain efficient and relevant to business needs.

- **Minimizing waste and maximizing resource utilization**: Cloud operational excellence organizations minimize resource waste and maximize resource utilization. Automation and IaC enable rapid resource provisioning and de-provisioning, ensuring that resources are only active when needed. This "just-in-time" approach to resource management reduces costs and eliminates unnecessary spending on idle or unused resources.

Cost visibility

Empowering informed decision-making and optimal resource allocation.

Cost visibility is a foundation principle within Azure Fundamentals for FinOps, serving as a critical driver for efficient cloud financial management. This principle involves understanding cloud usage and spending patterns to give organizations actionable cost optimization and strategic decision-making insights.

Following are the key points for the cost visibility:

- **Azure Cost Management and Billing**: Azure offers a suite of tools and services, Azure Cost Management and Billing, which forms of achieving cost visibility. This complete platform provides real-time and granular insights into resource consumption and cost allocation across Azure subscriptions. By leveraging Azure Cost Management and Billing, businesses can view detailed reports, create customizable dashboards, and perform deep analyses of their cloud spending.

- **Detailed cost reports**: Detailed cost reports offer a complete breakdown of cloud expenses, clearly showing where and how resources are utilized. Organizations can access cost reports categorized by services, regions, and periods. This level of granularity allows Businesses to identify specific cost drivers and allocate resources more effectively.

- **Customizable dashboards**: Azure Cost Management and Billing enables organizations to build customizable dashboards for their needs and priorities. These dashboards can be designed to display critical cost metrics and trends in real-time. By visualizing data through interactive graphs and charts, teams gain valuable insights that facilitate better cost monitoring and decision-making.

- **Resource tagging**: One of the key features that contribute to cost visibility is resource tagging. Azure allows organizations to apply custom metadata labels (tags) to cloud resources like virtual machines, databases, or storage accounts. Businesses can attribute costs to specific departments, projects, or teams by tagging resources. This level of cost allocation enables responsibility and enables more accurate financial planning.

- **Insights across departments and projects**: Cost visibility further expands individual resources, enabling organizations to track costs across different departments and projects. Spending patterns help stakeholders understand the financial impact of various initiatives and make data-driven decisions when allocating resources.

- Identifying cost drivers: By analyzing cost data with the help of Azure Cost Management and Billing, organizations can identify the key cost drivers within their cloud infrastructure. These cost drivers could be specific services, regions, or usage patterns contributing significantly to cloud expenses. Businesses can devise targeted cost optimization strategies to address areas of significant spending.

- **Informed decision-making**: Cost visibility is a fundamental component of informed decision-making in cloud financial management. With real-time data and insights, organizations can make proactive and well-informed choices to optimize cloud resources, streamline operations, and align cloud spending with their budget goals.

Cost optimization

Maximizing value while minimizing cloud expenditure. Cost optimization is a central and critical element of Azure Fundamentals for FinOps, the perfect balance between cost-efficiency and performance within the cloud environment. Organizations can continuously review and refine their cloud infrastructure to ensure their cloud spending aligns with business objectives without compromising operational excellence.

Following are the key points for the cost optimization:

- **Leveraging Azure's cost-saving features**: Azure offers various cost-saving features designed to help organizations optimize their cloud spending. One of the key strategies is leveraging **Reserved Instances (RIs)**, which allow businesses to commit to using specific virtual machine instances over a predetermined period. By making this commitment, organizations can unlock substantial discounts compared to pay-as-you-go pricing, resulting in significant cost savings for long-term and stable workloads.

- **Spot Instances and Spot VMs**: Another cost-saving option is Azure Spot Instances or **Spot Virtual Machines (VMs)**. These are spare compute capacity instances offered at a considerable discount. Organizations can achieve significant cost reductions by using Spot Instances for workloads.

- **Dynamic resource scaling with autoscaling**: Azure Fundamentals for FinOps the importance of dynamic resource scaling through autoscaling. Autoscaling enables organizations to adjust the number of resources (for example, VM instances) based on real-time demand. Autoscaling also helps avoid overprovisioning during low-traffic periods, preventing unnecessary expenses.

- **Serverless architectures and managed services:** Serverless architectures managed services is another cost optimization strategy. Serverless computing, such as Azure Functions or Logic Apps, allows businesses to execute code or tasks without managing underlying servers. With serverless, users are only billed for the actual execution time, reducing costs for applications with sporadic usage.

  Similarly, exploring managed services such as Azure SQL Database or Cosmos DB eliminates the need for organizations to maintain and manage the infrastructure for databases and other services.

- **Right-sizing resources:** The right-sizing resource is a fundamental part of cost optimization. Organizations should continuously assess their resource requirements and adjust the size and type of cloud instances accordingly. By provisioning resources that match workload demands, businesses can avoid overprovisioning and ensure optimal resource utilization, reducing unnecessary costs.

- **Cost optimization and continuous improvement**: Azure Fundamentals for FinOps enables organizations to continuously review and optimize their cloud resources, applications, and services by analyzing usage patterns, performance metrics, and cost data and implementing targeted cost optimization strategies to align cloud spending with budgetary goals effectively.

Cost control

Enforcing budget constraints and governance policies. Cost control is a critical principle within Azure Fundamentals for FinOps, aimed at ensuring that cloud spending remains aligned with budget constraints and organizational policies. Organizations can proactively manage their cloud resources by implementing cost control measures, avoiding unexpected cost overruns, and maintaining financial stability within the cloud environment.

Following are the key points for the cost control:

- **Establishing budgetary constraints**: A crucial part of cost control is the establishment of budget constraints. Azure Fundamentals for FinOps enables organizations to set clear and realistic budgets for their cloud operations. Businesses can gain greater control over cloud spending by defining budget limits for different departments or resource groups.

- **Implementing Azure Policy**: Azure Policy is a powerful tool that enables organizations to enforce governance policies. Organizations can define policies to ensure compliance with security and operational requirements. Azure Policy can enforce specific cost-related guidelines, such as stopping using certain expensive VM sizes or services that do not match cost-efficiency goals.

- **Role-Based Access Control (RBAC):** It is a vital part of cost control. Organizations can control access to cloud resources and services by assigning proper roles to users and groups. RBAC ensures that only authorized users can create, modify, or delete resources.

- **Budget alerts and thresholds**: Azure allows setting up budget alerts. Organizations can configure these alerts to notify Businesses when cloud spending exceeds thresholds. Budget alerts can be sent via email or SMS. By receiving these alerts, Businesses can instantly identify overspending and address costs.

- **Budget forecasting and variance analysis**: Cost control involves constant monitoring and analysis of budget forecasts and actual spending. Azure Cost Management enables organizations to protect their cloud spending based on documented data. By approximating budget forecasts with actual costs, organizations can perform variance analysis to understand variations and take corrective actions.

- **Continuous improvement and iterative cost control**: Cost control is a process. Azure Fundamentals for FinOps enables organizations to review and optimize cost control measures constantly. Through regular audits and performance evaluations, businesses can analyze their cost control and improve their financial management in the cloud environment.

Conclusion

In conclusion, Azure Cost Management and Billing is a crucial component of FinOps practices, offering businesses the tools and insights needed to optimize cloud spending, achieve financial control, and enhance resource utilization. The platform enables efficient tagging strategies, facilitating accurate cost allocation and transparent spending tracking. By setting budgets, businesses proactively manage cloud expenses, aligning spending with budgetary limits and strategic goals.

Organizations gain in-depth insights into cloud spending trends and drivers through robust cost analysis capabilities, identifying cost-saving opportunities and optimizing resource usage. Azure Cost Management and Billing fosters collaboration between FinOps teams and business stakeholders, ensuring cloud resources are aligned with business needs and supporting informed decision-making.

Businesses optimize resource allocation by identifying underutilized resources and implementing corrective actions, reducing cloud costs without compromising performance. In summary, Azure Cost Management and Billing empower businesses to make data-driven decisions, collaborate effectively, and drive cloud cost efficiency to achieve their strategic objectives and maximize the value of cloud investments.

In the next chapter, we will learn more about setting up cost management, Budgeting, and Subscriptions.

Join our book's Discord space

Join the book's Discord Workspace for Latest updates, Offers, Tech happenings around the world, New Release and Sessions with the Authors:

https://discord.bpbonline.com

CHAPTER 4

Cost Optimization Strategies

Introduction

Cost optimization strategies within cloud environments, specifically in Azure, are critical to operating expenses while maximizing resource utilization. In Azure, these strategies contain many strategies and tactics to achieve efficiency and cost-effectiveness in resource management.

One basic strategy revolves around right-sizing resources. This practice involves aligning the allocated resources, such as **virtual machines** (**VMs**) or storage, with the actual needs of the applications or workloads. By avoiding over-provisioning or underutilization, organizations can optimize costs without compromising performance. Continually monitoring and analyzing usage patterns are vital in determining the appropriate size and configuration adjustments.

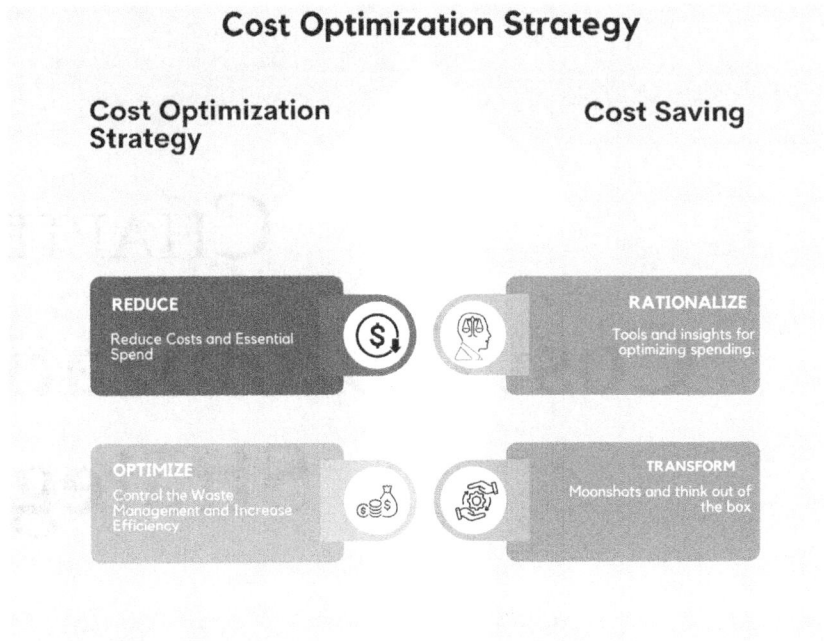

Figure 4.1: *Azure Cost Optimization strategy*

Structure

In this chapter, we will go through the following topics:

- Optimizing costs with reserved instances
- Right-sizing Azure resources
- Reserved instances and savings plans
- Azure Hybrid benefits
- Spot Instances and low-priority VMs

Objectives

By the end of this chapter, we will learn how to Right-sizing Azure Resources, how to purchase reservations for Azure services, and the process of buying Azure reservations. We will also learn about Azure Hybrid Benefits, Spot Instances, and low-priority VMs.

Optimizing costs with reserved instances

Another meaningful way for cost optimization is leveraging reserved instances and savings plans. These will allow organizations to commit to specific usage levels for a predetermined duration, resulting in significant cost savings compared to on-demand pricing. This commitment-based model offers flexibility while ensuring cost efficiency across various Azure services.

Ongoing monitoring and analysis of resource usage are indispensable. Organizations can identify inefficiencies, underutilized resources, or areas where optimization is possible by employing tools and analytics. Automation and scripting further improve cost optimization by facilitating resource deployment, management, and scaling processes, thereby reducing manual intervention and the potential for errors.

Designing architectures with a focus on cost efficiency is important. Adopting serverless computing, microservices, containers, and other scalable solutions can significantly reduce operational costs. Moreover, exploring vendor discounts, incentives, or negotiation options with cloud service providers can lead to better pricing based on usage volume or commitment.

Frequent review and optimization are essential parts of an effective cost-optimization strategy. Adapting to changing business needs, technological advancements, and developing pricing models from service providers is crucial for ongoing cost efficiency. Additionally, educating teams about cost implications related to resource usage and promoting best practices ensure a holistic approach to cost optimization across the organization.

Right-sizing Azure resources

Optimizing the cloud infrastructure is essential for success in a competitive business landscape. Azure rightsizing offers a powerful solution to accomplish this by ensuring your resources are perfectly aligned with your workload demands.

Think of a water faucet as an analogy for cloud resources. Just like a small faucet takes longer to fill a tank, small cloud resources can perform poorly. On the other hand, large faucets wastewater and cause inefficiencies; similarly, large cloud resources can be expensive and inefficient.

Azure rightsizing addresses this by analyzing your resource usage and adjusting them to match your needs. This proactive approach helps you:

- **Eliminate underutilized resources**: Stop paying for resources you are not fully utilizing, saving valuable costs.
- **Avoid overprovisioned resources**: Ensure your resources are adequately sized for peak loads without incurring unnecessary expenses, refer to the following figure.

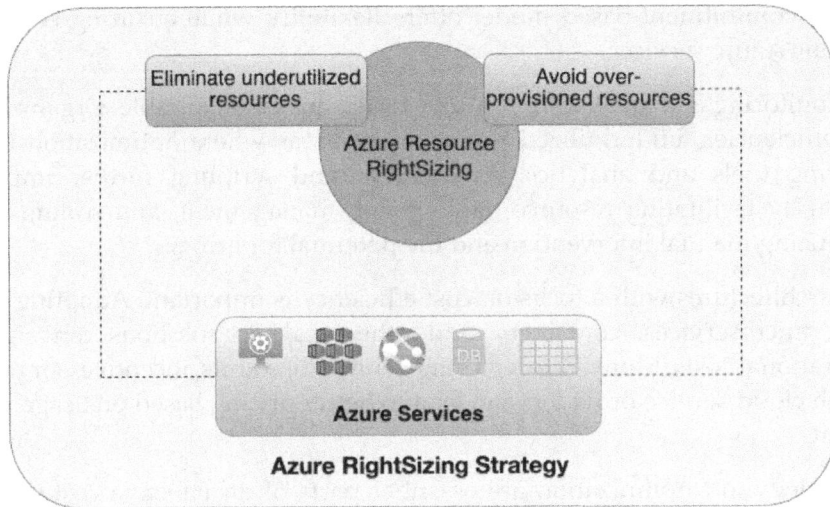

Figure 4.2: *Understanding Azure Rightsizing strategy*

Identifying candidates for Azure rightsizing

On a rightsizing initiative, strategically identifying suitable resources for optimization is critical. Start by analyzing the following Azure resources:

- **Virtual Machines (VMs):**
  - ○ **CPU utilization**: Analyze the average and peak CPU utilization. VMs with consistently low utilization (below 30%) are potential candidates for downsizing.
  - ○ **Memory utilization**: Monitor the average and peak memory consumption. VMs with consistently low memory utilization (below 70%) may benefit from downsizing.
  - ○ **Disk utilization**: Consider the used and available disk space. VMs with significant unused disk space might be suitable for downsizing storage options.
  - ○ **Performance bottlenecks**: If VMs show performance issues like slow response times, High Input/Output Operations Per Second (IOPS), consider upsizing or optimizing their configurations.

- **Azure SQL databases:**
  - ○ CPU utilization: Identify databases with consistently low (below 40%) or high (above 80%) CPU utilization. Low utilization indicates potential for downsizing, while high suggests the need for upsizing.

- o **Memory utilization**: Monitor the average memory consumption. Databases with consistently low memory utilization (below 80%) might be candidates for downsizing.

- o **Storage**: Analyze the used and available storage space. Databases with significant unused storage space might be suitable for downsizing storage options.

- o **Performance**: Evaluate query execution times and identify slow queries for potential optimization.

- **Azure app service plans:**

  - o **CPU utilization**: Analyze the average and peak CPU utilization. App service plans with consistently low (below 50%) or high (above 80%) CPU utilization might require adjustments.

  - o **Memory utilization**: Monitor the average memory consumption. App service plans with consistently low memory utilization (below 70%) might be suitable for downsizing.

  - o **Instance metrics**: Analyze the number of instances running and the average CPU and memory consumption per instance. This helps identify scaling opportunities.

- **Azure storage accounts:**

  - o **Storage capacity**: Analyze the used and available storage space. Storage accounts with significant unused space might be suitable for downsizing storage options.

  - o **IOPS**: Monitor the average and peak IOPS to identify potential bottlenecks or underutilized resources.

  - o **Network throughput**: Analyze the average and peak network throughput to identify potential bottlenecks or underutilized resources.

- **Azure Kubernetes Service clusters**

  - o **CPU utilization**: Review the average and peak CPU utilization across nodes. Nodes consistently underutilized (below 50%) are potential candidates for scaling down.

  - o **Memory utilization**: Analyze the average and peak memory utilization across nodes. Nodes consistently underutilized (below 70%) might be suitable for scaling down.

  - o **Node status**: Identify unhealthy or unresponsive nodes for potential troubleshooting or scaling down.

- **Additional considerations:**
    o **Workload patterns**: Analyze your workload patterns to identify peak and off-peak hours for potential scaling considerations.

    o **Cost analysis**: Use Azure Cost Management tools to identify resources with high costs and analyze potential savings through rightsizing.

    o **Business needs**: Prioritize rightsizing decisions based on your business needs and performance requirements.

By utilizing these insights and strategically analyzing your resources, you can efficiently identify candidates for Azure rightsizing and optimize your cloud environment for cost-effectiveness and performance. Remember, the key to successful rightsizing is continuous monitoring, evaluation, and adaptation.

Gathering utilization data

Once you have identified candidate resources for rightsizing, gathering the utilization data is essential. This data provides the foundation for making informed decisions and ensures your rightsizing efforts are helpful.

Here is how to effectively collect utilization data:

- **Data sources:**
    o **Azure monitor:** This monitoring service collects and analyzes data from your entire Azure environment, including virtual machines, Azure SQL databases, App Service plans, storage accounts, and **Azure Kubernetes Service (AKS)** clusters. Utilize Azure Monitor metrics, logs, and alerts to gain detailed insights into resource utilization patterns.

    o **Azure metrics:** This service delivers pre-configured metrics for various Azure resources, offering a suitable way to gather performance data. You can access metrics through the Azure portal, Azure CLI, or REST API.

    o **Third-party monitoring solutions:** Multiple third-party monitoring solutions integrate seamlessly with Azure and offer advanced features such as real-time monitoring, anomaly detection, and custom dashboards. Consider solutions like Datadog, Dynatrace, or Splunk for deeper insights and extensive monitoring capabilities.

    o **Data collection period**: The data collection period should be representative of your regular workload patterns. Aim to collect data for at least a month to capture seasonal variations and peak usage hours. For resources with predictable workloads, a shorter period might suffice.

- **Key metrics to collect:**

  o **CPU utilization:** This metric indicates the percentage of time the CPU is actively processing tasks. Monitor average and peak utilization to identify underutilized or overloaded resources.

  o **Memory utilization:** This metric shows the percentage of available memory currently used. Track average and peak memory consumption to identify resources requiring downsizing or upsizing.

  o **Disk utilization:** This metric indicates the percentage of currently available disk space. Analyze used and open space to optimize storage costs.

  o **Network throughput:** This metric calculates the amount of data transferred over the network. Monitor average and peak throughput to identify potential bottlenecks.

  o **IOPS:** This metric shows the number of read and write operations per second. Analyze IOPS to identify performance issues or optimize storage options.

  o **Instance metrics:** For resources like App Service plans and AKS clusters, monitor the number of running instances and their individual CPU and memory utilization. This data helps identify scaling opportunities.

- **Additional data points:**

  o **Cost data:** Utilize Azure Cost Management tools to analyze resource costs and identify potential savings through rightsizing.

  o **Application logs:** Review your application logs for performance issues or resource bottlenecks related to specific workloads.

  o **User activity data:** Analyze user activity data to understand usage patterns and identify potential peaks or periods of low activity.

By combining data from multiple sources and analyzing it over a representative period, you can comprehensively understand your resource utilization patterns and make informed decisions during the rightsizing process. Remember, the key is to collect relevant, accurate data and analyze it effectively to optimize your cloud environment for cost efficiency and performance.

Analyzing resource utilization

Having gathered comprehensive utilization data, it is time to delve deeper through a comprehensive analysis that identifies patterns, trends, and areas for improvement.

Here is an analysis of essential factors to take into consideration:

- **CPU utilization:**
  - ○ **Identify:** VMs or app service plans consistently exhibiting low CPU usage (below 30%) are candidates for downsizing. Conversely, instances experiencing regular spikes above allocated capacity might require upsizing.
  - ○ **Analyze:** Look for patterns in CPU usage across the day and week. Identify peak periods and potential underutilized times for scaling opportunities.
  - ○ **Correlate:** Consider if low CPU usage correlates with other metrics like memory or disk utilization to identify potential bottlenecks.

- **Memory utilization:**
  - ○ **Determine:** VMs or app service plans with excess memory (below 70% utilization) might be suitable for downsizing, freeing up resources for other applications.
  - ○ **Analyze:** Monitor memory usage trends and identify periods of high memory consumption that could benefit from upsizing or workload optimization.
  - ○ **Correlate:** Analyze if memory utilization spikes coincide with CPU or disk usage spikes to pinpoint potential resource bottlenecks.

- **Disk utilization:**
  - ○ **Analyze:** Evaluate disk read/write metrics to identify potential bottlenecks or underutilized storage options.
  - ○ **Identify:** VMs or databases experiencing high read/write activity might require faster storage types, while those with significant unused storage space could be downsized.
  - ○ **Optimize:** Consider implementing storage optimization strategies like data tiering or archiving older data to optimize costs.

- **Network throughput:**
  - ○ **Evaluate:** Network metrics to identify potential bottlenecks or excessive bandwidth utilization impacting performance.
  - ○ **Identify:** Resources experiencing high network throughput might benefit from upgraded network tiers or optimized application network configurations.
  - ○ **Trend analysis:** Track network usage trends over time to identify peak periods and potential opportunities for scaling network resources.

- **Cost optimization:**
  - ○ **Calculate:** Assess the potential cost savings achievable by downsizing resources or optimizing their configurations.

- o **Consider:** Include the cost of downtime and potential performance impacts when making rightsizing decisions.
  - o **Prioritize:** Implement rightsizing strategies that optimize costs while ensuring adequate performance and reliability for your workloads.
- **Additional analysis tips:**
  - o **Visualize data:** Utilize charts and graphs to visualize resource utilization trends and identify patterns more easily.
  - o **Compare resources:** Compare utilization data across similar resources to identify outliers and optimize resource allocation.
  - o **Consider application requirements:** Ensure rightsizing decisions align with your application's performance needs and resource requirements.
  - o **Utilize Azure tools:** Leverage tools like Azure Advisor and Azure Cost Management to analyze resource utilization and receive optimization recommendations.

By analyzing your resource utilization data and considering these important factors, you can effectively identify areas for improvement and implement rightsizing strategies that optimize your cloud environment for performance, cost efficiency, and scalability. Remember, continuous monitoring and analysis are vital to ensure your rightsizing efforts remain effective and aligned with your evolving business needs.

Azure rightsizing strategies: Optimizing resources

Based on your thorough utilization analysis, it is time to implement rightsizing strategies that optimize your resources for cost-effectiveness and performance:

- **Upsizing:**
  - o **When to apply**: If a resource consistently operates at or near capacity (above 80% CPU or 90% memory utilization), consider upgrading to a larger or higher performance tier to avoid performance bottlenecks.
  - o **Benefits**: This strategy ensures smooth operation, prevents performance degradation, and improves user experience.
  - o **Considerations**: Carefully evaluate the cost implications of upsizing and ensure it aligns with your budget and Return on Investment (ROI) expectations.
- **Downsizing:**
  - o **When to apply**: If a resource is significantly underutilized (below 30% CPU or 70% memory utilization), downsizing to a smaller or lower performance tier can optimize costs.
  - o **Benefits**: This strategy reduces unnecessary cloud spending and frees up resources for other applications.

- o **Considerations**: Carefully analyze the potential impact of downsizing on performance and ensure it does not negatively affect your applications.

- **Horizontal scaling:**
  - o **When to apply**: Instead of simply upsizing a single resource, consider distributing the workload across multiple instances or VMs. This strategy is beneficial for applications with burst workloads or high availability requirements.
  - o **Benefits**: Horizontal scaling improves resource utilization, enhances application scalability, and facilitates load balancing for better performance.
  - o **Considerations**: Manage the increased complexity of managing multiple instances and ensure your network infrastructure can handle the increased traffic.

- **Vertical scaling:**
  - o **When to apply**: When your resource requires adjustments but scaling horizontally is not suitable, consider vertical scaling. This refers to modifying the size or settings of a resource while keeping the number of instances unchanged. For example, you could increase memory allocation for a database or CPU allocation for a VM.
  - o **Benefits**: Vertical scaling offers a more granular approach to resource allocation and can address specific performance bottlenecks.
  - o **Considerations**: Evaluate the cost implications of increased resource allocation and ensure it is cost-effective compared to alternative options.

- **Automation:**
  - o **Benefits**: Automating the rightsizing process saves time and effort, ensures consistency across deployments, and minimizes the risk of human error.
  - o **Tools**: Leverage Azure Automation or **Infrastructure as Code (IaC)** tools like **Azure Resource Manager (ARM)** templates to automate scaling processes based on predefined rules and thresholds.
  - o **Considerations**: Invest in setting up robust automation workflows and ensure they are adequately tested and monitored to prevent unintended consequences.

- **Additional strategies:**
  - o **Utilize azure advisor and cost management**: Leverage these tools to receive recommendations and insights into resource optimization opportunities.
  - o **Implement autoscaling**: You should explore utilizing Azure VMs Autoscaling, which can automatically adjust the resource capacity up or down in real-time based on the resource demands.

- o **Optimize application configuration**: Review your application configuration and implement optimization techniques to reduce resource consumption.
- o **Monitor and refine**: Monitor your resource utilization and adjust your rightsizing strategies to ensure optimal performance and cost efficiency.

By implementing a proactive approach to rightsizing, you can optimize your Azure resources and achieve the desired balance between performance, cost-effectiveness, and scalability. Remember, rightsizing is an ongoing process, and continuous monitoring, analysis, and adaptation are crucial for maximizing its benefits and ensuring the long-term success of your cloud deployments.

Azure implement right sizing change

Once you have chosen the rightsizing strategies for your Azure resources, it is crucial to follow best practices for implementation to ensure a smooth and effective transition:

- **Backups:**
  - o **Importance**: Before modifying your resources, prioritize taking recent backups of critical data and configurations. This safeguard ensures you can recover quickly in case of unexpected data loss or service disruptions during the rightsizing process.
  - o **Backup options**: Utilize Azure Backup services like Azure Backup Service or Azure Backup for VMs to create reliable and secure backups of your data and configurations.
- **Staging environment testing:**
  - o **Benefits**: Deploy the rightsized resources in a separate staging or test environment before implementing them in production. This allows you to validate the functionality and performance of the rightsized resources.

    Identify and address any potential issues before impacting your production environment.

    Ensure the transition to the new resource configuration is seamless and without disruptions.
  - o **Considerations**: Configure your staging environment to resemble your production environment for accurate testing and validation.
- **Continuous monitoring and optimization:**
  - o **Importance**: Continuously monitor the performance and utilization of your rightsized resources after implementation. This helps you identify potential issues, performance bottlenecks, or unexpected resource needs.

- o **Monitoring tools**: Utilize Azure Monitor, Azure Metrics, or third-party monitoring solutions to track resource utilization, performance metrics, and application logs.

  - o **Proactive optimization**: Based on your monitoring data, adjust your rightsizing configurations to accommodate changing workloads, optimize performance, and maintain cost efficiency.

- **Regular reviews:**
  - o **Benefits**: Conducting periodic reviews of your Azure resources helps you identify new candidates for rightsizing as your workloads and utilization patterns evolve.

  - o **Review frequency**: Schedule regular reviews based on the dynamism of your workloads and the potential for significant changes in resource needs.

  - o **Proactive approach**: By proactively identifying new rightsizing opportunities, you can ensure your cloud environment remains optimized and cost-effective.

- **Additional best practices:**
  - o **Communicate changes**: To ensure a smooth transition and to minimize the potential for disruptions, it is essential to inform all relevant stakeholders about the planned rightsizing changes. This will help everyone be prepared and aware of the changes happening.

  - o **Document changes**: Document the changes made during rightsizing and the rationale behind them for future reference and troubleshooting.

  - o **Automate tasks**: Utilize tools like Azure Automation or Terraform to automate rightsizing functions for efficiency and consistency.

  - o **Seek support**: If needed, consider seeking assistance from Azure experts or consulting with experienced cloud architects to ensure optimal rightsizing strategies for your specific environment.

By using these best practices and adopting a proactive approach to implementation and monitoring, you can successfully implement rightsizing changes and maximize the benefits for your Azure environment. Remember, rightsizing is a continuous process, and ongoing vigilance and adaptation are essential to maintain a cost-effective, performant, and scalable cloud infrastructure.

Reserved instances and savings plans

Azure Reservations saves you money by saving to one-year or three-year plans for multiple Azure Services. Saving permits, you get a discount on the services you use. Azure Reservations can reduce your resource costs by up to 70% from pay-as-you-go prices. Reservations deliver a billing discount and do not impact the runtime state of your resources. After you purchase a reservation, the discount is automatically used to match resources.

You can spend for a reservation upfront or monthly. The cost of up-front and monthly reservations is the same, and you do not need to spend any extra fees when you select to pay monthly. Monthly payment is known for Azure reservations, not third-party products.

There are many reasons to buy an Azure reservation, but the main one is to save money. By committing to a one-year or three-year plan for Azure resources, you can get discounts of up to 72% off the pay-as-you-go rates. This can be a considerable savings, mainly if you use Azure heavily.

Here are some other benefits of buying Azure reservations:

- **Predictable costs**: Reservations allow you to budget for your Azure costs, as you know exactly how much you will spend each month. This can be useful for businesses that need to keep their IT costs under control.

- **Improved resource availability**: Reservations can help you confirm that the Azure resources you need are available when you need them. This can be important for mission-critical applications.

- **Simplified billing**: Reservations can streamline your Azure bill by consolidating your charges into a monthly payment.

There are also some things to believe before buying Azure reservations. For example, you must use your reserve resources for the entire reservation term. Otherwise, you could save money. You also need to make sure you choose the right reservation type for your needs. Several different types of reservations are available, each with its terms and conditions.

Overall, Azure reservations can be a great way to save money on your Azure costs. However, weighing the pros and cons carefully before purchasing is essential.

Here are some additional things to keep in mind:

- Reservations are not a one-size-fits-all solution. They may only be suitable for some.

- Buying the **Reserved Instance (RI)** as shared is always recommended to ensure the use of the RI at Maximum.

- If you are still determining whether reservations are right for you, you can contact Microsoft for help.

- Several tools and resources are available to help you choose the right type of reservation and calculate your potential savings.

Purchasing reservation on Azure Services

Following are the Azure Resource types where you can buy the reservation Instance. You can buy the RI using Portal, PowerShell, or **command line (CLI)**.

- App Service
- App Service: JBoss EA Integrated Support
- Azure Backup
- Azure Cache for Redis
- Azure Data Factory
- Azure Database for MariaDB
- Azure Database for MySQL
- Azure Database for PostgreSQL
- Azure Blob storage
- Azure Files
- Azure Vmware Solution
- Azure Cosmos DB
- Azure SQL Edge
- Databricks
- Data Explorer
- Dedicated Host
- Disk Storage
- Microsoft Fabric
- SAP HANA Large Instances
- Software plans
- SQL Database
- Synapse Analytics: Data warehouse
- Synapse Analytics: Prepurchase
- Virtual machines
- Virtual machine software

Buying Azure Reservation instance

If you're a business that uses Azure services, Buying Azure Reservations can save you money compared to the pay-as-you-go billing option. You save to a one-year or three-year term for specific Azure resources, which helps with budgeting and financial planning, particularly for organizations with predictable workloads. Azure Reservations protects various services, including virtual machines, database services, storage, and analytics, providing flexibility and cost efficiency for all your cloud computing needs.

Whether you're a small business looking to optimize your cloud costs or a large enterprise aiming for cost-effective scalability, purchasing Azure Reservations is a significant first step.

1. Sign-in to Azure Portal.

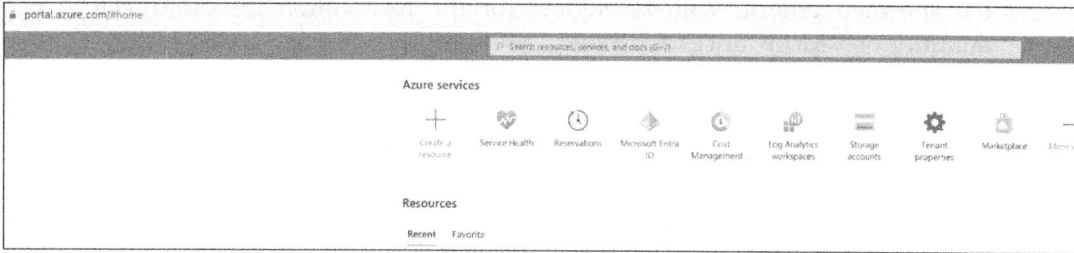

Figure 4.3: *Sign in Azure Portal*

2. Go to **All Service | Reservation**.

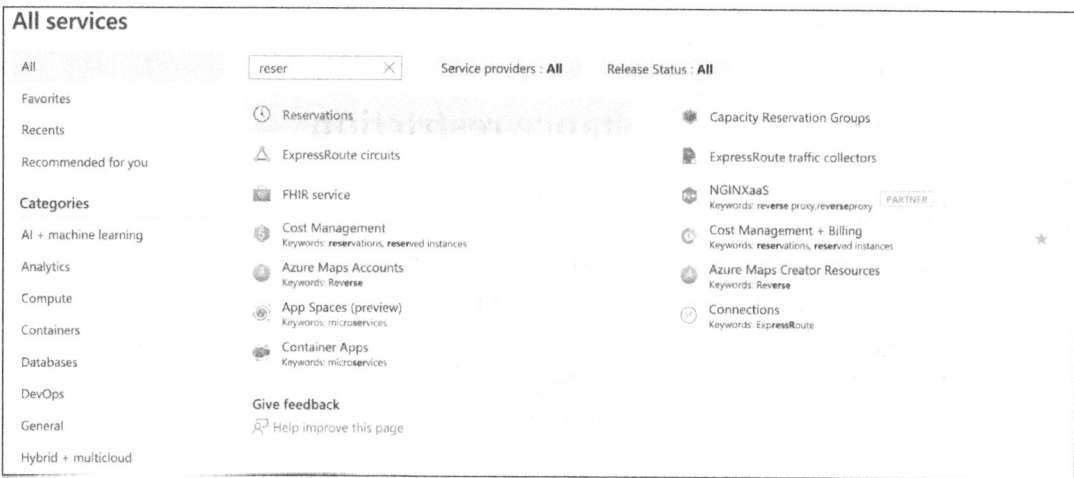

Figure 4.4: *Azure Reservation*

3. Add to buy a new reservation, let us say *virtual machine* here.

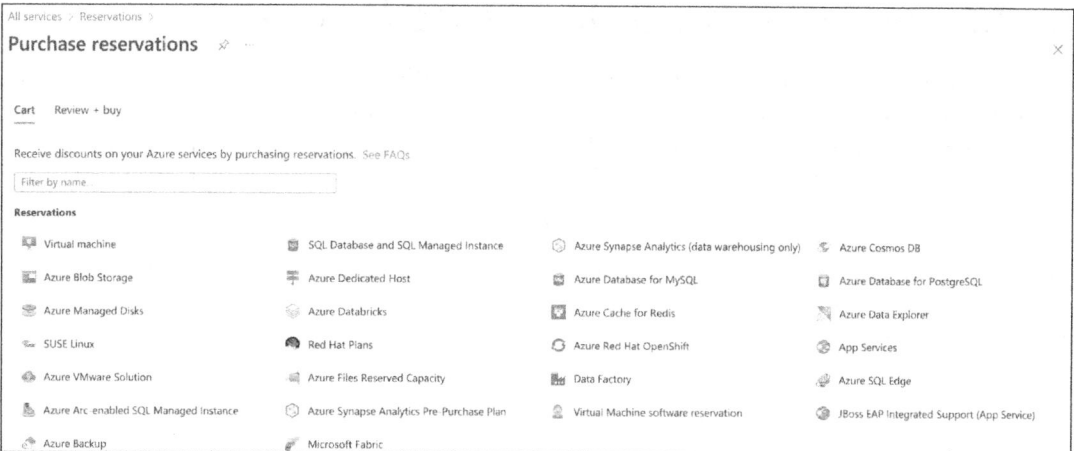

Figure 4.5: *Azure Reservation Services*

4. Provide the necessary information in the designated fields. VM instances meeting the specified criteria will be eligible for the reservation discount. The actual quantity of VM instances receiving the discount will vary based on the chosen scope and quantity.

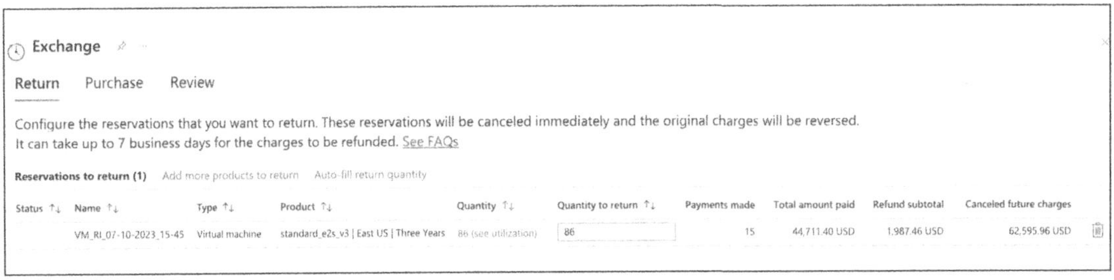

Figure 4.6: Azure Reservation purchase details

Purchasing Reserved Instance restriction

Reserved Instance (RI) is available for most of the VM size. There are some VMs where the RI discount does not apply:

- **VM series**: A-series and G Series do not support RI.
- **Preview or Promo VMs**: Any preview VM series or size.
- **Insufficient quota**: A reservation can be scoped only to the vCPU quota available in the single subscription. For example, if the subscription has a quota limit of 10 vCPUs for D-Series, then you cannot buy a reservation for 11 Standard_D1 instances.
- **Capacity restrictions**: In rare cases, Azure can limit the purchase of new reservations for a subset of VM sizes because of low capacity in a region.

Exchange and refund the Azure Reservation

Azure Reservation can allow interchange if the reservation is the same type. For example, you can exchange multiple compute reservations, which include Azure Dedicated Host, Azure VMware Solution, and Azure VM size. You can exchange database types, such as SQL database reservation types, including SQL managed instances and elastic pool, with each other.

However, you cannot exchange different reservations, such as you cannot exchange cosmos DB for SQL database. Exchange Azure Reservation will give the option to change the region. For example, you can exchange the RI from the West US to the East US.

When you exchange the reservation, you can change the term from one year to three years, or you can change it from three to one year. There is an option to refund the Azure RI, but the sum of all canceled RI commitments can be USD 50,000 in a 12-month rolling window.

The following RI is not eligible for refunds:

- Azure Databricks reserved capacity.
- Synapse Analytics Pre-purchase plan
- Azure VMware solution by CloudSimple
- Azure Red Hat Open Shift
- Red Hat plans
- SUSE Linux plans

Step-by-step process to exchange or refund an existing reservation:

1. Select the RI that you want to exchange and select **Exchange**:

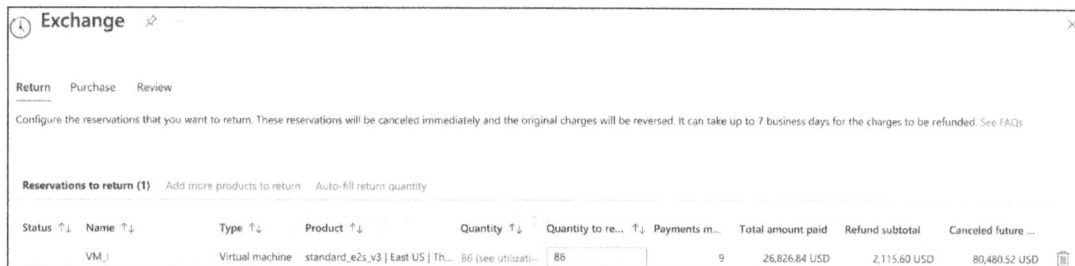

Figure 4.7: Azure Reservation Return

2. Select the RI that you want to purchase and make sure the new RI cost should be more than the return cost:

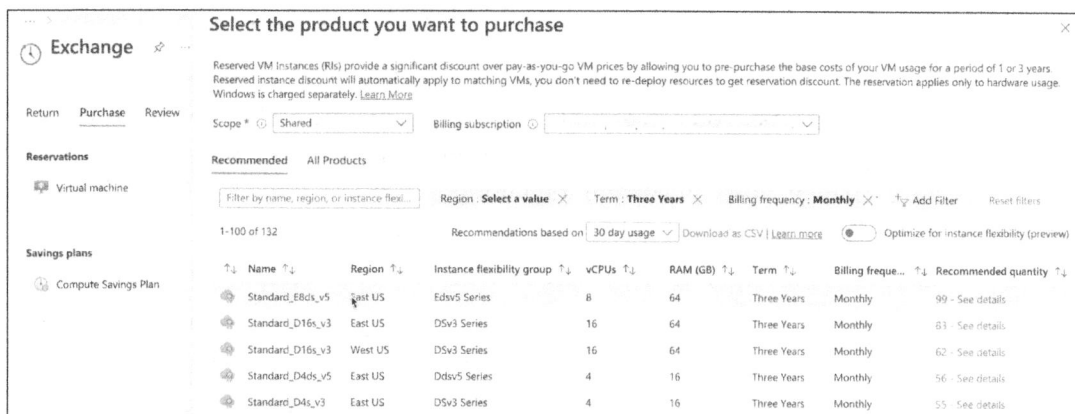

Figure 4.8: Azure Reservation Purchase

3. At the end, review the change and click on **Exchange**.

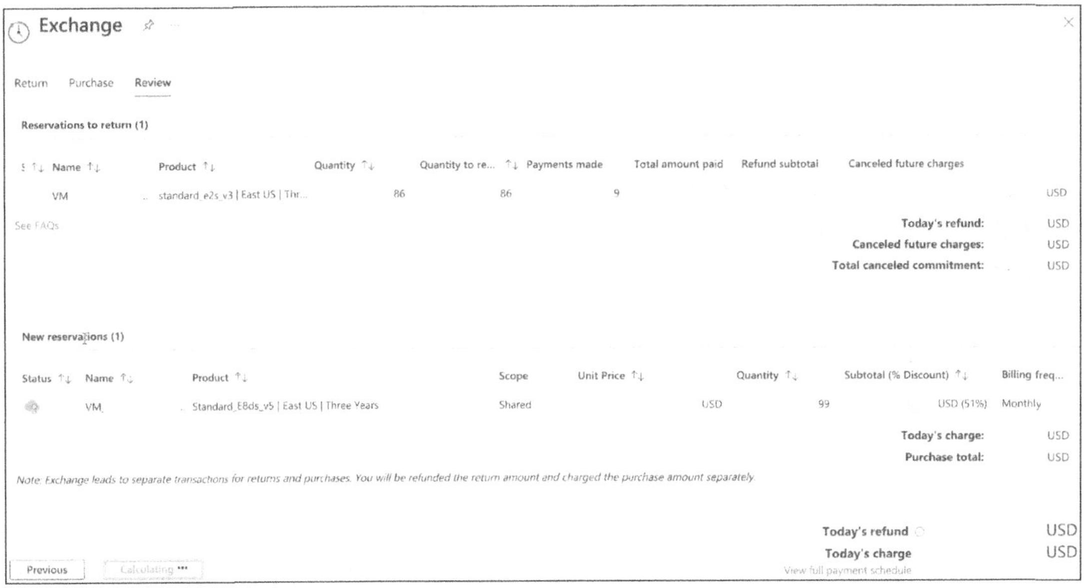

Figure 4.9: Azure Reservation Review

Exchange, refund, and cancel reservation policies

Understanding the reservation policies for exchanging, refunding, and canceling Azure Reservations is essential to modifying your cloud services to meet your business needs. Azure delivers a collection of rules that customers can use to change their reservations without incurring excessive costs or service disruptions.

*   Exchange policies:
    o   You can return multiple existing reservations to purchase one new reservation of the same type. You can exchange the different kinds of RI. For example, you cannot return an App Service reservation to purchase an SQL reservation. In the exchange, you can change the family, series, version, SKU (Stock Keeping Unit), region, quantity, and term with an exchange.
    o   As part of the exchange will be started as a new term as part of the exchange.
    o   You can exchange or refund the expired enterprise agreement that was used to purchase and was renewed as a new contract.
    o   The new RI commitment should be equal to or greater than the returned RI's remaining commitment.
    o   There is no penalty if you do the exchange.

- There is an announcement from Microsoft that there will be no Exchange on RI for all compute reservations, such as Azure Dedicated Host reservations, Azure Reserved Virtual Machine Instances, and Azure App Services reservations. For example, if you made a three-year compute reservation before July 2024. You still can exchange the reservation on or after July 1, 2024. Because it is processed as a cancellation, refund, and new purchase, the reservation is no longer exchangeable.

- You can still exchange the RI for a savings plan, and there are no time limits.

- Refund policies:

  - Currently, MS is not charging an early termination fee, but in the future, MS might be charged 12% as an early termination fee for RI cancellation.

  - Refunds are calculated on the lowest price of your purchase or the current value of reservations.

  - Canceled commitment cannot exceed 50,000 USD in a 12-month rolling window for a billing or single enrollment. Azure does not process any refund which exceeds the 50,000 USD limit in 12-month window.

  - Only RI owners have access to refund the Azure RI.

Azure Saving Plan

Azure savings plan for computing is an elastic pricing model. It delivers savings of up to 65% off pay-as-you-go pricing when you commit to spending a specified hourly amount on computing services for one or three years. Reserving to a savings plan permits you to obtain discounts, up to the hourly commitment amount, on the resources you utilize. The savings plan commitment is priced in USD for **Microsoft Customer Agreement (MCA)**, **Cloud Solution Provider (CSP)**, and **Enterprise Agreement (EA)** customers. Savings plan discounts vary by meter and commitment term (1-year or 3-year), not the commitment amount. Savings plans deliver a billing discount and do not affect the runtime condition of your resources.

You can spend for a savings plan upfront or monthly. The total cost of the up-front and monthly are the same.

Buying a savings plan permits you to reduce your costs if you have consistent computing spending but use disparate resources that make reservations infeasible. For example, assume you consistently pay at least $X every hour, but your use comes from different resources and data center regions. In that case, you cannot protect these costs with reservations. Your hourly use, up to your commitment amount, is discounted when you purchase a savings plan. For this usage, you are no longer charged at the pay-as-you-go rates.

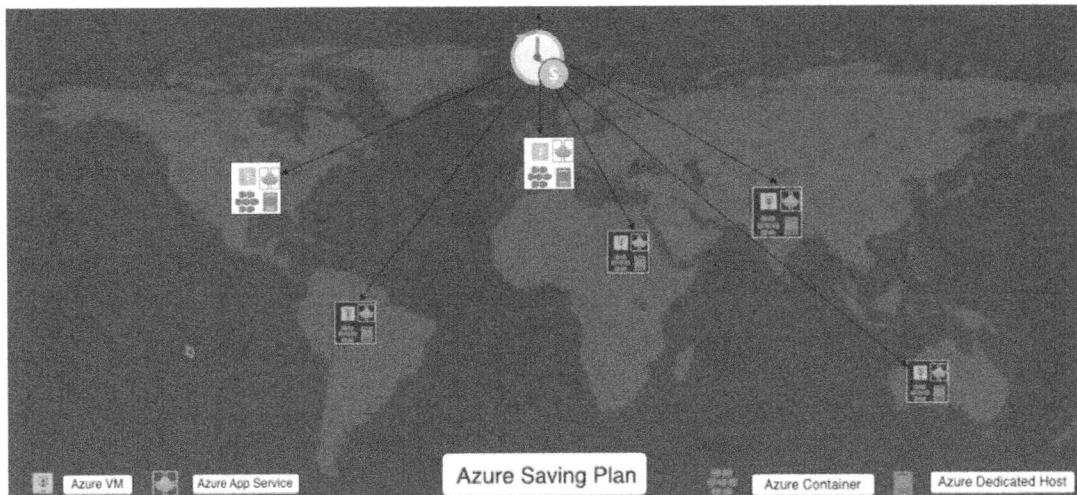

Figure 4.10: Azure Saving Plan

Eligible Azure Services for Saving Plan:

- Azure Virtual Machine
- Azure App Service (App Service Plan Version 3 Only)
- Azure Functions Premium Plan
- Azure Container Instances
- Azure Dedicated Host
- Azure Container App

Virtual Machines used with both **Azure Kubernetes Service (AKS)** and **Azure Virtual Desktop (AVD)** are eligible for the savings plan. Saving Plan discounts apply only to compute or infrastructure costs, not software costs. If you use Windows VMs and you have a savings plan. You do not have Azure hybrid benefits for your VMs, which means you will be charged for the software meter.

Understanding Azure Saving Plan purchase

Suppose a company uses ten qty of **Standard_d2as_v4**, **Standard_E8ds_v5**, and **Standard_L16as_v3**. There will be different list prices: 0.188 for the D series, 0.944 for the E series, and 1.984 for the L series. However, there will be another discount from MS for the client with their agreement. The total Pay-As-You-Go for our example is $ 23.06.

Compute Resources	Standard_D2as_v4	Standard_E8ds_v5	Standard_L16as_v3
Qty	10	10	10
Pay As you Go List Price rate per hour	0.188	0.944	1.984
Pay as you go with discounted rate per hour (26% Discount)	0.139	0.699	1.468
Pay as go Total Price	1.39	6.99	14.68

Figure 4.11: Azure Saving Plan purchase 1

Now, we will apply the savings plan discount, which would be for each of these three compute resources. A discount will be applied to the one that receives the highest discount.

Our example assumes a $13 hourly commitment for the savings plan. The resource would get the biggest discount on the L series, which would be 60% off. The E series would get a discount of 54.94%, and the M series would get a discount of 54.93%.That amounts to a saving plan hourly rate of 0.084 for the D series, 0.425 for the E series, and 0.793 for the L series.

Compute Resources	Standard_D2as_v4	Standard_E8ds_v5	Standard_L16as_v3
Saving Plan Discount in %	54.93%	54.94%	60%
Saving Plan Hourly	0.084	0.425	0.7936

Figure 4.12: Azure Saving Plan purchase 2

All 10 L series would be covered by a $13 hourly commitment with $5.064 remaining. The remaining hourly commitment would then be applied to the E series. $5.064 is sufficient to cover all 10 E series VM with the remaining $0.814.

Compute Resources	Standard_D2as_v4	Standard_E8ds_v5	Standard_L16as_v3
Hour Commitment		$13.00	
Qty	10	10	10
Saving Plan Discount in %	54.93%	54.94%	60%
Saving Hourly Rate	0.084	0.425	0.7936
Saving Plan Benefit Required for L16as_v3		7.936	
Covered by Available Hourly Commitment		100%	
Hourly Consumed Commitment		7.936	
Hourly Remaning Commitment		5.064	

Figure 4.13: Azure Saving Plan purchase 3

Compute Resources	Standard_D2as_v4	Standard_E8ds_v5	Standard_L16as_v3
Qty	10	10	10
Saving Plan Discount in %	54.93%	54.94%	60%
Saving Hourly Rate	0.084	0.425	0.7936
Saving Plan Benefit Required for E8ds_v5		4.25	
Covered by Available Hourly Commitment		100%	
Hourly Consumed Commitment		4.25	
Hourly Remaning Commitment		0.814	

Figure 4.14: Azure Saving Plan purchase 4

The remaining $0.814 hourly commitment is sufficient to cover 97% of D series. The remaining 0.026 will be the Pay-As-You-Go.

Compute Resources	Standard_D2as_v4	Standard_E8ds_v5	Standard_L16as_v3
Qty	10	10	10
Saving Plan Discount in %	54.93%	54.94%	60%
Saving Hourly Rate	0.084	0.425	0.7936
Saving Plan Benefit Required for d2as_v4		0.84	
Covered by Available Hourly Commitment		97%	
Hourly Consumed Commitment		0.814	
Hourly Remaning Commitment		0	

Figure 4.15: Azure Saving Plan purchase 5

In this scenario, MS will be charged $13.03 to run all the VM with pay-as-you-go. The company will save $10.03, which is around 44% of savings over the on-demand price.

Pay as you go	$23.06
Hourly Saving Plan Commitment	$13
Pay as you go after Saving Plan	0.026
Total Charge	$13.03
Amount Saved with Saving Plan	$10.03
Saving %	44%

Figure 4.16: Azure Saving Plan purchase 6

Step-by-step buying Azure Saving Plan

Azure Savings Plan is a pricing model that offers discounted rates on Azure services in exchange for saving to use a constant amount of service, measured in dollars per hour, for one or three years. This model benefits workloads with predictable resource requirements and is intended for long-term use.

To benefit from the Azure Savings Plan, follow these steps:

1. Login to the Azure Portal:

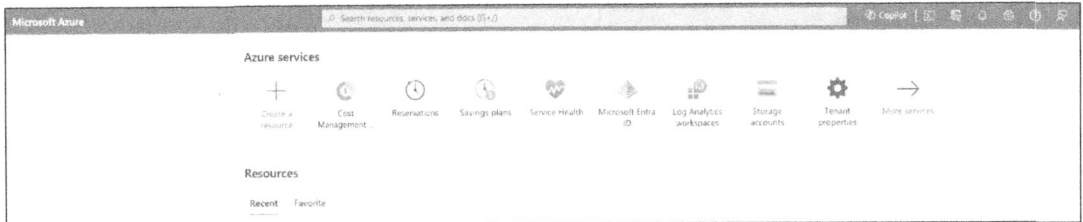

Figure 4.17: Azure Portal Login

2. Search the **Savings plans** in a global search:

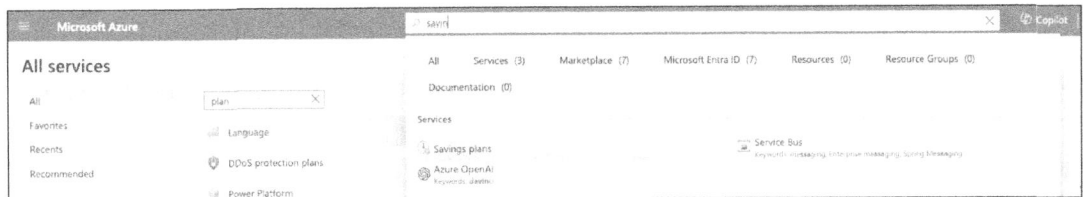

Figure 4.18: Azure Portal saving plan search

3. Select **Add** to purchase a new savings plan:

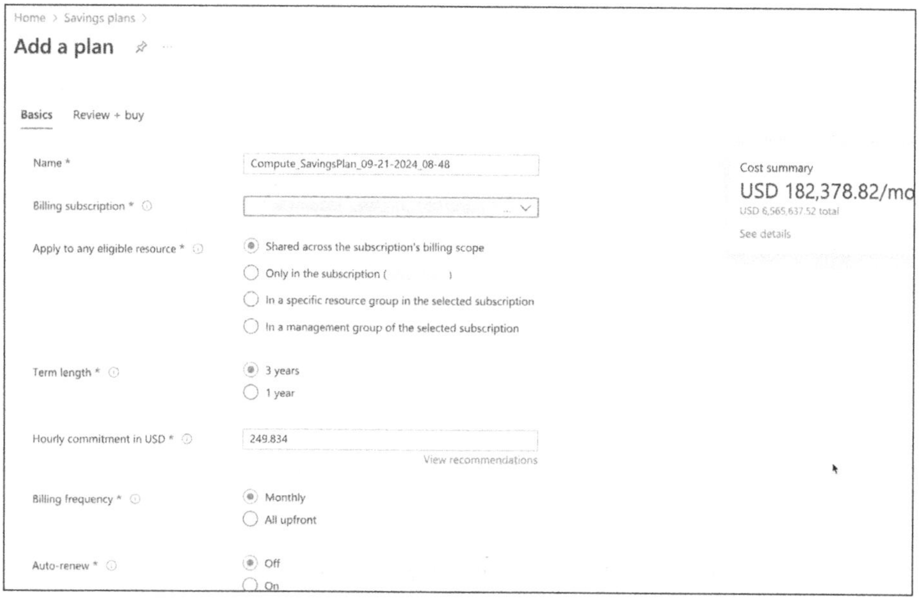

Home > Savings plans >

Add a plan ✎ ···

Basics   Review + buy

Name *   Compute_SavingsPlan_09-21-2024_08-48

Billing subscription * ⓘ

Apply to any eligible resource * ⓘ   ⦿ Shared across the subscription's billing scope
                                      ○ Only in the subscription (   )
                                      ○ In a specific resource group in the selected subscription
                                      ○ In a management group of the selected subscription

Term length * ⓘ   ⦿ 3 years
                                      ○ 1 year

Hourly commitment in USD * ⓘ   249.834
                                                        View recommendations

Billing frequency * ⓘ   ⦿ Monthly
                                      ○ All upfront

Auto-renew * ⓘ   ⦿ Off
                                      ○ On

Cost summary
USD 182,378.82/mo
USD 6,565,637.52 total
See details

Figure 4.19: Azure Portal saving plan provision

4. Complete all the required field:

- **Name**: Provide the friendly name for the saving Plan.

- **Billing subscription**: Subscription which is used to pay for the Saving Plan.

- **Apply to any eligible resources**: Scope of resources that are eligible for the saving plan. Such as shared scope, single subscription, resource group and management group.

- **Term length**: Three years or one year.

- **Hourly commitment in USD**: The amount will be available through the savings plan each hour. The Azure portal will provide up to 10 recommendations based on the last 30 days' usage. Also, these recommendations are based on scope specific. Currently, Azure does not provide recommendations for management groups. Each recommendation contains:

  o An hourly commitment.

  o The possible savings percentage is approximated to on-demand costs for the commitment.

  o The percentage of the selected scope compute usage that the new savings plan would cover. It contains the commitment amount plus any other previously purchased savings plan or reservation.

- **Billing frequency:** All upfront or monthly.

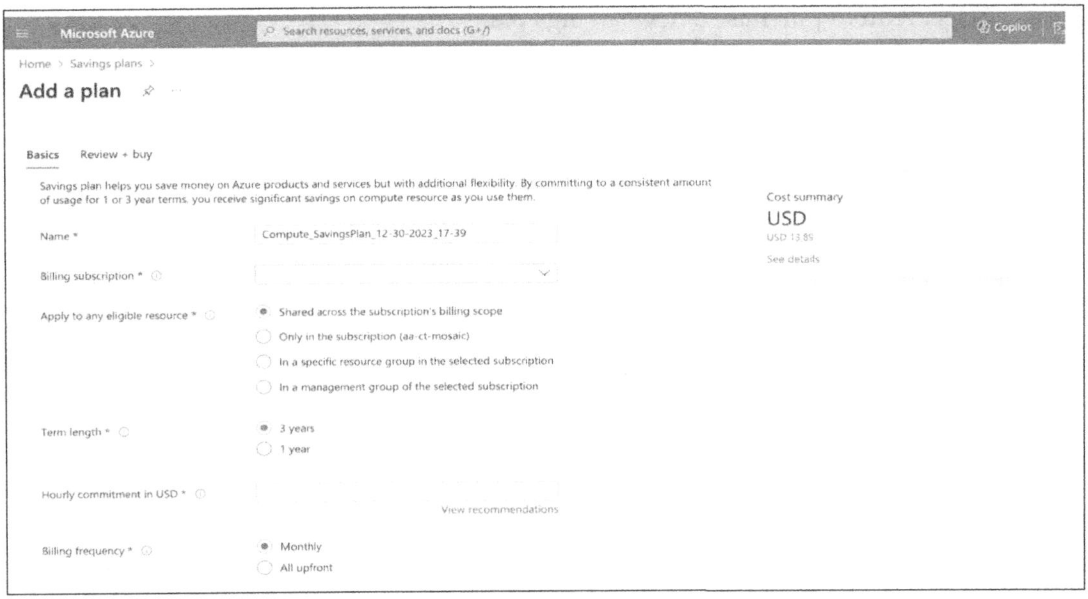

Figure 4.20: Azure Portal saving plan required fields.

Note: There are no to cancel, exchange, or refund savings plans.

Difference between Azure Reservation and Saving Plan

Azure offers two cost-saving mechanisms:

- Reservations
- Savings Plans

With Azure Reservations, you commit to a specific resource type in a particular region to obtain a discount. This is suitable for predictable, steady workloads. On the other hand, Azure Savings Plans provide discounts based on an overall hourly commitment to Azure services, offering flexibility across various services and regions. This plan is ideal for dynamic, changing workloads. Both plans help reduce costs compared to pay-as-you-go rates and can be committed to on a 1-year or 3-year basis.

Feature	Azure Reservations	Azure Savings Plans
Commitment type	Specific VM type and region.	Spend a fixed hourly amount on compute services.
Ideal usage	Highly stable, continuous workloads with no expected changes in machine series or region.	Dynamic workloads, different VM sizes, or frequently changing regions.

Feature	Azure Reservations	Azure Savings Plans
Scope of application	Only to the identified compute service and region.	Across all participating compute services globally, up to the hourly commitment.
Savings	Provides the greatest savings for specific resources.	Offers flexibility with savings, automatic optimization, beneficial for varied and changing usage.
Flexibility and optimization	Less flexible, best when there are no changes expected.	Provides flexible benefit application and automatic optimization for changing needs. This means you can use any type of compute service such as VM, Container and App Service.

Table 4.1: Features of Azure Reservations and Azure Savings Plans

Azure Hybrid benefits

Azure Hybrid benefit is a critical cost-saving measure provided by Microsoft. It is desired to help users maximize the value from their existing on-premises licenses when they move to the Azure cloud. This program expands to Windows and SQL Server licenses and benefits Linux customers, offering a comprehensive approach to cost savings and efficiency in cloud deployments. We will discuss and explore the various elements of Azure Hybrid Benefit for Windows Server, SQL Server, and Linux deployments.

- **Azure Hybrid Benefit for Windows Server**: Azure Hybrid Benefit for Windows Server users can lower the costs of operating virtual machines on Azure. By using existing on-premises Windows Server licenses with **Software Assurance (SA)** or preparing subscriptions to Azure, users only pay the base to compute rate for the VMs. This rate is equivalent to the Linux rate, eliminating the additional costs typically associated with Windows Server licensing. It is highly beneficial for organizations with stable, continuous workloads that can predictably utilize these VMs over time.

- **Azure Hybrid Benefit for SQL Server**: Azure Hybrid Benefit extends to SQL Server, offering savings. Users can utilize their existing SQL Server licenses with SA to migrate or manage their SQL workloads on Azure SQL Database, Azure SQL Managed Instance, or SQL Server on Azure VMs. This effort will reduce costs and remove the need for additional SQL Server licenses in the cloud. The benefit is incredibly impactful due to the significant costs associated with database licensing, offering an efficient path for businesses to scale their databases with the flexibility and advanced features of Azure's cloud services.

- **Azure Hybrid Benefit for Linux**: Azure Hybrid Benefit provides value for Linux users as well. Azure works with various Linux distributors to provide integrated support and a seamless experience for Linux-based deployments. At the same time, you have Azure VM running on Red Hat Linux VM and existing RedHat server licenses with SA to migrate or manage their RedHat workloads.

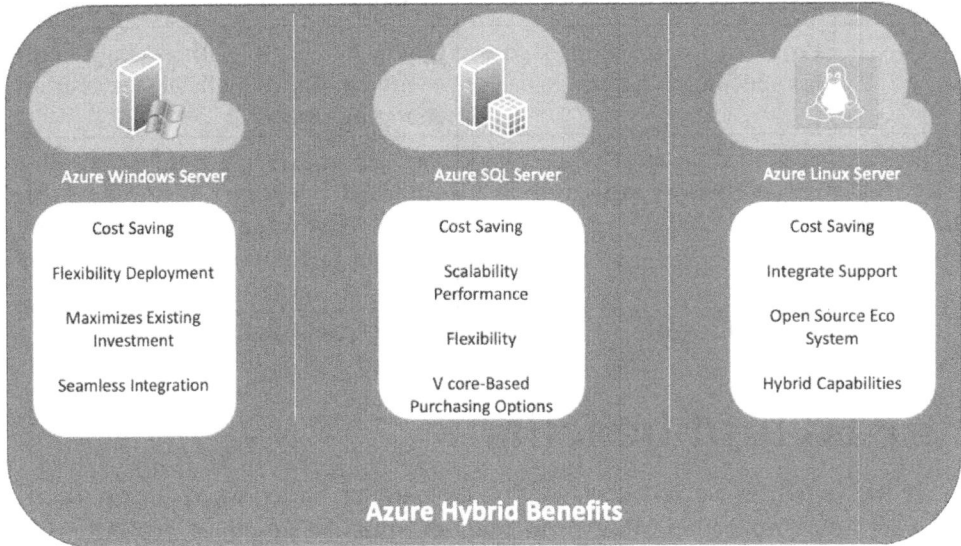

Figure 4.21: Azure Hybrid benefit

- **Additional benefits and flexibility**: The Azure Hybrid Benefit program is created with flexibility, allowing users to support hybrid environments during the change to the cloud. Users can simultaneously use their benefits on-premises and in the cloud, offering a buffer during migration phases. Additionally, Azure provides tools and services for Windows Server, SQL Server, and Linux workloads that enhance performance, security, and scalability, maximizing the return on cloud investments.

Enforcing Azure Hybrid Licenses Policy

1. Login to Azure Portal.
2. Navigate to the All services and search policy.

Figure 4.22: Azure policy search

3. Create a new policy definition:

a. Click on **Definitions** and then **Add definition**.

b. Definition **Location** (choose the managed group/subscription or resource group)

c. Provide the name, the definition and put the description.

d. Choose the create new in the category.

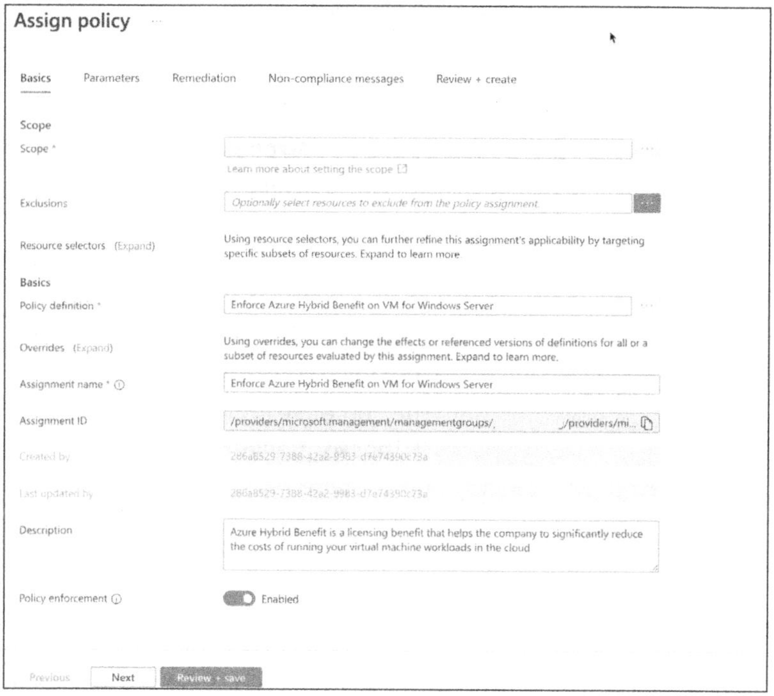

Figure 4.23: Azure policy name and description

4. Provide the policy rule as follows:

```
{
    "mode": "Indexed", // The policy is in "Indexed" mode, which
    means it will only evaluate resources that support tags and
    location.
    "policyRule": { // This defines the actual rule for the policy.
        "if": { // The "if" block specifies the conditions under
        which the policy rule applies.
            "allOf": [ // All conditions in this array must be met
            for the policy to be applied.
                {
                    "equals": "Microsoft.Compute/virtualMachines",
```

```
        "field": "type" // The resource type must be
        virtual machines.
    },
    {

        "anyOf": [ // One of the conditions in this
        array must be met.
            {
                "exists": false,
                "field": "Microsoft.Compute/licenseType"
                // The licenseType field must not exist.
            },
            {

                "field": "Microsoft.Compute/licenseType",
                "notEquals": "Windows_Server" //
                The licenseType field must not equal
                "Windows_Server".

            }
        ]
    },
    {

        "allOf": [ // All conditions in this nested
        array must be met.
            {
                "anyOf": [ // One of the conditions in
                this array must be met.
                    {
                        "equals": "MicrosoftWindowsServer",
                        "field": "Microsoft.Compute/
                        imagePublisher" // The image
                        publisher must be Microsoft
                        Windows Server.
                    },
                    {
                        "contains": "Windows",
```

```
                                    "field": "Microsoft.Compute/
                                    imagePublisher" // The image
                                    publisher must contain
                                    "Windows".
                             },
                             {

                                    "contains": "MicrosoftSQLServer",
                                    "field": "Microsoft.Compute/
                                    imagePublisher" // The image
                                    publisher must contain
                                    "Microsoft SQL Server".
                             },
                             {

                                    "equals": "Windows",
                                    "field": "Microsoft.Compute/
                                    virtualMachines/storageProfile.
                                    osDisk.osType" // The OS type
                                    must be Windows.
                             }
                      ]
               },
               {

                      "not": {
                             "equals": "MicrosoftWindowsDesktop",
                             "field": "Microsoft.Compute/
                             imagePublisher" // The image
                             publisher must not be Microsoft
                             Windows Desktop.
                      }
               }
        ]
    }
  ]
},
```

```
        "then": { // The "then" block specifies what to do when the
        conditions are met.
            "details": {
                "conflictEffect": "deny", // If the policy rule is in
                conflict with the resource, the action will be to
                deny the deployment.
                "operations": [ // Operations to perform if the
                conditions are met.
                    {
                        "field": "Microsoft.Compute/virtualMachines/
                        licenseType",
                        "operation": "addOrReplace",
                        "value": "Windows_Server" // This will add
                        or replace the licenseType with "Windows_
                        Server".
                    }
                ],
                "roleDefinitionIds": [ // Role definitions that are
                granted permissions to the resources under this
                policy.
                    "/providers/microsoft.authorization/
                    roleDefinitions/9980e02c-c2be-4d73-94e8-
                    173b1dc7cf3c"
                ]
            },
            "effect": "[parameters('effect')]" // The effect of the
            policy, which is determined by a parameter that can be
            modified.
        }
    },
    "parameters": { // Parameters for the policy.
        "effect": { // Defines the "effect" parameter.
```

```
    "type": "String", // The type of the parameter is a
    string.
    "metadata": { // Metadata for the parameter.
        "displayName": "Effect", // The display name for the
        parameter.
        "description": "Enable or disable the execution of
        the policy" // Description of what the parameter
        does.
    },
    "allowedValues": [ // Allowed values for the "effect"
    parameter.
        "Modify",
        "Disabled"
    ],
    "defaultValue": "Modify" // The default value for the
    "effect" parameter is "Modify".
        }
      }
    }
```

5. Click on **Save** the definition. Now you have the definition saved and need to create the assignment for the policy.

6. Click on **Assign policy** and provide the below details:

   a. **Scope**: Provide the Scope such as Managed Group, Subscription, or Resource Group.

   b. **Exclusion (Optional)**: To exclude from the policy, provide the scope here.

   c. **Policy Definition**: Browse the policy which we need to add in this assignment.

   d. **Assignment**: Provide the assignment name

   e. **Description (Optional):** Provide the description of the assignment.

   f. **Policy Enforcement**: Move the toggle button to enabled.

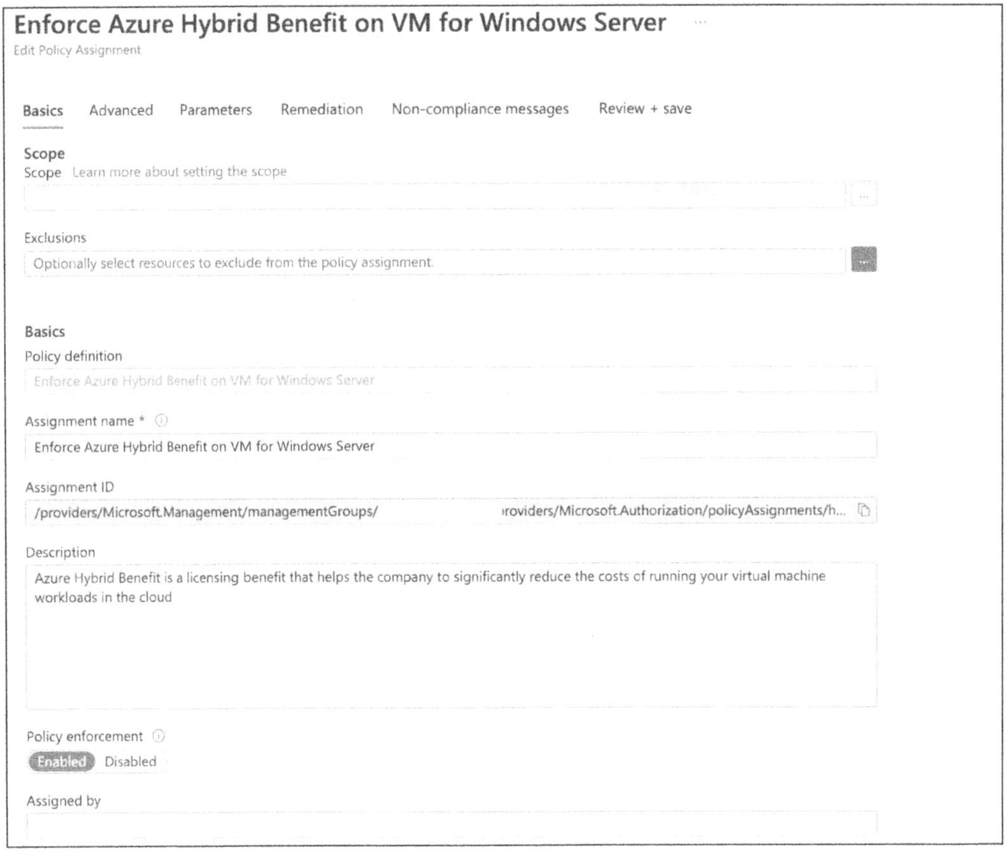

Figure 4.24: Azure Policy assignment basic

7. Leave all the fields as default and move to the non-compliance message. This message will be populated as an error if the user does not select the hybrid license.

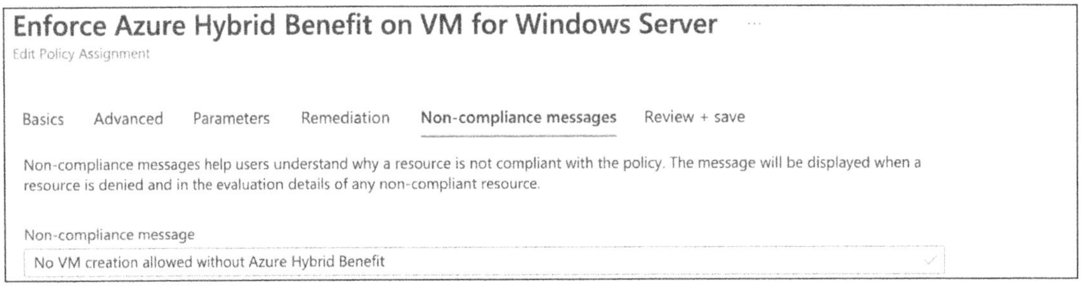

Figure 4.25: Azure Policy Assignment Non-Compliance Message

8. At the end, click on **Review + Save**. Normally it will take up to 120 min to see the policy effect.

The policy assignment will be the same for the Linux and SQL Server. The only change which is required is policy rule.

Policy rule for **Red Hat Enterprise Linux (RHEL)** Linux Server:

```
{
    "mode": "All", // The policy applies to all resources, not just
    those that support tags and locations.
    "policyRule": { // The main structure defining the rule.
      "if": { // The "if" block specifies the conditions for applying the
      policy.
        "allOf": [ // All of the following conditions must be met.
          {
            "equals": "Microsoft.Compute/virtualMachines",
            "field": "type" // The resource must be a virtual machine.
          },
          {
            "equals": "Linux",
            "field": "Microsoft.Compute/virtualMachines/storageProfile.
            osDisk.osType" // The OS type on the VM's OS disk must be
            Linux.
          },
          {
            "anyOf": [ // One of the following conditions must be met.
              {
                "exists": false,
                "field": "Microsoft.Compute/virtualMachines/licenseType"
                // The licenseType field must not exist on the VM.
              },
              {
                "field": "Microsoft.Compute/virtualMachines/licenseType",
                "notEquals": "RHEL_BYOS" // The licenseType for the VM
                must not be RHEL_BYOS.
              }
            ]
          },
          {
            "anyOf": [ // One of the following conditions must be met.
              {
                "equals": "RedHat",
                "field": "Microsoft.Compute/imagePublisher" // The image
                publisher must be RedHat.
              },
```

```
          {
            "contains": "RHEL",
            "field": "Microsoft.Compute/imageOffer" // The image offer
            must contain RHEL.
          },
          {
            "contains": "RedHat",
            "field": "Microsoft.Compute/virtualMachines/
            imagePublisher" // The image publisher on the VM must
            contain RedHat.
          },
          {
            "contains": "RHEL",
            "field": "Microsoft.Compute/virtualMachines/imageOffer" //
            The image offer on the VM must contain RHEL.
          },
          {
            "equals": "RedHat",
            "field": "Microsoft.Compute/virtualMachines/instanceView.
            osName" // The OS name in the VM's instance view must be
            RedHat.
          }
        ]
      }
    ]
  },
  "then": { // The action to take if the conditions above are met.
    "details": {
      "conflictEffect": "deny", // If the policy rule conflicts with
      existing resources, it will deny the creation or update.
      "operations": [ // Defines the operations to take when the "if"
      conditions are satisfied.
        {
          "field": "Microsoft.Compute/virtualMachines/licenseType",
          "operation": "addOrReplace",
          "value": "RHEL_BYOS" // Add or replace the licenseType to
          RHEL_BYOS.
        }
      ],
```

```
        "roleDefinitionIds": [ // Defines the roles that are granted
        permissions under this policy.
          "/providers/microsoft.authorization/roleDefinitions/9980e02c-
          c2be-4d73-94e8-173b1dc7cf3c"
        ]
      },
      "effect": "[parameters('effect')]" // The effect of the policy,
      which can be modified by a provided parameter.
    }
  },
  "parameters": { // Parameters that can be passed to the policy.
    "effect": { // Defines the "effect" parameter.
      "type": "String", // The data type of the parameter is a string.
      "metadata": { // Metadata providing more information about the
      parameter.
        "displayName": "Effect",
        "description": "Enable or disable the execution of the policy"
        // A description of what the parameter does.
      },
      "allowedValues": [ // The possible values for this parameter.
        "Modify",
        "Disabled"
      ],
      "defaultValue": "Modify" // The default value of the parameter.
    }
  }
}
```

Policy rule for Azure SQL Server:

```
{
    "mode": "All", // The enforcement mode for the policy rule.
    "policyRule": {
      "if": {
        "allOf": [
          {
            "equals": "Microsoft.Sql/servers/databases",
            "field": "type" // The resource type field.
          },
          {
```

```
        "field": "name",
        "notEquals": "master" // Ensuring the database name is not
        'master'.
},
{
  "anyOf": [
    {
      "equals": "GeneralPurpose",
      "field": "Microsoft.Sql/servers/databases/sku.tier" //
      Check for GeneralPurpose SKU tier.
    },
    {
      "equals": "Hyperscale",
      "field": "Microsoft.Sql/servers/databases/sku.tier" //
      Check for Hyperscale SKU tier.
    },
    {
      "equals": "BusinessCritical",
      "field": "Microsoft.Sql/servers/databases/sku.tier" //
      Check for BusinessCritical SKU tier.
    },
    {
      "contains": "GP_",
      "field": "Microsoft.Sql/servers/databases/sku.name" //
      Check for SKUs starting with GP_.
    },
    {
      "contains": "BC_",
      "field": "Microsoft.Sql/servers/databases/sku.name" //
      Check for SKUs starting with BC_.
    },
    {
      "contains": "HS_",
      "field": "Microsoft.Sql/servers/databases/sku.name" //
      Check for SKUs starting with HS_.
    }
  ]
},
```

```
      {
        "field": "Microsoft.Sql/servers/databases/licenseType",
        "notEquals": "BasePrice" // The field indicating license type
        is not BasePrice.
      },
      {
        "not": {
          "anyOf": [
            {
              "equals": "ElasticPool",
              "field": "Microsoft.Sql/servers/databases/sku.name" //
              Ensure it's not an ElasticPool.
            },
            {
              "contains": "GP_S_",
              "field": "Microsoft.Sql/servers/databases/sku.name" //
              Ensure SKU name does not contain GP_S_.
            },
            {
              "contains": "pool",
          "field": "kind" // Ensure the kind does not contain 'pool'.
            },
            {
              "contains": "serverless",
              "field": "kind" // Ensure the kind is not 'serverless'.
            }
          ]
        }
      }
    ]
  },
  "then": {
    "details": {
      "conflictEffect": "deny", // The effect to apply if there's a
      conflict.
      "operations": [
        {
          "field": "Microsoft.Sql/servers/databases/licenseType",
```

```
            "operation": "addOrReplace",
            "value": "BasePrice" // The operation to adjust the
            license type to BasePrice.
          }
        ],
        "roleDefinitionIds": [
          "/providers/microsoft.authorization/roleDefinitions/6d8ee4ec-
          f05a-4a1d-8b00-a9b17e38b437" // The role definition ID.
        ]
      },
      "effect": "[parameters('effect')]" // The effect based on
      parameters.
    }
  },
  "parameters": {
    "effect": {
      "type": "String", // The data type of the parameter.
      "metadata": {
        "displayName": "Effect", // The display name of the parameter.
        "description": "Enable or disable the execution of the policy"
        // Description of the parameter.
      },
      "allowedValues": [
        "Modify",
        "Disabled"
      ],
      "defaultValue": "Modify" // The default value of the parameter.
    }
  }
}
```

Spot Instances and low-priority virtual machines

In cloud computing, cost optimization remains highly preferred for businesses leveraging cloud resources. Microsoft Azure offers two features for cost-conscious consumers:

- Spot Instances
- Low-Priority VMs

These services are developed to utilize Azure's unused capacity at a significantly lower cost than regular instances.

Azure Spot Instances

It is a flexible, cost-saving option. Azure Spot Instances allow users to bid for unused Azure capacity. The pricing is variable, based on real-time supply and demand, and is often relatively lower than standard rates. Spot Instances are ideal for workloads tolerant of interruptions, such as batch processing jobs, development and testing environments, or any non-critical background tasks.

The main trade-off with Spot Instances is their need for higher availability guarantees. Azure has the right to reclaim these instances with minimal notice, typically around 30 seconds. This makes them inappropriate for critical applications that require constant uptime. However, for flexible tasks, the cost savings can be significant, with discounts of up to 90% off the pay-as-you-go pricing.

Users can set a maximum price they are willing to pay, and if the market price exceeds this point, the instance can be automatically evicted. Alternatively, setting the max price to -1 ensures that the instance will not be evicted for pricing reasons if Azure has the capacity.

Low-priority virtual machines

Low-priority VMs were Azure's initial charge into cost-saving computing options, offering customers a balanced discount on computing resources by utilizing Azure's spare capacity. However, Microsoft has since transitioned these to Spot Instances, getting more flexibility and variable pricing to the model. This change reflects Azure's commitment to providing more competitive pricing options in the market.

Strategic use cases and best practices: The strategic deployment of these VMs can lead to considerable cost savings. They are highly effective for specific types of workloads:

- **Development and testing**: DevOps teams can utilize Spot Instances for development, testing, and quality assurance without incurring the total costs of regular instances.

- **Big data and analytics**: Large-scale data processing tasks, which can be spread across multiple instances and tolerate interruptions, are ideal candidates for Spot Instances.

- **Batch jobs**: Workloads that process data in batches, such as video encoding or scientific simulations, can be scheduled to run on Spot Instances.

- **Disaster recovery**: Users can use Spot Instances as part of their disaster recovery strategy, keeping costs low during normal operations and only scaling up to full-price instances when needed.

Organizations should implement vital monitoring and automation tools to use Spot Instances and Low-Priority VMs effectively. These tools can help manage instance lifecycles, handle evictions gracefully, and shift workloads as necessary to ensure continuity.

Conclusion

In conclusion, the journey through various cost optimization strategies within Azure presents a complete approach to managing and reducing cloud costs. From right-sizing resources to ensure that each Azure service is provided to actual usage needs to leveraging Reserved Instances and Savings Plans for budget predictability and cost savings, organizations can make informed decisions about their cloud infrastructure. The ability to determine between Azure Reservation and Saving Plans allows for solutions based on unique workload demands. Additionally, organizations can maximize their existing on-premises licenses by employing Azure Hybrid Benefits and understanding the complex processes of enforcing Azure Hybrid Licenses using Azure Policy. Lastly, utilizing Spot Instances and Low-Priority VMs offers a strategic avenue for running workloads at a significantly reduced cost when start and end times are flexible. These strategies signify Azure's commitment to providing a flexible, cost-effective cloud environment that can adapt to the diverse financial objectives of businesses.

This concludes the chapter and underscores the importance of each strategy in the broader context of financial efficiency and cloud resource management.

In the next chapter, we will discuss the following topics:

- Azure Monitor helps you understand how your applications are performing and proactively identifies issues affecting them and the resources they depend on.

- Azure Log Analytics is a tool within Azure Monitor that collects and aggregates data from monitored resources into a comprehensive search platform. This is one of the expensive Azure services and needs to be optimized to control the cost.

- Azure Monitor will help to create the dashboard that allows you to display the most relevant monitoring data and insights for your team, project, or operations, ensuring quick access to the health and performance of your resources.

Join our book's Discord space

Join the book's Discord Workspace for Latest updates, Offers, Tech happenings around the world, New Release and Sessions with the Authors:

https://discord.bpbonline.com

CHAPTER 5

Azure Monitoring

Introduction

In the dynamic landscape of cloud computing, the power to monitor, analyze, and respond to system performance data is essential. This section explains the powerful abilities of Azure monitor and metrics, which form the backbone of functional insights for applications and infrastructure on Azure. We will analyze log analytics and Azure monitor workbooks, which provide developed analytics and interactive reporting features, enabling you to explore into your data. Next, we will show you through the method of creating and customizing dashboards, allowing for a tailored view that aligns with your operational goals and needs. Lastly, we will cover reporting and data visualization, which converts raw data into effective visual narratives, making it easier to understand trends, identify issues, and make informed decisions. Each of these elements plays a key role in optimizing the performance and reliability of your Azure services.

Structure

In this chapter, we will go through the following topics:

- Monitoring reporting
- Azure Monitor and metrics
- Log analytics and Azure monitor workbooks

- Creating and customizing dashboards
- Reporting and data visualization

Objectives

This section will allow you to know how to use Azure's monitoring and analytics services to manage your cloud environment. You will learn how to track your system's performance in real-time using Azure monitor and metrics. Additionally, you will learn how to explore data in detail using log analytics and Azure monitor workbooks. You will also learn how to create and customize dashboards that fit your monitoring needs. Lastly, you will explore tools for reporting and data visualization that help you understand trends, identify issues, and make educated decisions.

Monitoring reporting

Azure Monitor is a monitoring and control service offered by Azure. It allows the team to observe the performance of the team's resources hosted on the Azure cloud. The goal of Azure Monitor is to confirm that the team has visibility into the application's performance and cost management.

The following figure shows how Azure Monitor works. It is a tool that allows you to collect and analyze data from your cloud and on-premises. In this course, you can deliver your applications to run smoothly and fix problems. The picture shows how the data flows from different sources like Azure resources, subscriptions, tenants, applications, and operating systems. Then, it demonstrates how the data is collected, analyzed, and used to make decisions. Finally, it shows how the tool automatically sends alerts and scales resources if needed.

This figure demonstrates Azure Monitor's ability to gather and analyze data from sources like Azure resources, subscriptions, tenants, applications, and operating systems. It highlights how Azure Monitor uses metrics and logs for visualization, analysis, insights, integration, and response, ensuring optimized performance and proactive management of Azure environments.

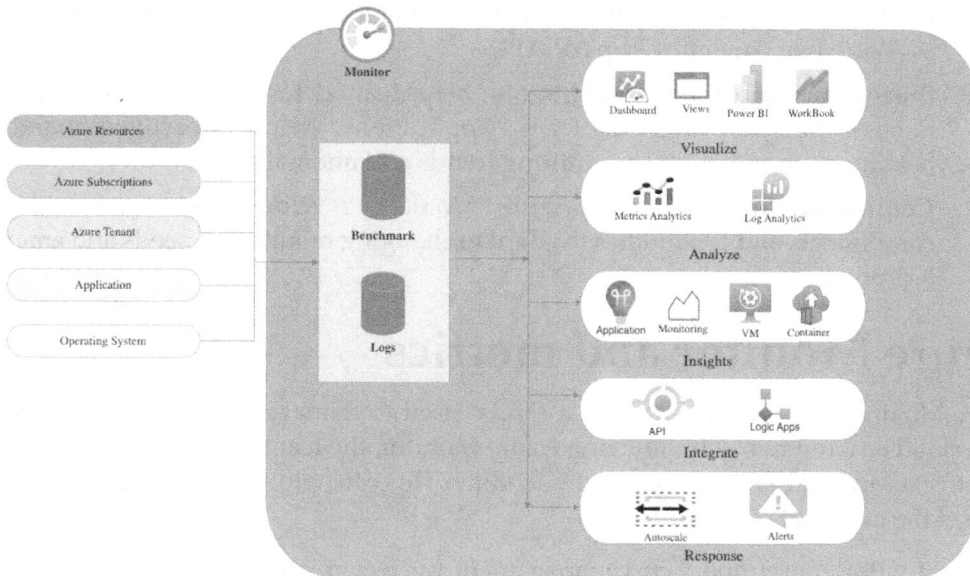

Figure 5.1: *Function principle of Azure Monitor*

Here are some fundamental principles and features of Azure Monitor:

- **Data collection**: Azure Monitor manages data from various origins, including Azure resources, applications, and external sources. It contains metrics, logs, and traces to deliver understanding into the environment.

- **Metrics**: Azure Monitor captures metrics such as **central processing unit (CPU)** usage, memory utilization, network traffic, etc. These metrics are managed at regular intervals and can be used to analyze the performance of resources over time.

- **Logs**: Azure Monitor captures logs from Azure resources and applications. These logs can include data about application events, errors, and other diagnostic data.

- **Alerts and notifications**: Azure Monitor permits the team to set up alerts based on predefined conditions. When these conditions are met, the system can send notifications via various communication channels, helping the team respond to issues promptly.

- **Dashboards and visualization**: Azure Monitor provides tools for creating customized dashboards. Team can create visual presentations of data to better understand application's health and implementation.

- **Application insights**: Azure Monitor integrates with Application Insights, a service that helps team watch the performance of the team's applications. It delivers a thorough knowledge of application manners, user interactions, and dependencies.

- **Autoscaling**: Azure Monitor can initiate autoscaling actions based on performance metrics. This enables the team's applications to dynamically change their resources to satisfy demand.

- **Integration:** Azure Monitor can combine with other Azure services and tools, such as Azure Log Analytics Apps or API.

- **Proactive monitoring**: Azure Monitor helps team determine and address possible issues before they affect the team's applications. We can proactively maintain a healthy environment by monitoring trends and anomalies.

- **Continuous improvement**: Azure Monitor develops over time with new components and capabilities to adapt to changing monitoring needs and emerging technologies.

Azure Monitor and metrics

Azure Monitor is an effective tool that can be used to manage, analyze, and act on data from cloud environments. By utilizing Azure Monitor, the team can achieve visibility into Azure costs and take steps to optimize spending. This can help save money on Azure costs and get the most out of investment.

Azure Monitor can support cost management by recognizing underutilized resources. Azure Monitor can follow resource usage metrics like CPU, memory, and network usage. Azure Monitor can also support team notice of cost anomalies. It can support identifying sudden points in unexpected costs. If a cost anomaly, the team can analyze the issue to determine the cause. This can help to avoid overspending on resources.

The following figure demonstrates how Azure Monitor works. It is a tool that allows you collect and understand data from your cloud and on-premises. This way, you can deliver your applications easily and fix problems when they happen. The image shows how the data flows from different sources like Azure resources, applications, and operating systems. Then, it shows how the tool collects, analyzes, and uses the data to make decisions. Finally, it shows how the tool automatically sends alerts and adjusts resources if needed. Overall, it is a helpful tool that makes it easier to manage your IT infrastructure, refer to the following figure:

The figure shows how the Azure Monitoring Agent enhances security and efficiency, simplifies administration, lowers costs, and uses a single monitoring agent. It demonstrates how Azure's unified monitoring system boosts operational efficiency and cost-effectiveness while ensuring strong security.

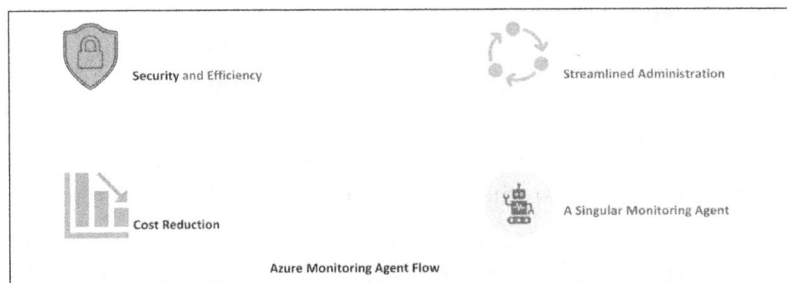

Figure 5.2: Azure Monitor flow

Identifying underutilized resources and seeing cost anomalies, Azure Monitor can also assist in setting budgets and alerts for Azure resources. This can help to remain on path with spending and to be informed when the team is exceeding the team's budget.

Monitoring and reporting in Azure for cost optimization is about turning raw usage data into actionable insights. It's changing cloud cost from a black box into a transparent, manageable, and well-understood element of the team's operations. Power of these tools and practices, Teams can achieve greater control over their Azure spending, identify opportunities for savings, and align their cloud usage with goals.

Finally, Azure Monitor combines a combination of cost-saving features, such as reserved instances and azure spot instances. These features can allow the team to reduce costs by up to 70%. By using Azure Monitor, the team can achieve visibility into Azure costs and bring steps to optimize the team's spending.

Metrics in Azure Monitor

Metrics from Azure Monitor is a vital and complete monitoring and control service offered by Azure. Cloud-based applications and resources, metrics provide essential data that gives valuable understanding into the behavior, performance, and utilization of various resources across Azure environments. These metrics help systems, permitting their health and making instructed findings to ensure extreme performance and uninterrupted availability.

Metrics

Metrics are a type of data that Azure Monitor collects from the team's Azure resources. They are values gathered at standard intervals and represent some system element at a particular time. For example, a metric can provide the CPU utilization of a virtual machine and the free space in a storage account.

Importance of metrics

Metrics are essential because they provide a complete view of the team's Azure environment. They can track resources' implementation, utilization, and conduct over time. This data can be used to determine problems, troubleshoot issues, and optimize resources.

Types of metrics available

Azure Monitor contains a combination of metrics from the team's Azure resources. Below are the metrics into two categories:

- **Platform metrics**: Platform metrics are compiled from Azure resources. They are known for all Azure resources and do not need any configuration.

- **Custom metrics**: Custom metrics are compiled from resources that the team configures. The team can configure custom metrics for any resource that supports them, such as virtual machines, applications, and services.

How to use metrics?

Azure Monitor provides a combination of tools for using metrics. These tools can be used to:

- **View metrics**: Azure Monitor delivers a metrics explorer that permits the team to consider metrics for Azure resources. The team can use the metrics explorer to follow resources' performance, utilization, and behavior over time.
- **Create alerts**: Azure Monitor can be utilized to create alerts based on metrics. This lets the team know when a metric exceeds a certain threshold. This can help the team identify and resolve problems before they cause outages or other issues.
- **Visualize metrics**: Azure Monitor can visualize metrics utilizing charts and dashboards. This permits the team to see trends and patterns in data. This information can be used to determine problems, troubleshoot issues, and optimize resources.

The following figure shows how Azure Monitor works. It is a tool that helps you understand data from sources like Azure resources and applications. This way, when there are any problems, you can quickly fix them. The tool collects data from different sources and then analyzes it. It helps you make decisions and sends alerts if needed. Overall, the tool makes it easier to manage your IT infrastructure.

The figure illustrates the merging of multiple data sources with Azure Monitor Metrics. It depicts how data from REST APIs, Azure Resources, and Kubernetes (K8) clusters are categorized into Custom, Platform, and Innovator through Azure Monitor Metrics. This processed information is subsequently visualized and observed using Azure Workbooks, Dashboards, Metrics, Alerts, and Grafana, providing thorough monitoring and alerting functionalities.

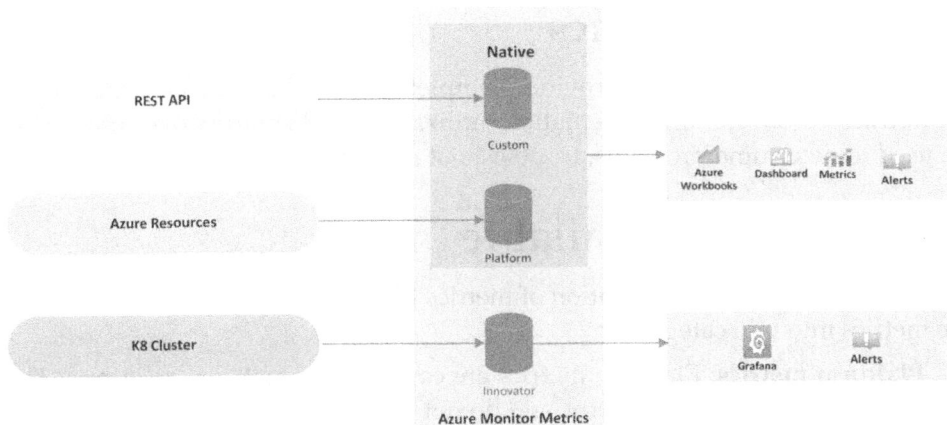

Figure 5.3: *Azure Monitor Metrics*

Key characteristics of metrics

Following are the key characteristics of metrics:

- **Measurement parameters in metrics**: Azure Monitor measurement parameters are the different features or variables that Metrics grab to quantify and evaluate the performance and manners of the team's cloud resources. These parameters act as the building blocks of understanding, allowing team to gain an understanding of various parts of applications and infrastructure.

- **Mixed dimensions of measurement**: Metrics are like windows through which teams can peer into the complex workings of the cloud environment.. These windows, shaped by measure parameters, show different dimensions of resource manners. Here are some essential measurement parameters and insights:

  - **CPU utilization:** This parameter measures the percentage of the CPU a resource uses. High CPU utilization could mean a resource-intensive task or the need for extra computing capacity.

  - **Memory consumption:** Metrics related to memory utilization deliver an understanding of how much memory the team's resources are using. Oversized memory consumption might conduct to performance bottlenecks or application crashes.

  - **Network throughput:** This parameter measures the volume of data transmitted over a network. Observing network throughput helps determine possible congestion or network-related problems.

  - **Response times:** Response time metrics show how long it takes for a resource to respond to a request. Slow response times could mean performance issues or inefficiencies within applications.

  - **Storage occupancy:** Metrics associated with storage occupancy follow how much data is stored on an individual storage resource. Observing storage occupancy is required to prevent resource overutilization and potential data loss.

  - **Request rates:** Request rate metrics show the number of incoming requests over a specific timeframe for web applications or APIs. High request rates could affect application response.

  - **Error rates**: Error rate metrics quantify the frequency of errors or failures experienced by cloud resources. Tracking error rates helps determine issues impacting user experience.

  - **Latency:** Latency metrics measure the time data transits from the source to the destination. High latency can negatively affect application performance, especially in real-time applications.

- **Specialized insights**: Each measurement parameter shows a specialized lens via which the team can keep a typical dimension of the team's resource behavior. Observing these parameters collectively provides the team with an entire view of how their resources function, interact, and respond to varying workloads.

- **Data-driven decision making**: Measurement parameters transform raw data into actionable insights. For instance, if a team observes high CPU utilization and slow response times, the team might suppose that the team's application's performance is delayed by CPU-intensive jobs. Armed with this information, the team can take targeted measures to optimize the team's application's efficiency.

- **Adapting to unique needs**: Azure Monitor's flexibility permits the team to describe custom measurement parameters tailored to the team's application's specific essentials. This customization assigns the team to observe the attributes that matter most to the team's business logic and performance goals.

- **Granularity: Capturing of time and change**: Metrics lie not only in the data team capture but also in the context they deliver through granularity. Granularity guides the level of the point at which data points are gathered and recorded. In Azure Monitor, granularity is a vital tool that allows team to examine and understand the team's strategy's performance across various timeframes and systems.

- **Multifaceted perspective through granularity**: Metrics are significantly amplified by their ability to grab data at varying phases of granularity. This means team can select the frequency at which Metrics are organized, whether per minute, per hour, or at custom gaps that align with the team's application's needs. This multifaceted view improves the team's performance of the team's plan's manners by delivering insights into short-term and long-term implementation dynamics.

- **Unveiling transient fluctuations**: Metrics documented at sufficient intervals, such as per minute, deliver an exact lens into the team's system's manners over short timeframes. This level of granularity allows the team to capture rapid changes that might occur in minutes.

- **Identifying long-term trends**: On the other end of the range, Metrics followed over more extended breaks, such as per hour or day, enable the team to recognize and assess long-term movements. These trends contain gradual changes in resource utilization and performance practices that might occur over extended periods.

- **Empowering proactive management**: By having the ability to select the right granularity, the team is assigned to perform proactive management. For instance, Metrics can help the team see anomalies and swiftly react to potential issues that require immediate alerts.

- **Customizing granularity for precision**: Azure Monitor understands that every application and design have unique monitoring requirements. This is why it allows the team to customize the granularity of Metrics according to the team's application's difficulties. Custom intervals can be to the team's business logic and resource utilization patterns, ensuring the team grabs data points that truly matter.

Data collection

Data collection is vital in Azure Monitor's functionality, allowing the team to capture and functional understandings about the implementation and behavior of the team's resources. This frequent process involves orchestrating the collection of Metric data from various resources hosted within the Azure environment.

Mechanism of regular polling

Azure Monitor uses an organized method to collect Metric data from resources. This method concerns regular polling, where the monitoring system gets out to various resources at predetermined intervals to recover specific metrics.

Wide array of resources

Data collection is extensive, spanning various resources containing virtual machines, databases, web applications, containers, and more. Azure Monitor releases its net across this landscape, ensuring that no critical team infrastructure goes unnoticed.

Capturing performance parameters

During polling, Azure Monitor grabs mixed performance parameters based on the metrics team has selected for monitoring. These parameters include CPU usage, memory utilization, network traffic, response times, and other metrics that deliver insights.

Aggregation and storage: Uniting the data puzzle

Data is collected. It is not just a series of isolated data points. Azure Monitor aggregates the gathered data, creating a cohesive and complete view of the team system's implementation over time. This collection process might affect calculating averages or other statistical efforts to better represent the team's resource's behavior.

Here is how Azure Monitor facilitates this process:

1. **Harnessing data for insights and action**: The aggregated data is then kept in a structured format helping with analysis and visualization. This data repository allows the team to investigate historical implementation trends, identify anomalies, and make informed decisions to enhance the application's performance.

2. **Analysis, visualization, and trend identification**: The organized and aggregated data needs to be indicated to remain static. Azure Monitor provides the team with tools to analyze and visualize this data.

3. **Predicting the future**: With historical data, the team can employ predictive analytics to predict future behavior. By determining regular practices and trends, the team can make strategic conclusions that help the team's system achieve optimally despite varying demands.

4. **Empowering informed action**: Azure Monitor's entire data collection method is created to assign teams with actionable insights. These understandings authorize the team to take informed actions, scale resources to satisfy peak demand and fine-tuning application configurations.

Enable the metrics in Azure Monitor

In this section, we will learn how to enable the metrics in Azure Cloud. Following are the steps to enable the metrics:

1. Select **Metrics** from the Azure Monitor menu or the resource menu's **Monitoring** section in the Azure portal. Then select a scope to open the scope selector.

2. Use the scope selector to select objects and metrics. The scope should be created if the Azure Metrics Explorer is opened in the resources menu, refer to the following figure:

   The screenshot illustrates how users can choose a scope for metrics within the Azure Monitor interface. From the Azure Monitor dashboard, users go to the "Metrics" section and are asked to select a scope to access specific metrics data. The "Select a scope" panel lets users filter and refine the monitoring data by choosing from different subscriptions, resource types, and locations. This functionality assists in tailoring the metrics view to concentrate on the most pertinent resources and information.

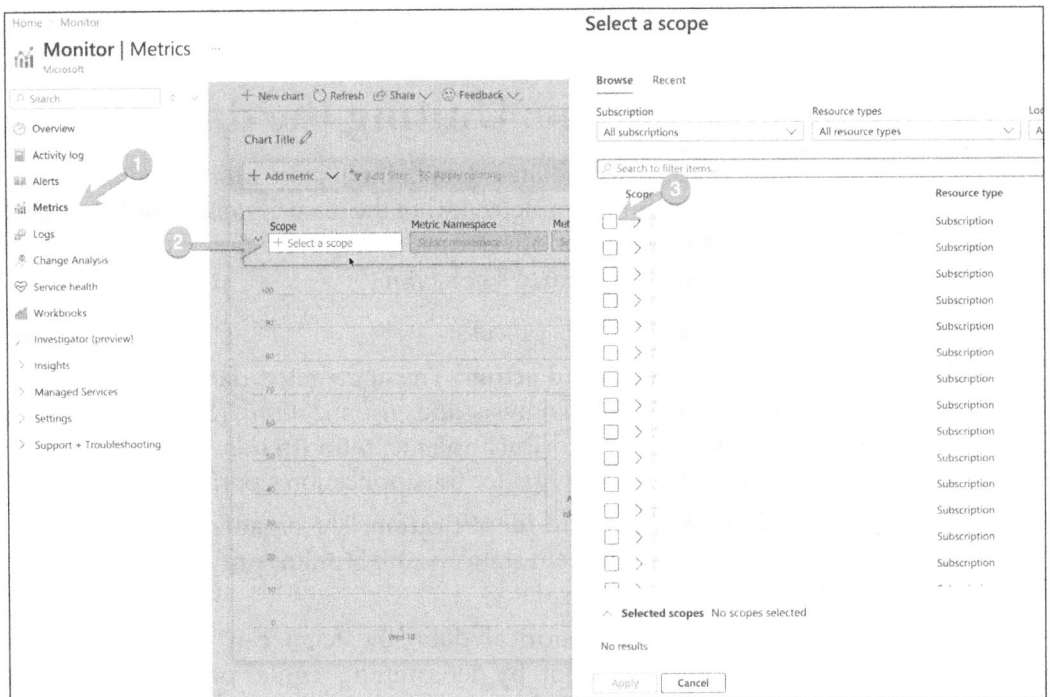

Figure 5.4: Azure Monitor Metrics (Select a scope)

3. Choose the preferred subscription, then select the resource type and the specific resource you wish to monitor:

The screenshot presents the "Select a scope" interface in Azure Monitor, enabling users to choose resources for metric monitoring. Users can narrow the scope by selecting a specific resource type, such as "App Services," then picking a particular service and location. This interface helps users filter and target specific resources for performance analysis. It also mentions that multi-selection for App Service resources is not currently supported, encouraging users to vote for this feature. Once choices are made, users can click "Apply" to establish the chosen monitoring scope.

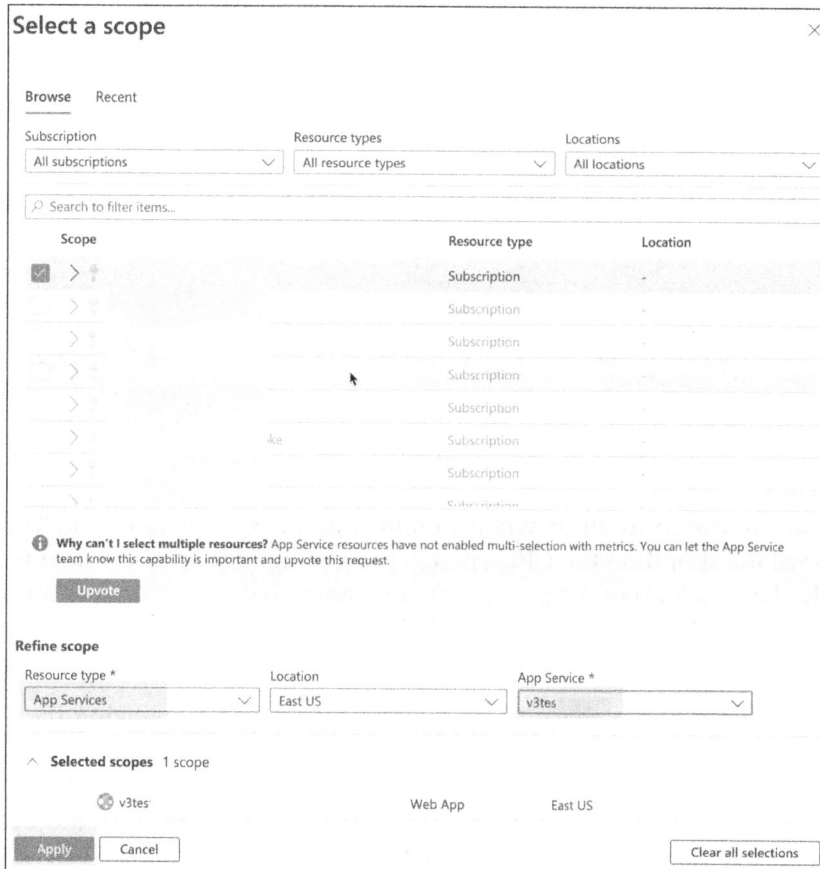

Figure 5.5: Azure Monitor Metrics (Select the Resource type)

4. Upon selecting a resource, choose the metrics you intend to monitor. This will lead you to a graph displaying the metric values, which can be effectively monitored:

The screenshot shows the Azure Monitor Metrics interface, where users can build custom charts to visualize specific metrics. In the "Chart Title" section, with the scope set to "dev-ms365," users can choose a metric namespace like "App Service standard." They can pick metrics such as "Average memory working set" or "CPU Time" and apply aggregations for time-based analysis. Users can also add filters, plot multiple metrics, create custom dashboards, and set up alerts to monitor Azure resource performance effectively.

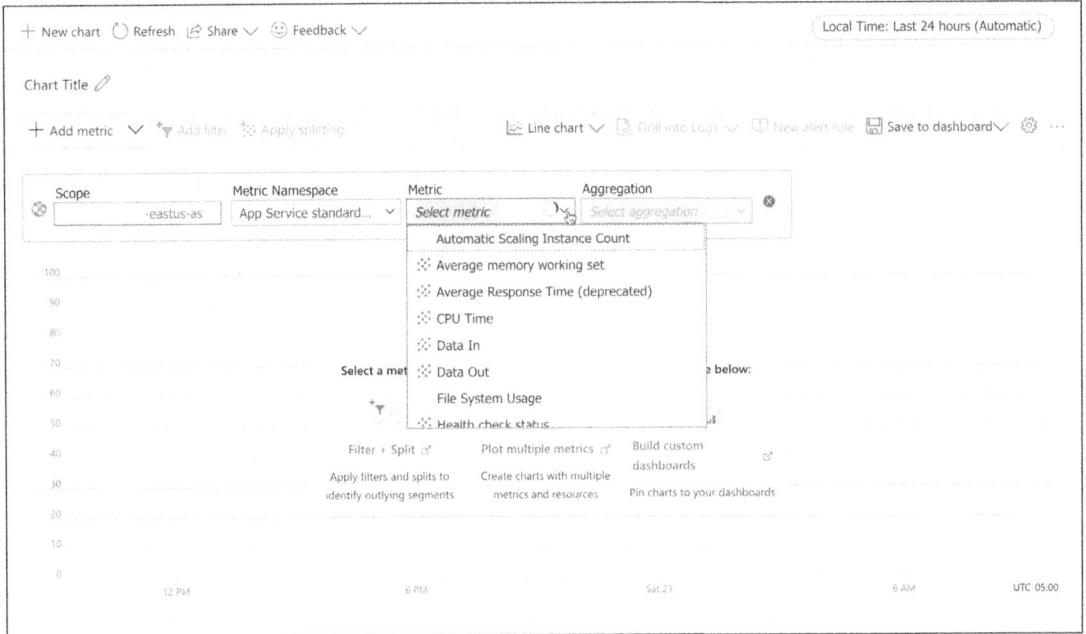

Figure 5.6: Azure Monitor Metrics (Select a Metric)

One important metric to monitor when monitoring an App service is CPU Time. This measures the amount of time the CPU spends processing requests. The data is calculated using a method called Sum of Aggregates, which makes it easier to understand. The chart shows how many milliseconds (MS) the CPU uses, clearly showing how much resources are consumed.

The screenshot shows a line chart in Azure Monitor Metrics visualizing the "Sum CPU Time" for the resource "dev-ms365groupmanagement" over the last 24 hours. The chart displays the total CPU time consumed using the "Sum" metric aggregation. The graph shows fluctuations in CPU usage over time, providing insights into the application's performance. The bottom left corner highlights a data point indicating a total CPU time of 1.22 minutes, helping users monitor and analyze the resource's computational load and identify periods of high or low activity.

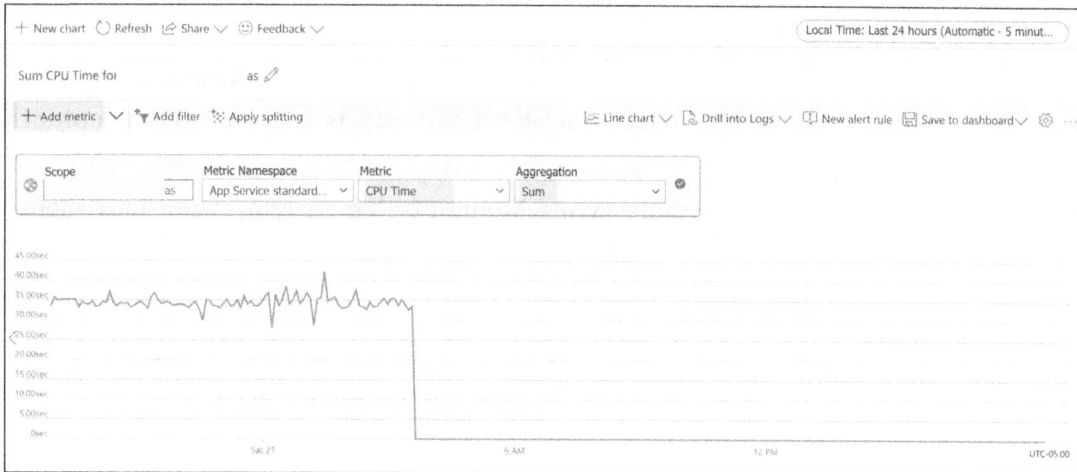

Figure 5.7: *Azure Monitor Metrics (Display graph)*

Log analytics and Azure Monitor workbooks

Log Analytics is an essential tool in the Azure portal. Azure Monitor Logs make it easier to create and manage log queries against the data residing in the storage.

Teams have the flexibility to complete queries of differing degrees of difficulty. For example, an easy query can be created to retrieve annotated logs. Now, log analytics assigns a team to leverage its full functionality. This includes carefully organizing, skillfully filtering, and analyzing data. This technique allows for unlocking valuable insights that might otherwise remain hidden.

If a team's analytics purposes require an advanced approach, log analytics easily meets this need. The team can go further into preparing complex questions that facilitate statistical analysis. The result of this step is how the team can manage the team's findings. This data visualization allows the team to determine and identify specific trends, a powerful capacity to assess patterns that lead to decision-making.

The use of log analytics expands further individual query functions. Whether the team interacts with query results or weaves them into the fabric of other Azure Monitor applications, such as creating log query alerts or advanced workbooks, log analysis remains the cornerstone of the team's workflow and the breadth of the application from creating queries to repeating test plans. This powerful tool gives the team the tools to refine the team's queries and then turn the results into actionable insights, thus helping tremendously with the team's holistic research efforts in the Azure ecosystem, the more comprehensive system.

Starting log analytics

To enable log analytics in the Azure portal, select Logs from the Azure Monitor menu. You will also find this option in the menus of most Azure products. Log analytics determines where data is available.

When you start log analytics from the Azure Monitor or log analytics workspace menu, you have access to all records in the workspace. If you select Logs from another resource, your data will only be logging data for that resource. The team needs to select the scope by choosing the desired subscription.

The image showcases the interface for selecting content within Azure Monitor's log feature. This step is critical as it determines the context for the data queries and log analysis. It allows users to focus on specific subscriptions, resource groups, resource types, and locations for detailed monitoring.

The screenshot shows Azure Monitor's "Logs" section, where users can analyze log data. It prompts users to "Select a scope" for querying logs from specific resources. The selection pane allows filtering by subscription, resource group, resource type, and location, helping target specific Azure resources for efficient monitoring and troubleshooting.

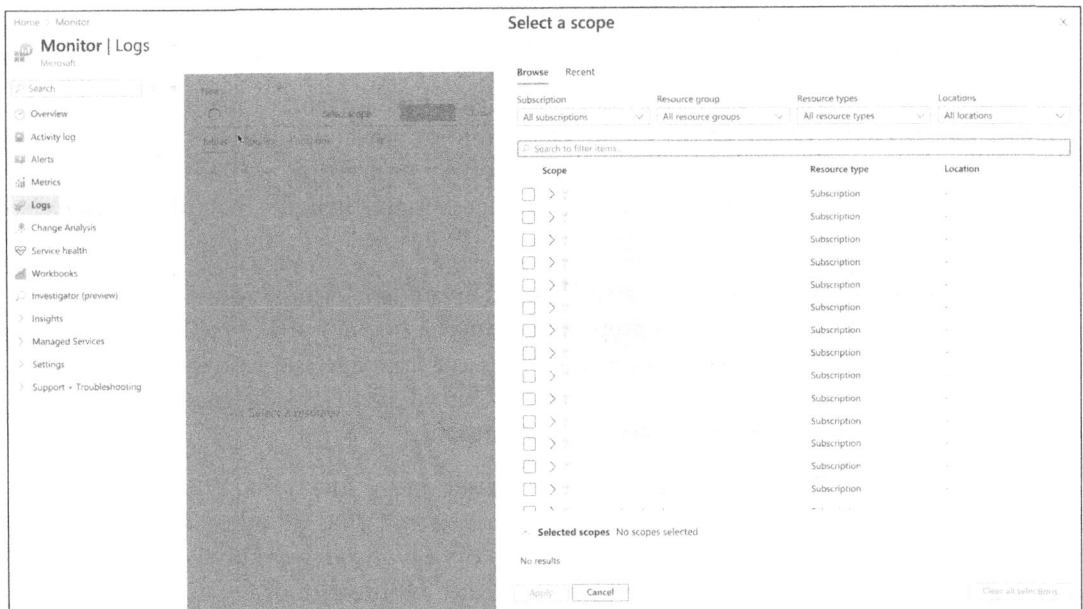

Figure 5.8: Azure Log Analytics (Select Subscription)

When you use Azure Monitor's Log feature, you'll see a screen that lets you choose the data you want to analyze. This is really important because it helps you focus on specific things you want to monitor. You can choose things like subscriptions, resource groups, and locations to help you find exactly what you need. There are some pre-made queries that you can use, or you can modify them to fit your needs.

The screenshot depicts the "Queries" section within the Logs feature of Azure Monitor. This interface enables users to execute predefined queries on various Azure resources for log data analysis. On the left panel, users can choose from resource types such as "API Management," "App Services," or "Application Gateway" to access pertinent queries. Each query tile, like "Number of requests," "Logs of the last 100 calls," "Number of calls by APIs," and "Bandwidth consumed," offers specific insights into the resource's activity and performance. By clicking the "Run" button next to each query, users can execute it and obtain the required log data, facilitating monitoring and troubleshooting activities.

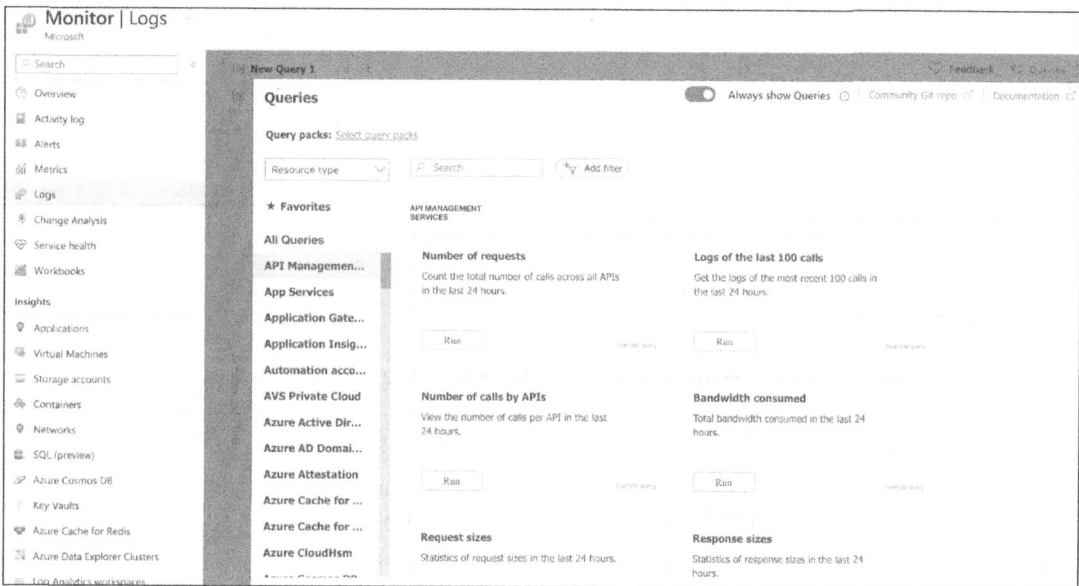

Figure 5.9: *Azure Log Analytics (Select Query)*

If the team wants to begin with an empty script and write it yourself, close the standard queries.

Log analytics interface

Azure Monitor Logs enabled telemetry data from your Azure resources. It offers tools to create and execute queries on log data, which helps identify trends, resolve problems, and enhance resource performance. The interface supports multiple data sources, allowing in-depth analysis and customized monitoring.

The figure below shows how to run queries using the Azure Monitor Logs interface. It demonstrates selecting a data scope, picking specific tables, writing and executing a query, and reviewing results to efficiently monitor and analyze Azure resource activities.

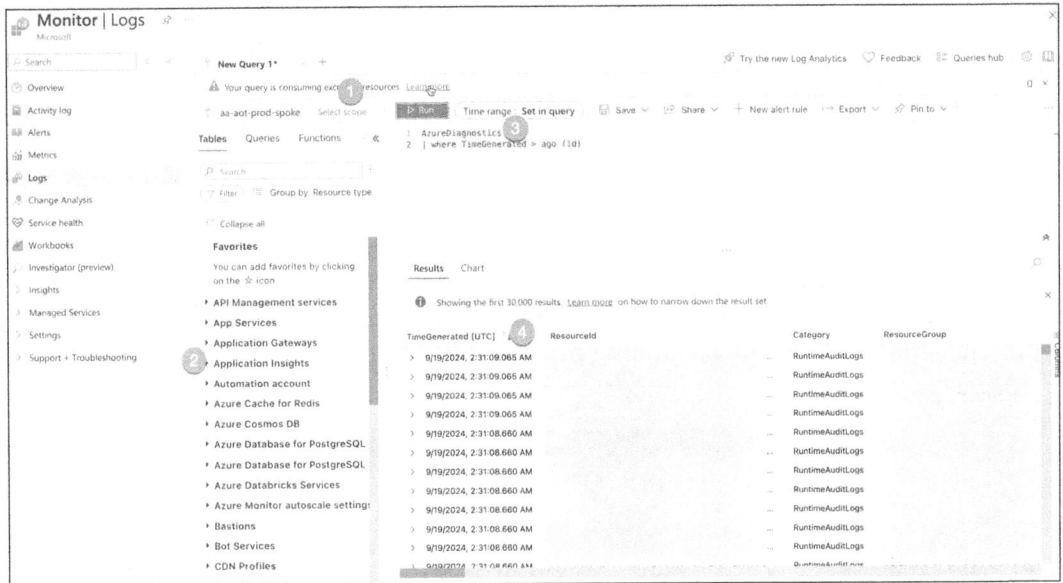

Figure 5.10: *Azure Log Analytics (Getting result)*

Top action bar

The top bar contains the controls you use in queries in the query window.

Function	Description
Run button	Execute the selected query in the query window. You can also choose *Shift + Enter* to execute the query.
Scope	Specifies the content of data used for the query. This could be data for a specific resource across multiple workspaces.
Save button	Save the query to the workspace.
New alert rule button	Empty Query in new tab.
Export button	Export the query results to a CSV file.
Pin to button	Save the query results to an Azure dashboard or an Azure workbook.
Format query button	Organize the specified text for readability.
Example queries button	Open the sample queries dialog that appears when open Log Analytics.
Query Explorer button	Open Query Explorer to save queries in the workspace.
Copy button	Query text or the query results to the clipboard.
Time picker	The time range for the data available to the query.

Table 5.1: *Azure Log Analytics Action Steps*

Left side bar

The sidebar on the left displays tables, sample queries, and filter options for the current query.

The table gives an outline of how to use the Azure Monitor Logs interface. It explains how to select and manipulate data tables, make, and run queries, and use filters to refine search results. This information is essential for using the platform to check and analyze data about cloud resources effectively.

Tab	Description
Tables	You have to choose where you go. Change the grouping of tables. There are options to manually place the table name and display a dialog with a table description to view its documentation and preview its data. Expand the table to see its columns. You need to Double -click to get the term and column name to add in query.
Queries	A list of example queries that you can open in the query window. This list is what seems when you open log analytics. Set group by to edit the groups of questions. Double-click the question to add it to the question window.
Filter	Create filter options based on the results of the query. Once you run the query, lines with different values will appear from the results. Select one or more values, then choose **Apply & Run**, add the where command to the query, and run again.

Table 5.2: Different Aspects in Azure Monitor Logs

Query window

The query window is option to edit your query. **Kusto Query Language** (**KQL**) commands and character encoding increase readability. Select **+** at the top of the window to open a new tab.

Numerous queries can be entered in a single window. Queries cannot include blank lines, so you can separate multiple queries in a window with one or more blank lines. The current question is where the cursor is positioned. Select the **Run** button or press *Shift + Enter* to run the current query.

Results view

The results view displays the query effects in a table sorted alphabetically. Left click the row to extend its values. Choose the **Columns** dropdown to adjust the color list. Select the column name and sort the results. Clear the filters and rerun the query and reconfigure the settings.

Select the **Group** columns to specify the group column above the query result. Drag the results onto the ribbon and group each color.

Chart view

The chart view displays the results as one of several available charts. You can specify chart type in the render command in your query. You can also select from the visualization type drop-down list.

The following table outlines various components that are essential in creating a data visualization, particularly a chart:

Option	Description
Visualization type	Type of chart
X-axis	Column for the x-axis.
Y-axis	Column for the y-axis. A numeric column.
Split by	Results that define the series in the chart.
Aggregation	Aggregation to perform on the numeric values in the y-axis.

Table 5.3: Chart Configuration Parameters

Log query in Azure Monitor

When running a log query in Log Analytics in the Azure portal, the data the query tests rely on the scope and timing. To access the Log Analytics workspaces, you would need to have Microsoft Operational Insights/Workspaces/Query/*/Read permissions.

Query scope

The query defines the records that the query searches for. This typically includes all records in a log analytics workspace or Application insights application. Log analytics also permits you to configure the scope of a specific Azure object that is managed. This allows resource owners to focus solely on their data, even if that resource writes to multiple workstations.

The scope is always shown in the upper left corner of the log analytics. Each icon points to a new Azure object.

The image shows what the Azure Monitor logs interface looks like. It's a place where users can manage and run their queries. The **Favorites** section is for services you use often so that you can find them quickly. The **Queries History** section keeps track of recent queries you have made and shows how many results you got. This helps you monitor your system and find what you need faster.

The screenshot displays the "Tables" pane in Azure Monitor Logs, enabling users to choose data sources for queries. Users can favorite resources like "API Management services," "App Services," and "Application Insights" by clicking the star icon for quick access. The "Queries History" section shows past queries for easy reference.

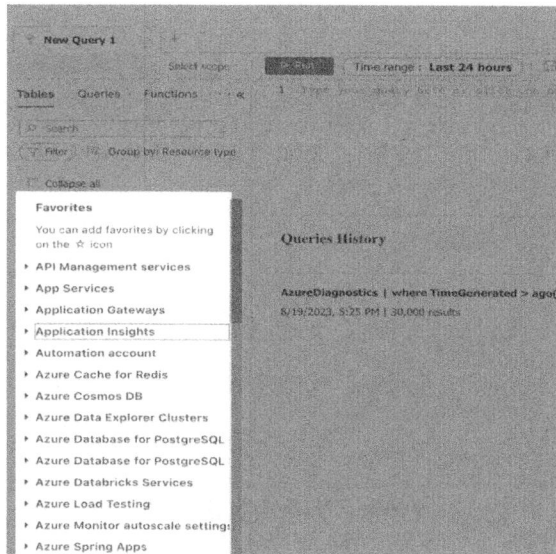

Figure 5.11: *Azure Log Analytics Scope*

The scope is determined by how you start Log Analytics, and you can change the scope. The table lists the types of scopes used and the various descriptions of each:

Query scope	Records in scope	How to select	Changing Scope
Log Analytics workspace	All records in the log analytics workspace.	Azure Monitor menu or the log analytics workspaces menu.	Can change scope to any other resource type.
Application Insights application	All records in the application insights application.	Application insights menu for the application.	Can only change scope to Application Insights application.
Resource group	Resources in the resource group.	Logs from the resource group menu.	Cannot change scope.
Subscription	All resources in the subscription.	Logs from the subscription menu.	Cannot change scope.
Azure resources	Records oxalated by the resource.	Logs from the resource menu,	Can only change scope to same resource type.

Table 5.4: *Query Scope Selection and Limitations in Azure Monitor*

Sample log queries using Kusto Query Language

The section *Number of VMs created in the last seven days* provides insight into the recent virtual machine deployment within your Azure infrastructure.

Sample code:

```
VMComputer
| where TimeGenerated >= ago(7d)
| summarize dcount(Computer) by endofweek(TimeGenerated)
```

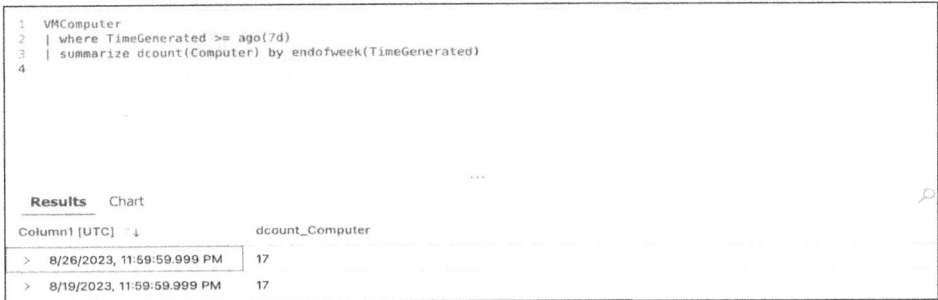

```
1   VMComputer
2   | where TimeGenerated >= ago(7d)
3   | summarize dcount(Computer) by endofweek(TimeGenerated)
4

                                        ...

Results    Chart

Column1 [UTC]    ↓              dcount_Computer

>   8/26/2023, 11:59:59.999 PM    17

>   8/19/2023, 11:59:59.999 PM    17
```

Figure 5.12: Sample Query 1

List of the VMs created in last seven days sorted with VM name, IP address, subscription ID and resource group name.

Sample code:

```
VMComputer
| where TimeGenerated >= ago(7d)
| project Computer,Ipv4Addresses,AzureSubscriptionId,AzureResourceGroup
```

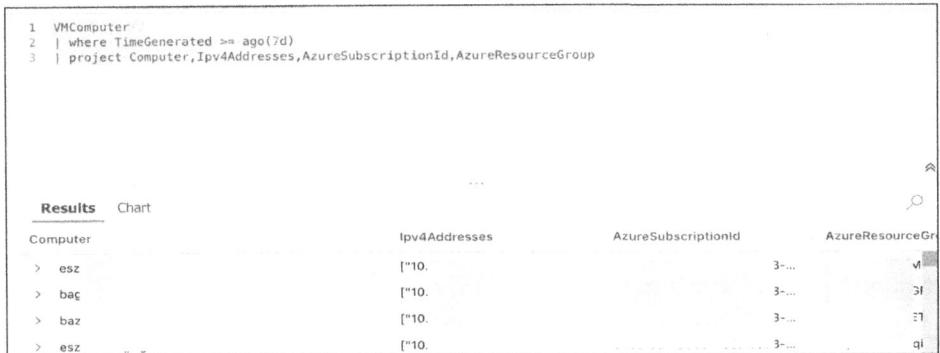

```
1   VMComputer
2   | where TimeGenerated >= ago(7d)
3   | project Computer,Ipv4Addresses,AzureSubscriptionId,AzureResourceGroup

                                        ...

Results    Chart

Computer           Ipv4Addresses    AzureSubscriptionId    AzureResourceGr

>   esz            ["10.            3-...                  vl

>   baç            ["10.            3-...                  3l

>   baz            ["10.            3-...                  E1

>   esz            ["10.            3-...                  q1
```

Figure 5.13: Sample Query 2

List of VM's which have not reported a heartbeat in the last 5 minutes in the Azure infrastructure

Sample code:

```
Heartbeat
| where TimeGenerated > ago(24h)
| summarize LastCall = max(TimeGenerated) by Computer, _ResourceId
| where LastCall < ago(5m)
```

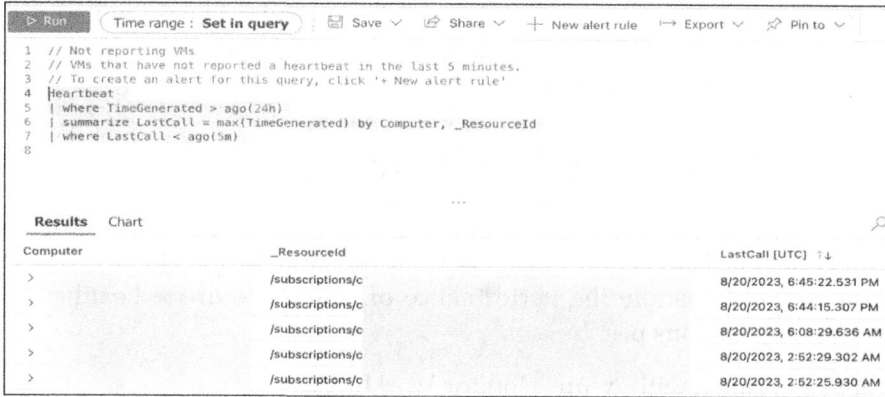

Figure 5.14: Sample Query 3

Response time trend provides an analysis of the durations for requests made to services over the previous 12 hours. This snapshot is essential for identifying patterns or issues in application performance that may affect user experience.

Sample code:

```
requests
| where timestamp > ago(12h)
| summarize avgRequestDuration=avg(duration) by bin(timestamp, 10m) //
use a time grain of 10 minutes
| render timechart
```

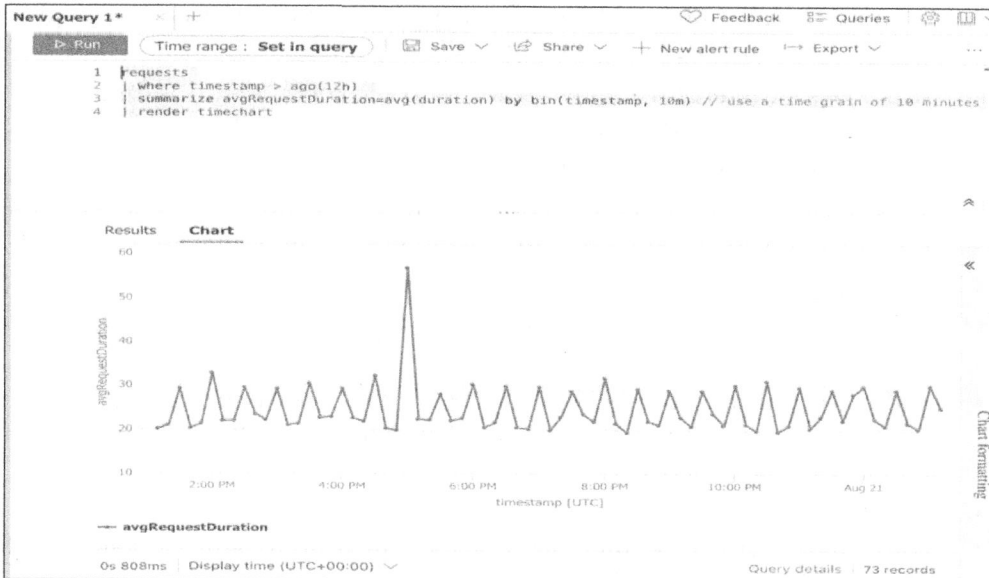

Figure 5.15: Sample Query 4

The **Performance chart** section is designed to display a graphical representation of request volumes coming from the top 10 states, offering a clear perspective on regional demand and activity within a specified timeframe.

Azure Workbook in Monitor

Azure Monitor Workbooks is a data visualization tool that permits teams to create custom reports and dashboards to acquire insights from the data Azure Monitor. These reports and dashboards often handle the performance of Azure resources, health, and overall condition after applications use.

Key concepts associated with Azure Monitor Workbooks:

- Workbooks can pull data from different sources, including Azure Monitor Logs, Application Insights, Azure Metrics, and custom data sources. Data will be used to draw the graphics and dashboard.

- Azure Monitor Workbooks provides a gallery of pre-made templates that the team can use as a starting point to make the team's custom reports. These concepts cover various topics, such as operating virtual machines, web applications, and databases.

- Azure Workbooks are written using KQL, a powerful language for querying and exploring data. The team can use KQL queries to retrieve detailed data from the team's chosen data source and then use aggregate and visualize that data in the workbook.

- Workbooks keep a wide range of graphics, including tables, charts (lines, bars, pies, etc.), maps, and text blocks. The team can use these visuals to display the team's data meaningfully and thoughtfully.

- Workbooks are interactive, allowing teams to add controls such as dropdown lists, time range options, and checkboxes. These controls permit the team to use the data displayed in real-time, making it easier to analyze parts of your data.

- The team creates a workbook and can share it with your team members or stakeholders. This encourages unity, and others benefit from your insight.

- The team can join organized workbook data updates to ensure up-to-date data is displayed. Additionally, the team can set up alerts to notify when typical conditions are met, helping stay on top of the necessary information.

- Workbooks can be embedded in Azure Dashboards, customizable displays of tiles describing various objects and insights. This integration allows the team to create suitable viewing experiences.

- Azure Monitor Workbooks is an effective tool for custom visualizations and reports based on your Azure data. It allows the team to manage their inventory, solve problems, and make informed determinations based on insights from your data.

Gallery

The gallery displays all saved workbooks and templates for your workspace. Easily create, organize, and manage all workbooks.

The gallery section is like a centralized hub where you can keep and manage all your saved workbooks and templates in one place. It makes things easier for you by letting you create, organize, and customize these resources according to your monitoring and analysis needs.

The screenshot displays the "Workbooks Gallery" in Azure Monitor, where users can create and access interactive reports and dashboards to monitor Azure resources. The gallery includes templates and categories like "Virtual Machines," "Synapse," "Containers," and "Applications," offering predefined workbooks such as "Key Metrics," "Performance," "Resource Picker," and "Availability." These workbooks enable users to visualize and analyze performance data, monitor health, and troubleshoot issues across Azure services.

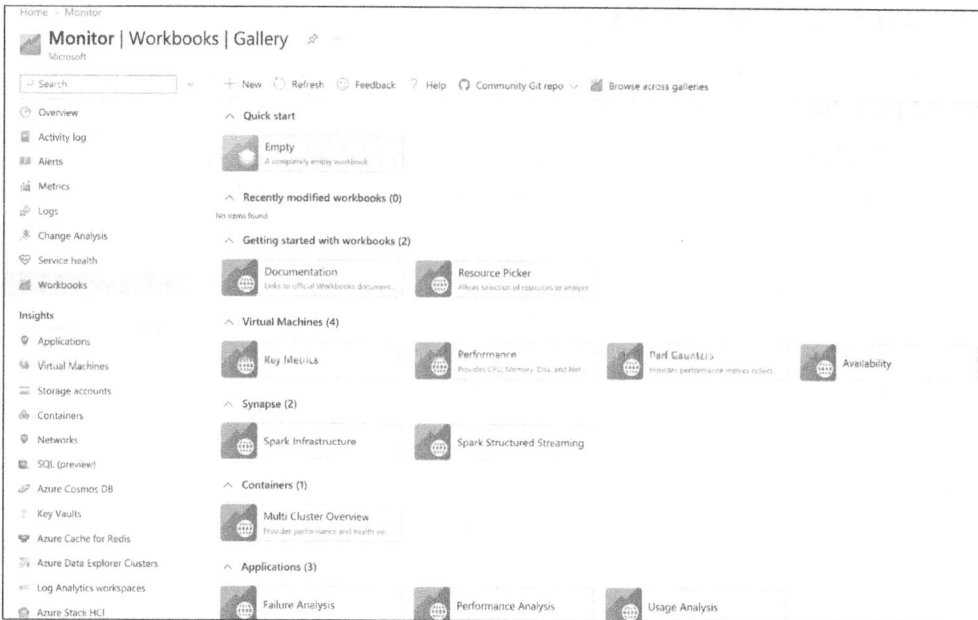

Figure 5.16: Sample Azure Workbooks

Gallery tabs

There are four tabs in the gallery to help organize workbooks:

Tab	Description
All	It displays the top four resources for workbooks, public reviews, and my reviews. The workbooks are organized by modified date, so you will see the eight most recently modified workbooks.

Tab	Description
Workbooks	Identify all existing workbooks that you have created or shared.
Public templates	Displays a list of all available ready-to-use starter workbook templates published by Microsoft and grouped by group.
My templates	Identify all available workbook template inserts you have created or shared.

Table 5.5: *Workbook and Template Organization in Azure Monitor*

Introduction to Azure Workbooks

In this section, we will learn about Azure Workbooks. We will learn how to create or open a Workbook.

Accessing Azure Monitor

In the Azure portal, you can access Azure Monitor by searching for it in the search bar or selecting it from the Azure services menu.

Once in Azure Monitor, look for the **Workbook** option in the left navigation pane or under the **Monitoring** section. Click to access **Workbooks**, refer to the following figure:

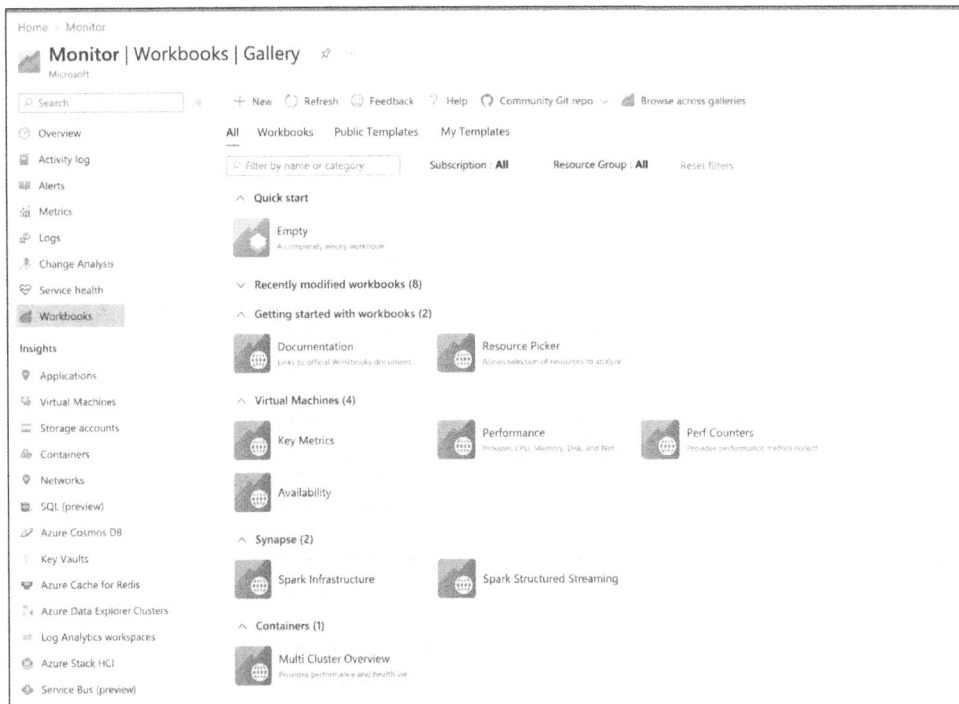

Figure 5.17: *Access Azure Workbooks*

Creating or opening a workbook

The following figure has an option **+ Add** to add a piece of data to the Azure workbook with text, parameters, links/tabs, queries, metrics, and groups. It includes where we can store, share, edit settings, and view code, refer to the following figure:

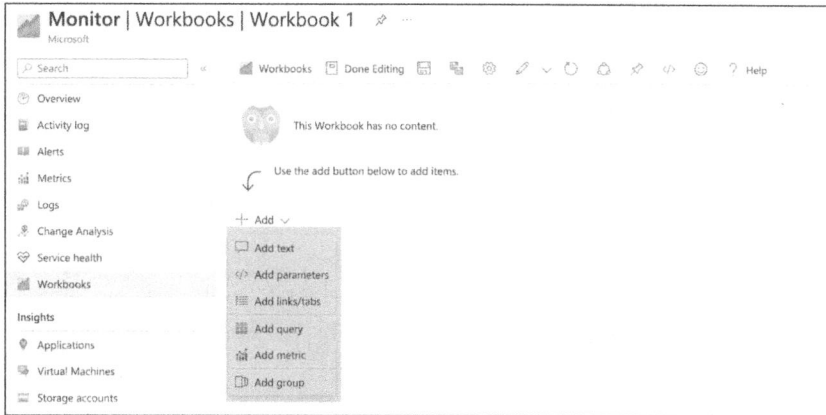

Figure 5.18: Access Azure Workbooks

Adding text

Workbooks allow the user to add summaries to their workbooks. Texts can include human reviews of telemetry, comments to help users interpret the data, section titles and more.

Text can be added through a Markdown control where users can add their text. A user can use the full formatting abilities of markdown. These include additional header or font styles, hyperlinks, tables, and so on. Markdown allows users to create rich word or portal-like reports. Text markdown text can have parameter values, and those parameter references will be made new when parameters change.

Edit

Edit mode gives you flexibility that we can put the Azure Workbook Heading.

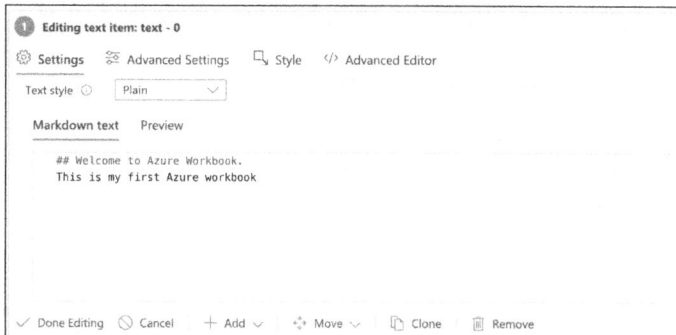

Figure 5.19: Edit Text Azure Workbook

Preview will show the heading for the Azure workbook.

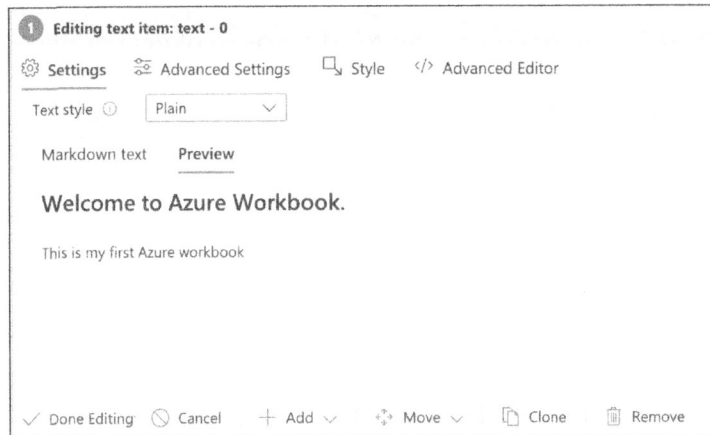

Figure 5.20: *Preview Text Azure Workbook*

Adding queries

Queries can allow to run the query with the supported data source:

1. Convert the edit mode by choosing the **Edit** option from the toolbar. Add a query by doing any one step:

   a. Click **Add** and add query below an existing element of the workbook.

   b. Click on three dots (...) the **Edit** button next to any one element in the workbook and then click add and add query.

2. From the list, you need to select the data source for the query. The other fields are depending on the data source you choose.

3. Choose any required other important values based on the selected data source.

4. Choose the visualization for the workbook.

5. Run the query.

6. User should see the result in the below pane:

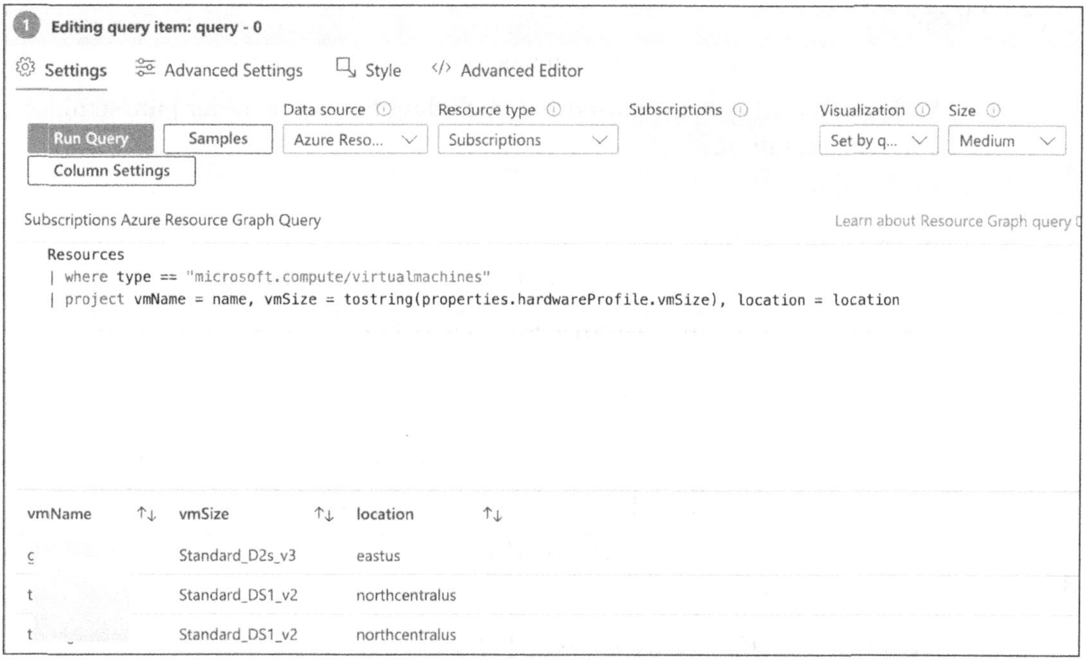

Figure 5.21: *Execution Azure Query*

Data sources

Workbooks can extract the data from the below data source:

- Logs:
    - Azure Monitor Logs (Application Insights object and Log Analytics workspace).
    - Data focus (activity log).
    - Queries in KQL manipulate resource data to generate images.
- Azure resource graph:
    - Supports Azure Resource Manager REST operations for querying management. azure.com.
    - Use the data source dropdown to select Azure Resource Manager.
- Azure Data Explorer:
    - Query data from Azure Data Explorer clusters using Kusto query language.
    - Specify the cluster name followed by the region.
- JSON Format Result:
    - Create query results from static JSON content.
    - Useful for dropdown parameters of static values.

- Merge:
  - Combine data from different sources for enhanced insights.
  - Various merge types are supported, including inner join, outer join, semi-join, anti-join, and more.
- Custom endpoint:
  - Retrieve data from external sources.
  - Use the data source dropdown and select Custom Endpoint.
  - Ensure **Cross-Origin Resource Sharing** (**CORS**) support for external data sources.
- Azure resource health:
  - Retrieve Azure resource health data and combine it with other sources.
  - Use the query type dropdown and select Azure health.
- Azure **role -based access control (RBAC)**:
  - Check permissions on resources using RBAC.
  - Commonly used to verify RBAC setups.
  - Supports both string and array operations.
- Change analysis (preview):
  - Use application change analysis as a data source.
  - Filter changes for the last 14 days and specify importance levels.
- Prometheus (preview):
  - Collect Prometheus metrics for Kubernetes clusters using Azure Monitor.
  - Select Prometheus from the data source dropdown and use Prometheus Query Language (PromQL) queries.

Creating first Azure FinOps Workbook

If you want to keep track of your Azure spending, you need to create a workbook. It's like a special tool that helps you organize and analyze your data. With an Azure FinOps workbook, you get a better understanding of how much you're spending on the cloud and where you can save money. This helps you stay within your budget and make smarter decisions about your cloud resources. By using these workbooks, you can get the most out of your investment in Azure and save money in the long run.

Use case: The Azure workbook helps identify and manage non-orphaned disks and unused app service projects. It offers significant cost savings primarily by determining and managing redundancies, thereby reducing Azure costs, and encouraging more efficient use of resources. Automation features streamline operations, ensuring costs are consistent and effective.

Additionally, the workbook simplifies data-driven decision-making by systematically identifying orphans through real-time detection, eliminating unnecessary costs, and increasing operational efficiency. It causes detailed costs by creating opportunities for efficiencies, which aid in budgeting and cost control. Additionally, it strengthens security and compliance by addressing abandoned items, reducing potential security risks.

Our workbook will identify the orphaned resources (disk and app service) with subscription, resources group, resource name, and tags. These workbooks will help to determine the resource owner and can be cleaned up as required.

Following are the steps for the creation of an orphaned Azure Workbook:

1. **Add text:**

   The screenshot displays the editing interface in an Azure Monitor workbook, where a text item titled "Orphaned Resources" is edited. It explains that this workbook helps identify and clean up unused resources to minimize waste and reduce costs. The editor offers markdown formatting and various settings to customize the text.

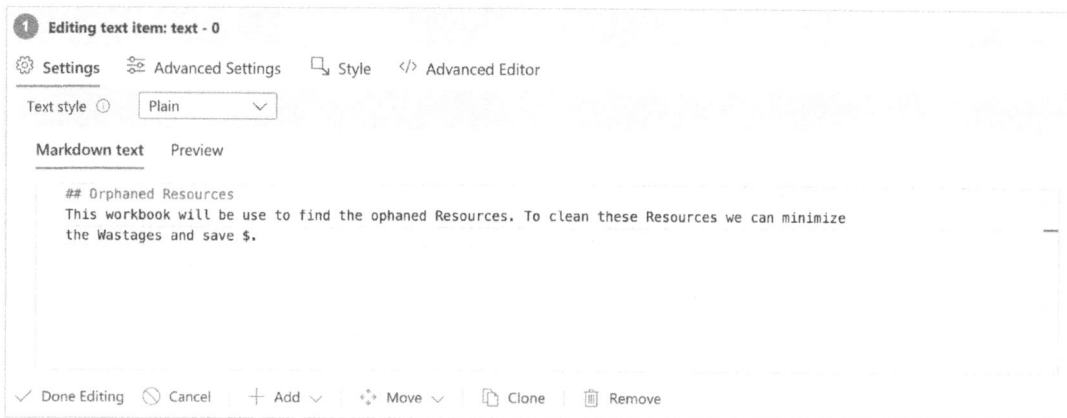

Figure 5.22: Add Text Azure Workbook

2. **Add parameter:**

   The screenshot displays a custom workbook setup in Azure Monitor, featuring sections for text editing and parameter creation. The text item focuses on identifying and removing orphaned resources to reduce costs. The "New Parameter" panel enables the configuration of parameters, such as choosing subscriptions, for customized data analysis.

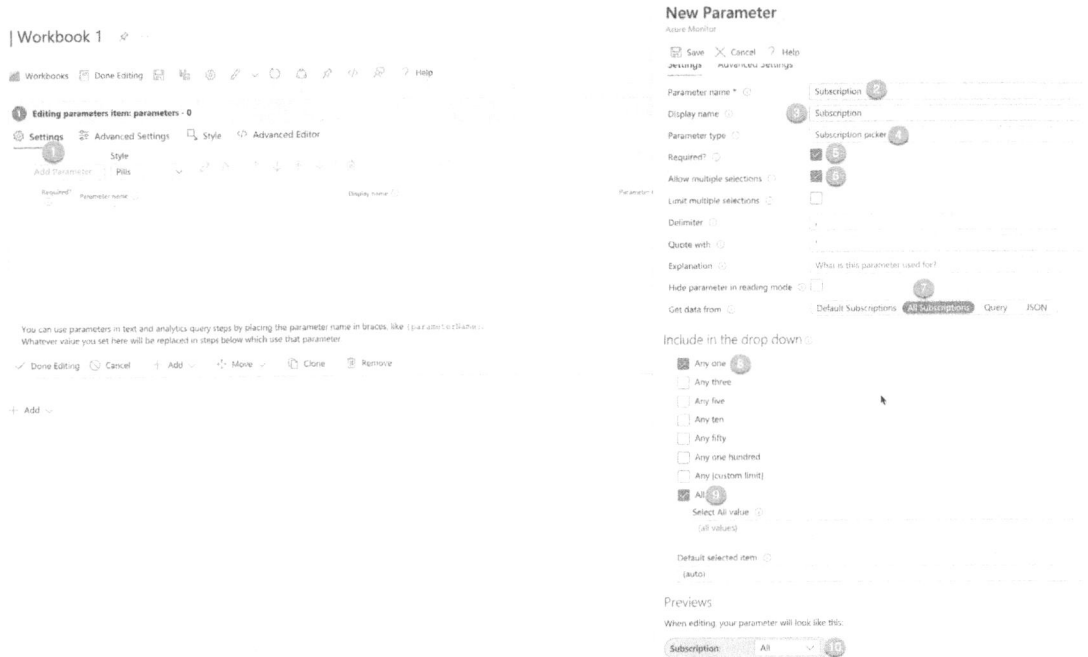

Figure 5.23 Add Parameter Azure Workbook

The screenshot displays the "Editing parameters" section within an Azure Monitor workbook. It includes a parameter configuration for selecting subscriptions, with choices for adding, changing, or deleting parameters. The "Subscription picker" parameter lets users filter data according to selected subscriptions, thereby enhancing the customization of workbook reports.

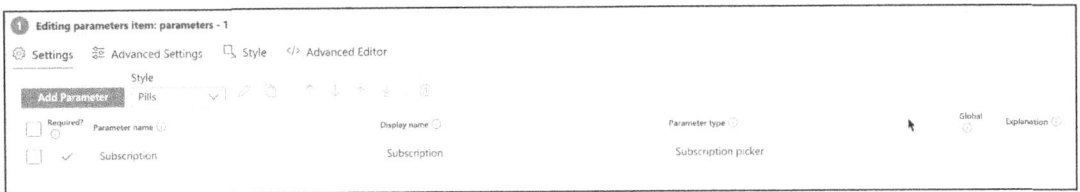

Figure 5.24: Add Parameter Azure Workbook

3. Add Tabs/Links:

The screenshot shows the "Editing link items" section in an Azure Monitor workbook. It allows users to create and configure navigation tabs, such as "Overview," "Disks," and "App Service Plans." Each tab is linked to specific actions and parameter values, helping users easily navigate between different sections of the workbook and customize the display of data based on selected parameters.

Figure 5.25: *Add Tabs/Links Azure Workbook*

4. Add text:

   The screenshot displays the "Editing text item" interface in an Azure Monitor workbook, with a markdown-formatted title: "Overview Azure Orphan Resources (Disk and App Service Plan)." This likely serves as a header for a section on identifying and managing orphaned Azure resources to improve cost and resource efficiency.

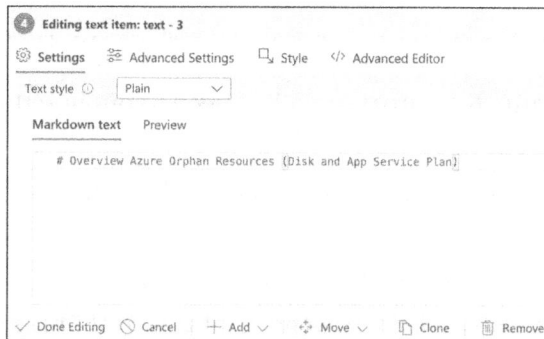

Figure 5.26: *Add Text for Overview Message Azure Workbook*

5. Add Query for disks count:

   The screenshot shows an Azure Monitor workbook aimed at spotting orphan resources like disks and app service plans. It features subscription filters and tabs for various resource types, with a KQL query editor at the bottom to find and count orphaned disks. The right panel offers formatting options for titles, colors, and display settings, enabling a customized presentation of data and insights.

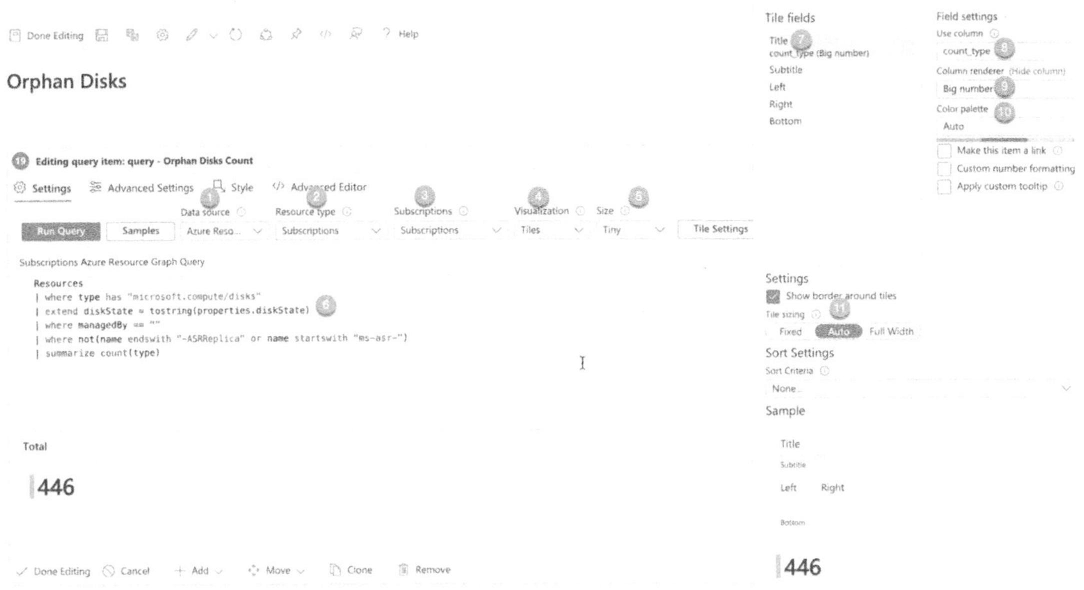

Figure 5.27: Add the orphaned disk count Azure Workbook

Data sources: Azure Resource Graph You need to put in setting in the Data Source.

Chart name: Orphaned Disks

Following is the query to get the orphaned disks count:

```
Resources
| where type has "microsoft.compute/disks"
| extend diskState = tostring(properties.diskState)
| where managedBy == ""
| where not(name endswith "-ASRReplica" or name startswith "ms-asr-")
| summarize count(type)
```

6. Same as need to create the count for App Service Plan:

    The screenshot displays an Azure Monitor workbook for finding orphaned resources like disks and app service plans. It shows a query that lists 379 orphaned disks and has tabs to view different resources. The bottom includes a KQL script to retrieve orphaned Azure resources, while the right panel offers customization options for titles, fields, and colors.

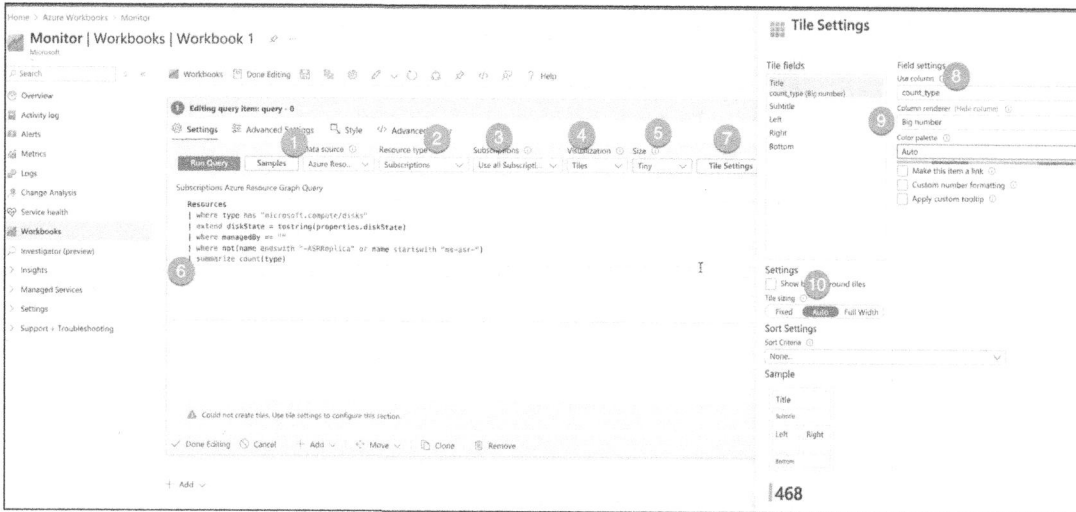

Figure 5.28: Add the orphaned App Service Plan count Azure Workbook

Data Source: Azure Workbooks permit you to analyze and visualize data from various sources. Here are some key data sources you can use:

1. **Azure Monitor Logs**: This queries and visualizes logs from services like VMs and applications.

2. **Azure Metrics**: For performance metrics of Azure resources.

3. **Application Insights**: For detailed telemetry of instrumented applications.

4. **Azure Resource Graph**: This is for querying across Azure resources for management and compliance.

5. **Azure Log Integration**: To integrate logs into Workbooks from external SIEM tools.

6. **Azure Cosmos DB**: For data from Cosmos DB accounts.

7. Custom APIs and External Data: Supports data integration via Azure Logic Apps or Functions.

8. **GitHub**: To track metrics related to GitHub projects.

Following is the query to get the orphaned App Service Plan:

```
Resources
| where type =~ "microsoft.web/serverfarms"
| where properties.numberOfSites == 0
| summarize count(type)
```

1. Add Text Azure Orphaned Disks:

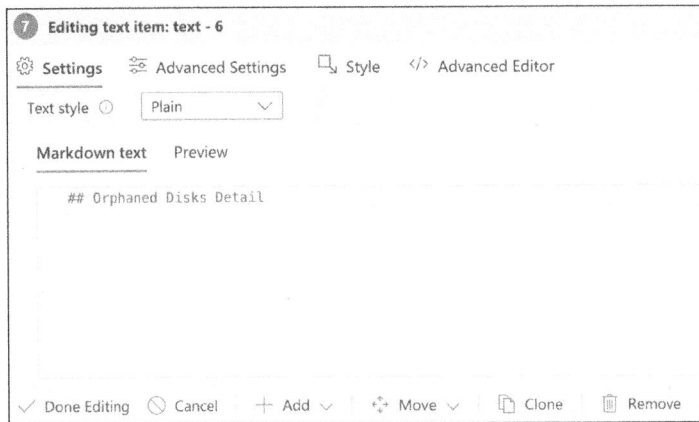

Figure 5.29: *Add Text for orphaned Disk Detail Azure Workbook*

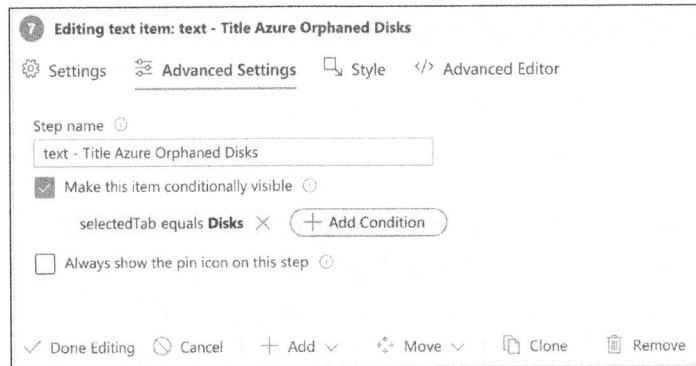

Figure 5.30: *Add Text for orphaned disk detail advance setting Azure Workbook*

2. Add Query Azure orphaned disks detail:

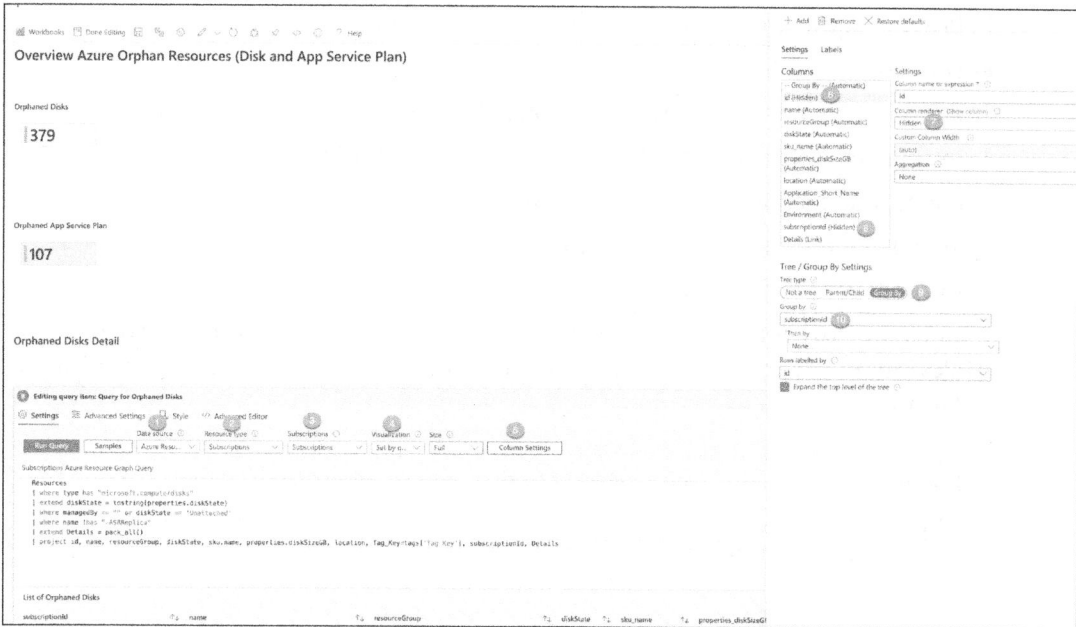

Figure 5.31: *Add Query for orphaned disk detail Azure Workbook*

3. Change the advance setting for export:

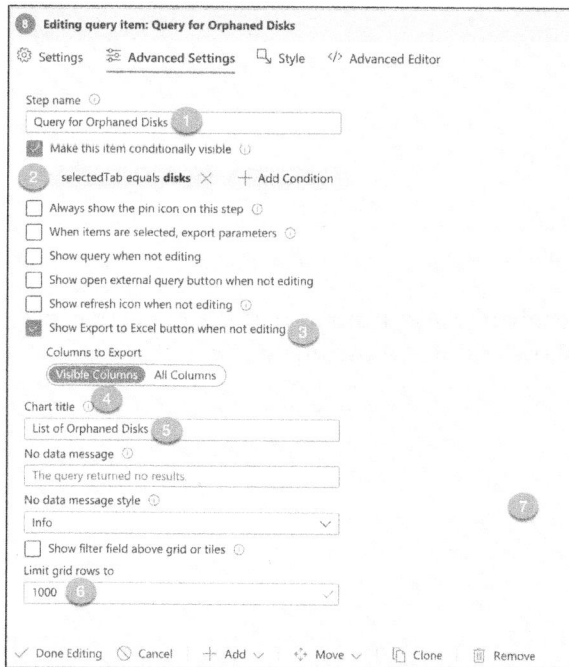

Figure 5.32: *Add query for orphaned disk detail export excel Azure Workbook*

Following is the query for the orphaned disk details:

```
Resources
| where type has "microsoft.compute/disks"
| extend diskState = tostring(properties.diskState)
| where managedBy == "" or diskState == 'Unattached'
| where name !has "-ASRReplica"
| extend Details = pack_all()
| project id, name, resourceGroup, diskState, sku.name, properties.
diskSizeGB, location, Tag_Key*=tags['Tag Key'*], subscriptionId,
Details
```

```
*Change the Tag Key according to the environment.
```

4. Add text azure orphaned app service plan:

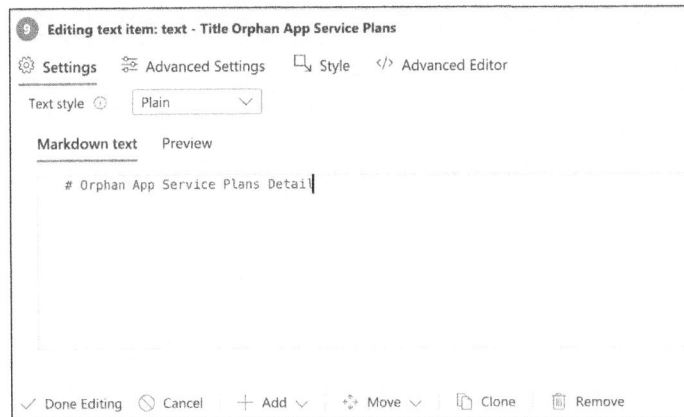

Figure 5.33: Add text for orphaned application service plan detail Azure Workbook

5. Add Text for orphaned Application Service Plan Advance Setting Detail Azure Workbook as shown in the following figure:

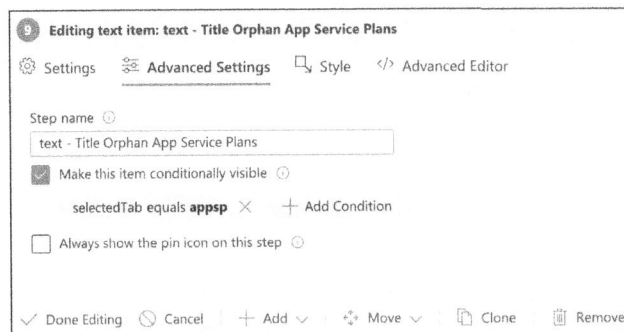

Figure 5.34: Add Text for orphaned Application Service Plan Advance Setting Detail Azure Workbook

Creating and customizing dashboards

Azure dashboard is a useful tool to manage your Azure resources. It is a way to monitor the health, performance, and status of Azure resources in one place. The most helpful part is that it is completely customizable. User can make numerous dashboards, individually with a different view, such as one for user's VM, storage accounts, and application services.

Each dashboard consists of tiles, which show various types of data, such as charts, graphs, and metrics. Users can customize the dashboard and add and remove tiles as needed. And the most useful part is that it is easy to use, the user can launch tasks and get instant communication right from the dashboard. So, whether you are an experienced Azure user or just starting out, Azure Dashboard is absolutely worth a look.

Azure dashboards are private by default. However, user can share their dashboard with additional users in the Azure organization.

Here are the benefits of Azure dashboards:

- Azure dashboards deliver a centralized view of users' Azure resources, making it straightforward to observe the health and performance.
- Azure dashboards are mostly customizable, so users can make dashboards that satisfy users specific needs.
- Azure dashboards are interactive, so users can look into data from the dashboard and start operations.

Here are examples of how users can use Azure dashboards:

- Create a dashboard to track the health and performance of applications. Dashboards can have tiles that show the number of users, error rates, and response times.
- Create a dashboard to observe the usage of your Azure resources. This dashboard can consist of tiles that show CPU usage, memory usage, and disk usage of virtual machines.
- Create a dashboard to follow the progress of Azure services. This dashboard can have tiles showing the project level, defect rates, and estimated completion dates.
- Create a dashboard to set up Azure products. This dashboard can have tiles that display error logs, performance metrics, and system health information.

In the end, Azure dashboards are a powerful tool that can help you manage your Azure resources more effectively.

Creating key performance indicator dashboards

In this section, we will go through the steps of creating KPI dashboards:

1. In the menu on the left in the Azure portal, select **Dashboard**:

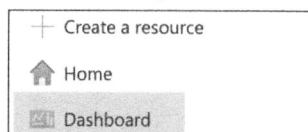

Figure 5.35: *Azure Dashboard Creation*

2. At the **Tile Gallery** for various tiles that user can add to your dashboard.

   o **Azure Inventory**: Shows a summary of your Azure resources, useful for tracking and managing them.

   o **Cosmos DB Health**: Displays health and performance metrics of your Cosmos DB, important for ensuring its reliability.

   o **Application Insights**: Visualize application performance and usage data, including error rates, response times, and user metrics.

   o **SQL Database Health**: Monitor the health, performance, and availability of your Azure SQL Databases, including query statistics and resource usage.

   o **VM Scale Set**: Track the health, performance, and scaling of your Virtual Machine Scale Sets, ensuring they meet demand efficiently.

   o **App Service Tracking**: Monitor the health and performance of your Azure App Services, including HTTP error rates, response times, and throughput.

   o **IoT Hub**: Visualize IoT Hub metrics such as device connections, messages, and errors, crucial for managing IoT applications and devices.

3. On the dashboard user needs to select **Create a dashboard** | **Azure Inventory**.

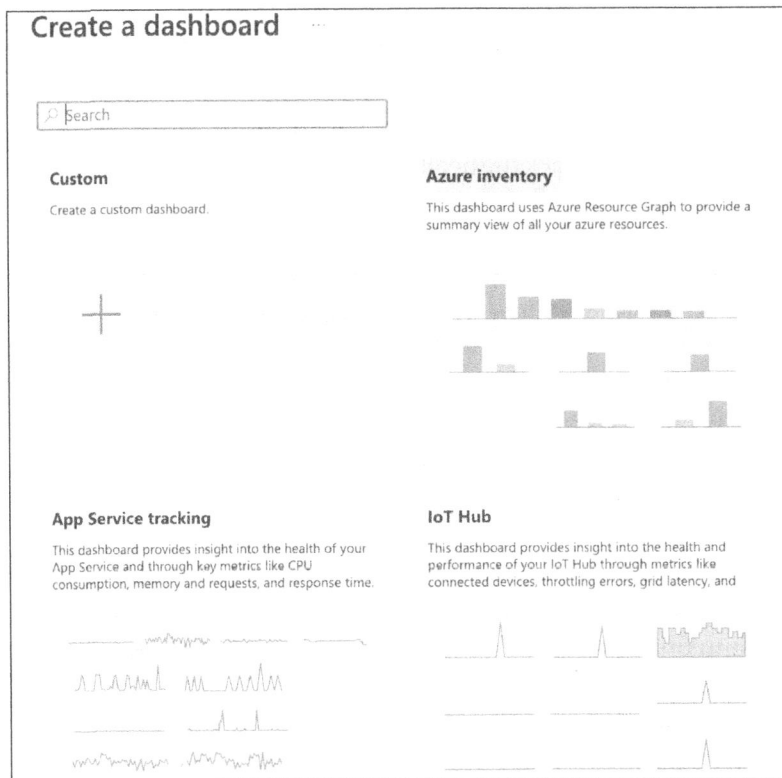

Create a dashboard ...

Search

Custom

Create a custom dashboard.

Azure inventory

This dashboard uses Azure Resource Graph to provide a summary view of all your azure resources.

App Service tracking

This dashboard provides insight into the health of your App Service and through key metrics like CPU consumption, memory and requests, and response time.

IoT Hub

This dashboard provides insight into the health and performance of your IoT Hub through metrics like connected devices, throttling errors, grid latency, and

Figure 5.36: Azure Dashboard Custom Tiles

4. Provide a name for the Dashboard:

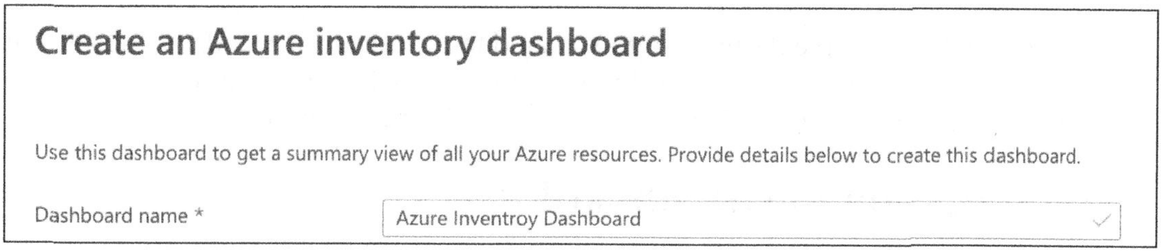

Create an Azure inventory dashboard

Use this dashboard to get a summary view of all your Azure resources. Provide details below to create this dashboard.

Dashboard name * | Azure Inventroy Dashboard

Figure 5.37: Azure Dashboard Name

It delivers an understanding of resource counts, service counts, OS accounts, family counts, resource manager counts, and other service counts (App services, database counts). This information can be used to identify potential areas and ensure that the Azure environment meets the organization's needs.

The dashboard is easy to use and understand, with clear and concise graphics. It is also scalable, allowing users to display more personalized information.

The Azure Environment Dashboard is a valuable tool for any Azure deployment. It is necessary for anyone who wants to keep their Azure environment safe and efficient.

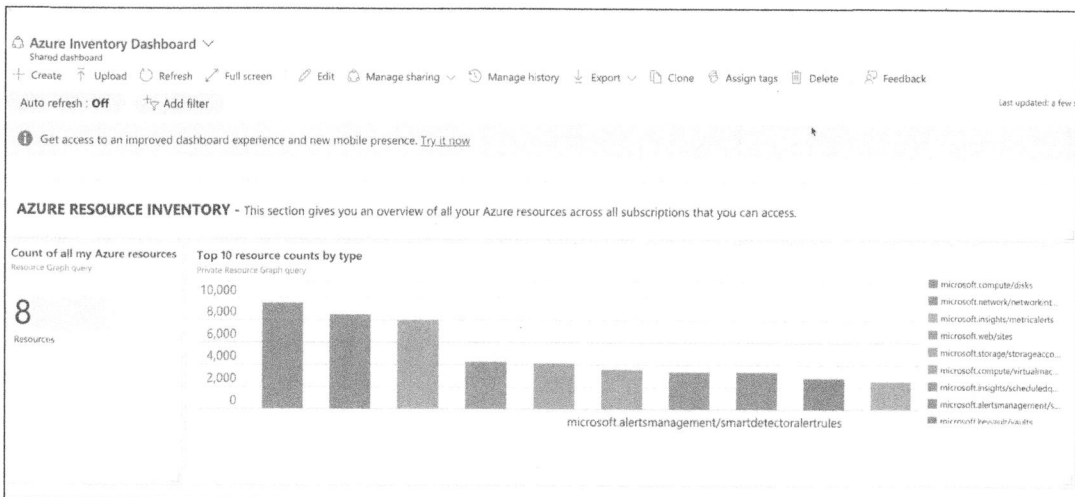

Figure 5.38: Azure Inventory Dashboard

Editing KPI dashboards

Now, let us edit the example dashboard you created to include, resize, and create tiles that display Azure resources or other helpful information. We will start by implementing the Tile Gallery and then explore different ways to customize the dashboards.

Adding tiles on the dashboard

To add tiles to a dashboard by using the Tile Gallery, follow the below steps:

1. Click on **Edit** from the dashboard's page header:

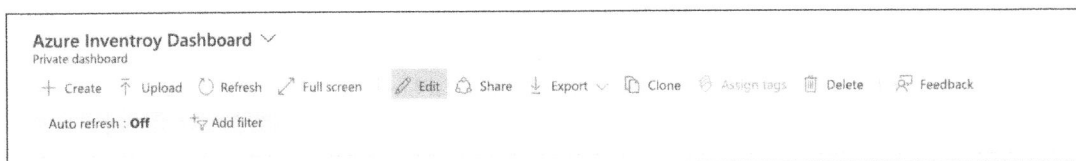

Figure 5.39: Azure Inventory Dashboard Edit

2. We need to browse the Tile Gallery or use the search field to find a specific tile. Select the tile to add to your dashboard.

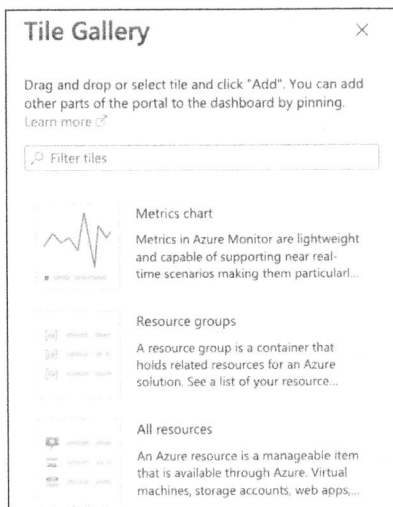

Figure 5.40: Azure Inventory Dashboard Tiles

3. Select **Add** to add a tile to the dashboard with a custom size and position or drag the tile onto the grid and place it where we want it.

4. We can also choose **Preview** and save the changes without viewing. This preview mode also lets you see how the filters affect your tiles. From the preview screen, you can choose Save to save changes, cancel to remove them or edit to return to the editing options and make further changes:

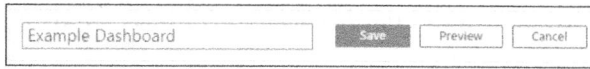

Figure 5.41: *Azure Inventory Dashboard saving*

Publishing on the dashboard

If we want to share access to a dashboard, we must publish first. After working on these, other users in your organization can access and change the dashboard based on their Azure RBAC roles.

To share an Azure Dashboard using Azure RBAC, you must observe these steps to ensure the intended users have the appropriate access permissions. Azure RBAC allows you to manage who has access to Azure resources, what they can do with those resources, and what areas they can access.

1. In the dashboard, click on **Share**.

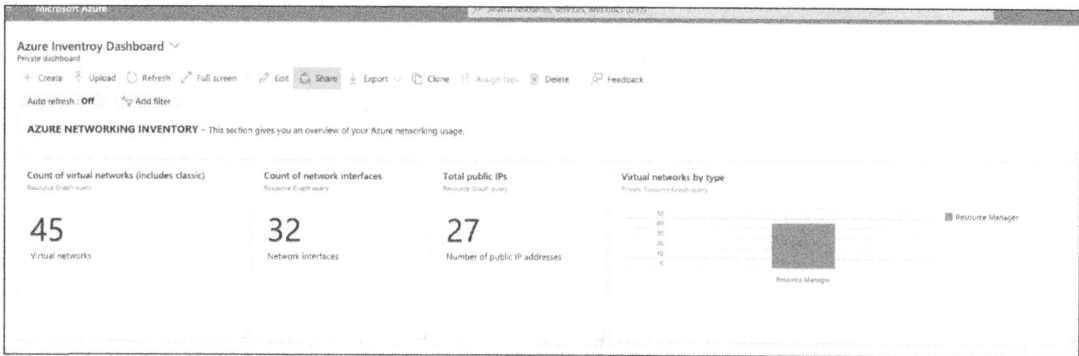

Figure 5.42: *Azure Inventory Dashboard share*

2. In **Sharing + access control**, click on **Publish**.

   By default, share publishes the dashboard to a resource group called dashboard. To select a new object group, clear the check box.

3. To **Add** the tags on the dashboard, we need to add the **Key and Value** pairs.

4. At the end we need to click on **Publish**.

Our dashboard is now published, and users inherit the subscription property.

Assigning access on the dashboard

We can allocate built-in Azure RBAC services to service groups (or individual users) for the individual dashboards we publish. This permits them to use those users in the dashboard, even if their subscription-level permissions would not allow it:

1. Once we publish the dashboard, click on **Manage sharing,** then select **Access control**:

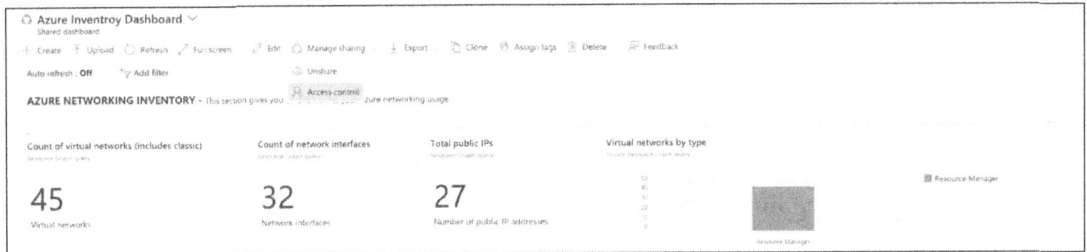

Figure 5.43: *Azure Inventory Dashboard Manage sharing*

2. In **Access Control**, select role assignments to view existing users who have already been assigned roles for this dashboard.

3. To add the user, click on **Add** and then **Add role assignments**.

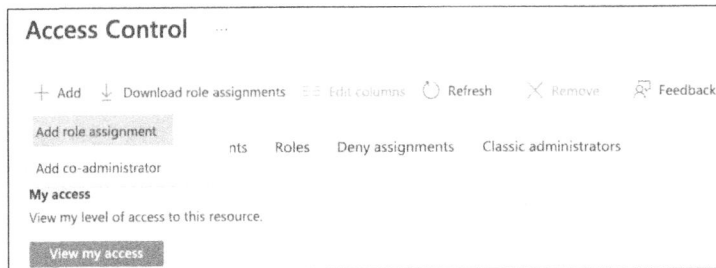

Figure 5.44: *Azure Inventory Dashboard Access Control*

4. We can select the role which we need to grant, such as owner, reader, or contributor. \

5. We will select the members; we can select the multiple users from Azure Active Directory.

6. Select **Review + assign** to complete the assignment.

As mentioned above, individual tiles in the dashboard can assess their access control requirements based on the features of the tile. If users need to view data for a particular tile, ensure they have the appropriate permissions for the underlying objects the tile accesses.

Reporting and data visualization

Azure Monitor delivers a combination of reporting and data visualization components, including dashboards, workbooks, alerts, and insights. These components can be utilized to build reports and dashboards for detailed audiences, such as developers, IT operations professionals, or stakeholders. Azure Monitor also combines with other Azure services and third-party tools for reporting and data visualization.

Dashboards for documentation

Dashboards are views that can be utilized to display metrics, logs, and other monitoring data in A Single pane of glass. We can create dashboards for products, services, or services or for general purposes such as monitoring the system's overall health. Dashboards can be shared with Azure users and deployed to web browsers and applications.

If we want to create a dashboard, we can select an existing dashboard from the Azure Monitor. We can customize the dashboard by adding and removing tiles and changing the tiles' layout.

Tiles can show metrics, logs, charts, and tables. We can insert the text and images into the dashboard.

Once we make the dashboard, we can share it with other Azure users via the web link.

Workbooks

Workbooks are an excellent tool for exploring data and creating custom visualizations. They contain text, rules, charts, and tables and can be specific audiences, developers, IT operations professionals, or interns.

Creating a workbook is easy, select a previously created workbook from the Azure Monitor gallery and customize it by adding or removing elements or changing their order. Workbooks can develop different types of reports, such as trends, comparisons, troubleshooting, and ad hoc reports. Once we have created a workbook, we can share it with other Azure users as a PDF file or a link.

Workbooks can be utilized to complete a combination of different types of reports, such as:

- Trend reports indicate how metrics have varied over time.
- Comparison reports liken two or more metrics.
- Troubleshooting reports help you to identify and troubleshoot issues.
- Ad hoc reports can be used to create custom reports that meet your needs.

Alerts

Alerts are a great way to stay informed when specific conditions are met, such as when a metric surpasses a certain threshold or when a log event happens. You can customize alerts through various notification channels, like email or SMS.

To set up an alert, you must select a rule summarizing the typical conditions needed to trigger the alert. After putting up a rule, you can act when the alert is triggered.

Actions can include sending notifications, starting a workflow, or running a script.

Alerts can be used to notify you of a variety of different events, such as:

- When a metric exceeds a threshold
- When a log event occurs
- When a resource becomes unavailable
- When a performance problem is detected

Insights

Insights are pre-built workbooks that offer valuable insights and analytics into the health and performance of your resources and applications. They can assist you in identifying potential problems, troubleshooting issues, and optimizing your environment. To access these insights, simply navigate to the Insights tab located in the Azure Monitor menu.

Insights are available for a variety of different Azure resources and applications, including:

- Virtual machines
- App Services
- SQL Server
- Kubernetes
- Azure Database for PostgreSQL
- Azure Database for MySQL

Integration with Azure services and third-party tools

Azure Monitor integrates with various other Azure services and third-party tools for reporting and data visualization. For example, we can use Power BI to create interactive reports and dashboards from Azure Monitor data or Grafana to create custom visualizations.

To integrate Azure Monitor with another service, we must first create a connection between the two services. Once we have created a connection, we can use the other service to access and visualize your Azure Monitor data.

Here are some examples of how Azure Monitor can be integrated with other services:

- **Power BI:** We can use Power BI to make interactive reports and dashboards from Azure Monitor data. Power BI delivers a combination of features for data analysis and visualization, such as charts, tables, and maps.
- **Grafana:** We can use Grafana to make custom visualizations of your Azure Monitor data.

Conclusion

Azure Monitor is a complete monitoring answer for managing, analyzing, and responding to monitoring data from Azure Services. It allows to maximize the availability and performance of applications and services.

Azure Monitor gathers and aggregates the data from each layer and component of the system across multiple Azure and non-Azure subscriptions and tenants. This contains data from infrastructure, applications, and networks.

Azure Monitor delivers a combination of features for monitoring and managing systems, including:

- Metrics
- Logs
- Insights
- Alerts

Azure Monitor enables integration with other Azure services and third-party tools to provide monitoring solutions. For example, we can deploy the Azure Monitor to monitor your virtual machines, App Services, SQL Server, and Kubernetes clusters.

Azure Monitor is a powerful solution to manage and monitor your systems more effectively.

In the next chapter, we will learn more about Azure cost allocation and chargeback features, such as resource group tagging, automated cost reporting, show back, chargeback, and role-based access. In short, Azure cost allocation and chargeback features can help you better understand and manage your Azure costs.

Join our book's Discord space

Join the book's Discord Workspace for Latest updates, Offers, Tech happenings around the world, New Release and Sessions with the Authors:

https://discord.bpbonline.com

CHAPTER 6

Cost Allocation and Chargebacks

Introduction

Cloud cost management is important for multi-departmental business teams that are using Azure. Azure is consumption-based, which means there needs to be a clear system of debt tracking/cost assignment to different departments or projects. Tagging can be used for anything from categorizing resources in spending reports and showing how much each department, project, or environment is spending, all the way to simple metadata of resources themselves. This is done to allot the exact billing to each department or project. Also, Azure Cost Management and Billing offer spending views to help you analyze costs, as well as budget definitions and alerts. This feature provides tracking of costs by tag and the ability to do chargebacks, enabling users to analyze spending in multiple dimensions as needed to make sure they know what they are spending and where.

This means that by setting budgets and defining alerts, organizations can look after their spending proactively and get notified as soon as limits are about to be touched or even violated, preventing budget overruns and keeping departments. In addition, other tools like Azure Policy and automation are critical to managing cost, compliance, and resource optimization. Automation of these tasks can represent a significant part of your savings, for instance, shutting down your VMs during non-business, removing any unused resources, and so on. This 360 degree approach leads to a culture of transparency and perpetual improvement that drives the frugal use of Azure services. Refer to the following figure:

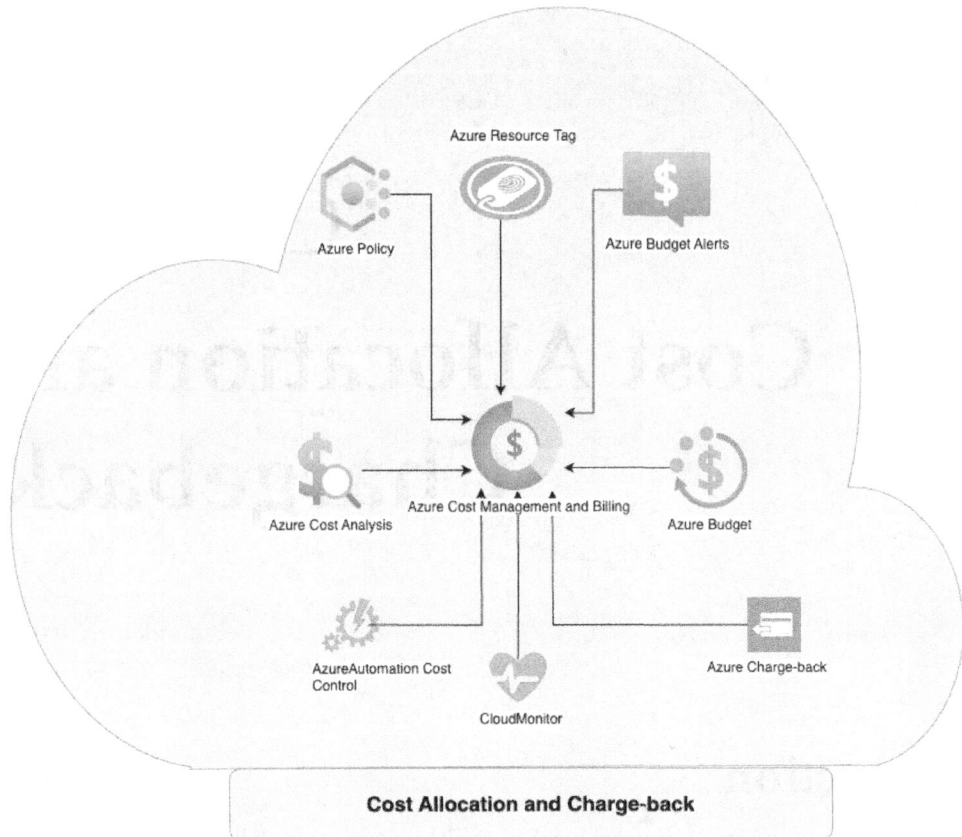

Cost Allocation and Charge-back

Figure 6.1: *Azure Cost Allocation and Chargeback*

Structure

In this chapter, we will go through the following topics:

- Azure Resource group tagging and cost allocation
- Azure Cost Management APIs and automation
- Implementing showback and chargeback models
- Azure RBAC for cost management

Objectives

Enterprises, for instance, often administer Azure services or resources from a central location. However, the reality is that they may have fewer servers, yet they may be using other internal departments or business units. Most of the time, the central organizing team would like to outsource these services to the internal departments or organizational business units that operate them.

This chapter will cover an important topic in cost management - the cost allocation rule. Basically, cost allocation allows us to figure out how to distribute the costs of our services using the basic building blocks we installed (compute, storage, caching). Such expenses related to Subscriptions, Resource Groups, or Tags charged that are delimited for organization-related Subscriptions, Resource Groups and Tags. Cost allocation supports management and demonstrates cost accountability from one point of another.

First thing, cost allocation is to amuck at the charge back. No charges, chargeback occurs within your organization outside Azure. This process helps you reassign or distribute costs and allows you to charge back the costs.

Azure Resource group tagging and cost allocation

Resource group tagging is a process of labeling or tagging cloud resources. These tags are like labels which consist of a key-value pair. These labels can be attached to different types of resources like virtual machines, databases, and storage accounts. These tags help to categorize resources in different ways, such as based on their purpose, owner, environment (like development, testing, production), or any other criteria that are helpful for the organization. Using tags makes resource management easy, especially in environments that have many resources, by allowing the filtering and grouping of resources based on their tags.

If you have a complex cloud-based deployment, organizing your resources is essential. You can do this by using naming and tagging standards, which can help you manage your resources more effectively in the following ways:

- **Resource management**: By organizing your resources, you can quickly locate resources that are associated with specific workloads, environments, ownership groups, or other important information. This is critical to assigning organizational roles and access permissions for resource management.

- **Cost management and optimization**: Tagging your resources will help you understand the resources and workloads that each team uses, which is essential for making business groups aware of the consumption of cloud resources. Additionally, cost-related tags can help with cloud accounting models, **Return on Investment (RoI)** calculations, cost tracking, budgets, alerts, recurring spend tracking and reporting, post-implementation optimizations, and cost-optimization tactics.

- **Operations management**: By tagging resources, you can have visibility on business commitments and SLAs, which is critical to ongoing operations for the operations management team.

- **Security**: Tagging resources can help you classify data and determine the security impact when breaches or other security issues arise.

- **Governance and regulatory compliance:** Tagging resources can help you maintain consistency across resources and identify divergence from policies. You can use tagging patterns to deploy governance practices and evaluate regulatory compliance.

- **Automation:** A proper organizational scheme enables you to take advantage of automation as part of creating resources, monitoring operations, and creating DevOps processes. Automation makes resources easier for IT to manage.

- **Workload optimization:** Tagging can help you identify patterns and resolve broad issues. It can also help you identify the assets that a single workload requires. Tagging all assets that are associated with each workload enables deeper analysis of your mission-critical workloads, which helps you to make sound architectural decisions.

Tagging decision guide

When it comes to keeping track of your IT assets, using a tagging system that aligns with your IT setup can make things simpler. For example, tagging based on workload, application, or environment can reduce the complexity of monitoring assets. This can help you make management decisions based on operational requirements with ease.

However, if you want to align your tagging system with your business operations, you might have to invest more time. Creating tagging standards that reflect business interests and maintaining them can take more effort, but it can also yield better results. By connecting an asset's business value to its operating cost, you can get a better understanding of the costs and value of your IT assets to the business. This can help change the prediction of IT from a cost center to an asset within your organization.

The below image gives a detailed figure of the Tag Decision Guide, which smartly categorizes the consideration aspects for the right tagging to be used in cloud environments. It focuses on the core design principles, base naming conventions, scope, function, type, and tagging elements required when building and managing resources within a cloud-based system. The whole purpose of this guide is to provide a framework and enable you to make the decisions you need, from all the factors that are important to manage resources optimally and allocate costs properly.

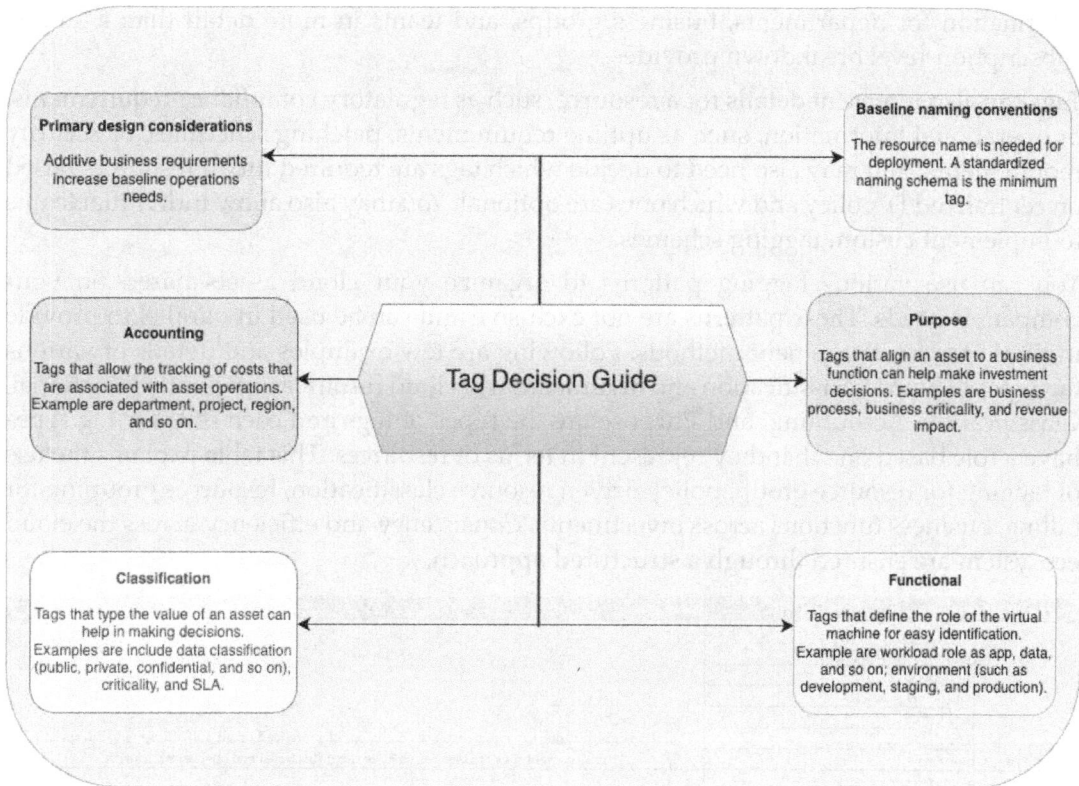

Figure 6.2: *Tag decision guide*

Baseline naming conventions

When you store your data on the cloud, it is important to name your resources in a consistent and organized way. This helps you manage and keep track of them easily. If your organization already has a naming system for IT resources, think about whether you should use the same naming conventions for your cloud resources or come up with new ones specifically for the cloud. Either way, having a good naming convention is essential.

Resource tagging patterns

To keep your cloud resources organized in a refined manner, you can make use of tags. These metadata elements consist of key-value pairs attached to your resources. You can choose the values you want to include in these pairs.

It is essential to have a comprehensive naming and tagging policy, and applying a consistent set of global tags is a critical part of it. Before you start tagging your resources, you need to determine what types of information the tags should support.

For instance, you may need to integrate your naming and tagging policies with existing policies within your company. Suppose you plan to implement a chargeback or showback accounting system. In that case, you may need to associate resources with accounting information for departments, business groups, and teams in more detail than a simple subscription-level breakdown provides.

Tags can also represent details for a resource, such as regulatory compliance requirements, or operational information, such as uptime requirements, patching schedules, or security requirements. You may also need to decide which tags are required for all resources based on centralized IT policy and which ones are optional. You may also allow individual teams to implement custom tagging schemes.

You can use various tagging patterns to organize your cloud assets based on your company's needs. These patterns are not exclusive and can be used in parallel to provide multiple asset management methods. Following are few examples and details of various tag types to help in classification and organization of cloud resources efficiently Functional, Classification, Accounting, and Purpose are the types of tags and each of these tag types have a role based on what they represent in terms of resources. This table explains the use of tagging for resource group, policy driven resource classification, resources grouping for billing, business functions across investments. Consistency and efficiency across the cloud ecosystem are ensured through a structured approach.

Tag type	Examples	Description
Functional	app = catalogsearch1 tier = web webserver = apache env = prod env = staging env = dev	In simpler terms, one can group resources based on their intended usage within a system, the specific environment they are being used in, or other functional and operational aspects.
Classification	confidentiality = private SLA = 24hours	Classifies a resource by policies.
Accounting	department = finance program = business-initiative region = northamerica	Associates a resource for billing purposes for Groups.
Purpose	businessprocess = support businessimpact = moderate revenueimpact = high	Business functions support investment decisions.

Figure 6.3: Tag types and descriptions

Apply tag on Azure Resources

There is different type of ways to add the tag on resources:
- Portal
- Azure CLI
- Azure PowerShell
- Python

Portal

The steps below can be executed from the portal (**https://azure.com**).

1. Refer to the overview section to check the tags associated with a resource or resource group. If no tags have been assigned previously, the list will appear empty.

Tag type	Examples	Description
Functional	app = catalogsearch1 tier = web webserver = apache env = prod env = staging env = dev	In simpler terms, one can group resources based on their intended usage within a system, the specific enviroment being used in, or other functional and operational aspects.
Classification	confidentiality = private SLA = 24hours	Classifies a resource by policies.
Accounting	department = finance program = business-initiative region = northamerica	Associates a resource for billing purposes for Groups.
Purpose	businessprocess = support businessimpact = moderate revenueimpact = high	Business functions support investment decisions.

Figure 6.4: Add Tag on Resource

2. Click on **Add Tag**.

3. Provide the **Key and Value**:

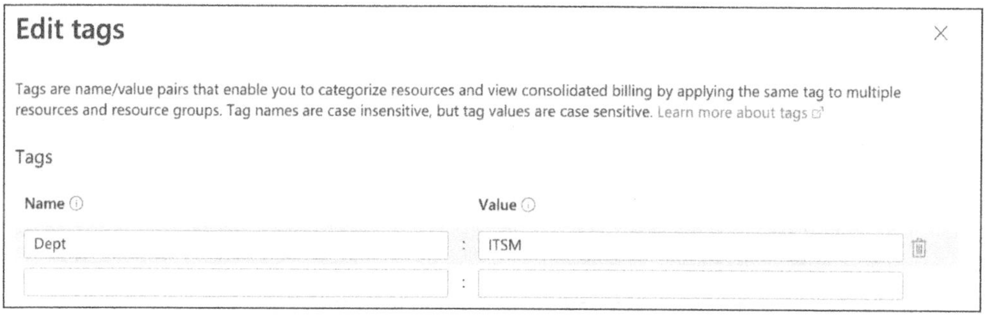

Figure 6.5: Tag Key and Value

4. Click on **Save** to add the tag:

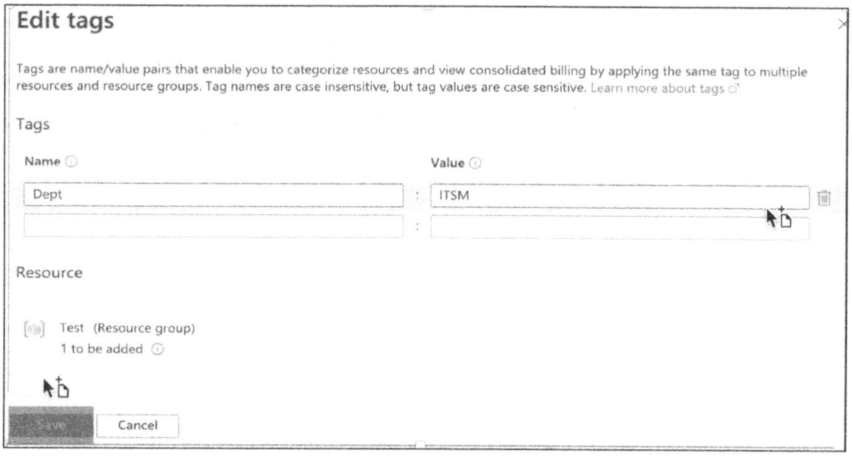

Figure 6.6: Save the tag

5. The tag should be displayed at the **Resource Group**:

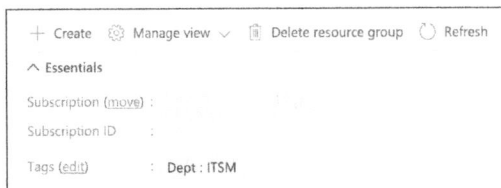

Figure 6.7: Validation of the tag

Assign tags on multiple resources

The steps below will help assign multiple tags to Azure Resources. These steps will save the effort of updating the tags one by one:

1. Select the list of the targeted **Resources** and then click on the **Assign tags**:

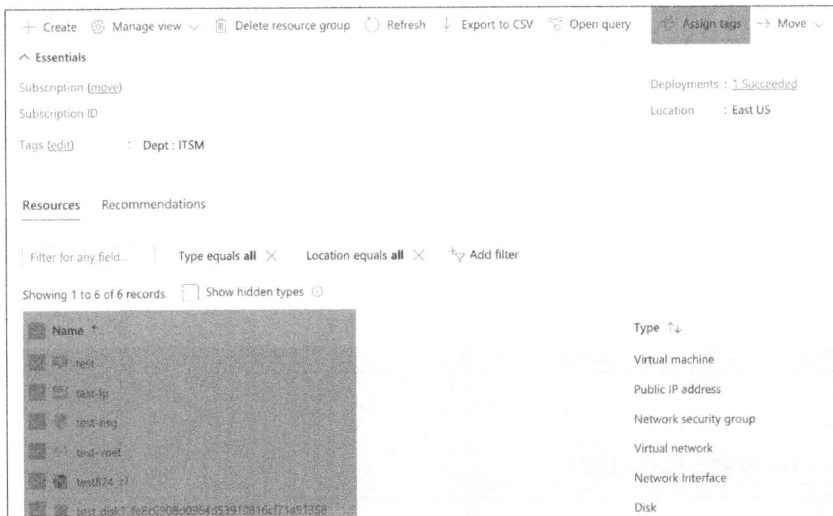

Figure 6.8: Selection of multiple resources

2. Provide the tag key and values for the resources:

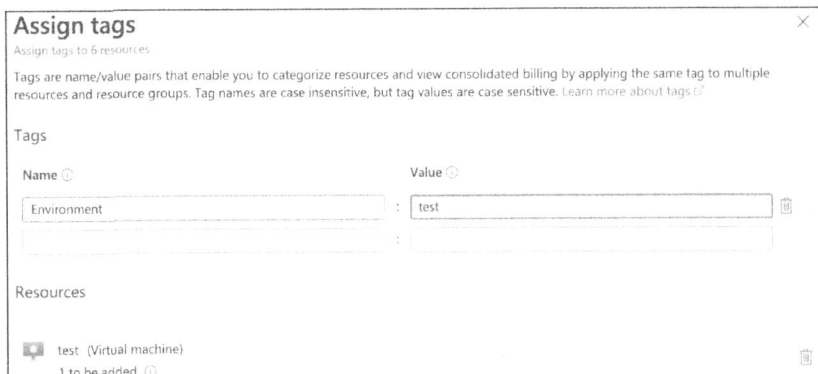

Figure 6.9: Tag keys and value

3. Click on the save button to save the value:

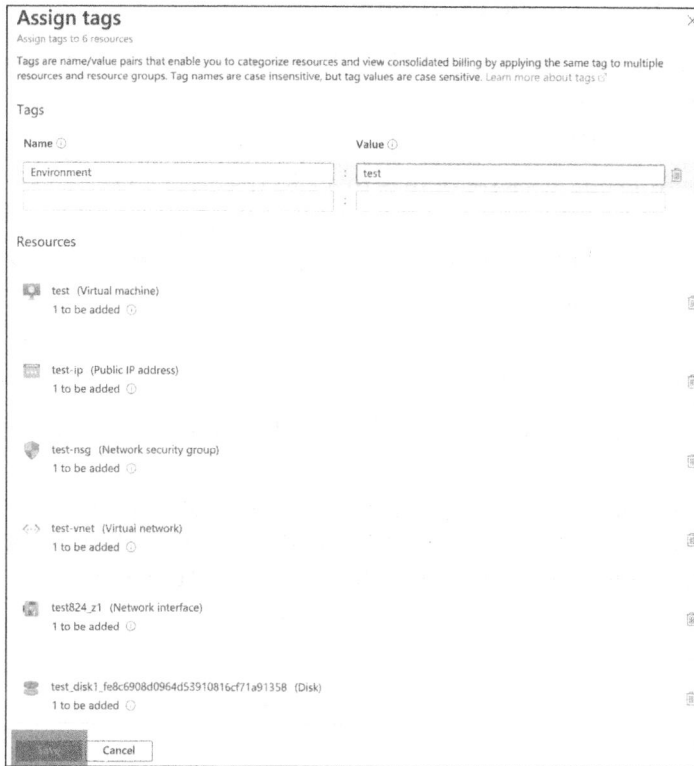

Figure 6.10: *Save tag keys and value*

4. Validate the new tags on the resources.

Figure 6.11: *Validate tag keys and value*

Azure Command-Line Interface

If you want to apply tags in the Azure **command-line interface (CLI)**, two commands are available: `az tag create` and `az tag update`. To use these commands, ensure you have the Azure CLI version 2.10.0 or later installed on your system. You can validate the current version by running the command **az version**.

If you want to replace all the tags associated with a resource, resource group, or subscription, you can use the **az tag create** command. To use this command, you need to pass the resource ID of the entity you want to tag.

The following example applies a set of tags to a VM disk:

```
$ resource=$(az resource show -g TEST -n test_disk1_
fe8c6908d0964d53910816cf71a91358 --resource-type Microsoft.Compute/disks
--query "id" --output tsv)


$ az tag create --resource-id $resource --tags Dept=Finance
```

This will provide the output as JSON. It will validate that the resource gets the tag.

```
{
    "id": "/providers//subscriptions/7dac628a-a608-4a53-9315-64d5346fadc6/
    resourceGroups/TEST/providers/Microsoft.Compute/disks/test_disk1_
    fe8c6908d0964d53910816cf71a91358/providers/Microsoft.Resources/tags/
    default",
    "name": "default",
    "properties": {
      "tags": {
        "Dept": "Finance"
      }
    },
    "type": "Microsoft.Resources/tags"
}
```

When using **az create**, all the existing tags from the resource and tags with the new tag will be removed.

Figure 6.12: Validate tag keys and value

If you want to add new tags to a resource that already has tags, you can use the **az tag update** command. To do this, you need to set the --operation parameter to Merge. If you want to replace all the tags associated with a resource, resource group, or subscription, you can use the **az tag create** command. To use this command, you need to pass the resource ID of the entity you want to tag:

```
$ az tag update --resource-id $resource  --operation Merge --tags
Environment=dev Status=Normal
```

Notice that the existing tags grow with the addition of the two new tags:

```
{
    "id": "/providers//subscriptions/7dac628a-a608-4a53-9315-64d5346fadc6/
    resourceGroups/TEST/providers/Microsoft.Compute/disks/test_disk1_
    fe8c6908d0964d53910816cf71a91358/providers/Microsoft.Resources/tags/
    default",
    "name": "default",
    "properties": {
      "tags": {
        "Dept": "Finance",
        "Environment": "dev",
        "Status": "Normal"
      }
    },
    "type": "Microsoft.Resources/tags"
}
```

The following image shows the VM tagged to the tags of **Dept: Finance**, **Environment: dev**, and **Status: Normal**

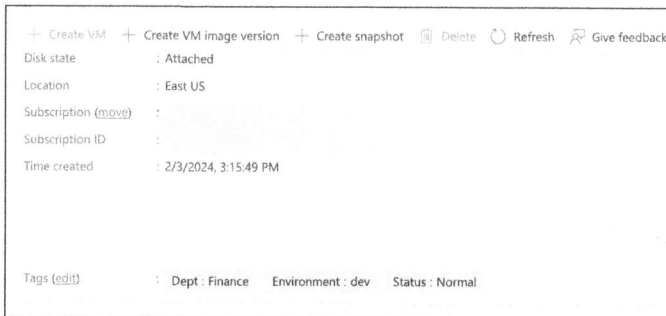

Figure 6.13: *Validate tag keys and value*

Yes, that is correct. When you use the **az tag update** command and set the **--operation** parameter to Replace, the new set of tags will replace the existing tags associated with the resource, resource group, or subscription. Any previously assigned tags will be removed and replaced with a new set.

```
$ az tag update --resource-id $resource --operation Replace --tags
Environment=test Status=Normal Dept=Finance
```

Notice that the output will have new values on the tag:

```
{
    "id": "/providers//subscriptions/7dac628a-a608-4a53-9315-64d5346fadc6/
    resourceGroups/TEST/providers/Microsoft.Compute/disks/test_disk1_
    fe8c6908d0964d53910816cf71a91358/providers/Microsoft.Resources/tags/
    default",
    "name": "default",
    "properties": {
      "tags": {
        "Dept": "Finance",
        "Environment": "test",
        "Status": "Normal"
      }
    },
    "type": "Microsoft.Resources/tags"
}
```

The following image shows the VM tagged to the tags of **Dept: Finance**, **Environment: test**, and **Status: Normal**. We have updated only the Environment here.

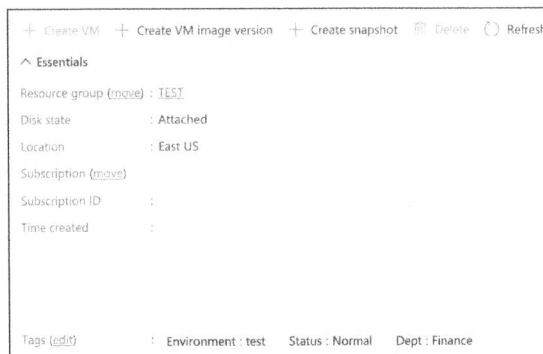

Figure 6.14: Validate tag keys and value

Azure PowerShell and want to apply tags, there are two commands you can use:

- **New-AzTag**
- **Update-AzTag**

However, you need to have the **Az.Resources** module version 1.12.0 or higher. To check your version, you can use the command **Get-InstalledModule -Name Az.Resources**.

If you do not have the required module, install it or update it to Azure PowerShell version 3.6.1 or later.

When you use the **New-AzTag** command, it will replace all the existing tags on the resource, resource group, or subscription. To apply tags to a specific resource, you should provide the resource ID of that entity as an input parameter when calling the command.

The following example applies a set of tags to a VM disk:

```
$ tags = @{"Dept"="Finance"; "Status"="Normal"}
$ resource = Get-AzResource -Name "test_disk1_
fe8c6908d0964d53910816cf71a91358" -ResourceGroupName TEST
New-AzTag -ResourceId $resource.id -Tag $tags
```

Notice when you execute the command, and you will see the resource has two tags:

```
Properties :
        Name    Value
        ======  =======
        Dept    Finance
        Status  Normal
```

The following image shows the VM tagged **Dept: Finance** and **Status: Normal**. We have deleted only the Environment here.

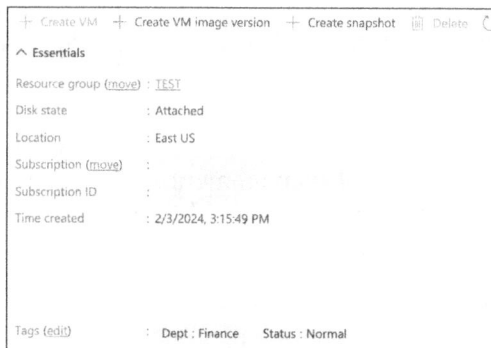

Figure 6.15: Validate tag keys and value

If we run the same command with different tag keys and values. You will notice that earlier tags disappear.

```
$tags = @{"Team"="Compliance"; "Environment"="Production"}
$resource = Get-AzResource -Name "test_disk1_
fe8c6908d0964d53910816cf71a91358" -ResourceGroupName TEST
New-AzTag -ResourceId $resource.id -Tag $tags
```

Notice when you execute the command, you will see the resource has two new tags and earlier has been removed:

```
Properties :
        Name          Value

        ===========   ==========

        Team          Compliance

        Environment   Production
```

The following image shows the VM tagged **Team: Compliance** and **Environment: Production**. We have deleted the earlier tags and replaced them with new tags.

Figure 6.16: Validate tag keys and value

If we want to add tags to a resource that already has some tags, we can use a command called `Update-AzTag`. Just remember to set the `-operation` parameter to merge.

Azure cost allocation using tag inheritance

Tags are used to group costs based on different business units, departments, and so on, allowing businesses to manage and allocate costs efficiently. This section explains how we can use the tag inheritance in cost management. With tag inheritance, you can apply billing, resource group, and subscription tags to child resource usage records without the need to tag every resource individually.

Tag inheritance is available for below account types:

- **Enterprise Agreement (EA)**
- **Microsoft Customer Agreement (MCA)**
- **Microsoft Partner Agreement (MPA)**

To access subscriptions:

- **Read permission to cost management reader**: Granting readers read permission allows users only to view data in an Azure subscription, not the ability to perform unavoidable updates and operations on it. Crucial for stakeholders where they need to see cost allocation and usage but should not have editing capabilities.

- **Cost management contributor (edit)**: Grants users the ability to view cost and edit and manage cost information for Azure subscriptions. This is important for maintaining precise chargeback and cost tracking, which those in charge of setting up tag inheritance policy and partitions depend on.

For EA billing accounts:

- **Read-only Enterprise Administrator permission**: People with this permission see all cost and billing data for the EA accounts. Administrators who need to monitor to confirm that costs are properly enforced, and that tag inheritance is behaving as expected but does not have the permissions to make changes.
- **Edit Enterprise Administrator**: Full read/write access to Cost and Usage data for EA accounts It allows operators with this role to define and edit tag inheritance strategies to assign cost correctly and bless billing accuracy.

MCA billing profiles:

- **View billing profiles**: Billing profile reader permission to view Accounts with MCA and related cost data. Users need this visibility to understand how costs are charged, and how costs are managed through the tag inheritance.
- Edit billing profile contributor permission only allows MCA users to edit and manage billing profiles. Users can use tag inheritance policies at the point of application to ensure cost distribution is as per organization policies.

The following figure illustrates how tag inheritance works:

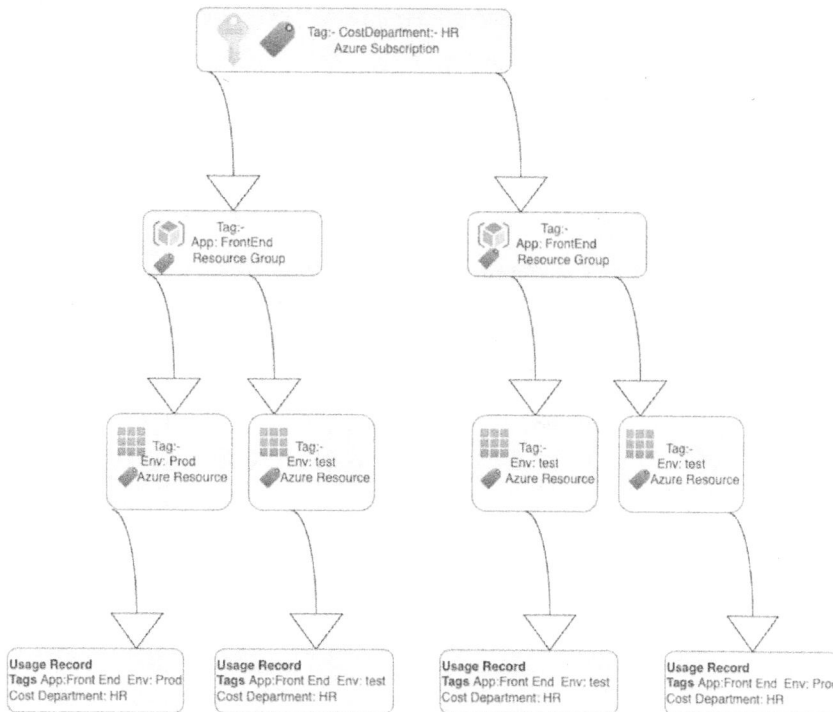

Figure 6.17: Tags with cost usage

Enable tag inheritance in Azure portal

Tag inheritance is a very useful feature in Azure. It allows tags to be applied higher up the resource hierarchy (at the resource group or subscription level) and automatically inherited by resources further down the hierarchy. This provides consistency and makes managing tags throughout your cloud footprint simple. Tag Inheritance reduces the number of tags required for better cost allocation and monitoring and managing your resources.

1. Select the scope.

2. On the left, locate the setting and click on **Configuration**.

3. Under **Tag inheritance** click on **Edit**.

   In the following image, you can see the Cost Management section of the Azure portal, which highlights the Tag Inheritance capability. This means that you can create tags at a subscription or resource group level and then rely on Tag Inheritance to automatically apply those tags to associated resources.

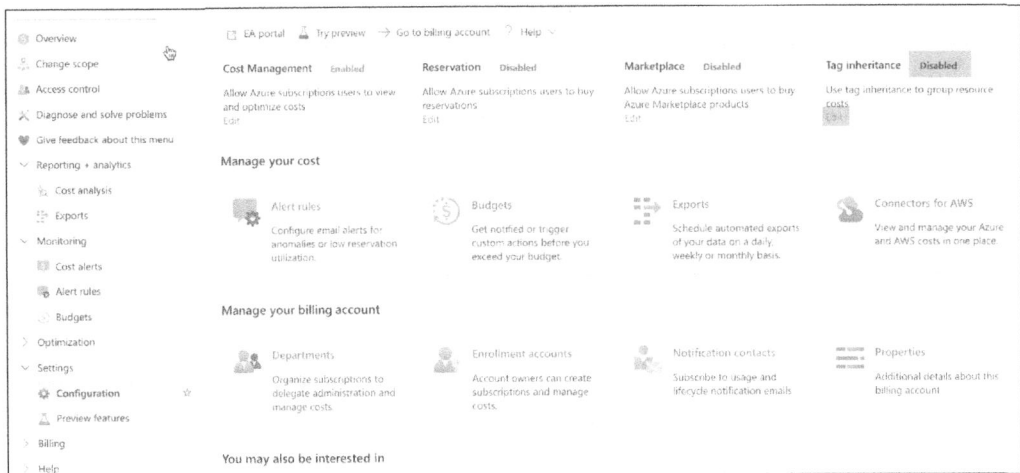

Figure 6.18: Enable Tag inheritance

4. In the **Tag inheritance**, click on automatically apply billing, subscription, and resource group tags to new usage data as below:

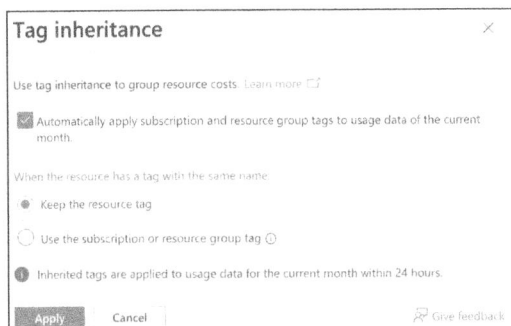

Figure 6.19: Enable Tag inheritance

After the inheritance is enabled, the billing profile, Subscription, invoice section and resource group tags are applied to the child resources record for the current month within 24 hours.

View the costs grouped by tag

The tag-based cost view in Azure helps you review costs and track spending on a resource or project, which in turn makes it convenient to keep a more coherent tab on your budget and spending. The main goal of cost organization costs is to show you exactly which department, environment, or project is using the most significant resources.

1. In the portal, select the cost management.
2. On the left of the menu, select the cost analysis.
3. Click on the scope.
4. In **Group by** list, select the tag and you can see the cost for the tag group by.

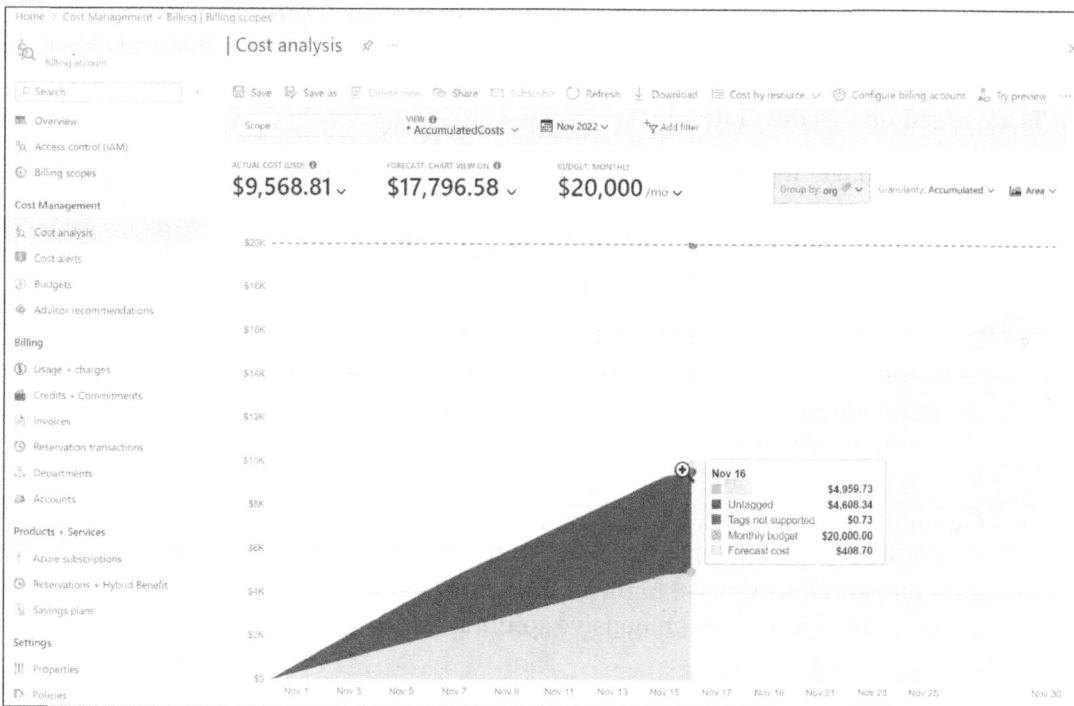

Figure 6.20: *Costs grouped by tag*

Azure Cost Management APIs and automation

You can utilize the Azure Cost Management APIs to access data about your usage and expenses. These APIs (Application Programming Interfaces) allow you to create custom reports, set up budget alerts, and automate cost management tasks for your Azure account.

You can use Azure Logic Apps or Azure Functions to automate actions based on the data you retrieve from the cost management APIs. For instance, you can trigger a notification when your spending reaches a specific limit or optimize your resources to reduce costs based on usage patterns.

Available APIs

Several APIs help you access and manage your Azure usage and expenses. Each API has unique functions and capabilities, and you may need multiple APIs to achieve your desired outcome. You can check out the API specification articles to learn how to use each API. Additionally, you can refer to the scenarios outlined later for further guidance on utilizing the available APIs for your specific needs.

Cost details APIs

These APIs can help you get detailed information about your Azure expenses, previously called usage details. Cost details are the most thorough records of your usage and expenses that you can access within Azure. The cost management features in the Azure portal and APIs are based on this raw dataset.

To efficiently manage and analyze your Azure cost data, you have several options for exporting and generating detailed reports. These methods ensure that you can keep track of your usage and expenses in a structured and accessible format.

Following are two key methods to consider:

- **Exports API**: If you want to get a comprehensive understanding of your Azure usage and expenses, you can set up a recurring task to export your cost details data to Azure storage on a daily, weekly, or monthly basis. Exported data can be in CSV format, which is easy to analyze. This is the most recommended solution for managing cost data and is ideal for large enterprises as it is highly scalable.

- **Generate cost details**: On-demand download is an excellent option for downloading cost details data in CSV format for smaller datasets with specific date ranges. However, we highly recommend using Exports for larger workloads as they offer a more comprehensive solution for managing cost data.

Pricing APIs

Microsoft Azure Pricing **APIs (Application Programming Interfaces)** offer some cool features for fetching and controlling pricing-related data for different Azure services. These APIs allow organizations to incorporate pricing data into their own applications and systems to realize costs in real time and plan for their financials. Utilizing the Pricing APIs, enterprises can ensure they are accountable for their business and optimize Cloud spend based on the latest pricing details.

- **Azure Retail Prices**: Retrieve the meter rates that correspond to pay-as-you-go pricing. You may combine this information with your resource usage data to manually estimate your anticipated bill.

- **Price sheet API**: You can obtain personalized pricing information for all the meters you use. Enterprises can combine this data with their usage details and marketplace usage information to estimate costs manually. This can be done by utilizing their usage and marketplace data.

Budgets and alerts APIs

This article examines how to manage and monitor cloud spending with the Budgets and Alerts APIs on Azure. With these APIs, organizations can set resource cost thresholds, monitor spending, and receive alerts when costs are close to or exceed budgeted limits. Using these APIs, companies will exercise more control over their cloud budgets, reduce unforeseen costs, and make informed financial decisions.

- **Budgets API**: With the help of personalized pricing information, you can create cost budgets for your resources, resource groups, or billing meters. Once you have completed budgets, you can put up alerts to notify you when you exceed the specified budget thresholds. Additionally, you can configure actions to occur when you've reached the budget amounts. This will help you manage your costs and stay within your budget limits.

- **Alerts APIs**: You can keep track of all the alerts that have been set up by budget and other alerting systems in Azure and manage them accordingly.

Invoicing APIs

An invoicing API allows companies to create, send, manage, and reconcile invoices and track related payments end to end.

- **Invoices API**: The API should give us a brief overview of all the invoices, such as the total amount and payment status, and a link to download a PDF copy of each invoice.

- **Transactions API**: The API allows you to obtain an invoice's line items. This will enable you to retrieve all the purchases, refunds, and credits included in the invoice. However, please note that customers with a billing account can only access the API under the Microsoft Customer Agreement or Microsoft Partner Agreement.

Reservation APIs

In Azure, Reservation APIs are a set of APIs to manage Azure Reserved Instances. With these APIs, customers can view, purchase, and manage reserved instances, which are cost-saving options when you commit to a one—or three-year term for a virtual machine, SQL database, and other resources.

- **Reservation details API**: You can use the reservation details API to get more information about the resource consumption associated with your reservation purchases. It will give you a thorough breakdown of all the details.

- **Reservation Transactions API**: You can use the Reservation Transactions API to get all the purchase and management transactions related to your reservations.

- **Reservation recommendations API**: The reservation recommendations API allows you to get recommendations for future reservation purchases and information about expected savings.

- **Reservation recommendation details API**: To perform a what-if analysis, you can use the reservation recommendation details API to get detailed information for specific reservation purchases.

Azure Cost Management APIs

Azure Cost Management APIs are a set of tools provided by Microsoft Azure to help users manage and optimize their cloud spending. These APIs allow users to track and control their Azure costs by providing detailed insights and control mechanisms over their cloud expenses.

- **Get the list of billing accounts:** To get the list of billing accounts in Azure, you can use the Azure Cost Management API with the following details:

  Method: GET

  URI: https://management.azure.com/providers/Microsoft.Billing/
  billingAccounts?api-version=2019-10-01-preview

- **Get the list of customers:** To get the list of customers for a specific billing account in Azure, you can use the Azure Cost Management API with the following details:

  Method: GET

  URI:

  https://management.azure.com/providers/Microsoft.Billing/
  billingAccounts/{billingAccountName}/customers?api-version=2019-10-
  01-preview

- **List of subscriptions:** To get the list of billing subscriptions for a specific billing account in Azure, you can use the Azure Cost Management API with the following details:

  Method: GET

  URI: https://management.azure.com/providers/Microsoft.Billing/
  billingAccounts/{billingAccountName}/billingSubscriptions?api-
  version=2019-10-01-preview

- **Get the invoice list for the time period:** To get the invoice list for a specific period in Azure, you can use the Azure Cost Management API with the following details:

Method: GET

URI:

```
https://management.azure.com/providers/Microsoft.Billing/
billingAccounts/{billingAccountName}/invoices?api-version=2019-10-
01-preview&periodStartDate={periodStartDate}&periodEndDate={periodEn
dDate}
```

- **Get the list of Reserved Instance (RI):** To get the list of Reserved Instances (RI) in Azure, you can use the Azure API with the following details:

Method: GET

URI:

```
https://management.azure.com/{scope}/providers/Microsoft.Capacity/
reservationOrders?api-version=2019-04-01
```

- **Get the budget information:** To get the budget information for a specific subscription in Azure, you can use the Azure Consumption API with the following details:

Method: GET

URI:

```
https://management.azure.com/subscriptions/{subscriptionId}/
providers/Microsoft.Consumption/budgets/{budgetName}?api-
version=2019-10-01
```

- **Create the anomaly alert:** To create an anomaly alert in Azure, you can use the Azure Monitor API with the following details:

Method: PUT

URI:

```
https://management.azure.com/{resourceUri}/providers/Microsoft.
Insights/scheduledQueryRules/{ruleName}?api-version=2018-04-16
```

- **Get the cost of the resource group for the last 30 days:** To get the cost of a resource group for the last 30 days in Azure, you can use the Azure Cost Management API with the following details:

Method: POST

URI:

```
https://management.azure.com/subscriptions/{subscriptionId}/
resourceGroups/{resourceGroupName}/providers/Microsoft.
CostManagement/query?api-version=2019-11-01
```

JSON body:

```
{
  "type": "ActualCost",
```

```
    "timeframe": "Last30Days",
    "dataset": {
      "granularity": "None",
      "aggregation": {
        "totalCost": {
          "name": "PreTaxCost",
          "function": "Sum"
        }
      },
      "grouping": [
        {
          "type": "Dimension",
          "name": "ResourceGroup"
        }
      ]
    }
}
```

- **Get the cost of Azure service for the last 30 days:** To get the cost of a specific Azure service for the last 30 days, you can use the Azure Cost Management API with the following details:

Method: POST

URI:

```
https://management.azure.com/subscriptions/{subscriptionId}/
resourceGroups/{resourceGroupName}/providers/Microsoft.
CostManagement/query?api-version=2019-11-01
```

JSON body:

```
{
    "type": "ActualCost",
    "timeframe": "Last30Days",
    "dataset": {
      "granularity": "Daily",
      "aggregation": {
        "totalCost": {
          "name": "PreTaxCost",
          "function": "Sum"
```

```
            }
        },
        "filter": {
          "And": [
            {
              "Dimension": {
                "name": "ResourceType",
                "operator": "In",
                "values": [
                  "Microsoft.ServiceName/serviceType" // Replace with
                  the actual service name/type
                ]
              }
            },
            {
              "Dimension": {
                "name": "Date",
                "operator": "InLast",
                "values": [
                  "P30D" // P30D represents the last 30 days
                ]
              }
            }
          ]
        }
      }
    }
}
```

- **Get the top 10 highest spender resource groups in the last 30 days**: To get the top 10 highest spending resource groups in the last 30 days in Azure, you can use the Azure Cost Management API with the following details:

Method: POST

URI:

```
https://management.azure.com/subscriptions/{subscriptionId}/
providers/Microsoft.CostManagement/query?api-version=2019-11-01
```

JSON body:

```
{
  "type": "Usage",
  "timeframe": "Last30Days",
  "dataset": {
    "granularity": "None",
    "aggregation": {
      "totalCost": {
        "name": "PreTaxCost",
        "function": "Sum"
      }
    },
    "sorting": [
      {
        "direction": "descending",
        "name": "PreTaxCost"
      }
    ],
    "grouping": [
      {
        "type": "Dimension",
        "name": "ResourceGroup"
      }
    ]
  },
  "datasetConfiguration": {
    "top": 10
  }
}
```

Implementing showback and chargeback models

Having showback and chargeback models is crucial for effective cloud management. These models offer detailed cost information, which can help enterprises promote responsible usage, optimize costs, and align cloud investments with business outcomes. Engaging stakeholders, undertaking careful planning, and using the appropriate tools and policies are vital to implement these models. By doing so, organizations can enjoy enhanced transparency, accountability, and financial management.

Importance of showback and chargeback model

Showback and chargeback models effectively bring financial clarity within organizations by highlighting the direct relationship between resource consumption and expenditure. This increased visibility of cloud spending empowers each department to understand its financial impact within the larger organizational context, promoting budget-conscious behavior and fiscal responsibility. The improved visibility makes it harder to ignore the cost implications of one's cloud activities, which deters wasteful practices.

These models also encourage a culture of justification and rationalization for cloud expenditures, urging departments to assess and validate their resource demands critically. This cultivates a robust fiscal governance and stewardship framework, where teams actively engage in cost-saving strategies and eliminate unnecessary spending.

When it comes to managing costs through these models, it is not just about reducing expenses. It is also about finding the right balance between cost, performance, and capacity. By using analytics to analyze consumption data, organizations can make better investment decisions in cloud services. For example, they can choose scalable solutions that match their needs, avoid overspending, and ensure resources are utilized effectively.

Showback and chargeback models are also transformative tools for financial forecasting, providing a predictive lens through which future costs can be anticipated with a higher degree of accuracy. Financial planning thus evolves from a reactive to a proactive exercise, characterized by strategic foresight and adaptability.

Finally, the equitable distribution of costs achieved through these models is fundamental to fostering a fair and just internal economy. By mapping costs to the respective consuming entities, the organization can dispel any inequities in financial responsibility, promoting a culture of efficiency and merit-based resource distribution. This enhances overall operational efficiency by ensuring that resource allocation reflects contribution to the enterprise's strategic objectives.

Implementing showback and chargeback model

In this section, we will learn how to implement showback and chargeback model:

- **Define objectives:** When setting up showback and chargeback models, it is essential to define your goals to support your organization's overall objectives. This can involve different aims, such as fostering a culture of careful spending, creating a fair cost distribution system, or encouraging teams to collaborate more effectively. It is also important to consider objectives that promote efficiency and innovation while staying within budget constraints. For example, this might involve aligning costs with business value or optimizing cloud spending through cross-departmental collaboration. By setting clear goals, your organization can maximize showback and chargeback models to achieve its broader strategic aims.

- **Stakeholder engagement:** Engaging stakeholders is more than just getting them to agree on policies; it is about making sure that those policies are based on the actual working conditions of each department. It involves educating stakeholders about the significance of cost management and its effect on the business's financial outcomes. Successful engagement leads to policies that are not just fair but also adaptable to the evolving demands of the organization, encouraging a cost-conscious culture across all levels.

- **Tagging strategy:** A comprehensive tagging strategy enables a multi-dimensional analysis of cloud costs, facilitating detailed insight into spending by service, department, project, or even individual resources. Tags should be standardized across the organization for consistent reporting and should include considerations for future scalability. Proper tagging enables the attribution of costs to the right entities, thereby ensuring that the data driving financial decisions is both accurate and actionable.

- **Choose a model**: When choosing between showback and chargeback models, there are a few things to consider. The main factors are how ready the organization is for this change and what kind of impact you want to have on behavior. Showback models are a good choice if you're looking to educate employees about cost accountability before enforcing any financial implications. This can be a good first step towards creating a culture of cost-consciousness. Chargeback models, on the other hand, tie consumption directly to departmental budgets and have a more immediate impact on behavior. When deciding which model to choose, you should think about how mature your organization's cost management practices are and how quickly you want to see cultural change.

- **Tooling:** Selecting the appropriate tools for showback and chargeback models is crucial for their effectiveness. Azure Cost Management tools are a great option, providing built-in support for managing and tracking costs. However, third-party tools can be used to expand the ecosystem and offer specialized analytics, advanced reporting, or integration with enterprise financial systems. To ensure the success of these models, it is important to choose tools that can automate processes, combine them with systems, and be flexible enough to suit the organization's specific needs.

- **Reporting:** Reporting should not be limited to just allocating costs; it should go further and provide helpful insights and recommendations. Reports should be effortless to understand and actionable, enabling departments to analyze their spending habits and identify potential cost-saving opportunities. Additionally, reports should be customizable to cater to the specific needs of different stakeholders, making them more valuable and user-friendly.

- **Feedback loop:** Establishing a feedback loop means opening communication channels about cost management, allowing for ongoing improvement of the showback and chargeback processes. This can be performed through traditional meetings, surveys, or a dedicated feedback channel. The goal is to create a flexible system where departments can discuss any discrepancies, offer suggestions for improvements, and align their consumption practices with the organization's overall goals. The aim is to promote a responsive system that encourages continuous improvement and helps achieve cost-consciousness.

Steps to show back and chargeback

In this section, we will learn some steps to showback and chargeback:

- **Tagging resources**: Creating a strong cost management framework requires thorough tagging of resources. This means labeling them with basic metadata and providing context, such as the environment they belong to (production, staging, test), the application or service they support, and even the individual resource owner. The aim is to create a tagging system that reflects the complex nature of cloud expenses and allows for precise tracking of costs to the appropriate organizational unit. By implementing detailed tagging protocols, organizations can analyze cloud expenses at a granular level, enabling them to make informed decisions and gain valuable insights.

- **Azure policies**: Azure policies go beyond just monitoring compliance; they help organizations enforce their standards and best practices in the cloud environment. By using policy definitions that require tagging, organizations can automate governance and ensure consistent application of tags. These policies can be set up to audit, deny, or append tags, making sure that resources are not only labeled consistently but also that untagged resources are quickly identified and fixed, preserving the accuracy of cost management practices.

- **Azure Cost Management + Billing:** Azure's cost management suite effectively allows organizations to keep track of their finances, offering more than just cost reports. It provides advanced analytics, budgeting, and forecasting features, allowing customized views and allocations of cloud spend. This enables stakeholders to analyze data according to their specific requirements. By using its comprehensive functionality, organizations can delve deeper into their cloud spend, identifying trends, anomalies, and areas for optimization.

- **Automate:** When it comes to showback and chargeback models for cloud usage, automation goes beyond just generating reports. It involves creating workflows that can adapt to the organization's usage patterns and provide real-time data and alerts. Automation can also be used to adjust resources in response to demand, which helps cut costs. This approach ensures that stakeholders receive timely and relevant information and keeps the organization agile in its financial management.

- **Educate:** Education plays a crucial role in effectively managing costs. It is insufficient for teams to receive reports; they need to comprehend the consequences of their cloud usage and have the expertise to make informed decisions about their resource consumption. Education programs should cover topics such as the principles of cloud economics, the impact of various cloud services and pricing models, and strategies for cost optimization. When teams are equipped with this knowledge, organizations promote a proactive culture of cost accountability.

- **Iterate**: It is essential to regularly review showback and chargeback models to make sure they are still working effectively. This means looking at how costs are allocated, checking that chargeback bills are accurate, and getting feedback from everyone involved. These reviews should consider any changes in pricing models for cloud services, the introduction of new services, and any shifts in the organization's structure or goals. By doing this regularly, you can ensure the models stay relevant to the organization's needs and continue to have the desired impact on behavior and finances.

Benefits of showback and chargeback

When managing finances in the cloud, cost visibility is crucial. It helps organizations understand exactly where their money is going and make informed decisions about allocating resources. This transparency promotes the efficient use of cloud resources and eliminates waste. It also enables decision-makers to optimize financial planning and invest every dollar in the organization's growth and innovation.

Cost visibility promotes accountability and responsibility in managing cloud resources, which leads to increased resource efficiency. Teams are learning more about how they use the cloud and are being encouraged to closely examine every service, instance, or application to make sure they are valuable and cost-effective. This helps create a culture of efficiency where everyone is responsible for making sure the cloud is being used in a sustainable way by reducing waste and finding cost-effective solutions.

When IT expenditures align with the broader business objectives, it leads to a harmonious synergy between them. By mapping costs to specific business activities, organizations can understand the value derived from each service and make informed decisions about allocating resources. This makes IT a strategic partner in achieving business outcomes and repositions it as a pivotal contributor to the organization's success. Such alignment goes beyond the traditional view of IT as a mere cost center.

When stakeholders from different departments clearly understand the financial implications of their cloud usage, it fosters a shared sense of fiscal responsibility across the organization. Showback and chargeback models provide cost visibility and encourage everyone to use the organization's financial resources wisely. This responsibility goes beyond just sticking to the budget. It creates a mindset where every action regarding its financial impact is considered, leading to a financially smart workforce.

Chargeback models have an intrinsic function of cost recovery, a practical approach for IT departments to manage their budgets effectively. By attributing costs directly to the consuming departments, IT can ensure that the financial burden of services is distributed fairly. This promotes the efficient use of cloud resources and encourages departments to evaluate the necessity and efficiency of their cloud usage. As a result, chargeback models serve as a financial tool that helps balance the investment and consumption within the organization, ensuring that every unit contributes its fair share to the technological enablement of the enterprise.

Azure RBAC for cost management

Operating costs in cloud environments can be a challenge. That is the reason **Role-Based Access Control (RBAC)** is essential. RBAC helps teams decide who can see and control costs in their cloud environment.

Using RBAC, teams can manage their costs effectively and stay in charge of their cloud spending.

Organizations that need to master their cloud spend should roll out a RBAC system defining roles and permissions for each area is an important tool for organizations to provide cost management tools and data access to their teams while keeping it secure and accountable. There are biggest things that RBAC provides in cloud cost management.

- **Defining roles and responsibilities**: Organizations need to establish various roles within their cost management strategy to manage operating costs in cloud environments efficiently. These roles can range from cost viewers, who can only view cost data, to cost managers, who can allocate budgets and implement spending caps. By defining these roles, organizations can ensure that their teams have access to and control over costs in their cloud environment. This enables them to manage their costs effectively and stay in charge of their cloud spending.

- **Granular access control**: RBAC, or Role-Based Access Control, permits organizations to control access to their cloud environment. It assigns specific permissions to different roles. This allows for granular access control, where a project manager can only view the costs related to their project, while a department head can view costs across multiple projects. By doing this, organizations can ensure that their teams can access the right information and control costs in their cloud environment. This helps them manage their costs efficiently and stay in charge of their cloud spending.

- **Custom roles**: Apart from the pre-defined roles, organizations using Azure can also create custom roles that align with their unique cost management requirements. These custom roles can be personalized with specific permissions to view or manage costs, apply tags, and leverage cost management tools.

- **Secure budget management**: Azure's RBAC feature helps organizations secure their budget management processes by allowing only users with the appropriate roles to create or modify budgets. This ensures that budgetary controls are not bypassed and helps maintain the integrity of the budgeting process.

- **Ensuring compliance:** Azure's RBAC permits teams to manage keys to their resources by giving each team member access only to the areas they require to work in. This allows support compliance with company policies and standards and implements the principle of least privilege, which suggests that users can access only those resources necessary for their job roles. It is beneficial in budget management as it provides cost control and contains unauthorized access to sensitive financial data. By limiting access to financial details based on job roles, RBAC helps secure the company's financial information. It's like showing each team member a key to only the rooms they need to enter so they can do their job effectively without blundering into areas they do not need to be in. RBAC ensures that the team operates smoothly without unnecessary crossovers or confusion.

- **Audit and accountability**: RBAC is very helpful in tracking and monitoring cost-related activities, and it helps keep everyone accountable for their actions. With RBAC, you can easily record who made changes to budgets, approved certain expenses, and the like. This information is very useful for both internal audits and external compliance requirements. By keeping track of such details, RBAC ensures that everyone knows their responsibilities and that the team operates smoothly.

- **Integration with organizational structure**: RBAC is very helpful in tracking and monitoring cost-related activities, and it helps keep everyone accountable for their actions. With RBAC, you can easily record who made changes to budgets, approved certain expenses, and the like. This information is very useful for both internal audits and external compliance requirements. By keeping track of such details, RBAC ensures that everyone knows their responsibilities and that the team operates smoothly.

Assign the roles to users

As a best practice, it is always recommended to provide role-based access to the users so that the control and management of access and permissions will be in place on the Azure side. This will then give each member of your team the right amount of access they need to carry out their tasks efficiently, remaining secure and compliant.

This is done in the following steps to assign roles to users in Azure:

1. Navigate to the Azure Portal.

2. Select the scope you want to control access to, such as **Management Groups**, **Subscriptions**, or **Resource Groups**.

3. Go to the **Access control (IAM)** section.

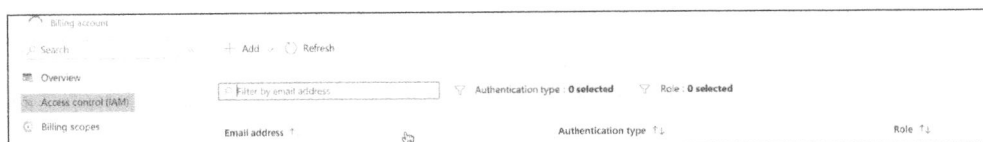

Figure 6.21: Access control (IAM)

4. Click on **Add role assignment**.

5. Select the role you want to assign and choose the user/group/service principal to assign it to.

The following figure shows how we can map roles on users on Azure Portal. By defining the user email, choosing the right kind of authentication, and fine-tuning the notification settings, the admin can guarantee that the proper access requirements are granted to the team while keeping their security and compliance levels in check.

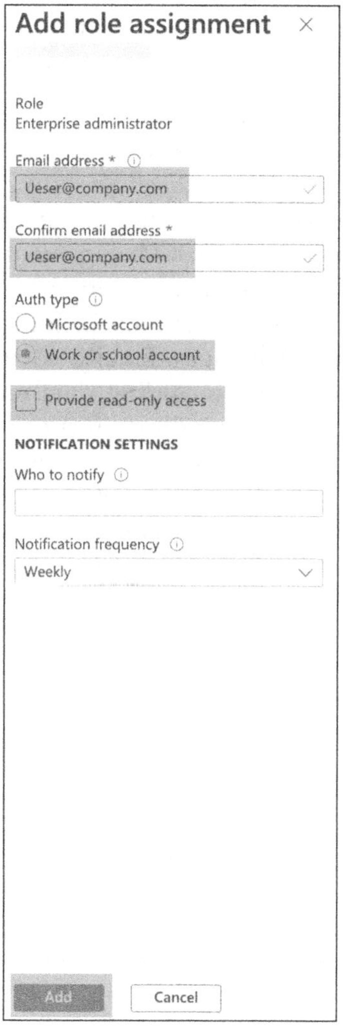

Figure 6.22: Add User IAM

6. Click **Save** to apply the role assignment.

Conclusion

Azure's cost management guide provides an in-depth look at how to accurately allocate costs and chargebacks within the Azure platform. The chapter covers everything from creating and managing cost allocation rules to the strategic use of tagging in resource groups to streamline cost tracking. Additionally, the chapter explores the technical aspects of Azure Cost Management APIs and the role of automation in cost management processes. A significant part of the chapter is dedicated to implementing showback and chargeback models, which help promote financial accountability. Finally, the chapter discusses how assigning roles to users through Azure RBAC can help improve governance and control over financial aspects of Azure resource usage.

The next chapter, Governance and Compliance in Azure, provides guidelines and strategies to uphold strong policies, manage costs, ensure reliable security practices, and comply with regulatory standards. chapter discusses how Azure Policy can help automate compliance, maintain cost management discipline, and enforce operational rules. The chapter explores the integration of Azure Cost Management with the Azure Security Center and how they can work together to balance security measures with cost-effectiveness. It focuses on compliance and regulatory obligations, including global standards like GDPR, and industry-specific compliance challenges. Finally, covers data protection and privacy principles and practices within Azure, including data encryption, access controls, and privacy strategies to ensure that data handling in Azure aligns with legal and ethical standards. The chapter provides a comprehensive view of governance and compliance in Azure, emphasizing the critical relationship between cost management, security, and compliance to maintain a secure and efficient cloud infrastructure.

Join our book's Discord space

Join the book's Discord Workspace for Latest updates, Offers, Tech happenings around the world, New Release and Sessions with the Authors:

https://discord.bpbonline.com

CHAPTER 7

Governance and Compliance

Introduction

In managing any cloud environment, its level of governance and compliance are the most important. Azure has a wide array of tools and services that help organizations meet these goals, we will describe a few of them briefly. Azure Policy is a service in Azure that you use to create, assign, and manage policies. It also enforces how resources are made and used in managing expenses.

Integrating Azure Cost Management with Azure Security Center is critical to achieving a complete picture of financial status. The integration lets enterprises view consumption costs and security threats on the cloud.

Cost management + security = A comprehensive view of the edge

Cloud environment, balancing cost management and robust security measures is paramount for gaining a comprehensive view of the edge. Organizations can now gain financial visibility at the same edges where they derive security insights. Understanding and managing your financial and security landscape at the edge means you can better leverage and serve your resources and fulfill compliance as internal and external policies require.

In addition, compliance and regulatory considerations provide a reason to comply with the law.

Azure is committed to data security and privacy, offering extensive compliance offerings. It enhances data protection with enterprise-grade encryption, access controls, and data loss prevention. This security level complies with privacy laws and regulations, ensuring your company can keep customer data safe, protect your brand, and avoid data privacy breaches. It is a testament to Azure's dedication to data security and privacy compliance.

These components help lay the groundwork for controlling resources, protecting data, and maintaining compliance in the cloud. With Azure, you get a comprehensive end-to-end governance and compliance toolkit, gateways to integrate your existing infra, and extra templates to ensure your cloud environment is secure, efficient, consistent, and compliant with the relevant standards.

Structure

In this chapter, we will go through the following topics:

- Azure Policy and Cost Management
- Azure Cost Management and Azure Security Center
- Compliance and regulatory considerations
- Data protection and privacy

Objectives

The objective of this chapter is to provide an overview of governance, cost management and security in Azure with help on how you can have effective execution from the tools provided by azure for these services. This chapter covers combining Azure Policy and Cost Management where the integration here is how these tools are accelerating to enforce governance & cost-saving effectively. It will also explore the essential integration between Azure Cost Management and Azure Security Center, allowing organizations to view their financial status as well as its safety all indicated in one location.

Additionally, we will also explore important compliance and regulatory considerations organizations must consider with regards to industry standards that need it be adhered to and legal requirements. It will also cover the best practices to govern data security and privacy in cloud infrastructures. Readers will have gained the knowledge and skills required to design strong governance frameworks, cost management strategy designs, improve security best practices and controls as well help in ensuring data compliance/privacy on their azure environment.

Azure Policy and Cost Management

Cloud environment needs to be managed with governance and compliance. They maintain overall financial responsibility, cost control, and the security and privacy of the data they touch. In this respect, Azure provides many tools and services to aid organizations in pursuing these goals. Together with Azure Policy and Cost Management, we can use all these to apply the rules and reduce costs. Through Azure Policy, administrators can create, assign, and manage policies that enforce organization standards and evaluate compliance at scale. Elasticity manages a budget by maintaining resources within their guidelines of use both in deployment as well as in use.

Management is an important part of any cloud infrastructure; cost governance is an inherent piece of that. Azure Policy is a powerful tool that can assist with taking care of cost governance in your Azure environment. Azure Policy enables you to create and enforce policies to control costs, monitor usage, and manage resources. These policies can ensure that no non-cost-saving measure-compliant resources are created or tag the created resources as cost-related. Policies can also be used to monitor the usage of resources and set up alerts for conditions that hit certain thresholds, which can then be used to take steps to comply, review, or operationalize your resource consumption and costs reopening.

In the following section, we will learn about the sample of Azure Policies for cost optimization.

Azure Policy for naming convention

A good naming convention is key to successful cost governance in a cloud environment. The name helps you identify what exactly the service is doing and how we can classify costs around that. A standardized naming convention helps to identify which resources are for which project, the hash of a project, and the room of a project or department and how they are utilized. This transparency helps to understand how clouds are being used and what can be optimized in terms of cost.

For example, a solid naming convention allows one to easily distinguish the resources used for development and testing from those used for production. This distinction allows you to ensure resources are used efficiently rather than over-provisioning them for development and testing, saving you money.

Additionally, the same naming-swapping approach should help you track usage and spending more easily in the long run. This makes generating reports and analyzing usage trends easier, which is a key element for organizations pursuing further cost optimization.

In conclusion, a clear naming convention is one of the most important parts of cost governance in the cloud—or even in the data center. It helps with Resource-Level tagging and grouping, Resource usage and spending detail tracking, and over-the-period cost optimization.

The following policy can enforce the naming convention using Azure Policy:

```
"policyRule": {
    "if": {
```

```
"anyOf": [ {
    "allOf": [ {
        "field": "type",
            "equals": "Microsoft.Compute/virtualMachines"
    }


    ,
        {
        "field": "location",
            "equals": "centralindia"
    }


    ,
        {
        "not": {
            "anyOf": [ {
                "field": "name",
                    "match": "ind-prd-net-###"
            }

            ]
        }
    }

    ]
}

]
}

,
"then": {
    "effect": "deny"
}
```

```
}
```

One task may be determining whether a **Virtual Machine (VM)** will be deployed in Central India. If so, it needs to meet the naming convention **ind-prd-vm-###**, where **###** is any three-digit suffix. This method uses the match operator, which specifies that **#** represents any number. For characters, you can use numbers or characters

Alternatively, we could use the like operator with the pattern **ind-prd-vm-**. In this pattern, the **""** character allows any sequence of characters to follow. By placing * after the -, it signifies **"** *match anything that comes after this."*

Storage accounts in non-production environments

If you look at many enterprises' Azure Setups, you will commonly find GRS, ZRS, and even RA-GRS storage accounts in non-production environments. Sometimes, this is on purpose, and sometimes, it is not. This can become expensive and ineffective for storing non-production workloads like development and QA.

For non-production environments, **Locally Redundant Storage (LRS)** accounts could come to dollars for less dollars and keep the environment as available as production. It combines high durability and availability and copes inside one data center, which also means it can be used for development and testing when geo-redundancy is unnecessary. So, using LRS storage accounts can help us reduce costs to a bare minimum without compromising data safety and accessibility.

Opting for LRS for non-production will save companies significant money and not compromise on data availability and durability. LRS accounts can be easily implemented and maintained for non-critical scenarios simply to remain cost-effective.

The following policy can enforce the LRS storage policy for non-prod using Azure Policy:

```
"policyRule": {
    "if": {
      "allOf": [
        {
          "field": "type",
          "equals": "Microsoft.Storage/storageAccounts"
        },
        {
          "field": "Microsoft.Storage/storageAccounts/sku.name",
          "notEquals": "Standard_LRS"
        }
      ]
```

```
    },
    "then": {
      "effect": "deny"

    }

  }
}
```

The critical aspect of cost management is choosing the proper storage redundancy level based on the environment's needs. This makes LRS perfect for non-production environments, which do not need as high redundancy as production environments. Such an adjustment will save huge costs without sacrificing the appropriate data security and availability.

Auditing orphan resources

In the right hands, orphaned resources are a key focus for cost optimization in a cloud environment. This will help in finding and clearing out resources that are no longer used but are still being billed for. Resources that are not associated with a project, application, or user but are still consuming resources and incurring costs are referred to as orphaned resources. These can be stand-alone disks, orphaned App Service Plans, or other unused resources that keep generating charges.

Even if orphaned resources are not consuming actual costs (for example, idle resources), it is still a best practice to identify and right-size these resources for various reasons, including security, compliance, and governance. Unutilized cloud resources can act as soft attack vectors and can be easily overlooked in security updates and audits. Furthermore, a neat and tidy cloud environment helps meet compliance demands with corporate policies and regulatory bodies.

It helps identify and delete orphan resources, maintaining a clean and cost-efficient cloud environment. For example, if a particular unattached disk is not in use, it must be audited to be either reattached with a new VM, or it needs to be deleted to procure any unnecessary charges. Similarly, you should probably remove or switch the App Service Plans pricing tier with no associated App Services.

The following is an example of Azure Policy to audit unattached disks and orphaned App Service Plans:

```
{
  "policyRule": {
    "if": {
      "anyOf": [
        {
          "allOf": [
```

```
      {
        "field": "type",
        "equals": "Microsoft.Compute/disks"
      },
      {
        "not": {
          "anyOf": [
            {
              "field": "Microsoft.Compute/disks/diskState",
              "equals": "Attached"
            },
            {
              "field": "Microsoft.Compute/disks/diskState",
              "equals": "Reserved"
            }
          ]
        }
      }
    ]
  },
  {
    "allOf": [
      {
        "field": "type",
        "equals": "Microsoft.Web/serverfarms"
      },
      {
        "not": {
          "field": "Microsoft.Web/serverfarms/sku.tier",
          "equals": "Free"
        }
      },
      {
        "count": {
```

```
                        "field": "Microsoft.Web/sites/serverFarmId",
                        "where": {
                          "field": "Microsoft.Web/sites/serverFarmId",
                          "equals": "[field('Microsoft.Web/serverfarms/id')]"
                        }
                      },
                      "equals": 0
                    }
                  ]
                }
              ]
            },
            "then": {
              "effect": "audit"
            }
          }
        }
```

This policy performs the following checks:

- It audits unattached or unreserved disks by checking the **Microsoft.Compute/ disks** type and ensure the disk state is neither attached nor reserved.

- It identifies orphaned App Service Plans by checking the **Microsoft.Web/ serverfarms** type, ensuring the **Stock Keeping Unit (SKU)** tier is not Free, and verifying that there are no associated App Services (**Microsoft.Web/sites**) with the App Service Plan.

Implementing such policies helps maintain a cost-effective, secure, and compliant cloud environment.

Azure Hybrid Benefit

Users can use their Windows Server and SQL Server on-premises licenses with **Azure Hybrid Benefit (AHUB)** to run workloads in Azure. This allows customers to save up to 40% on the cost of running Windows Server and SQL Server workloads in Azure.

It is essential to audit the utilization of these benefits to make sure you are utilizing AHUB in the right way. Audit AHUB usage, to verify the use of correct licensing options to counter such that VMs or **Virtual Machine Scale Sets (VMSS)** are using the only needed resources to ensure better cost-saving opportunities.

You can audit the AHUB usage using Azure Policy. An example of a policy that audits, whether VMs or VMSS are using the *Windows_Server* ImageSKU value with the `Windows_Server` license type, is as follows. If it is not, then your AHUB is disabled. Also, include other SKUs you use in your environment.

```
{
    "policyRule": {
      "if": {
        "allOf": [
          {
            "field": "type",
            "equals": "Microsoft.Compute/virtualMachines"
          },
          {
            "anyOf": [
              {
                "field": "Microsoft.Compute/virtualMachines/
                storageProfile.imageReference.sku",
                "equals": "2016-Datacenter"
              },
              {
                "field": "Microsoft.Compute/virtualMachines/
                storageProfile.imageReference.sku",
                "equals": "2019-Datacenter"
              }
            ]
          },
          {
            "not": {
              "field": "Microsoft.Compute/virtualMachines/licenseType",
              "equals": "Windows_Server"
            }
          }
        ]
      },
      "then": {
```

```
        "effect": "audit"
      }
    }
  }
```

This policy checks the following:

- If the resource type is **Microsoft.Compute/virtualMachines**.
- If the **ImageSKU** is either 2016-Datacenter or 2019-Datacenter.
- If the **licenseType** is not set to **Windows_Server**.

By auditing AHUB usage, you can ensure that all eligible VMs take advantage of Azure Hybrid Benefit's cost-saving benefits.

You can create separate policies or a combined policy to enable AHUB for both Windows Server and SQL Server using Azure Policy. The following is an example of a combined policy that automatically sets the **licenseType** to **Windows_Server** for VMs and to AHUB for SQL Servers.

The following is combined Policy for Windows Server and SQL Server:

```
{
    "properties": {
      "displayName": "Enable Azure Hybrid Benefit for Windows Server and
      SQL Server",
      "policyType": "Custom",
      "mode": "All",
      "description": "This policy enables Azure Hybrid Benefit for
      Windows Server by setting the licenseType to Windows_Server for
      eligible virtual machines and to AHUB for SQL Servers.",
      "metadata": {
        "version": "1.0.0",
        "category": "Cost Management"
      },
      "parameters": {
        "windowsImageSku": {
          "type": "Array",
          "metadata": {
            "description": "The list of Image SKUs for Windows Server
            for which the Azure Hybrid Benefit should be enabled.",
            "displayName": "Windows Image SKUs"
```

```json
      },
      "allowedValues": [
        "2016-Datacenter",
        "2019-Datacenter"
      ],
      "defaultValue": [
        "2016-Datacenter",
        "2019-Datacenter"
      ]
    },
    "sqlImageSku": {
      "type": "Array",
      "metadata": {
        "description": "The list of Image SKUs for SQL Server for
        which the Azure Hybrid Benefit should be enabled.",
        "displayName": "SQL Image SKUs"
      },
      "allowedValues": [
        "SQL2016-WS2016",
        "SQL2017-WS2016",
        "SQL2019-WS2019"
      ],
      "defaultValue": [
        "SQL2016-WS2016",
        "SQL2017-WS2016",
        "SQL2019-WS2019"
      ]
    }
  },
  "policyRule": {
    "if": {
      "anyOf": [
        {
          "allOf": [
```

```
                          {
                            "field": "type",
                            "equals": "Microsoft.Compute/virtualMachines"
                          },
                          {
                            "anyOf": [
                              {
                                "field": "Microsoft.Compute/virtualMachines/
                                storageProfile.imageReference.sku",
                                "in": "[parameters('windowsImageSku')]"
                              }
                            ]
                          },
                          {
                            "not": {
                              "field": "Microsoft.Compute/virtualMachines/
                              licenseType",
                              "equals": "Windows_Server"
                            }
                          }
                        ]
                      },
                      {
                        "allOf": [
                          {
                            "field": "type",
                            "equals": "Microsoft.Sql/servers"
                          },
                          {
                            "field": "Microsoft.Sql/servers/sku.name",
                            "in": "[parameters('sqlImageSku')]"
                          },
                          {
```

```
                "not": {
                  "field": "Microsoft.Sql/servers/licenseType",
                  "equals": "AHUB"
                }
              }
            ]
          }
        ]
      },
      "then": {
        "effect": "modify",
        "details": {
          "roleDefinitionIds": [
            "/providers/microsoft.authorization/roleDefinitions/
            f1a07417-d97a-45cb-824c-7a7467783830"
          ],
          "operations": [
            {
              "operation": "addOrReplace",
              "field": "Microsoft.Compute/virtualMachines/licenseType",
              "value": "Windows_Server"
            },
            {
              "operation": "addOrReplace",
              "field": "Microsoft.Sql/servers/licenseType",
              "value": "AHUB"
            }
          ]
        }
      }
    }
  }
}
```

Explanation of the combined above policy

In this section, we will go through the combined policy explanation:

- **Properties**: Contains metadata about the policy, including its display name, description, and category.
- **Parameters:** Defines parameters used in the policy.
  - ○ **windowsImageSku**: Specifies the list of image SKUs for Windows Server.
  - ○ **sqlImageSku**: Specifies the list of image SKUs for SQL Server.
- **PolicyRule**: Defines the logic for the policy.
  - ○ **If:** Checks for VMs and SQL servers.

    For VMs:
    - ▪ Check if the type is Microsoft.Compute/virtualMachines.
    - ▪ Check if the imageReference.sku is in the list of specified Windows SKUs.
    - ▪ Check if the licenseType is not already set to Windows_Server.

    For SQL servers:
    - ▪ Check if the type is Microsoft.Sql/servers.
    - ▪ Check if the sku.name is in the list of specified SQL SKUs.
    - ▪ Check if the licenseType is not already set to AHUB.
  - ○ **Then**, apply the modifying effect to set the licenseType to Windows_Server for VMs and AHUB for SQL servers. This will check if all Windows VM and SQL Servers are using hybrid license.

This combined policy ensures that both Windows and SQL Server workloads use Azure Hybrid Benefit, optimizing your cloud costs.

Azure Cost Management and Azure Security Center

This security baseline extends guidance from the Microsoft Cloud security benchmark version 1.0 to Cost Management. The Microsoft cloud security benchmark give you ideas for securing Azure cloud solutions. The content is organized by Microsoft Cloud security benchmark security control and Cost Management-related recommendations for security control.

You can also track this security baseline and its recommendations using Microsoft Defender for Cloud. They appear in the Regulatory Compliance section of the Microsoft Defender for Cloud portal page. This helps you quickly evaluate your current compliance stance and respond with any necessary actions to comply with security standards.

Features with related Azure Policy Definitions are present in this baseline to assist you in assessing a given Microsoft cloud security benchmark control or recommendation. These policies offer proactive enforcement of security and governance rules in your Azure environment, ensuring all resources follow best practices and any regulatory requirements. With these policies in place, organizations can automate compliance checks and implementation of organizational standards and notify of deviations swiftly.

Certain security configurations are gated behind paid Microsoft Defender plans by design. Advanced security keeps your cloud environment safe and compliant. You can access several security features, including threat detection, vulnerability management, and proactive threat hunting. These additional security capabilities let you detect and respond to potential threats, thus allowing you to secure your cloud resources.

Compliance and security, as explained earlier, can help with compliance and security benefits and, in doing so, also help with cost savings. You can avoid extra costs and manage resource usage and configurations with policies to ensure that resources are used as they should. For instance, policies can help you pinpoint and clean up unused resources, such as unattached disks or app service plans that end up incurring costs when forgotten.

In addition, deploying these security controls and policies can help enhance your organization's security posture, eliminate the chances of data leaks, and keep your cloud environment compliant with industry standards and regulations:

- **Security profile:**
  - **Highlights**: Key actions of cost management with significant security implications, helping to address potential security concerns effectively.
- **Service behavior attributes:**
  - **Product category**: MGMT/Governance
  - **Customer access to HOST / OS**: No Access
  - **Deployable into customer's virtual network**: FALSE
  - **Stores customer content at rest**: TRUE
- **Network Security (NS-2):**
  - **Aspect**: Disable Public Network Access
  - **Description**: Enhances security by disabling public network access. Supports service-level IP **Access Control List (ACL)** filtering rules or a Disable Public Network Access toggle switch.
  - **Support**: FALSE
  - **Enabled by default**: Not applicable
  - **Configuration responsibility**: Not applicable
  - **Configuration guidance**: This feature is not supported to secure this service.

- **Identity management**:
  - IM-1: Use a centralized identity and authentication system
    - **Aspect**: Azure AD Authentication Required for Data Plane Access
    - **Description**: Supports Azure AD authentication for data plane access.
    - **Support**: TRUE
    - **Enabled by default**: TRUE
    - **Configuration responsibility**: Microsoft
    - **Feature notes**: Integrates with Azure **Active Directory (Azure AD)** and operates within the Azure Portal.
    - **Configuration guidance**: No extra configuration needed, as this feature is enabled by default during deployment.
  - IM-3: Manage application identities securely and automatically
    - **Aspect**: Managed identities
      - **Description**: Supports authentication using managed identities for data plane actions.
      - **Support**: FALSE
      - **Enabled by default**: Not applicable
      - **Configuration responsibility**: Not applicable
      - **Configuration guidance**: This feature is not supported to secure this service.
    - **Aspect:** Service principals
      - **Description**: Supports authentication using service principals for data plane actions.
      - **Support**: TRUE
      - **Enabled by default**: FALSE
      - **Configuration responsibility**: Customer
      - **Feature notes**: To use Azure Cost Management APIs, assign the appropriate permissions to an Azure service principal.
      - **Configuration guidance**: For services not supporting managed identities, use Azure AD to create a service principal with restricted permissions at the resource level. Configure service principals with certificate credentials and use client secrets as a fallback for authentication.

o **IM-7**: Restrict resource access based on conditions

  ▪ **Aspect:** Conditional access for data plane

  ▪ **Description**: Data plane access can be controlled using Azure AD Conditional Access Policies.

  ▪ **Support:** TRUE

  ▪ **Enabled by default**: FALSE

  ▪ **Configuration responsibility**: Customer

  ▪ **Feature notes**: Azure Cost Management is integrated with Azure AD.

  ▪ **Configuration guidance**: Define conditions and criteria for Azure AD conditional access based on workload requirements.

- **Privileged access**:

  o **PA-1**: Separate and limit highly privileged/administrative users

    ▪ **Aspect**: Local admin accounts

    ▪ **Description:** The service has the concept of a local administrative account.

    ▪ **Support**: FALSE

    ▪ **Enabled by default**: Not applicable

    ▪ **Configuration responsibility**: Not applicable

    ▪ **Configuration guidance**: This feature is not supported to secure this service.

  o **PA-7**: Follow just enough administration (least privilege) principle

    ▪ **Aspect**: Azure RBAC for Data Plane

    ▪ **Description: Azure Role-Based Access Control (Azure RBAC)** can manage access to the service's data plane actions.

    ▪ **Support**: TRUE

    ▪ **Enabled by default**: FALSE

    ▪ **Configuration responsibility**: Customer

    ▪ **Configuration guidance**: Use Azure RBAC to manage access to Azure resources through built-in role assignments.

Compliance and regulatory considerations

Meeting regulatory compliance requirements and benchmark standards can pose significant challenges in a cloud or hybrid environment. It can be difficult to determine what assessments are required, assess where they are, and address any gaps. One such mechanism is the Regulatory Compliance dashboard, which **Azure Security Center (ASC)** made available for public preview.

The regulatory compliance dashboard provides visibility into your compliance posture across a set of supported standards and regulations by continuously assessing your Azure environment. These assessments, run by Azure Security Center, check if you meet recommended security baselines to address risk in your hybrid cloud environment. The dashboard is mapped to Compliance Controls from Supported Standards, giving you a centralized view of the compliance of all assessments in your environment at the standard or regulation level.

You will see your compliance posture improve as you act on the recommendations and implement changes that reduce environmental risk factors. The dashboard helps you to evaluate the initial state and remediation guidance for key portions of your compliance status concerning the selected standard (for example, azure-cis, pci-dss-3.2, iso-27001, soc-tsp). The Compliance tab shows an overall compliance score and a breakdown between passing and failing assessments for each standard, helping you to know exactly where you stand so you can center your attention on what is most important.

Here is how the ASC regulatory compliance dashboard can help you better focus on compliance by resolving recommendations from within the dashboard. You can click through each recommendation to explore details, including specifics about the resources to which the recommendation should be applied. This information is very useful for auditing evidence to internal and external auditors about compliance with the supported standards.

The regulatory compliance dashboard streamlines the management and maintenance of compliance. It enhances compliance posture, simplifies compliance tracking across standards and regulations, and helps automate it. Centralizing compliance data and automating assessments helps organizations increase efficiency and accuracy in their compliance activities.

Additionally, the dashboard delivers actionable intelligence that helps to prioritize remediation based on an imported risk rating scoring model. By focusing on this first ordering of risk, the prioritization method also ensures that resources are used wisely to address the most important compliance issues first. It helps organizations monitor the progress of remediation activities and their effectiveness over time.

We are launching a new report builder within the regulatory compliance dashboard so you can build and export reports for easier sharing with your stakeholders. These reports will offer an exceptionally broad overview of compliance status, making them invaluable tools for communicating compliance work and successes to management, auditors, and regulatory centers. In addition, data from the ASC compliance dashboard will get integrated into Compliance Manager, delivering compliance assessments automation from Azure right into the Compliance Manager experience, minimizing manual steps required to seed a compliance report.

The regulatory compliance dashboard preview is part of Azure Security Center's standard pricing tier and comes with a 30-day free trial. This helps organizations analyze the dashboard's functionalities and advantages without spending extra money.

Cloud security and regulatory compliance Microsoft Defender for Cloud has many built-in capabilities with which you can assess your own levels of adherence, manage regulations requirements.

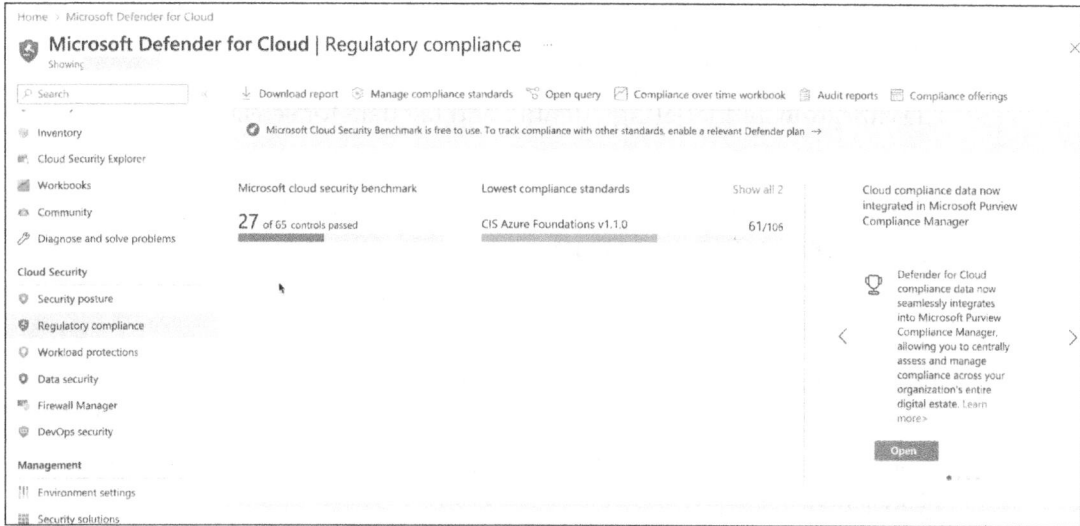

Figure 7.1: Azure Security Regulatory Compliance

Using the Azure Security Center regulatory compliance dashboard, organizations can streamline compliance management, improve their security help status, and ensure they meet industry standards and regulations. Such proactive compliance will not only mitigate risks but also help the operations win more trust from customers and stakeholders, proving that they are serious about a safe and healthy cloud environment.

Data protection and privacy

Azure provides various services and functions developed to fulfill data protection and privacy compliance. These services allow organizations to encrypt their data, stay compliant, and maintain privacy. These are all the high-level Azure service names and features to help you with data protection and privacy:

- **Azure Security Center:**
  - **Threat protection**: Offers modern threat detection and security recommendations.
  - **Compliance**: Helps you meet regulatory compliance requirements with compliance assessments and recommendations on what to do.

- **Azure Key Vault:**
  - **Secrets management**: Securely store and tightly control access to tokens, passwords, certificates, and other secrets
  - **Key management**: The service to manage cryptographic keys for encryption and decryption of data.
  - **Certificate management**: Issued, uploaded, and managed public and private SSL/TLS (Secure Socket Layer and Transport Layer Security) certificates.
- **Azure Information Protection (AIP):**
  - **Classification and labeling**: Identify and tag data for sensitivity.
  - **Encryption**: Encrypt data at rest and in motion.
  - **Rights management**: Limit or restrict how data is used and accessed.
- **Azure Active Directory (Azure AD):**
  - **Identity and access management**: Protect user identity and Reduce risk by providing secure access to your apps and data.
  - **Multi-Factor Authentication (MFA)**: Secure logs in with 2-factor authentications
  - **Conditional access**: Establish standards that permit users to access resources in specific ways.
- **Azure Disk Encryption:**
  - **VM Disk encryption**: Encrypt VM disks Windows and Linux VM disks with BitLocker and DM-Crypt.
  - **Key management**: Integrates with Azure Key Vault for managing encryption keys.
  - **Managed and unmanaged disks**: Supports encryption for both managed and unmanaged disks.
  - **Encryption-in-use**: Provides encryption-in-use capabilities with Azure Confidential Computing.
- **Azure Storage Encryption:**
  - **Encryption at rest**: Automatically encrypt data in Azure Blob Storage, Azure Files, and Azure Queue Storage.
  - **Key options**: Uses Microsoft-managed keys by default, with the option to use customer-managed keys.
  - **Integration with key vault**: Seamlessly integrates with Azure Key Vault for key management.

- o **Performance**: Encrypts both new and existing data without impacting performance.

- o **Role-Based Access Control**: Enables role-based access control (RBAC) for managing permissions for encryption key usage.

- o **Service encryption**: Supports Azure Storage Service Encryption (SSE) for end-to-end data protection.

- **Azure Backup**:

  - o **Data backup**: This offers a secure and reliable backup solution for Azure VMs, SQL databases, and other services.

  - o **Encryption for backups**: Encrypted backups to secure your data.

- **Azure Site Recovery**:

  - o **DR (Disaster Recovery)**: Replicate workloads to a secondary location for recovery from catastrophic disaster.

  - o **Encryption in transit and at rest**: Ensure the replicated data is encrypted both in transit and at rest.

- **Azure Policy**:

  - o **Governance and compliance**: Establish and enforce organizational standards; evaluate compliance at scale.

  - o **Data protection policies**: Implement policies for data protection and compliance.

- **Azure Monitor:**

  - o **Monitoring and alerts**: Watch your resources and create alerts on any suspicious activity or policy violations.

  - o **Log analytics**: An integration with Azure Monitor Logs to enable querying logs for security research and compliance.

  - o **Auditing**: To review logs and search service metadata with user actions.

- **Azure DDoS Protection**:

  - o **DDoS mitigation**: Defend Azure applications against **Distributed Denial of Service (DDoS)** attacks.

  - o **Traffic monitoring**: Continuously monitors traffic patterns to detect and mitigate potential threats in real-time.

  - o **Automatic Attack Mitigation**: Automatically mitigates DDoS attacks without user intervention.

  - o **Protection Plans**: Offers Basic and Standard protection plans to meet different security needs.

- **Azure Sentinel**:
  - **Security Information and Event Management (SIEM)**: Collect, detect, research, and respond to threats across the enterprise.
  - **Threat intelligence**: With the help of inbuilt AI analytics, process massive data for advanced detection of threats.
- **Azure Confidential Computing**
  - **Data in-use protection**: Safeguard data during processing in the cloud using hardware-based **trusted execution environments** (TEEs) to isolate computations.
- **Azure Private Link**:
  - **Private connectivity**: Connect privately to Azure services.
- **Azure Data Loss Prevention (DLP)**
  - **DLP policies**: Establish and apply policies to deter sensitive data's unauthorized or unauthorized transmission.
- **Azure GDPR Compliance**:
  - **GDPR readiness**: Tools and services to support compliance with SPF requirements.
  - **Data subject requests**: Tools to handle and address data subject requests

Together, these services and features help organizations secure data, protect privacy, and maintain regulatory compliance when using Azure cloud services. By using multiple of these services, you can build a compliance-level presentation tailored to your specific needs and be highly effective in protecting data and privacy.

Conclusion

Continuous compliance is a critical aspect of cloud management because, in the rapidly changing, ever-more complex world of the cloud, compliance ensures that the company avoids non-compliant risks, maintains financial responsibility, controls costs, and reaps the benefits of maintaining data privacy and security. Security & compliance: Azure offers various security and compliance tools and services like Azure Policy and Cost Management to create and enforce rules that ensure resources are used efficiently. Using these tools, administrators can create, assign, and manage policies that reflect organizational standards, evaluate compliance at scale, and help ensure resources are used efficiently, and costs are controlled.

A naming convention is one of the most critical aspects of Cost governance. It is crucial for labeling, organizing, and managing resources, giving the facility to track usage and spending. This transparency informs how the cloud is being utilized and where optimizations can be found. For example, isolating resources used for development and testing from production can help avoid over-provisioning and unnecessary costs.

Using **Locally Redundant Storage (LRS)** instead of more costly redundancy options in non-production environments is an easy win to decrease overall costs without sacrificing data availability and durability. Using policies, you can have an LRS for well-known workloads and an LRS for non-critical workloads that use local redundant storage, making the cost a good setup.

Another important Oracle audit cost optimization aspect is the audit for orphaned resources. Knowing and removing things you are no longer using will allow you to keep a cloud environment tidy and cost-effective. This practice saves money and improves security and compliance by eliminating possible attack vectors.

Utilizing AHUB allows organizations to apply their existing on-premises Windows Server and SQL Server licenses to Azure, leading to significant savings. Policies will ensure AHUB is being used correctly; this is key to improvements, provides incentives, and optimizes cloud costs.

This also enhances security and compliance by integrating Azure Cost Management with Azure AD, allowing you to configure conditional access policies. Azure RBAC provides you with the appropriate access level to resources you need to manage while securing your environment against unauthorized actions.

The regulatory compliance dashboard offers a fast track to monitoring posture and assisting in remediating compliance. The dashboard helps you manage compliance through real-time assessment of the environment against supported standards with actionable insights, thereby reducing compliance management efforts, improving security, and ensuring compliance with industry regulations.

Briefly, using Azure's comprehensive suite of products for governance, cost management, and compliance lowers costs while improving security and regulatory compliance. By following these best practices, you should create a secure, compliant, and economical cloud that will build trust with your customers and stakeholders while helping you be more efficient.

In the next chapter, the readers will be introduced to Infrastructure as Code (IaC), a method for provisioning infrastructure that allows them to manage resources in less time and at reduced costs. This chapter will also include Azure Functions and Automation which can be used with these technologies to automate your daily requirements, thereby improving operational efficiencies.

Readers will also learn the advantages of serverless computing and how it can help to save cost by using them when you need. By the end of this chapter, the readers will learn how to combine Azure DevOps with FinOps processes and demonstrate through that marriage it is possible to optimize financial management and operational workflows resulting in more efficient cloud operations at a lower cost.

Join our book's Discord space

Join the book's Discord Workspace for Latest updates, Offers, Tech happenings around the world, New Release and Sessions with the Authors:

https://discord.bpbonline.com

CHAPTER 8
Advanced Azure FinOps Techniques

Introduction

Advanced Azure FinOps techniques are a step forward in cloud technology and finance operations. It is not just about reducing costs but understanding how investments and cloud resource utilization are connected. This helps organizations manage costs strategically and efficiently. Azure's suite of analytics and cost-management tools provides insights into resource usage, enabling organizations to move towards an operational expenditure model with more agility and foresight. This is important for businesses that want to align their spending with earnings.

Advanced Azure FinOps is about cutting costs and maximizing the return on cloud investments. It encourages a proactive culture where finance and IT teams work together to optimize costs rather than just reacting to cost-cutting needs. With Azure's advanced analytical tools, teams can forecast spending trends, scrutinize cloud services' ROI (Return on Investment), and implement governance policies that preempt cost overruns.

Infrastructure as Code (IaC) further improves cost efficiency by allowing the design of repeatable and automated processes for infrastructure provisioning. It is about applying software development principles to infrastructure management, leading to a more economically efficient lifecycle for cloud resources.

Azure Functions are an example of the financial agility offered by cloud computing. They encapsulate complex applications into simple, single-purpose functions, allowing organizations to build highly responsive systems that can quickly adjust to changing market dynamics without the burden of inactive capacity.

Serverless cost optimization leverages the scalability and elasticity of the cloud, where costs are directly linked to consumption. This helps organizations achieve operational excellence and financial efficiency.

The fusion of Azure DevOps with FinOps is about embedding cost considerations into the software development process. It allows teams to iterate faster while maintaining a clear view of financial impact, fostering a culture of accountability where cost is an integral part of operational metrics.

Advanced Azure FinOps techniques are vital for sustainable growth (GreenOps) in today's cloud-centric IT landscape. They equip organizations with the tools to make data-driven decisions that balance technological and financial strategies, ensuring they remain grounded in economic reality. This balanced approach is the essence of modern cloud financial management and the cornerstone of a resilient, forward-looking enterprise.

Structure

In this chapter, we will go through the following topics:

- Infrastructure as Code for Cost Efficiency
- Azure Functions and Automation
- Serverless helps reduce costs in Azure
- Azure DevOps and FinOps Integration

Objectives

By the end of this chapter, readers will be presented with the enterprise-level view where advanced Azure FinOps features add more power to IT and finance. Both may become partners for life rather than just being cost-reduction outfits. Through Azure analytics and cost-management tools, they will learn how to manage cloud costs better, always spending in conjunction with business earnings, while any spending is being aligned towards creating a more proactive financial efficiency culture. The chapter also covers the principles of IaC that will help you in abstracting away and automating the lifecycle management of cloud resources. Finally, learn about serverless computing with Azure Functions and how to use it so you never have costs spike out of control. This highlights how Microsoft brings Azure DevOps and FinOps together, demonstrating how to bake cost-aware development into the **software development lifecycle (SDLC)**, improving velocity, responsibility, and financial visibility. Finally, in the second part of this chapter, we looked at how to architect your solution for scale efficiently (planet-scale), which is essential if you want to develop a new generation and more resilient financial enterprise powered by cloud-native technologies.

Infrastructure as Code for cost efficiency

In simple terms, IaC is a new way of placing up and managing IT infrastructure. Traditionally, this was accomplished manually, making it prone to errors and inconsistencies. IaC changes this by using a coding language to automate infrastructure setup. This depends on managing infrastructure in a coding task, making things much more efficient.

The figure below highlights the key benefits of adopting IaC in modern cloud environments. These advantages illustrate how IaC facilitates efficient, scalable, and secure IT infrastructure management, driving operational excellence and supporting organizational goals.

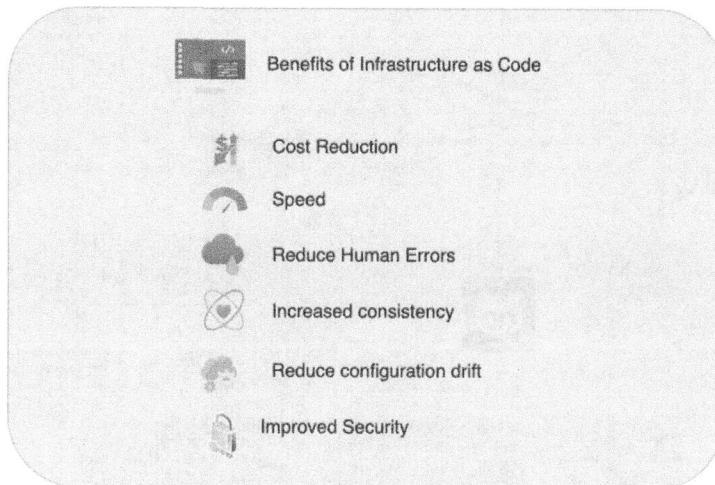

Benefits of Infrastructure as Code

Cost Reduction

Speed

Reduce Human Errors

Increased consistency

Reduce configuration drift

Improved Security

Figure 8.1: Benefits of IaC

Automated provisioning

Automated provisioning, made feasible by IaC, enables the setup of IT environments by automating the process. It reduces the time and labor needed to provision resources, resulting in significant cost savings. It is like a manufacturing group line for IT environments, ensuring that each deployment is consistent and predictable, minimizing the risks of human error and configuration issues. With IaC, businesses can deploy entire environments quickly and accurately, freeing IT staff to focus on more strategic tasks that add value to the business.

In addition to reducing labor costs, Automated Provisioning through IaC allows companies to respond more quickly to market demands. It speeds up the time-to-market for products by allowing for quick setup and tear-down of environments, which allows for better alignment of resources with project schedules and business opportunities. This responsiveness is not just about faster deployment; it is about the infrastructure's ability to adjust without incurring unnecessary overheads.

The following diagram shows the IaC workflow, which allows developers to code infrastructure configurations. This code is stored in version control, tested, and pushed/ pulled to an automation app or server, where the jobs deploy infrastructure across cloud or on-prem environments. The way we did it here describes how IaC can automate and make mandatory and efficient infrastructure management.

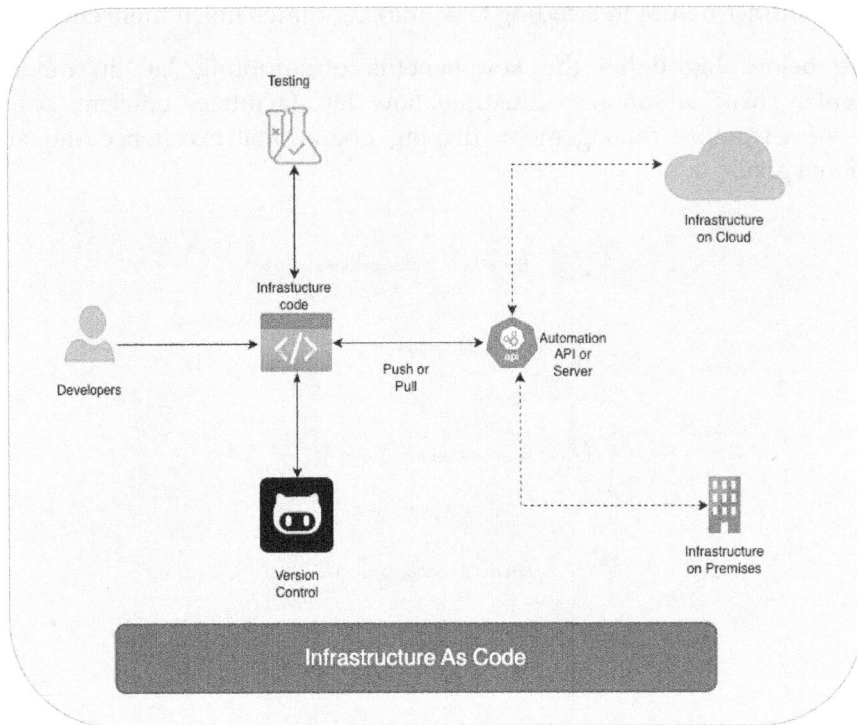

Figure 8.2: Automated Provisioning using IaC

Moreover, IaC optimizes resource allocation by dynamically adjusting to usage patterns and operational data. This suggests businesses can scale their infrastructure up or down based on real-time demands, ensuring efficient resource use and eliminating wasteful spending. Continuous integration and delivery pipelines help from this automation, allowing for the seamless introduction of changes and the maintenance of high-quality standards in production environments.

Automated Provisioning is the process of managing cloud resources that strengthen IaC, reduce costs, and improve operational agility and reliability. It's an investment in technology that delivers short—and long-term benefits by creating an infrastructure as active and scalable as the cloud.

Resource standardization and efficiency

Resource standardization and efficiency are IaC components that provide significant cost benefits and operational reliability. In IaC, businesses encode their infrastructure blueprints into version-controlled scripts or templates, ensuring a uniform setup across all environments. This uniformity is vital to reducing unique configurations that require special handling and can inflate operational costs.

Standardization mitigates the risk of environment drift, where slight differences between environments can lead to significant issues during deployment, often necessitating costly and time-consuming emergency fixes. IaC ensures that what is tested in development or staging will behave the same way in production, thus safeguarding against expensive downtime and the expenses associated with it by defining a single source of truth for infrastructure configurations.

Resource efficiency is enhanced as standardized environments are more accessible to monitor and optimize. Performance bottlenecks and over-provisioned resources become more apparent, enabling precise tuning and scaling. IaC is also about making more intelligent decisions regarding resource allocation, such as knowing when to opt for reserved instances versus on-demand instances or when to use burstable cases, which can lead to substantial cost savings.

Developers can also benefit from IaC as it promotes better time utilization. Standardized environments mean developers spend less time troubleshooting environment-specific issues and more time delivering value-added features. Additionally, the overhead costs associated with training new team members are reduced as they encounter a consistent infrastructure setup, irrespective of the project or environment they work on.

Codifying infrastructure also streamlines compliance and governance processes, as the templates used can include necessary regulatory controls, ensuring compliance is baked into every environment. This can prevent costly legal and reputational repercussions associated with non-compliance.

Overall, IaC is an approach that favors the bottom line and reinforces best practices in software deployment, resource management, and organizational efficiency. By treating infrastructure as a repeatable and consistent commodity rather than a bespoke creation, IaC aids in crafting a resilient, predictable, and cost-effective operational model.

Rapid scalability

IaC helps companies change their computer systems quickly and smartly to match their workload. Think of it like a water tap for your computer resources: turn it up when you need more power because things are busy, or turn it down and save money when things are quiet. This way, companies only pay for the computer power they use.

IaC automates this process, optimizing cloud costs and aligning resource consumption with actual needs rather than static predictions. During peak periods, infrastructure can expand to maintain performance levels without manual intervention, while during low utilization periods, scaling down occurs automatically, trimming costs without any loss of availability.

IaC's predictive capabilities allow it to anticipate scaling events before they happen, avoiding financial impacts such as lost sales or diminished user experience. This approach fosters innovation and experimentation, enabling development teams to trial new features or services at scale without the risk of prohibitive costs.

In summary, IaC's rapid scalability ensures that infrastructure perfectly fits a business's needs at any moment, providing a seamless, cost-effective scale supporting business objectives.

Version control and documentation

IaC collects details about your infrastructure, such as server configurations, networks, and databases. It is like managing software code changes. By keeping these configurations in version control systems, teams can track every change made, who made it, and why. This record-keeping is known as an **audit trail**.

The real power of using version control with IaC is when something goes wrong. If an update or configuration causes issues, the audit trail can help teams quickly identify the cause. This means that teams can understand what went wrong and why, making it easier to fix issues. If a change causes significant problems, teams can revert their infrastructure to a previous state that worked well, all with just a few commands.

This capability to quickly revert changes significantly reduces downtime and the associated costs. Instead of scrambling to undo changes or troubleshooting manually under pressure, teams can roll back to a stable state while figuring out a solution. This ensures that services remain available and reliable, crucial for maintaining customer trust and satisfaction.

In summary, by using IaC and storing infrastructure specifications in version control systems, organizations can efficiently track changes, solve problems quickly, and maintain stability in their IT environments. This approach minimizes downtime and enhances the overall agility and resilience of the infrastructure management processes.

Elimination of configuration drift

Picture having a recipe to make a cake, but every time someone makes it, they make small changes, like adding more sugar or baking it longer. Over time, the recipe varies so much that it is not even the exact cake anymore, and sometimes it depends poorly.

In the IT world, when we manage our computer systems manually, small changes often occur, just like tweaking the cake recipe. These changes can make our systems unstable or cause errors because they are no longer set up as originally intended. We call this **configuration drift**.

To bypass this problem, we use IaC. It is like owning an original cake recipe that everyone must follow strictly, no matter how many times they make it. With IaC, we note the instructions for setting up and keeping our computer systems in code. Every time we must set up a new system or make changes, we use that code, which ensures everything is done consistently. This makes our systems more reliable and reduces the need to fix unexpected problems caused by configuration drift.

By using IaC, teams can be sure that their IT environments are set up precisely as they should be every single time, which saves a lot of time and hassle in troubleshooting and maintenance.

Predictable and transparent costs

IaC is a way to manage computer resources using software code. It has excellent benefits, such as driving costs predictable and transparent. When paired with monitoring and analytics tools, IaC can deliver real-time data about how resources are utilized and where money is going. This helps businesses avoid overspending and wasting resources.

IaC shows businesses more useful control over their resources and lets them give them more efficiently. This helps them budget ideally and saves them money in the long run. Financial leaders and IT departments can perform jointly more effectively because they access the same information, leading to more informed decision-making.

By integrating IaC with business intelligence tools, businesses can make more accurate and timely reports. This can help stakeholders understand how IT investments impact the bottom line. Overall, integrating IaC with advanced monitoring and analytics transforms cost management in IT from a reactive to a proactive discipline. It helps businesses cut down on undeserved spending and encourages a culture of continuous improvement and fiscal responsibility.

Improved compliance and security

There are some essential advantages to remember regarding IaC. One of the most significant advantages is that IaC can improve compliance and security. Using code to turn rules into automated methods, IaC ensures that every part of your computer system is up to standards. This indicates there is minor room for human error, and you can be sure that your systems follow all the necessary laws and guidelines.

IaC can also support preventing problems before they happen. For example, suppose your organization has a detailed data protection rule that must be followed. In that case, IaC can automatically set up the necessary security measures whenever a system is deployed. This means you will likely face penalties for non-compliance because your system is prepared to comply with the rules immediately.

In addition, IaC documents every detail of the infrastructure setup in code, making it easier to audit and ensure compliance. Auditors can quickly review the design history to ensure every change aligns with compliance requirements. This level of transparency facilitates the audit process and helps improve security by making it easier to track and remedy any deviations quickly.

Ultimately, IaC can help keep your systems safe and secure, reduce the risk of costly non-compliance issues, and ensure that your business operates smoothly and legally.

Enhanced disaster recovery

Enhanced disaster recovery is another essential IaC benefit. When a disaster happens, whether a system crash, a security breach, or a natural catastrophe, IaC can help get things back to normal faster. Since all the infrastructure setup is saved as code, you can quickly rebuild your systems precisely as before using these predefined templates. This rapid redeployment can drastically reduce the time your systems are down, reducing the financial hit your business takes from being offline.

The ability to bounce back quickly is crucial. You could lose sales, productivity, and customer trust every minute your systems are down. With IaC, you are not starting from scratch to restore your services; you are just executing a script that automatically reconstructs your infrastructure. This speeds up recovery and eliminates the errors that can happen when things are done manually under the stress of a crisis.

Moreover, quick and reliable disaster recovery can also help with costs in the long run. Insurance premiums, for example, can be lower if you demonstrate that your business has adequate risk management strategies like rapid disaster recovery. This is because there is less risk of prolonged downtime or data loss, which are expensive to rectify and can lead to higher claims.

Using IaC secures your infrastructure more robustly. It ensures you can recover swiftly and cost-effectively from disruptions, keeping your business resilient and financially protected in the face of unexpected challenges.

Example of using Infrastructure as Code

Terraform is a popular tool that implements the principles of IaC. It uses a high-level configuration language called **HashiCorp Configuration Language (HCL)** to describe the desired state of infrastructure resources such as virtual machines, storage accounts, and networking interfaces. Terraform then generates a plan to achieve the desired state and executes the plan to build the infrastructure. This approach ensures consistency and repeatability across deployments.

Scaling resources based on demand

Implement IaC scripts that adjust the scale of resources automatically based on usage metrics. For example, you can scale down Azure VMs or Azure Function instances during off-peak hours to reduce costs, and scale them up during peak times to meet demand without manual intervention.

The following are the prerequisites:

- Terraform installed on your local machine.
- An Azure subscription.
- Azure CLI installed and configured with your account.

Terraform Script to Automate Scaling:

1. Define the provider:

```
provider "azurerm" {
  features {}
}
```

2. Define the resource group:

```
resource "azurerm_resource_group" "example" {
  name     = "autoscale-resources"
  location = "East US"
}
```

3. Create a virtual network and a subnet:

```
resource "azurerm_virtual_network" "example" {
  name                = "example-vnet"
  address_space       = ["10.0.0.0/16"]
  location            = azurerm_resource_group.example.location
  resource_group_name = azurerm_resource_group.example.name
}


resource "azurerm_subnet" "example" {
  name                 = "example-subnet"
  resource_group_name  = azurerm_resource_group.example.name
  virtual_network_name = azurerm_virtual_network.example.name
  address_prefixes     = ["10.0.2.0/24"]
}
```

4. Create a scale set:

```
resource "azurerm_linux_virtual_machine_scale_set" "example" {
  name                = "example-scaleset"
  location            = azurerm_resource_group.example.location
  resource_group_name = azurerm_resource_group.example.name
  sku                 = "Standard_F2"
  instances           = 1
  admin_username      = "adminuser"

  admin_ssh_key {
    username   = "adminuser"
    public_key = file("~/.ssh/id_rsa.pub")
  }

  source_image_reference {
    publisher = "Canonical"
    offer     = "UbuntuServer"
    sku       = "18.04-LTS"
    version   = "latest"
  }

  os_disk {
    caching              = "ReadWrite"
    storage_account_type = "Standard_LRS"
  }

  network_interface {
    name    = "example-nic"
    primary = true

    ip_configuration {
      name        = "internal"
```

```
        subnet_id = azurerm_subnet.example.id
        primary   = true
      }
    }


    upgrade_mode = "Manual"
  }
```

5. Define auto-scale settings:

```
resource "azurerm_monitor_autoscale_setting" "example" {
  name                = "example-autoscale"
  resource_group_name = azurerm_resource_group.example.name
  location            = azurerm_resource_group.example.location
  target_resource_id  = azurerm_linux_virtual_machine_scale_set.
    example.id

  profile {
    name = "defaultProfile"

    capacity {
      default = 1
      minimum = 1
      maximum = 10
    }

    rule {
      metric_trigger {
        time_window = "PT5M"
        metric_name        = "Percentage CPU"
        metric_resource_id = azurerm_linux_virtual_machine_scale_
        set.example.id
        time_grain         = "PT1M"
        statistic          = "Average"
        time_aggregation   = "Average"
```

```
      operator           = "GreaterThan"
      threshold          = 75
    }

  scale_action {
    direction = "Increase"
    type      = "ChangeCount"
    value     = "1"
    cooldown  = "PT1M"
  }
}

rule {
  metric_trigger {
    time_window = "PT5M"
    metric_name         = "Percentage CPU"
    metric_resource_id = azurerm_linux_virtual_machine_scale_
    set.example.id
    time_grain          = "PT1M"
    statistic           = "Average"
    time_aggregation    = "Average"
    operator            = "LessThan"
    threshold           = 25
  }

  scale_action {
    direction = "Decrease"
    type      = "ChangeCount"
    value     = "1"
    cooldown  = "PT1M"
  }
}
```

```
        }
    }
```

The following is the explanation of the above codes:

- This script sets up a virtual machine scale set and defines auto-scale settings based on CPU usage.
- The scale set will increase by one instance if the average CPU percentage exceeds 75% over a minute, and decrease by one if it falls below 25%.
- The minimum number of instances is set to 1, and the maximum is set to 10.

The following are the steps for deploying the code:

1. Run **terraform init** to initialize Terraform.
2. Validate the configuration with **terraform validate**.
3. Preview the changes with **terraform plan**.
4. Apply the configuration with **terraform apply**.
5. This setup ensures that your Azure resources scale dynamically based on demand, optimizing performance and cost.

Azure Functions and automation

Azure Functions is an intelligent assistant that takes care of all the complex task so you can focus on creating apps. It's a service that stays in the cloud, which means you can build your app without worrying about the servers running in the background. This is great because your apps can automatically adjust to more users without skipping a best and work fast.

So, if you want to get your app built and out there without getting bogged down in tech details, you should check out Azure Functions. It is all about making app development and letting you focus on creating Apps development.

Basic understanding of Azure Function

Azure Functions is a resource type provided by Azure that lets you run code without worrying about the infrastructure it runs on. It is ideal for tasks that need to run because of certain events and is built to handle those jobs quickly.

It's essential to think about what you need your code to do. Consider how often it will run, how quickly it reacts, and whether it needs to scale up when many people use it simultaneously. Answering these questions can help determine if Azure Functions fits your project like a glove.

Here is what makes Azure Functions special:

- **Triggers** your code like web page requests, scheduled times, or new messages in a queue can all start the action.

- **Bindings** connect your code to other services without a fuss, so it can easily use data from or send data to different places when it runs.

- **Resource limits** control the computing power and frequency with which functions can run, ensuring they do not run wildly.

Azure Functions supports a wide range of programming languages, so you can start building functions immediately if you are into .NET, Java, JavaScript, Python, C#, PowerShell, or others. With Microsoft's Function Composition, you can mix and match different bits of code from various languages in one project.

It is like having a multi-language conversation where everyone understands each other perfectly, allowing more complicated tasks to be done more efficiently. Azure Functions has security features, support for storing logs and data, and the ability to integrate with other Microsoft services.

Azure Functions is a feature for modern, cloud-based apps. It gives you tools to keep an eye on how your app is being used, to work with data smoothly, and to use AI and machine learning without needing to be tech.

Benefits of Azure Functions in cloud computing

Azure Functions occurs as a cost-efficient and user-friendly choice in cloud computing. This Azure service simplifies the deployment process, allowing code to be launched across various regions quickly, regardless of whether it is a single instance or multiple instances. The functions are designed to be responsive, activate upon specific events or schedules, and are capable of operating in both synchronous and asynchronous modes. This flexibility means you can mount your processes up or down to suit the fluctuating needs of your business without the commitment of infrastructure management.

Azure Functions stands out for its hassle-free approach to application management. Developers are limited by the complexities of setting up and maintaining operating systems. Instead, they can direct their effort toward their work and develop the coding. Azure Functions is further highlighted by its support for a suite of triggers, including message queues, blob storage, and event grids, all available right out of the box.

However, the benefits continue beyond that. Azure Functions is planned to be time-efficient, cutting down the groundwork required for service setup and thus simplifying application architecture.

Moreover, Azure Functions seamlessly integrates with widely used development frameworks such as Node.js and .NET Core, enabling developers to apply familiar tools and languages to create complex applications much more than traditional methods would allow.

The appeal of Azure Functions lies in its simplification of the developmental process, its robust feature set that caters to modern application requirements, and its ability to reduce operational complexities and costs. It represents an optimal solution for businesses searching for powerful yet economical ways to deploy and manage their applications, all while keeping developer workload to a minimum.

Cost effectiveness for the Azure Functions

For enterprises looking to maximize value while capitalizing on cloud service offerings, Azure Functions presents an excellent choice. It is a platform tailor-made for diverse tasks ranging from web app development to orchestrating machine learning workflows, all within a serverless environment. This means you can access just the right amount of computing resources without a full-scale server infrastructure overhead, often translating to substantial cost savings.

Azure Functions simplifies operations, eliminating the intricacies of managing physical servers. You're billed precisely for the resources your applications consume, sidestepping the costs associated with idle capacity. This pay-as-you-go model is inherently budget-friendly, aligning operational expenditure with actual usage.

The service also excels in scalability. It automatically adjusts resources to your application's demands, ensuring seamless performance during traffic surges or heavy processing loads. This adaptability ensures that services are readily available to meet customer needs at any moment, providing a buffer against unpredictable workloads.

Integration is another area where Azure Functions shines. It works harmoniously with existing Azure services, enabling you to connect to storage solutions, databases, and more with minimal setup. Built-in management features for tasks like logging and API management contribute to cost efficiency, reducing the need for additional solutions.

Additionally, Azure Functions supports a wide array of programming languages, including popular ones like JavaScript, C#, Python, Java, PHP, and PowerShell. This allows teams to leverage their existing skills and tools, avoiding unnecessary spending on new technology stacks or specialized expertise.

Different architecture for Azure Function App

In this section, we will learn about different architecture for Azure Function App:

Azure Functions in a Hybrid Environment

This reference architecture explores organizations with branches spread across various locations. Each branch is enabled with the Azure Function App, set up with the Premium plan, and selected to ensure the cloud region is near the branch. This strategic setup promises enhanced performance and reduced latency. Developers managing this architecture employ Azure Monitor as a centralized observation platform—a single pane of glass—to oversee the performance and health of all Azure Function Apps deployed across the organization's network.

The following diagram shows the architecture of Azure Functions Hybrid Environment. This shows how premium function apps are spread over several regions available in Azure (East US, West US, and Central US). The diagram also explains that these function apps are integrated with on-premises branches in many locations using a VPN link and how it works as a hybrid cloud. It also underscores Azure Monitor to monitor the performance and health of function apps and configuration for local development environments for faster deployment and operation.

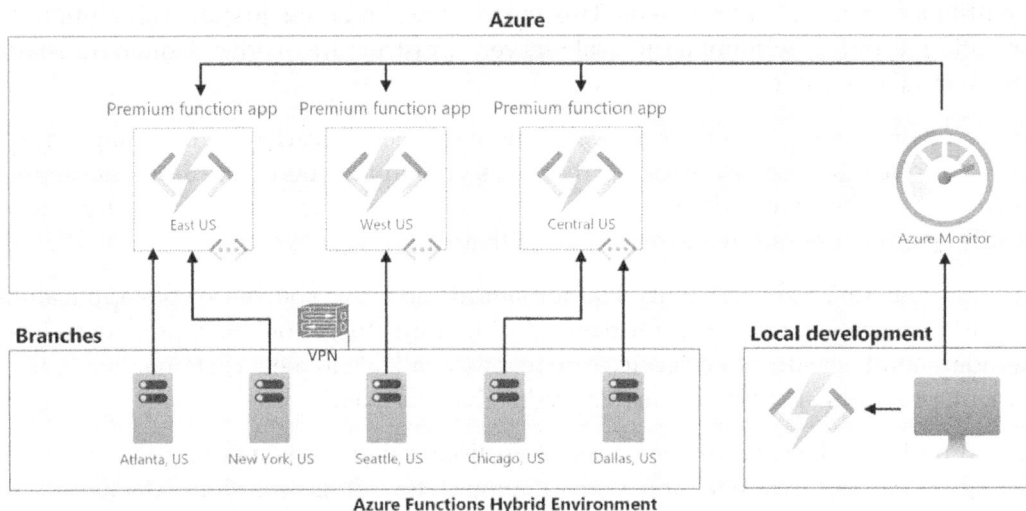

Figure 8.3: Azure Function App in Hybrid Environment

The following is the scenario about the flow. This architecture is beneficial for:

- **Multiple physical location organizations**: Architecture helps for using a network from Azure itself to communicate effectively with the animated Function in Azure. This architecture allows for an unbroken operation between sites around the globe.

- **Workloads under rapid growth**: This architecture helps these workloads because they can use Azure Functions locally and, simultaneously, scale up easily by simply changing to leverage on running in full bloom with local execution (or any cloud version of this) when high demand binds happen. This allows it to absorb peaks of work without negatively affecting the performance.

Components

This architecture includes several key components:

- **Azure functions**: Azure is a serverless platform provided by Azure that allows small, single-task pieces of code to run without the need to set up new infrastructure. The Premium plan of Azure Functions offers enhanced features, such as connecting to Azure Functions privately through a virtual network.

- **Azure Virtual Network**: These are private networks established within the Azure cloud platform, enabling Azure resources to communicate securely with each other. The networks are designed to ensure that Azure resources can only communicate through a secure virtual network backbone, enhancing security and connectivity.

- **On-premises network**: In this setup, the organization has developed a secure private network that links its various branches. This network is connected to the Azure virtual networks via a site-to-site connection, creating a seamless bridge between on-premise resources and cloud services.

- **Developer workstations:** Developers can work on the Azure Functions code either from within the secure private network or remotely. Regardless of their location, they have access to Azure Monitor, which allows them to track, query, and review metrics and logs associated with the function apps. This flexibility ensures that developers can maintain productivity and oversight wherever they are.

Event-based cloud automation

Using serverless technologies to automate workflows and repetitive tasks in the cloud can significantly boost the productivity of an organization's DevOps team. The serverless model is particularly effective for automation scenarios that rely on an event-driven approach, making it ideal for tasks that need to respond automatically to specific triggers or changes.

The image below shows the structure of the Event-Based Cloud Automation system on Azure. This demonstrates how the flow works from an event being triggered (that is, resource change or monitor alert) to the Event Grid. Then through an automation process using Logic Apps and Function Apps, ISPs can interact with a wide range of Azure services - such as Azure AD, or new and existing managed templates in the ITSM toolchain, connectivity to VPN management service; automation-based actions on various events from Slack notifications based issue/risk/consumption data. This architecture showcases how Azure can provide an ever-responsive cloud operation by Auto responding to events in the most automated, efficient way.

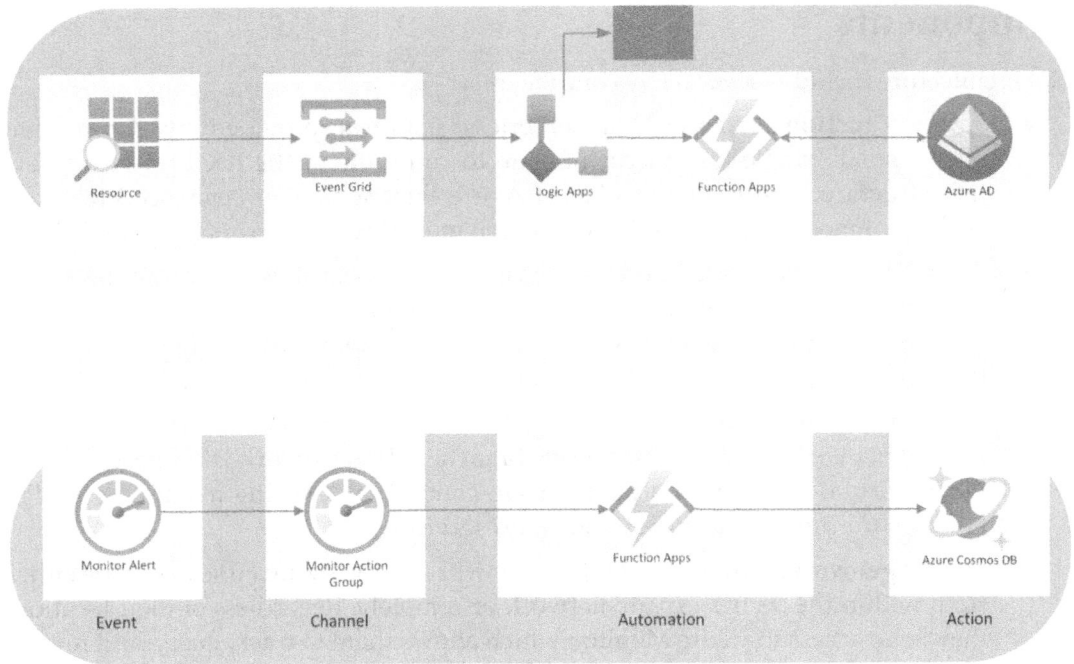

Figure 8.4: Event-based cloud automation

The following are the scenarios:

Cost center tagging is a method used to track the financial responsibility of each Azure resource. Here is how it works:

- **Azure Policy—Automatic tagging**: This service ensures that the name of a cost center ID tag is assigned to every resource created in any resource group and that it remains inactive using Azure policy. To make this happen, every resource will initially be tagged with the financial identifier when it is created, guaranteeing cost tracking from day 0.

- **Event Monitoring with AzureEventGrid**: Once the resources are added, we can set up our Azure event grid to monitor these creation events. This will, in turn, trigger an Azure function when a new resource is detected. This function validates the assigned cost center ID by connecting Microsoft Entra ID (old Azure Active Directory).

- **Properties Compliance**: If the Azure function detects a mismatch between the assigned cost center ID and the actual one as per Microsoft Entra ID, it will update the resource tags with the correct Cost Center ID. In addition, the function sends an email notification to a resource owner (**anonymous @ system**) informing them that some changes occurred; thus, manipulating cost-tracking data is not transparent, nor does it correspond with actuality.

- **Simplified simulated interactions**: The document states that the interactions with Microsoft Entra ID are simplified and not real life. So, in this case, the verification is not integrated completely at the synthesis level but emulated. These would all be seamlessly combined in a production environment using the Microsoft Graph PowerShell module or MSAL for Python. These tools would allow capabilities for any newly created Azure resource to be linked with Microsoft's matching Entra ID and billed without manual intervention.

A must-have for orgs that need to cost and track their spend through different departments or projects, making sure some financial discipline remains in the cloud estate.

Components

The architecture is built around several key components that work together to automate tasks in a cloud environment:

- **Azure functions**: These are the core of this architecture's event-driven, serverless computing capabilities. Functions are designed to execute automation tasks when specific events or alerts are triggered. For instance, in certain scenarios, a function might be activated by an HTTP request. To keep things efficient, each function is developed to be stateless and idempotent, meaning that no matter how many times you run the function, it will produce the same outcome. When scaling functions, especially under load (throttling scenarios), it is crucial to maintain simplicity to preserve this idempotency. For best practices in optimizing the performance and reliability of Azure Functions, it is recommended to consult specific Azure documentation.

- **Azure logic apps**: These are utilized for simpler, often routine tasks that can be automated using built-in connectors, such as sending email notifications or integrating with external management applications. Logic Apps offer a no-code or low-code visual designer, making them suitable for use in automation scenarios that do not require complex programming. For guidance on integrating Logic Apps with third-party applications, refer to Azure's basic enterprise integration materials. Comparing Azure Functions and Logic Apps will help determine which service fits a particular automation need.

- **Event grid**: Azure Event Grid supports events from Azure services and custom events. It facilitates the propagation of operational events, like resource creation, to the necessary automation function via a built-in mechanism. With its publish-subscribe model, Event Grid simplifies the automation of event handling, ensuring reliable event delivery over HTTPS.

- **Azure Monitor**: This service is crucial for monitoring critical conditions within the infrastructure. Azure Monitor's alerts and action groups can automatically trigger corrective actions in Azure Functions. This integration is particularly useful for addressing and resolving error conditions, such as database throttling.

- **Automation action**: This component represents the various services the function might interact with to execute its automation tasks. Depending on the scenario, it might involve Microsoft Entra ID for tag validation or a database service for resource provisioning.

Together, these components form a robust framework for automating and managing tasks in a cloud environment, streamlining operations, and ensuring efficient function execution across a distributed architecture.

Serverless Cost Optimization

Serverless technology, such as Azure Functions, provides several ways to help users reduce costs in Azure, primarily by optimizing resource usage and eliminating the need for manual scaling and infrastructure management. Here is how serverless technology achieves cost-efficiency:

- **Pay-only-for-what-you-use pricing model**: Serverless computing helps save money by removing the need to pay for servers that run constantly. You only pay for the server when your applications are using it. In the serverless model, you are billed for your functions' computing resources when running. If there is no code execution, there are no charges. This billing method can lead to substantial savings, especially compared to conventional cloud services, where you must pay for servers even if they are not actively utilized.

  This model is particularly advantageous for applications with fluctuating demand. For instance, if you have an app that only needs to run intensive computations at certain times of the day or in response to specific events, serverless computing ensures you are not wasting money on computing power that sits idle the rest of the time. It is like having electricity that you only pay for when you switch the lights on, which makes it an incredibly efficient way to manage and reduce costs in a cloud environment.

- **Automatic scaling**: Serverless technology is a type of cloud computing that automatically adjusts the computing resources your applications use based on their actual use. For example, Azure Functions is a serverless platform that can intelligently provide more computing power during high load times. Then, when things calm down, it will scale back the resources it is using to save you money. It also contributes to a better user experience. Regardless of the load, your applications remain responsive and performant without any lag that might prevent users. This reliability is important for maintaining user satisfaction and trust, particularly for services that handle varying levels of user interaction. The automatic scaling feature of serverless platforms like Azure Functions helps remove risks associated with under or over-provisioning resources. Under-provisioning can lead to low performance and downtime while over-provisioning wastes resources. By automating this process, Azure Functions allows your IT team to focus on innovation and improving application features rather than managing infrastructure.

- **Reduced operational overhead**: Serverless computing changes the way organizations manage their IT infrastructure. By removing responsibilities such as server provisioning, patching, and ongoing maintenance to the cloud provider, serverless platforms remove the burden of day-to-day IT tasks. This shift away from hands-on infrastructure management means that your IT staff can commit their time and expertise to more strategic initiatives that directly contribute to business goals, such as developing new features, enhancing security, or improving system efficiencies.

Workflow offered by serverless computing also accelerates development cycles. Developers can push updates and improvements quickly. This agility enables businesses to respond to market changes and customer needs, maintaining a competitive edge.

Serverless computing minimizes the risk of human error associated with manual server management. Automated processes are less to mistakes than manual interventions, which improves overall system reliability and security.

- **Improved resource utilization**: Serverless functions operate event-driven, springing into action only when needed due to specific triggers or events. This approach ensures that computing resources are not wastefully idling, which sharpens resource utilization efficiency. You only consume and pay for resources when your functions process tasks actively. This is especially advantageous for applications that do not have constant traffic but experience occasional bursts of activity.

For instance, an e-commerce website might only need significant computing power during special promotions or seasonal sales peaks while maintaining moderate traffic the rest of the time. Serverless computing caters perfectly to such scenarios by dynamically allocating resources during high-traffic periods and scaling down during quieter times, ensuring that each resource unit is used effectively.

Furthermore, this model reduces the need for over-provisioning. Traditionally, to handle peak loads, organizations might have had to invest in infrastructure capable of managing the highest expected demand, which would need to be more utilized most of the time. Serverless computing eliminates this inefficiency, allowing organizations to operate more leanly and responsively.

In addition to cost savings, this efficient use of resources can contribute to environmental sustainability by reducing your IT operations' overall energy consumption and carbon footprint. Less hardware is left running unnecessarily, conserving energy and extending the lifespan of physical equipment due to reduced wear and tear.

- **No idle capacity:** Serverless architectures fundamentally change the cost of running applications by eliminating idle capacity. In standard server-based setups, you usually must pay for computing resources regardless of use. This includes during nighttime hours, weekends, or other periods of low activity when your applications may need to do more. This can be costly, especially for businesses that operate seasonal services or those whose demand fluctuates unpredictably.

  With serverless computing, this problem is avoided. Resources are provisioned and paid for on-the-fly. If your application is not running or there is no demand, you are not charged for compute time or data processing. This pay-for-what-you-use model is incredibly efficient, aligning your costs directly with your usage.

  Idle capacity reduces costs and improves operational efficiency. It allows businesses to be flexible and responsive to shifts in demand without the need to predict traffic patterns or pre-provision resources that might not be needed.

  Reducing unnecessary resource usage can also be considered an environmentally friendly approach. By consuming only what you need, you contribute less to energy waste, often associated with underutilized servers sitting idle in data centers.

- **Development efficiency:** Serverless architectures are changing how developers approach project workflows. They can focus only on preparing code without the distractions of managing the underlying infrastructure. This shift significantly improves development efficiency, streamlining the process from start to deployment. By removing the limitations of server configuration, maintenance, and scaling, developers can launch new features and applications faster.

  This focus on coding rather than infrastructure management rules to a quicker reversal for development projects, directly impacting time to market. Faster deployment cycles mean businesses can respond more rapidly to market changes or customer needs, staying competitive and innovative in a fast-paced industry. Additionally, this efficiency reduces the lead time in iterating on feedback, allowing improvements and updates to be rolled out swiftly, further enhancing user satisfaction and engagement.

  A simplified operational model of serverless computing lowers the need for a large IT staff to maintain and monitor servers, thus decreasing overhead costs. With serverless, much of the operational responsibility moves to the cloud provider, releasing your team's time and resources. This cuts operational costs and permits developers and IT staff to allocate more time to higher-value tasks, directly contributing to business growth.

Azure DevOps and FinOps integration

Azure DevOps and FinOps integration is the partnership of software development, IT operations, and financial operations within the cloud. Azure DevOps provides a platform enabling software development, deployment, and maintenance. It contains various services, including code repositories, testing tools, and CI/CD pipelines, designed to foster collaboration and accelerate the development cycle.

FinOps, on the other hand, is the financial part of cloud operations. It highlights cost transparency, budgeting, and the efficient use of cloud resources. It is about ensuring that the financial importance of cloud services is transparent and managed proactively from the planning phase to the final deployment in production.

When integrated, Azure DevOps and FinOps create a vital framework where financial insights inform development decisions, leading to more cost-effective and value-driven outcomes. This intersection allows teams to continuously consider the financial impact of their workflows and resource use, ensuring that cloud spending aligns with business objectives and operational requirements. By doing so, organizations can maintain agility and innovation while remaining on budget and maximizing their return on investment in cloud technologies.

DevOps and FinOps for better resource management

DevOps is all about getting software developers and IT operations teams to work together to build, deploy, and manage software more efficiently for the business. With cloud-build-and-run software, FinOps is all about managing and optimizing cloud costs in the DevOps workflow. However, DevOps teams often find it challenging to adopt FinOps practices.

A DevOps team typically juggles designing software, writing code, testing it, handling the actual release, and keeping everything running smoothly. Keeping an eye on cloud spending and applying financial best practices from FinOps might feel like just one thing too many.

For DevOps teams to successfully incorporate FinOps, they should focus on best practices that help merge financial savvy with their tech expertise without overwhelming the workflow:

- **DevOps teams in on FinOps insights:** FinOps teams gather and analyze significant cloud worlds, keeping track of costs and figuring out how to maximize the cloud budget. When they share these insights with the DevOps, it can lead to more innovative, more cost-aware decisions in software development. Imagine the FinOps team scores a great deal on a certain kind of cloud container. If they tell the developers about this bargain, they can create software that takes advantage of those cheaper containers, saving money in the process.

- **Encourage teamwork between DevOps and FinOps:** DevOps folks need to be involved with the FinOps team. The developers and IT ops people know a lot about what kind of cloud services are necessary for the business's tech tasks.

  Conversely, those tech-savvy team members need to understand why cloud costs and the company's financial targets matter—stuff that FinOps teams are all about.

When both sides understand each other and work together, FinOps really starts to click.

- **Integrating cost analysis into regular DevOps meetings:** When the development and IT operations teams gather to discuss project progress and resolve tech issues, they should also discuss cloud costs. This is a good time to consider using cloud resources to save money and remember the financial goals the business aims for as they build stuff. When developing new software, they should consider how well it works and how reliable it is against its cost. They might ask questions like, *Do we need to spend extra on making this available all the time?*

- **Information exchange between DevOps and FinOps teams:** DevOps teams always monitor many different stats, such as the smoothness of their processes and the performance of the software. Sharing this information with the FinOps folks can help catch money issues or project slowdowns before they become too big. For instance, if developers are working on an API, they might keep track of how often the API is used or how fast it answers a request. If the number of people using the API increases and it starts slowing down, that's a heads-up for the FinOps team. They can then determine if it's time to beef up the cloud services to keep everything running smoothly without spending too much.

- **Obstacles in blending FinOps with DevOps:** FinOps has become an essential practice that helps businesses manage and understand cloud costs. However, introducing FinOps into a company can have challenges that impact both the DevOps teams and the broader business.

- **Challenges with gaining stakeholder support:** When a company specializes in FinOps, it can sometimes bump up against the do-it-yourself nature of using public cloud services. This clash leads to DevOps teams and business leaders not getting on board with FinOps methods. FinOps teams could begin with small, straightforward projects to get everyone on the same page. By showing quick, clear benefits and how FinOps can save cash and effort, they can convince DevOps and business folks that it is a smart move.

- **Addressing accountability issues:** If DevOps teams are not encouraged to adopt FinOps, they might not see any reason to follow its rules. Since FinOps is about controlling cloud usage, cutting costs, and ensuring business leaders monitor cloud budgets, companies need to set up policies and goals that support FinOps efforts.

- **Absence of impactful metrics:** DevOps teams can enhance their involvement in FinOps initiatives by sharing development and deployment metrics with FinOps teams. This data helps FinOps identify and address idle or underutilized cloud resources, ensuring efficient cloud spending. Without this crucial data, FinOps teams would be operating without complete insight, akin to working in the dark, which could hinder their ability to manage resources effectively.

- **Managing unpredictable cloud costs:** Effective FinOps depends on having detailed metrics about usage and deployment. However, managing workloads with unpredictable or fluctuating demands for cloud resources can be challenging for DevOps teams, even when FinOps oversees and guides. This complexity can sometimes lead DevOps staff to overlook or underestimate the importance of FinOps recommendations.

- **Addressing effective analytics:** FinOps proves its worth to business leaders by providing straightforward answers to crucial questions about cloud operations. It involves analyzing data from cloud usage to pinpoint wasteful practices and find opportunities for optimization. However, if the analytics could be better and more effective, DevOps teams might find it challenging to implement FinOps practices effectively.

Conclusion

In conclusion, Advanced Azure FinOps Techniques offer methods to optimize cloud expenditure and operational efficiency. IaC lays the foundation for cost efficiency by automating the provisioning and management of infrastructure, which cuts labor costs and reduces errors associated with manual processes.

Azure Functions and Automation take this a step further by providing a serverless environment where you pay only for the exact resources your code uses as it uses them. This event-driven execution ensures you are not wasting funds on idle capacity, with the added benefit of effortless scaling.

Serverless cost optimization builds upon this by fine-tuning the spending on cloud services, ensuring that the performance is maintained while costs are kept in check. This is particularly valuable for workloads that experience unpredictable bursts of activity.

Finally, integrating Azure DevOps with FinOps embeds cost management into the software development and deployment lifecycle.

In the next chapter, readers will explore cost optimization frameworks and deploy them to manage cloud expenses. They will delve into specifics around creating a FinOps culture within their enterprise and encourage IT and finance (and business) teams to work together collaboratively. Moreover, the chapter will discuss how to continuously iterate on these strategies to ensure that cloud resources are managed efficiently and sustainably over time. To summarize this chapter, readers will have learned how to provide financial accountability and operational excellence in their cloud contexts!

Join our book's Discord space

Join the book's Discord Workspace for Latest updates, Offers, Tech happenings around the world, New Release and Sessions with the Authors:

https://discord.bpbonline.com

CHAPTER 9
Azure FinOps Best Practices

Introduction

Azure FinOps best practices are about ensuring companies use Azure, which is like a big online warehouse where businesses can run their programs and store their data without spending more money than necessary.

Think of cost optimization frameworks as a budgeting app for the cloud. They help you pick out only the cloud services you really need, so you are not wasting cash on things you do not use

Building a FinOps Culture involves getting everyone, from the boss to the newest intern, to think about how to save money on cloud services. When everyone is looking for ways to be more efficient, it adds up to big savings.

It is crucial that the tech team and the money team are on the same page, and that is where collaboration and communication come in. By sharing info, they can make better choices about using the cloud in a way that makes sense for the business's budget.

Just like you would regularly check your bank account to ensure you are not overspending, continuous improvement and iterative optimization are about always looking for ways to improve things. If you are spending too much, you figure out how to spend less next time.

All these best practices together are like a smart strategy, ensuring that businesses get the most out of Azure without any wasted resources or unexpected costs.

Structure

In this chapter, we will go through the following topics:

- Cost optimization frameworks
- Building a FinOps culture
- Collaboration and communication
- Continuous improvement and iterative optimization

Objectives

Azure FinOps best practices aim to optimize cloud spending and gain operational efficiency throughout Azure. With a methodical means of cost optimization, businesses can make certain that their cloud investments are not only reduced but also aligned with business goals on the horizon. In other words, nurturing a FinOps culture throughout all teams (developers: finance) enables collective accountability for financial consciousness and expense tracking. Collaboration and communication create bridges between departments, and financial insights help make accurate decisions. By iterating on improvements over time, cloud services will always remain at peak efficiency and most closely aligned with business needs, resulting in a lower potential for waste, putting money where the value is.

Cost optimization framework

Cost optimization happens at different levels within an organization. It is crucial to see how your tasks support the organization's objectives and follow FinOps practices. By understanding the structure of business units, how resources are organized, and the centralized audit policies, you can adopt a consistent financial strategy for your tasks.

The figure below represents the major phases in formulating a complete cloud cost management strategy for the Azure ecosystem. The report underscores the following steps organizations must increasingly follow—from establishing cost-management discipline and designing for lower costs to optimizing usage/pricing while not forgetting ongoing monitoring/ refinement. By combining the four phases above, companies can keep their IT cost optimization sustainable and aligned with business objectives in the long run:

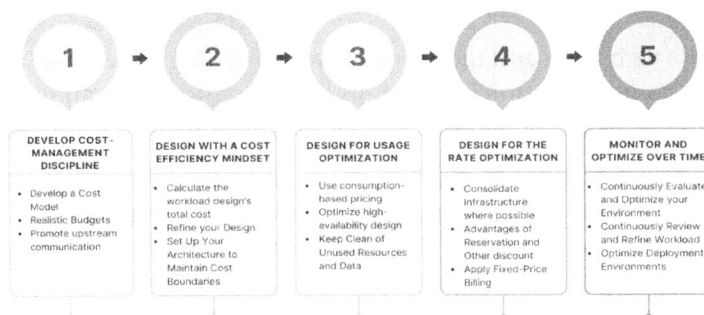

Figure 9.1: Cost optimization framework

Developing cost-management discipline

Developing a strong cost-management discipline is the first thing on your inflection path toward cloud savings. It is not a cost tracking or measurement discipline but rather one of understanding, classifying, and predicting costs associated with cloud services in an IT portfolio. A disciplined approach to managing these costs helps businesses control their ongoing spending and make better financial decisions that reflect future growth. We will deep dive into some specific principles and practices that can help you manage costs effectively in the cloud.

Develop a cost model

If you are running a business that involves cloud services, it is crucial to have a cost model to help you understand your finances. This is not just about recording expenses – it is about fully understanding the financial landscape of owning and operating your cloud infrastructure.

A well-crafted cost model will break your expenses into categories, allowing you to see where your money goes—from the infrastructure to the support services and setup process. This clarity is essential for identifying what is driving your costs and making accurate predictions about future expenses. You will also be able to see how changes in demand will impact your budget and overall financial health.

With this financial forecast, you will be better equipped to decide whether to scale up or down your resources. This means you can align your cloud strategy with your business growth trajectory. Having a financial tracking system in place is also crucial. It will help you stay informed and in control, steering your cloud services in a financially sound direction that aligns with your business objectives.

Realistic budgets

When running a business that involves cloud services, it's important to plan for the essentials and keep an eye on the future. You need to account for the must-haves, like the core functions of your cloud services, the features that keep everything running smoothly and securely, and the costs of having the right team on board. However, you also need to plan for growth and scaling to avoid problems down the line.

Once you have established your budget, it is like setting a spending cap to help you stay on track. You can set up notifications to alert you when costs start to climb too high, which can work at different levels for different parts of your cloud spending. This helps you avoid unexpected bills and keep your spending within the guardrails you have set.

Creating channels for effective communication between cloud solution architects and application owners is a crucial component of a strong Cost Optimization Framework. This approach ensures that the architects' knowledge and expertise trickle down to the application owners, empowering them to make informed decisions that balance operational needs and cost implications.

In simpler terms, this means that architects can provide valuable insights on building cost-effective and scalable cloud environments. When application owners receive this knowledge, they can more efficiently manage resources and avoid unnecessary expenses.

Acting on feedback, viewing it as a source of actionable intelligence, can lead to significant cost reductions. This feedback loop is essential and should be valued alongside quantitative analytics. By utilizing employees' observations and recommendations, companies can drive more realistic and financially sound design changes.

Promote upstream communication

Creating channels for effective communication between cloud solution architects and application owners is a crucial component of a strong cost optimization framework. This approach ensures that the architects' knowledge and expertise trickle down to the application owners, empowering them to make informed decisions that balance operational needs and cost implications.

In simpler terms, this means that architects can provide valuable insights on building cost-effective and scalable cloud environments. When application owners receive this knowledge, they can more efficiently manage resources and avoid unnecessary expenses.

Acting on feedback, viewing it as a source of actionable intelligence, can lead to significant cost reductions. This feedback loop is essential and should be valued alongside quantitative analytics. By utilizing employees' observations and recommendations, companies can drive more realistic and financially sound design changes.

A Cost Optimization Framework that fosters upstream communication contributes to a deeper understanding of cost drivers and leads to innovative strategies for reducing expenditure without compromising service quality. It ensures that cost considerations are integrated into every stage of the cloud service lifecycle, from architectural planning to daily management, creating a cost-aware culture that permeates every level of the organization.

Designing with a cost-efficiency mindset

With today being a very competitive cloud world, it is crucial for businesses to be cost-conscious when designing from a cheaper infrastructure perspective while gaining 10x or beyond on their returns and remaining scalable and flexible in the future. It goes further than cost containment; it necessitates thinking about the long-term value, flexibility, and how technology decisions fit with company strategy. This is an area where we delve into principles that are key for organizations building cloud architectures for both a price factor and scalable and flexible to sustain in the long run.

Calculate the workload design's total cost

When calculating the total cost of your workload design, it is vital to consider all the costs associated with your technology and automation choices. This retains the upfront costs and the long-term effect on your **return on investment (ROI)**. Ensure your design meets all necessary functional and non-functional requirements and is within budget.

It is also vital for your design to be flexible enough to adapt to future changes. Being adaptable can save you from costly overhauls down the road. Remember to include the costs of acquiring new technology, training your team, and managing the change process across your organization.

A balanced approach that considers ROI can prevent you from overengineering your solutions. Overengineering often leads to unnecessary expenses without adding enough value. By focusing on what truly brings value and ensuring your design is future-ready, you can maintain a cost-effective balance that aligns with your business goals and promotes sustainable growth.

Refine your design

To make your workload design more cost-efficient, you need to carefully select services and features that align with your business model and offer high ROI. It is essential to focus on choices that do not require significant new investments or that do not drastically affect your project's functionality.

In the refinement process, consider exploring more economical options that still meet your needs. For example, you can find solutions that offer greater resource flexibility or dynamic scaling capabilities, which can adjust to workload demands without manual intervention. This can help you save costs significantly over time. You should also consider extending the value of your existing investments rather than purchasing new solutions.

While prioritizing, consider the costs associated with maintaining critical operations and functionalities. It is important to consider direct and indirect costs that improve team efficiency and reduce time wastage. Considering these factors, you can fine-tune your design to make it cost-effective and robust, capable of effectively supporting your business objectives.

Set up your architecture to maintain cost boundaries

Creating an architecture that includes cost guardrails is essential to ensure you spend your time on cloud services. This can be achieved by incorporating platform solutions, setting clear policies, using specific infrastructure and application design patterns, and automating certain processes.

You can establish these guardrails by directly implementing your applications' governance policies and design principles. These mechanisms help prevent unexpected or unauthorized charges by setting limits and rules that govern resource usage and expenditures. This approach enables you to keep your costs predictable and ensures that your spending is aligned with your strategic business objectives so that your expenses add value and support growth.

Design for usage optimization

The manner of best utilizing the cloud is an important aspect of the cost management process, where we must make sure resources are being used effectively, and costs do not get out of hand. Optimizing usage involves matching your cloud services to actual demand, selecting pricing models that align with realistic utilization patterns, and adopting tactics aimed at making the most out of resources. This helps you save extra expenditures and makes your cloud infrastructure more efficient & reliable in a whole fashion. This chapter covers how and best supports plans to design a cloud environment that helps control costs, reduce waste, and ensure your resources are used effectively.

Use consumption-based pricing

When spending on cloud services, using consumption-based pricing wherever possible is a good idea. This pricing model benefits services where you only pay for what you use. You can turn off the service when it is not in use and avoid unnecessary costs. This approach is ideal for parts of your workload that are only required occasionally rather than continuously.

By choosing consumption-based pricing, you can significantly reduce unnecessary expenses compared to traditional models, where you pay for a service all year round, regardless of usage. This is an excellent option for scenarios where your computing needs fluctuate or are only high during specific periods. By aligning your payment structure with your actual usage, you can optimize your operational budget to match your real needs and manage your resources more efficiently.

Optimize high-availability design

To make sure your systems stay up and running even during failures or when there is a lot of demand, it is important to use certain strategies. One important way to do this is through load balancing, which spreads out incoming traffic across different servers so that no single server is available. This makes things run better and ensures that everything keeps working by dividing the work between servers. Another important strategy is failover clustering, which provides a backup - if one server fails, another one takes over, making sure everything keeps running smoothly for users.

Another way to ensure your systems stay available is to spread them across different locations or data centers. This means that if one place has a problem, the others can keep things going. Automatic failover and recovery are also important because they can quickly switch to backup resources if something goes wrong, ensuring services are restored fast and there's as little downtime as possible. Regular checks and automatic alerts can help find and fix issues before they cause problems for your system.

Keep clean of unused resources and data

Keeping a clean and efficient cloud environment is vital to managing costs effectively. It's essential to regularly review your deployments to identify and decommission resources and data that are no longer in use. Sometimes, resources and data become redundant over time and accumulate costs even if they are no longer needed. This wasteful expenditure can weigh down your budget unnecessarily.

To prevent this unnecessary expense, you must be proactive and vigilant in auditing your cloud resources. Establishing a routine where your team periodically scans the cloud environment to spot unused or idle resources and data can help. Once identified, shutting down these resources and deleting obsolete data not only cleans up your environment but also significantly reduces costs.

This practice not only helps cut down unnecessary expenses but also improves the performance and security of your cloud environment. With fewer cluttered resources, managing and securing your cloud infrastructure becomes more straightforward, allowing your team to focus on optimizing and scaling operations effectively.

Keeping your cloud environment free of unused resources and data is like regular housekeeping; it keeps your digital space efficient, secure, and cost-effective. This ensures that your financial resources are allocated to active and essential elements that genuinely add value to your business.

Designing for the rate optimization

In this section, we will learn how to design for rate optimization:

- **Consolidate infrastructure where possible**: If you want to enhance the efficiency of your cloud operations and reduce costs, think of consolidating your infrastructure. This strategy involves merging workloads, resources, and teams to use your cloud assets more densely and efficiently. Choose services that support effective consolidation, helping you get the most out of every asset.

  However, consolidation comes with its challenges, especially around security. When you combine workloads with different security needs, managing compliance and risks can get tricky. It is important to carefully evaluate how these changes might impact your security measures and ensure you still meet all regulatory and security standards.

  Beyond saving money, reducing your infrastructure can streamline how you collect your resources, freeing up your team to focus on more strategic projects. Additionally, using fewer resources more effectively can show energy savings and reduce your environmental impact, which is vital in today's increasingly eco-aware business world.

- **Advantages of reservation and other discounts**: Consider using reservations and other infrastructure discounts to save money on your cloud expenses. This involves committing to specific resources for a longer period and pre-purchasing them to take advantage of lower rates offered by Microsoft for predictable resource use. It is best to use this approach for resources you know your organization will need over time and where costs and usage levels are stable.

  To make this work, you must work closely with your licensing team. They are responsible for negotiating purchase agreements and renewals. By keeping them informed about your current and anticipated resource needs, they can tailor these agreements to better match your actual usage. This ensures you are not overcommitting or underutilizing resources and helps secure the best terms during negotiations.

  When your licensing team has accurate projections, they can negotiate better pricing structures that reflect your organization's usage patterns. This can lead to discounts that benefit not only your specific projects but also other teams and departments. By proactively managing commitments and collaborating with your licensing team, you can optimize your cloud budget more effectively and ensure that your cloud infrastructure costs align with your organizational needs and financial goals.

- **Apply fixed-price billing**: If you use specific resources frequently and can predict your usage, it might be worth considering switching to a fixed-price billing plan instead of a pay-as-you-go plan. This can be a wise decision if your service offers this billing option. Fixed-price plans usually come at a lower cost and include additional features unavailable with consumption-based options. By choosing a fixed-price billing plan, you can better predict and manage your expenses, leading to higher ROI. This billing method simplifies budget planning and can save significant costs, especially for essential services critical to your day-to-day operations.

Monitor and optimize over time

Cloud cost management is a discipline that never ends. It must be monitored and tweaked to keep pace with changes in your business so you can continue getting the most value possible for what you spend on cloud infrastructure. However, as usage patterns evolve and new technologies are introduced, you must update your cloud strategy regularly to control cost wherever possible without compromising functionality. Ongoing monitoring enables organizations to tune resource allocation, optimize pricing models, and renegotiate contracts as necessary. This section is about practices necessary for the long term and how you need to return on your strategic investments by optimizing cloud cost.

Continuously evaluate and optimize your environment

Maintaining a cost-efficient operation is crucial to tracking your spending on cloud resources, data storage, and paid support services. Use your cost tracking system to regularly assess whether the resources you are paying for are fully utilized or if some need to be used and could be downsized or replaced.

Knowing how different pricing models affect your overall costs is essential. This knowledge can help you make informed decisions that align with your financial objectives and potentially save you money. For example, resizing resources to match usage or switching to different service plans offering better terms can reduce your monthly bills.

You should also examine your support contracts with technology providers more closely. As your usage changes, you may find opportunities to renegotiate these agreements or adjust the levels of support, aligning service costs more closely with actual needs. This can be another effective way to cut expenses without compromising the necessary support and maintenance of your technological infrastructure.

By continually evaluating and adjusting your use of cloud and technology services, you control costs and improve operational efficiency, ensuring that every dollar spent drives value for your organization.

Continuously review and refine workload

To get the most out of your technology investments, it is vital to regularly check how your systems are working and how much they cost. This ongoing review allows you to make changes that save money and increase efficiency.

This includes monitoring resource usage, evaluating how well your code is performing, and assessing the effectiveness of your workflows. By analyzing these areas, you can find areas that can be improved to make your systems more efficient and cost-effective.

For example, you might realize that you are using more resources than you need, or you could find ways to make your code run more smoothly. By making these changes, you can save money and improve the performance of your applications.

By incorporating these reviews into your routine, you can ensure your technology meets your business goals and needs. This helps you control costs while adapting to changes in your business environment.

Optimize deployment environments

It is essential to check how your systems work and how much they cost to save money and improve application performance. This will allow you to make changes that increase efficiency and reduce expenses.

One way to do this is by tailoring each environment to specific needs. For instance, the environment where your applications are live and being used by customers should be the most robust and can be the most significant cost driver. On the other hand, non-production environments like development, testing, and staging do not need to be as high-powered as production. You can use lower-tier and less expensive resources since these environments are typically used for testing and not for serving real users.

You can also consider implementing on-demand pre-production environments, which can be spun up for final testing phases and decommissioned. This saves costs for running these environments 24/7 and aligns resource usage more closely with actual needs.

By selectively allocating resources, you can cut costs and optimize the performance of your development and testing activities. Overall, optimizing your deployment environments is a key strategy for managing costs effectively and ensuring your technology keeps up with your business goals and needs.

Building a FinOps culture

Creating a FinOps culture means ensuring everyone understands and focuses on using cloud technology efficiently to add value to the business. It involves promoting a mindset where managing costs is essential, but the main goal is to see how these efforts contribute to the business's overall success.

To specify this culture, you must start by highlighting the importance of being aware of costs to save money and, more importantly, improve business performance. It's essential to set clear, possible goals for all team members. These goals should align with the organization's mission and inspire team members to take responsibility for the outcomes of their actions.

Data is essential in this culture. By using data to guide decisions, you ensure that success is measured and that these metrics are directly linked to the goals of individual teams. This approach helps identify areas of success and opportunities for improvement.

FinOps culture brings the organization together to streamline processes and improve team collaboration. This agreement leads to better decision-making and enhances the organization's ability to adjust to new challenges and opportunities. Everyone in the company becomes better prepared to make intelligent, well-informed choices to contribute to the business's long-term success.

Getting started

When you are just starting out with establishing a FinOps culture, it is common to encounter stakeholders who are unfamiliar with FinOps and their roles within it. Here is how you can successfully initiate and expand your FinOps efforts:

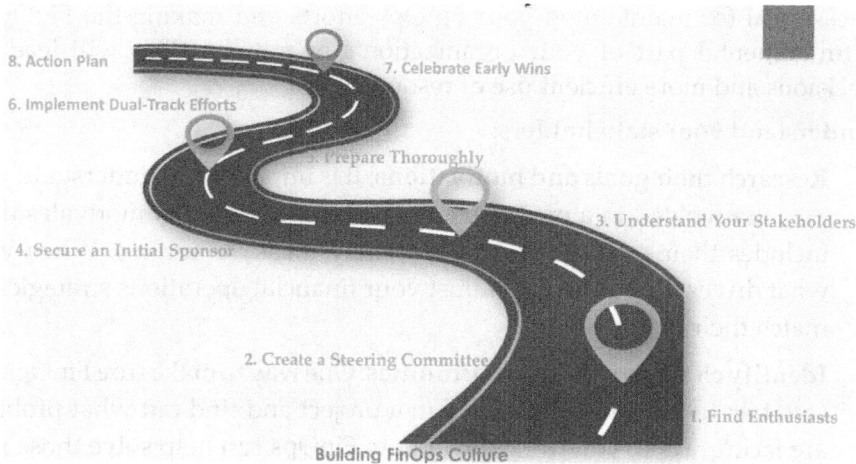

Figure 9.2: Building FinOps culture

1. **Find enthusiasts:** To establish your FinOps culture, start by finding people in your organization who are excited about using technology more efficiently and reducing costs without sacrificing performance. Look for colleagues who are keen on using data to enhance business decisions and passionate about innovation and progress.

    These individuals will be the main drivers of your FinOps initiative. They will play a key role in promoting the initiative, increasing awareness, and getting others involved. Their enthusiasm and expertise are essential—they can offer valuable insights, suggest practical solutions, and adapt FinOps strategies to meet your organization's specific needs.

    By assembling this group of motivated individuals, you create a solid foundation for a culture that recognizes the significance of financial operations in cloud technology. Their dedication and drive will be vital as you establish and refine your FinOps practices.

2. **Create a steering committee**: To ensure that your FinOps culture is strong and effective, you should create a steering committee of people passionate about FinOps. This group should be informal and encourage open discussion and collaboration. You should schedule regular meetings, so everyone stays involved and focused. During these meetings, the committee can work together to set shared goals, develop strategies, and plan how to implement these ideas.

    This steering committee will be the heart of your FinOps efforts. They will ensure that your FinOps practices are not just talked about but also implemented throughout your organization. They will align FinOps ambitions with your business goals, address any issues, and ensure that the FinOps culture is present in all relevant areas of your organization.

    By involving passionate and knowledgeable individuals in this committee, you can create a sense of ownership and accountability among team members. This is essential for maintaining your FinOps efforts and making the FinOps culture a fundamental part of your organization's operations. This will lead to better decisions and more efficient use of resources.

3. **Understand your stakeholders:**

   a. **Research their goals and motivations**: It is important to understand what each person involved in a project wants to achieve and what motivates them. This includes their main goals and how they measure success. When you know what drives them, you can adjust your financial operations strategies to better match their objectives.

   b. **Identify challenges and opportunities**: One way to make sure FinOps is helpful is to talk to the people involved in a project and find out what problems they are facing. Then, you can explain how FinOps can help solve those problems. For example, FinOps can help make things cost less or use resources better. This shows how valuable FinOps can be and positions it as a solution to real-world challenges.

   c. **Spot potential supporters**: Knowing who might support or oppose your efforts to make FinOps work is essential. That way, you can understand their reasons and see things from their point of view. This can help you figure out how to work with them to make FinOps successful. For people who favor FinOps, please find out how you can use their support to improve things. For those who are skeptical, listen to their concerns and try to address them. This way, everyone feels like they are being heard, and FinOps can be successful for everyone.

   By taking these steps, you can build a FinOps culture that is not only informed by the needs and dynamics of your organization but also one that is embraced by its key players, fostering a collaborative and proactive environment.

4. **Secure an initial sponsor**: To effectively kick off your FinOps initiatives, securing a sponsor who is a leader or influencer within your organization is crucial. Start by identifying someone with the necessary authority and open to innovative approaches that enhance operational efficiency. Once you have a potential sponsor in mind, prepare a compelling pitch that clearly outlines how FinOps practices can positively impact the organization's specific missions and success criteria. Highlight how these practices can lead to better resource management, cost savings, and a more robust bottom line. Be explicit in your pitch about what you're asking for—funding, resources, or advocacy. Also, provide a detailed action plan that includes the steps required to roll out FinOps, key milestones, and the expected outcomes. This structured approach demonstrates the potential benefits and shows your sponsor that you have a clear and actionable path forward, making it easier for them to support and champion your initiative within the organization.

5. **Prepare thoroughly**: When introducing FinOps into your organization, it is crucial to approach it with the exact level of care and attention you would, if you were starting a new business. This suggests being well-prepared for every meeting and relations, gathering detailed information, and ensuring you understand the current practices and potential improvements that FinOps can bring.

   You can use resources like the FinOps Foundation to help guide you through the process and offer you the best practices and case studies relevant to your efforts. You can also learn from other FinOps practitioners and communities, who can give you valuable insights and advice based on their experiences.

   By preparing and equipping yourself with the right resources and community support, you can ensure your FinOps initiative is well-informed and strategically sound right from the start. This preparation will help you make a compelling case for stakeholders and set a strong foundation for the successful integration of FinOps practices within your company.

6. **Implement dual-track efforts**: When looking for someone to sponsor your FinOps project, you must be clear about what you need from them. That could be money, additional team members, specific tools or software, or even just their public support. Whatever it is, explain it clearly so they understand what is required and can assess whether they can help.

   You should also outline the steps you plan to take to implement FinOps practices effectively. This means detailing the resources you will need, like time, personnel, and technology. For example, you might need new software to track costs, training for your staff, or regular meetings to review financial metrics.

   Make sure you explain the expected impact of their support. Show how their backing will enable these changes and what outcomes you anticipate. This might include saving money, using cloud resources more effectively, or making better decisions. Presenting a clear plan with defined expectations makes it easier for a sponsor to commit to supporting your FinOps initiatives.

7. **Celebrate early wins**: The FinOps project has started showing positive results, so it's important to celebrate and share those achievements with your team and the rest of the organization. This motivates the team involved and helps others understand the benefits of FinOps.

   You can highlight achievements like cost savings, better resource use, or faster and better decision-making. Share these successes through internal newsletters, company meetings, or intranet posts. You can also include testimonials or case studies from teams that benefited from these practices. This will create a buzz around FinOps and help gain support across the organization.

   Celebrating these milestones will also help sustain interest in FinOps practices. It shows that the support from stakeholders and sponsors is yielding real and impactful results, and it encourages others to get involved. Make sure to link the success to the specific FinOps practices that facilitated these results so that everyone understands the cause-and-effect relationship. This approach fosters a culture of recognition and celebration and reinforces the value of FinOps within your company.

8. **Action plan**: Implementing FinOps practices and creating a detailed roadmap is required. This roadmap should include specific timelines, key milestones, and what results to expect at each stage. With this plan, your stakeholders will obviously understand the steps you will take when you take them and what results to expect.

To create your plan, divide the process into manageable stages. For each stage, define the objectives and the actions required to achieve them. Assign a realistic timeline to each action, ensuring that you have enough time for thorough execution while also maintaining momentum.

Identify critical milestones within these stages. Significant points in the project will indicate progress, such as achieving a cost reduction target or successfully integrating a new tool. Celebrate these milestones to keep enthusiasm and support throughout the organization.

This could include improved cost transparency, more efficient resource use, or better alignment between IT spending and business goals. Explain how these results will benefit the organization and link them directly to the broader business objectives.

The following figure illustrates building FinOps with the basics:

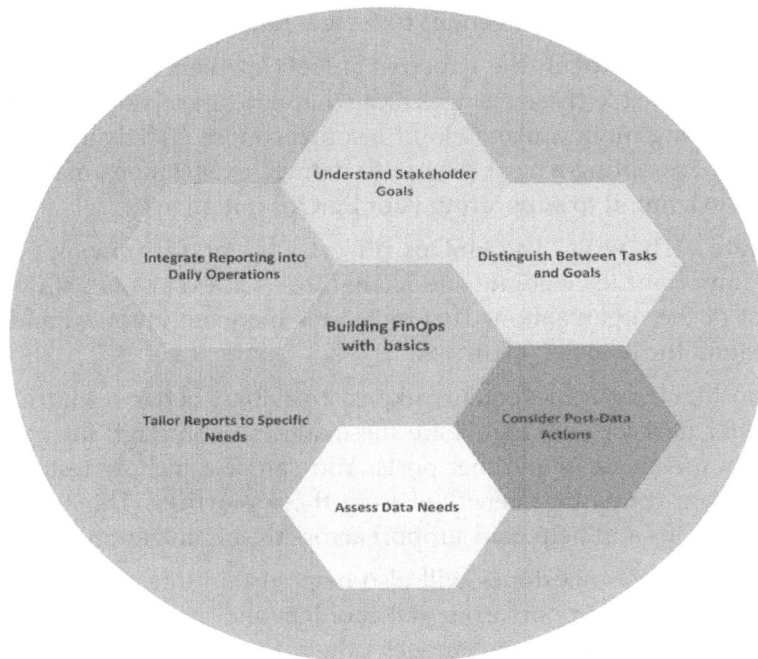

Figure 9.3: Building FinOps with basic

1. **Understand stakeholder goals**: It is essential to have open and detailed discussions with your stakeholders to understand their goals fully. These conversations should uncover what they want to achieve and the reasons behind their objectives. This will help you better understand their priorities, challenges, and expectations. Doing so makes your strategies and efforts more effective, ensuring they align well with what your stakeholders want to complete. This will also support building trust and facilitate smoother collaboration, making it easier to address any concerns or adjustments needed as your projects progress.

2. **Distinguish between tasks and goals**: When making plans, it's essential to understand the difference between tasks and goals. Tasks are the items you do to reach your goals, and they might change as technology and methods improve. Goals are your long-term plans that stay the same no matter what tools or methods you use. By understanding this difference, you can be flexible in your strategies while staying focused on your main objectives.

3. **Consider post-data actions**: After providing data to stakeholders, consider how they will use it to make decisions. Consider ways to make their tasks more accessible, such as automating processes or providing quick access to additional tools and reports. Also, explore opportunities for them to compare cost data with other business metrics. This can help them see the broader value of their resources and make more informed decisions. By streamlining these post-data actions, you can enhance their ability to utilize the information and drive better business outcomes efficiently.

4. **Assess data needs**: Evaluating your data needs is essential to ensure that you're effectively supporting your stakeholders' goals. Check whether you have all the necessary data at your disposal. If gaps exist, consider integrating additional datasets to enhance your analysis and simplify workflows. This might mean moving beyond basic in-portal reporting to more advanced, customized, or third-party solutions. Such an upgrade can provide more comprehensive insights and improve decision-making processes, aligning better with your organization's strategic objectives.

5. **Tailor reports to specific needs**:

   Develop reports that:

   o Provide detailed cost breakdowns according to allocation metadata and hierarchies.

   o Offer optimization insights for specific services and pricing models.

   o Show how well commitment-based discounts are being utilized and track chargebacks.

   o Allow stakeholders to drill into key performance indicators (KPIs) for various capabilities.

6. **Integrate reporting into daily operations**:

   o Regularly feature dashboards and KPIs in meetings and reviews.

   o Use both grassroots and executive-level strategies to promote data-driven decision-making.

   o Implement alert systems and use collaboration tools to keep everyone informed about costs.

Collaboration and communication

Collaboration in FinOps involves the joint efforts of finance, operations, and technology teams working together to manage and optimize cloud spending. This synergy ensures that cloud investments align with business objectives, balancing cost, efficiency, and scalability. Communication in FinOps refers to the clear and continuous exchange of information among finance, technology, and business teams about cloud usage, expenses, and operational impacts. Effective communication is crucial for transparency, enabling informed decision-making and strategic adjustments in real time.

The figure below shows the core principles of FinOps, which focus on collaboration and communication among different stakeholders in cloud cost management. They advocate for multidisciplinary teamwork, where finance and ops work with technology teams to cost-optimize clouds collectively, enrich decision-making substantively, and synchronize cloud investments mutually along the contours of business goals. Effective communication and collaboration are ways to bridge this gap so that all departments will cooperate with a unified strategy, contributing to optimizing cloud expenses and financial optimizations in general.

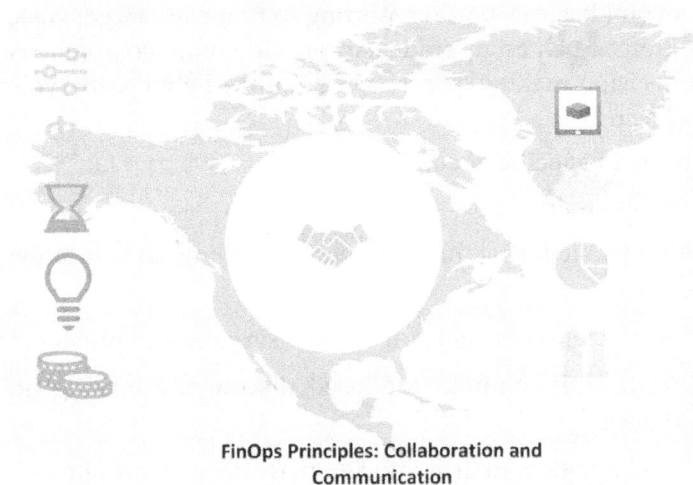

FinOps Principles: Collaboration and Communication

Figure 9.4: Collaboration and communication with FinOps

Collaboration and communication in FinOps

In FinOps, collaboration means that finance, technology, and business teams work together to manage and improve cloud spending and resources. It is like a team where each member has a specific role: finance monitors the budget; technology ensures resource efficiency, and business units define their needs and expectations. They all work together to balance cost, quality, and speed to get the most out of their cloud investments.

Excellent communication is essential in FinOps because it ensures everyone involved, such as engineers, IT professionals, financial analysts, and business managers, understands what's happening. For example, if the tech team wants to test new cloud services that might cost more, they must talk to the finance and business teams to ensure everyone knows the benefits and risks. This way, everyone can make better decisions together.

Framework for collaboration and communication

A successful model of cloud financial management always targets the known framework for collaboration and communication, focusing on where exactly major roles live while also seeing that they access key channels effectively. The opposite is true; this framework creates an information-sharing environment that allows teams to collaborate and act on the best decisions for financial/operational success. Within FinOps, it is important for every role to understand what their job entails, and that communication moves freely throughout the organization.

The following outlines the key roles involved in this framework and the communication channels that support their collaboration:

- **Key roles**:
  - **Executive leadership**: Think of them as the captains of the ship. They set the direction and ensure everyone has what they need to work together smoothly.
  - **Project managers**: They are like the organizers of a big event. They plan the work, ensure everything runs on time, and help different teams work together effectively.
  - **IT and technical support**: These are the tech experts who ensure everyone has the tools they need to communicate and collaborate without hiccups, like ensuring everyone can join video calls or access shared documents.
  - **Team leaders and members**: Team leaders and members do the day-to-day work. They focus on completing their tasks and reaching the team's goals.
  - **Cloud custodian**: This role is like a guardian of the cloud environment. They ensure the organization's cloud resources are used wisely and kept secure, what monitoring costs, and ensure data safety.

- **Communication channels:**
  - **Meetings**: These are regular catchups where everyone comes together, online or face-to-face. Here, the team discusses what is going well, what needs engagement, and plans. It's a time to ensure everyone is on the same page and dive into any significant issues.

  - **Instant messaging and emails**: Consider these as the everyday chats and notes you pass. They keep everyone connected and informed about what's happening daily. Whether it's a short update, a reminder, or a question, these tools help keep the discussion going.

  - **Collaborative tools:** These digital tools permit teams to collaborate and share information. Applications like Slack, Microsoft Teams, or Asana makes it easy to keep track of projects, share files, and communicate regardless of where team members are located.

  - **Feedback systems:** Imagine having a suggestion box or a regular check-in where you can say what's working and what's not. Everyone can voice their opinions through surveys, suggestion boxes, and review meetings. This helps the team understand how well they communicate and collaborate and what they can improve.

- **Collective processes:**
  - **Goal setting and alignment sessions:** Imagine a meeting where a team gets together to plan their strategy. During this meeting, people from different roles discuss their goals and how they will work together. The goal of this meeting is to ensure that everyone is working towards the same goal.

  - **Cross-functional teams:** Imagine a group project where people with different skills—like a tech whiz, a numbers guru, and a creative thinker—come together to tackle a problem. These teams mix talents across the organization to develop more innovative, well-rounded solutions.

  - **Knowledge sharing sessions:** These are like show-and-tell for grown-ups. Periodically, everyone meets to share what they have learned, whether it's a cool new tech trend, a project post-mortem, or industry news. It is a chance for the team to learn from each other's experiences and stay sharp.

  - **Innovation labs:** Think of this as a sandbox where you can build castles without worrying about making a mess. It is a dedicated space and time where teams can try out new ideas and experiment with creative solutions in a supportive environment. Even if something does not work out, it is all part of the learning process.

- **Role of the cloud custodian:**
  - **Policy enforcement:** The cloud Custodian is like the rule keeper of the cloud world. They ensure that everything happening in the cloud follows the organization's rules and the law. It's like ensuring everyone plays fair in the playground.
  - **Cost management:** This person is like a smart buyer for cloud services. They monitor spending on cloud resources, look for ways to cut costs without offering quality, and ensure the company gets the best charge for its dollar.
  - **Security and compliance:** Just as a security guard protects a building, the Cloud Custodian protects the company's data in the cloud. They ensure that all digital doors are locked tight and that the company meets all security standards, keeping hackers and data breaches at bay.
  - **Performance monitoring:** They are coaches who always watch how the team plays. The Cloud Custodian regularly checks how well the cloud services are performing and suggests ways to make them faster and more efficient.
  - **Stakeholder communication:** The Cloud Custodian also bridges the techy cloud team and everyone else in the company. They help explain complex cloud issues more straightforwardly and ensure everyone understands any changes or updates in the cloud strategy.
- **Evaluation and improvement:**
  - **Performance metrics:** Imagine if you checked how well you're doing at a video game or a sport every few months. That's what performance metrics are like in the workplace. Teams regularly look at specific scores—like how fast they complete projects, how happy everyone feels at work, and whether they're sticking to their budgets. These scores help them see how well they're working together and communicating.
  - **Continuous improvement:** Consider this a never-ending effort to improve at something you care about. This means constantly asking for everyone's opinions on what's working and what is not—from the boss to the newest hire. This feedback helps the team make minor tweaks and changes all the time so they can keep getting better at working together and reaching their goals.

The following are the benefits of collaboration and communication:

- **Projects finish faster:** when employees work together and understand their roles clearly, they can finish work projects more quickly and meet deadlines more efficiently.
- **Better ideas come up:** when people share their ideas and thoughts at work, they can develop innovative solutions and ideas they might not have considered.

- **Everyone feels part of the team:** when everyone at work contributes and their efforts are appreciated, they feel more valued and like they belong. This makes people happier and creates a more welcoming workplace.

- **Fewer mistakes:** People communicate clearly, and everyone knows what's happening; there's less chance of making mistakes, and things will go well.

- **Increased flexibility and adaptability:** The team communicates effectively, and you can easily adjust your gameplay and tactics based on how the game is going. Good communication helps teams manage new challenges and changes in the workplace, making the organization more adaptable and better prepared to deal with any unexpected situations.

- **Stronger relationships:** Regular team meetings and open communication help build stronger relationships among team members, making working together more enjoyable and improving teamwork.

Continuous improvement and iterative optimization

Continuous improvement and optimization in FinOps are all about never standing still. It is a perpetual cycle of examining, adjusting, and enhancing how money is spent on cloud services. This is crucial because the cloud environment and business needs are constantly changing.

In practice, this means teams are always on their toes, regularly reviewing cloud usage and costs to ensure every dollar spent is needed and effectively used. They look at detailed reports, spot any areas where they can cut back without losing performance, and adjust to keep up with the business's evolving needs.

Additionally, this process is deeply rooted in a culture of learning. Everyone involved in FinOps is encouraged to learn from past experiences and experiment with new ways to optimize cloud resources. This involves trying out new tools or strategies that could offer better results for less money.

Data plays a huge role here, too. Real-time data about cloud usage and costs helps the team make informed decisions quickly. This is crucial for staying agile—shifting strategies immediately as market conditions or business needs change.

Ultimately, continuous improvement in FinOps helps ensure that an organization's investment in the cloud always aligns with its financial goals, driving efficiency and cost savings while supporting growth and innovation.

Setting up your FinOps iteration

When preparing for your next FinOps cycle, clearly defining what you will focus on is crucial. This helps make sure your goals are realistic and achievable. If this is your first cycle, a good strategy is to start small—pick three to five key FinOps capabilities to concentrate on. You might stick with these initial capabilities for later cycles or add a couple more to expand your scope.

Below is a guide to help you choose the right FinOps capabilities based on your role, your experience, and what's currently most important for your team. This is not an exhaustive list, but it should serve as a good starting point. Feel free to pick capabilities from one group or mix and match based on your requirements.

For teams new to FinOps, particularly those with little to moderate experience in managing and optimizing costs, you might want to begin with the fundamentals:

- Data analysis
- Forecasting
- Budget management
- Resource utilization and efficiency
- Managing anomalies

If you are setting up a new FinOps team or want to boost awareness and adoption of FinOps practices, start with the following:

- Creating a decision-making and accountability framework (like a steering committee)
- Onboarding workloads
- Building a FinOps culture
- Educating and enabling your team on FinOps practices

For teams already comfortable with essential FinOps tools, especially those managing costs in large, diverse organizations, you might consider focusing on:

- Allocating costs
- Managing shared costs
- Implementing show-back and chargeback mechanisms
- Using commitment-based discounts

If your team is ready to tackle advanced reporting challenges, like managing costs across different clouds or integrating them with business data, look into the following:

- Data ingestion and normalization
- Advanced cost allocation (especially with metadata)
- Deepening data analysis and showing back strategies

For teams that understand the basics and are looking to delve deeper into optimization through advanced automation, think about the following:

- Enhancing resource utilization and efficiency
- Leveraging commitment-based discounts
- Automating workload management
- Strengthening cloud policy and governance
- Identifying and managing anomalies
- Refining budget management strategies

If your team knows the basics but needs to link cloud spending more directly to business value, you might focus on the following:

- Measuring unit costs
- Managing shared costs
- Applying show back and chargeback
- Streamlining budget management

The team has evolved in the dimension of cloud cost management; the next step is to tie spending on cloud resources more solidly back to business value. It must take a sophisticated view that looks beyond the nuts and bolts of finance, in line with corporate strategy. Keeping this in mind, you can help optimize cloud spend by honing your cost management processes and establishing clear goals towards which cloud usage should contribute - so that every dollar spent relates back directly to business value:

- **Define your goals:**
  - **Knowledge**: Start by understanding what you are dealing with. If it is new to you, learn the basics and get a clear idea of its purpose.
  - **Process**: Once the basics are down, it is time to get organized. Document a step-by-step process that everyone involved can follow. Make sure it is repeatable and includes roles, responsibilities, and how success will be measured.
  - **Metrics**: Think about what success looks like in concrete terms. Identify key metrics that will show whether you are achieving your goals. Start tracking them and consider automating the process to save time.
  - **Adoption**: Share what you are doing with others and get their input. Test your process on a small scale and refine it based on feedback. As it matures, aim for broader adoption across teams.
  - **Automation**: Look for ways to streamline your process. Identify tasks that can be automated to reduce manual effort. Keep an updated list of automation opportunities and prioritize those with the most significant impact.

- **Plan your action**: Now, it is time to put your plan into motion. Whether you're diving into learning the basics, refining a process for wider implementation, or driving full adoption and automation, use the FinOps Framework guidance to steer your efforts.

- **Review your progress**: As you wrap up this iteration, take a moment to reflect on your progress. Did you achieve the goals you set out for the identified capabilities? What aspects went smoothly, and where did you encounter challenges? Reflecting on these questions internally and reviewing them at the end of each iteration can help refine your process and address any issues. After closing out this iteration, remember that you can revisit this tutorial to guide you through subsequent iterations of the FinOps lifecycle. Restarting the tutorial can help you prepare for the next phase of your efforts. Do not hesitate to provide feedback on this page after each iteration, sharing whether you found the information helpful and any suggestions for improvement.

Conclusion

To effectively manage expenses and get the most out of Azure resources, organizations need to establish clear cost optimization frameworks. They should also create a culture around this framework that encourages people to take ownership of cloud costs and provide education on the principles of cost optimization. Collaboration and communication are crucial to achieve the desired results. Using tools for monitoring expenses and setting guidelines can help organizations manage their cloud expenses better. Organizations should continuously review and refine their cost management strategies and be open to experimentation and learning to foster a culture of innovation. By doing so, they can optimize their Azure spending, maximize returns on their cloud investments, and operate more efficiently.

In the next chapter, readers will get into real-world applications of FinOps principles through a series of case studies. Each case study will provide practical insights into different aspects of cloud cost management. You will explore strategies for optimizing costs in web applications, learn about the complexities of cost allocation and chargeback in large enterprises, and understand how effective collaboration between DevOps and FinOps teams can drive financial efficiency. These case studies will equip you with actionable knowledge and examples to apply to your cloud financial management practices.

Join our book's Discord space

Join the book's Discord Workspace for Latest updates, Offers, Tech happenings around the world, New Release and Sessions with the Authors:

https://discord.bpbonline.com

CHAPTER 10
Azure Case Studies and Real-world Examples

Introduction

In today's rapidly evolving digital landscape, the cloud has become an essential component of modern enterprises. Organizations across industries leverage cloud technologies to enhance agility, scalability, and efficiency. However, with the growing reliance on cloud services comes the challenge of managing and optimizing cloud costs. This is where the principles of FinOps, or Cloud Financial Management, come into play.

FinOps is a discipline that merges financial accountability with cloud operations, providing a robust framework for managing, monitoring, and optimizing cloud expenditures. It underscores the importance of visibility into cloud usage and costs, fosters team accountability, and advocates for proactive cost optimization strategies. The ultimate aim of FinOps is to ensure that every dollar invested in cloud services yields the maximum value for the organization, a goal that can significantly enhance operational efficiency and cost-effectiveness.

This write-up explores the successful implementation of FinOps principles through three distinct case studies. Each case study highlights a unique aspect of cloud financial management and demonstrates how effective FinOps practices can lead to substantial cost savings and improved operational efficiency.

Structure

In this chapter, we will go through the following topics:

- Case study 1: Cost optimization for Azure App Service
- Case study 2: Cost allocation and chargeback in a large enterprise
- Case study 3: DevOps and FinOps collaboration

Objectives

The objective is to clarify the value of applying FinOps ideas within a cloud-first enterprise. By reviewing three unique case studies, this paper aims to uncover standard cloud cost management and optimization challenges — including costs going up too high, departments losing sight of what they are spending, or budget overrun. It uses real-world examples to demonstrate practical solutions and illustrate how FinOps strategies can solve these problems. It also stresses the (quantifiable) benefits of FinOps, such as cost reduction/savings, better use of resources, and increased operational efficiency. Doing so helps foster cross-functional collaboration between DevOps and FinOps teams, which can serve as a blueprint for other organizations to implement these best practices. Ultimately, it helps inform strategic decision-making by helping leaders understand how FinOps affects overall business success — leading to the most out of your cloud investments and longer-term growth.

Case study 1: FinOps cost optimization for Azure App Service

In today's digital generation, web applications are vital in providing services and engaging with customers. They are the backbone of modern businesses, providing platforms for e-commerce, customer service, and various digital interactions. However, as these applications scale, the complexity and cost of managing cloud infrastructure can grow exponentially. Cloud costs can spiral out of control without proper oversight and optimization, impacting profitability and operational efficiency.

FinOps, a financial management domain for cloud services, is a critical strategy for addressing these challenges. It integrates financial accountability with operational efficiency, enabling organizations to optimize their cloud spending while maintaining the necessary performance and reliability. FinOps practices involve ongoing monitoring, cost analysis, and implementing optimization techniques to ensure that every dollar spent on cloud services is explained.

This case study explores how an in-house team implemented FinOps principles to optimize costs for a web application hosted on Microsoft Azure. Through a structured and strategic approach, the team delivered substantial savings and improved operational efficiency, demonstrating the powerful impact of FinOps in cloud financial management.

Key challenges

A leading e-commerce company faced escalating cloud costs as its web application traffic surged. The company utilized multiple Azure services, including App Services, SQL Databases, Storage Accounts, and VMs, for hosting, storage, and processing. However, it needed a comprehensive view of its cloud costs, making identifying and controlling cost drivers difficult.

The following are the key issues included:

- **Visibility gaps**: The absence of detailed cost reporting and analytics made it challenging to understand where and how money was being spent.
- **Resource over-provisioning**: Many services were provisioned with higher capacities than necessary to handle peak loads, leading to underutilization during normal operations.
- **Idle resources**: Several resources, such as App Services, ran continuously without active usage, contributing to unnecessary costs.
- **Orphaned services:** There were orphaned app service plans and other services that still incur charges despite not being actively used.
- **Lack of cost governance:** The organization needed formal processes to govern and optimize cloud spending, resulting in inefficiencies and wasted resources.

Rising costs significantly threatened the company's profitability, necessitating an urgent solution. The company needed a systematic approach to gain visibility into its Azure expenditures, identify cost-saving opportunities, and implement sustainable cost management practices. This was crucial to managing and optimizing its cloud spending without compromising performance and ensuring the company's financial health.

The solution

The in-house team was tasked with implementing a FinOps strategy on Azure. The approach included:

- **Assessment and analysis**: Conduct a thorough audit of the existing Azure infrastructure and expenditures using Azure **Kusto Query Language (KQL)** to query and analyze usage data. This allowed the team to identify ways, detect anomalies, and pinpoint areas where costs could be reduced. By leveraging KQL, they could create detailed reports and dashboards to visualize spending across various services and departments.

   This script efficiently iterates through each resource, applying specific tags such as "Environment" and "Department." Tagging resources is a best practice in cloud management, as it helps with cost allocation, resource organization, and compliance reporting. By implementing this script, organizations can ensure consistency in resource management and simplify governance processes. Here's how the script functions:

```
// Example KQL query to identify unused App Service Plans
AppServicePlans
| where TotalRequests == 0 and TimeGenerated > ago(30d)
| project AppServicePlanName, ResourceGroupName, SubscriptionId
```

- **Optimization strategy**: Develop an optimization strategy using Azure Workbooks to visualize and monitor resource utilization. The strategy focused on rightsizing resources by matching capacity with actual usage, identifying and addressing idle resources, and consolidating services to reduce redundancy. Azure Workbooks provided interactive and customizable visualizations that helped track real-time performance and cost metrics.

The following PowerShell script demonstrates how to assign tags to each resource programmatically within an Azure subscription. Tags like **Environment** and **Department** can be crucial for tracking resource usage, budgeting, and implementing governance policies. This script simplifies the process, ensuring all resources are correctly tagged and facilitating better resource organization and reporting. Here is how the script works:

```
// Example KQL query for Azure Workbook to track resource utilization
Perf
| where TimeGenerated > ago(30d)
| summarize avg(CounterValue) by bin(TimeGenerated, 1d), CounterName
| render timechart
```

- **Tools and automation**: Utilizing advanced tools like PowerShell scripts to automate the monitoring, prediction, and enforcement of cost-saving policies. PowerShell scripts were used to automate routine tasks such as scaling resources up or down based on demand, shutting down idle resources, and tagging resources for better management. Automation ensured that cost-saving measures were applied consistently and efficiently, minimizing manual intervention.

The following PowerShell script is utilized. This script iterates through each resource, extracting key details such as the resource name, type, location, and tags, and outputs this information in a structured format. This approach is handy for inventory management, auditing, and ensuring that resources are properly configured and tagged. Here is the script:

```
# PowerShell script to scale down idle App Services
$appServices = Get-AzWebApp | Where-Object { $_.State -eq 'Running'
-and $_.LastRequest -lt (Get-Date).AddDays(-30) }
```

```
foreach ($app in $appServices) {
    Stop-AzWebApp -ResourceGroupName $app.ResourceGroup -Name $app.
    Name

    Set-AzWebApp -ResourceGroupName $app.ResourceGroup -Name $app.
    Name -AppServicePlan "FreeTierPlan"
}
```

- **Training and governance**: The IT and finance teams were educated on FinOps principles and used tags to establish governance frameworks to sustain cost optimization and ensure proper resource allocation and tracking. Training sessions were conducted to familiarize teams with cost management tools and practices, while tagging policies were implemented to categorize and track resources based on usage and ownership. This governance framework helped maintain accountability and transparency in cloud spending.

The following PowerShell script is used to apply tags to all resources within a given subscription. By tagging resources with attributes such as **Owner** and **Environment**, organizations can better categorize and manage their cloud assets, enabling more efficient governance, cost management, and compliance monitoring. Here's the script:

```
# PowerShell script to tag resources

$resources = Get-AzResource

foreach ($resource in $resources) {
    New-AzTag -ResourceId $resource.Id -Tag @{"Owner" = "Finance";
    "Environment" = "Production"}
}
```

Cloud cost optimization

In this section, we will go through the challenges and remedies of cloud cost optimization:

- **Challenges:**
  - **Lack of visibility**: Difficulty in tracking and understanding Azure spending across various services and departments. Many organizations need more visibility into their cloud usage and costs. With a unified view, it becomes easier to pinpoint which services are driving costs and how they are being utilized. This lack of transparency hinders effective decision-making and cost control.
  - **Orphaned app service plans**: Unused App Service Plans still incur charges. As applications are decommissioned or moved, their associated App Service Plans can be forgotten and left running, incurring unnecessary charges. These

orphaned services should be more prominent in cost audits, leading to wasted expenditures.

- o **Idle app services**: Idle App Services running without traffic leads to unnecessary costs. Applications or services no longer in active use but have not been shut down continue to generate expenses. These idle resources consume the budget without providing value, highlighting the need for regular reviews and decommissioning of unused services.

- o **Complex pricing models**: Running complex Azure pricing models and identifying the most cost-effective options can be overwhelming. Azure offers a required of pricing options and configurations, which can be overwhelming to manage—understanding which pricing model or tier best suits the organization's usage patterns requires in-depth analysis and expertise.

- • **Remedies**:
  - o **Unified dashboard**: Executing a dashboard for real-time visibility into Azure spending and resource utilization, leveraging Azure Workbooks. This dashboard consolidates data from various sources, providing a comprehensive view of cloud spending and resource usage. It enables stakeholders to monitor costs in real time, identify trends, and make informed decisions.

The following script is designed to analyze Azure App Service resources by joining relevant data from the Azure resources dataset. It performs several key operations including filtering for specific resource types, calculating the number of running instances, and mapping the appropriate App Service Plan sizes to their recommended maximum application counts. This process ensures optimal resource utilization and provides insights into the current usage versus the recommended thresholds. Below is the detailed script:

This code snippet selects all resources of type **microsoft.web/hostingenvironments** and projects the **aseJoinId** column:

```
resources
    | where type == "microsoft.web/hostingenvironments"
    | project aseJoinId = toupper(id)
    | join kind=leftouter (
        resources
        | where type == "microsoft.web/serverfarms"
        | extend aseJoinId = toupper(properties.hostingEnvironmentId)
        | summarize ase_used_instances = sum(toint(sku.capacity)) by
        aseJoinId
    ) on $left.aseJoinId == $right.aseJoinId
```

This code snippet joins the **resources** table with itself, using a left outer join, to get the number of used instances for each app service environment.

```
| join kind=fullouter (
    resources
    | where type == "microsoft.web/serverfarms"
    | project id, tier = sku.tier, size = sku.size, instances
    = toint(sku.capacity), aseJoinId = toupper(properties.
    hostingEnvironmentId), aspJoinId = toupper(id)
    | project aseJoinId, aspJoinId, instances, tier, size
) on $left.aseJoinId == $right.aseJoinId
```

This code snippet joins the resources table with itself again, using a full outer join, to get the app service plan ID, tier, size, and number of instances for each app service environment.

```
| join kind=leftouter (
        resources
        | where type == "microsoft.web/sites" or type ==
        "microsoft.web/sites/slots"
        | extend aspJoinId = toupper(properties.serverFarmId),
        isRunning iif(properties.state == "Running", 1, 0)
        | summarize appCount=count(),
        runningCount=sum(isRunning), app_ids = make_set(id) by
        aspJoinId
) on $left.aspJoinId == $right.aspJoinId
```

This code snippet joins the resources table with itself again, using a left outer join, to get the number of apps, running apps, and app IDs for each app service plan:

```
| extend
    maxAppRecommendation =
        case(
            size == 'F1', 9999,
            size == 'B1', 8,
            size == 'S1', 8,
            size == 'P1v2', 8,
            size == 'I1', 8,
            size == 'B2', 16,
            size == 'S2', 16,
            size == 'P1v3', 16,
```

```
            size == 'P2v2', 16,
            size == 'I2', 16,
            size == 'I1v2', 16,
            size == 'B3', 32,
            size == 'S3', 32,
       size == 'P3v2', 32,
            size == 'P2v3', 32,
      size == 'I3', 32,
        size == 'I2v2', 32,
            size == 'P3v3', 64,
            size == 'I3v2', 64,
            size == 'I4v2', 128,
            size == 'I5v2', 256,
            size == 'I6v2', 512,
        0
    )
```

This code snippet calculates the maximum number of hybrid connections that can be hosted on each app service plan size:

```
| extend
    allowedHybridConnections = case(
        substring(size, 0, 1)  == 'B', 5,
        substring(size, 0, 1)  == 'S', 25,
        substring(size, 0, 1)  == 'P', 220,
        substring(size, 0, 1)  == 'I', 220,
        0
    )
```

This code snippet calculates the number of remaining app slots for each app service plan.

```
| extend
    remainingAppSlots = maxAppRecommendation - appCount,
    used_recommended_apps = min_of(maxAppRecommendation, appCount)
| extend
    remaining_recommended_apps = max_of(0, remainingAppSlots),
    over_recommended_apps =  -min_of(remainingAppSlots, 0)
| project
```

```
        aseId = aseJoinId,

        aspId = aspJoinId,

        tier,

        size,

        instances,

        appCount,

        runningCount,

        remaining_possible_instances = min_of(100 - instances, (200 -
        ase_used_instances)),

        used_recommended_apps,

        remaining_recommended_apps,

        over_recommended_apps,

        app_ids = app_ids,

        app_ids_json_string = tostring(app_ids),

        apps_label =
            strcat(
                case(remaining_recommended_apps > 0,
                strcat(tostring(used_recommended_apps), " (",
                tostring(remaining_recommended_apps), " remaining)"),
                ""),
                case(over_recommended_apps > 0, strcat(tostring(appCount),
                " (",tostring(over_recommended_apps), " over)"), "")
            ),
        allowedHybridConnections


| order by appCount, instances desc
```

- **Rightsizing and consolidation**: Regularly analyze and adjust resource allocations to match actual usage, including resizing apps to the free tier and consolidating multiple apps onto a single App Service Plan. This involves periodically reviewing resource usage and adjusting configurations to align with current demand. By consolidating apps into fewer service plans, the organization can maximize resource utilization and reduce overhead costs.

The following PowerShell script is designed to achieve this by moving applications from multiple source App Service Plans into a single, consolidated App Service Plan. By running this script, you can streamline your App Service infrastructure, leading to more efficient management and potentially significant cost savings. Below is the script that performs this consolidation:

```
# PowerShell script to consolidate multiple apps onto a single App
Service Plan
$sourceAppServicePlans = @("AppServicePlan1", "AppServicePlan2")
$destinationAppServicePlan = "ConsolidatedAppServicePlan"
$resourceGroupName = "ResourceGroup"

foreach ($sourcePlan in $sourceAppServicePlans) {
    $apps = Get-AzWebApp -ResourceGroupName $resourceGroupName |
    Where-Object {$_.AppServicePlanId -eq $sourcePlan }
    foreach ($app in $apps) {
        Set-AzWebApp -ResourceGroupName $resourceGroupName -Name
        $app.Name AppServicePlan $destinationAppServicePlan
    }
}
```

- **Automated policies**: Setting up computerized policies using PowerShell scripts to shut down or scale down unused or underutilized resources. Automation ensures that cost-saving measures are consistently applied without relying on manual intervention. Scripts can be scheduled to run regularly, checking for idle resources and taking appropriate actions to minimize costs.

- **Cost-aware development**: This encourages development practices considering cost implications, such as using serverless architectures and optimizing code for efficiency. Developers are trained to incorporate cost considerations into their workflow, selecting technologies and designing solutions that maximize resource usage. Serverless architectures, for example, can provide significant cost savings by scaling automatically based on demand.

Specific actions taken:

- **Identifying orphaned app service plans**: Used Azure KQL to detect and decommission orphaned App Service Plans that were no longer associated with any running applications.

```
AppServicePlans
| where TotalRequests == 0 and TimeGenerated > ago(30d)
| project AppServicePlanName, ResourceGroupName, SubscriptionId
```

- **Addressing idle app services**: Identified and scaled-down idle App Services to the free tier or lower-cost plans using PowerShell scripts.

```
$appServices = Get-AzWebApp | Where-Object { $_.State -eq 'Running'
-and $_.LastRequest -lt (Get-Date).AddDays(-30) }
foreach ($app in $appServices) {
```

```
    Stop-AzWebApp -ResourceGroupName $app.ResourceGroup -Name $app.
    Name

    Set-AzWebApp -ResourceGroupName $app.ResourceGroup -Name $app.
    Name AppServicePlan "FreeTierPlan"
}
```

- **Consolidating apps**: Moved two to three applications onto a single App Service Plan to maximize resource utilization and reduce costs.

```
# PowerShell script to consolidate multiple apps onto a single App
Service Plan

$sourceAppServicePlans = @("AppServicePlan1", "AppServicePlan2")

$destinationAppServicePlan = "ConsolidatedAppServicePlan"

$resourceGroupName = "ResourceGroup"


foreach ($sourcePlan in $sourceAppServicePlans) {

    $apps = Get-AzWebApp -ResourceGroupName $resourceGroupName |
    Where-Object { $_.AppServicePlanId -eq $sourcePlan }

    foreach ($app in $apps) {

        Set-AzWebApp -ResourceGroupName $resourceGroupName -Name
        $app.Name -AppServicePlan $destinationAppServicePlan

    }

}
```

Benefits and impact of the solutions and remedies

The following are the benefits and impact of the solutions and remedies:

- **Benefits:**
  - **Cost savings**: Completed a 30% reduction in monthly Azure spend within the first three months. This reduction was accomplished by identifying and decommissioning unused resources, rightsizing over-provisioned services, and consolidating multiple applications onto fewer App Service Plans.
  - **Improved efficiency:** Enhanced application performance by eliminating over-provisioned resources and optimizing usage. The performance of critical applications was enhanced by ensuring that resources were allocated based on actual demand rather than peak usage. This optimization also reduced the waste of resources, ensuring that the applications ran more efficiently.
  - **Predictable costs:** Established predictable cloud costs through better forecasting and budgeting practices. The team could accurately forecast future spending by implementing real-time monitoring and detailed reporting using

Azure Workbooks. This predictability allowed for more precise budgeting and financial planning, reducing unexpected costs, and improving financial management.

○ **Sustainability:** Created a sustainable cost management framework ensuring ongoing savings and efficiency. Implementing automated policies and regular audits ensured that cost-saving measures were not just one-time actions but part of a continuous process. This sustainability was vital to maintaining long-term financial health and operational efficiency.

- **Impact:**
  ○ **Financial:** The company saved approximately $1 million annually, significantly improving its profit margins. These savings were reinvested into other strategic initiatives, driving further growth and innovation.

  ○ **Operational:** Streamlined operations with better resource management and automation. Automating routine tasks such as scaling and tagging resources freed up valuable time for the IT team to focus on more strategic activities.

  ○ **Strategic:** Enabled the company to reinvest savings into innovation and growth initiatives. The company could allocate more resources towards developing new products and services with the realization of financial and operational benefits.

Case study 2: Cost allocation and chargeback in a large enterprise

In a large enterprise, managing cloud costs effectively is critical to maintaining financial health and operational efficiency. As organizations scale, the complexity of cloud environments increases, with multiple departments and business units utilizing shared cloud resources. This shared usage often challenges tracking, attributing, and managing costs. It isn't easy to allocate costs accurately and ensure that each department is easier to use without clearly understanding how resources are consumed and by whom.

However, implementing cost allocation and chargeback mechanisms can make this challenge an opportunity. They provide a structured approach to distribute cloud costs fairly among different departments and business units based on their usage. Implementing these mechanisms promotes cost transparency and encourages departments to use resources more efficiently, driving overall cost optimization and fostering a culture of financial responsibility.

This case study explores how an enterprise implemented a robust cost allocation and chargeback system using FinOps principles on Microsoft Azure. The enterprise achieved improved cost visibility, accountability, and financial management by leveraging Azure's powerful cost management tools, automated chargeback processes, and governance frameworks. The case study details the specific challenges faced, the solutions implemented, and the significant benefits realized, showcasing the impact of effective cost management practices in a large organization.

Key challenges

A global enterprise with various business units faced significant challenges in managing and allocating cloud costs. Multiple departments, including R&D, marketing, sales, and IT operations, used the shared cloud infrastructure on Microsoft Azure. These departments often had different requirements and usage practices, further complicating cost management.

The primary issues included:

- **Lack of cost visibility**: The enterprise needed help tracking cloud costs to specific departments and projects. With detailed insights into how resources were being consumed, it was easier to identify cost drivers and areas of inefficiency. The absence of cost data made deciding on resource allocation and budget planning complex.

- **Inefficient resource utilization**: Overprovisioned and underutilized resources lead to wasted costs. Departments usually request more resources than necessary to avoid potential performance issues, resulting in significant underutilization. This practice raises costs and makes it harder to identify and correct inefficiencies.

- **Cost accountability**: There needed to be a chargeback mechanism to hold departments accountable for their cloud usage. Without a formal system to allocate costs based on actual usage, departments had little incentive to monitor and optimize their resource consumption. This lack of accountability contributed to unchecked spending and inefficiencies.

- **Budget overruns**: The enterprise frequently experienced budget overruns due to unpredictable cloud spending and a lack of cost controls. Departments would exceed their allocated budgets, often without warning, leading to financial strain and reactive cost-cutting measures. This unpredictability made planning and managing the overall IT budget challenging.

The enterprise needed a systematic approach to allocate costs accurately, implement chargeback mechanisms, and ensure efficient use of cloud resources. A solution that provided detailed visibility into cloud spending, promoted resource optimization, and enforced cost accountability was essential to address these challenges and achieve sustainable financial management.

The solution

The FinOps team implemented a comprehensive cost allocation and chargeback strategy on Azure. The approach included:

- **Cost visibility and reporting**: Utilizing Azure Cost Management and Billing to gain detailed insights into cloud spending. Custom dashboards and reports were created to track costs by department, project, and resource type. These dashboards allowed for real-time monitoring and historical analysis, enabling better budgeting and forecasting.

The following KQL script is designed to create a cost report that breaks down expenses by department for the current month. By using this query, you can gain insights into departmental spending patterns, helping you to manage budgets and identify areas where cost optimization might be needed. Below is the KQL query that achieves this:

```
// Example KQL query to generate cost reports by department
Usage
| where TimeGenerated > startofmonth(now())
| summarize Cost = sum(PreTaxCost) by Department, bin(TimeGenerated,
1d)
| project Department, Cost, TimeGenerated
```

- **Tagging and resource grouping**: Implementing a comprehensive tagging strategy to categorize resources by department, project, and owner. Tags were enforced using policies to ensure consistency and accuracy in cost attribution. This approach enabled the team to attribute costs more precisely and facilitated easier reporting and analysis.

The following PowerShell script automates the process of tagging all resources within a subscription based on their department and owner. By applying these tags, you can easily categorize resources, streamline reporting, and ensure that each department's resource usage is accurately accounted for. Here's the script that handles this tagging:

```
# PowerShell script to tag resources by department
$resources = Get-AzResource
foreach ($resource in $resources) {
    New-AzTag -ResourceId $resource.Id -Tag @{"Department" =
    $resource.Department; "Owner" = $resource.Owner}
}
```

- **Automated chargeback mechanism:** Developing an automated chargeback system using Azure Automation and PowerShell scripts. The system calculated monthly costs for each department and generated chargeback reports, which integrated with the enterprise's financial systems. This automated approach ensured timely and accurate billing, reducing administrative overhead and minimizing errors.

The following PowerShell script automates the process of calculating the monthly costs for each department by leveraging Azure tags and generating a chargeback report. This report helps departments understand their cloud spending and ensures that costs are appropriately allocated. Below is the script that accomplishes this:

```powershell
# PowerShell script to calculate monthly costs and generate chargeback
reports
$departments = Get-AzTag -TagName "Department"
foreach ($department in $departments) {
    $costs = Get-AzConsumptionUsageDetail -StartDate (Get-Date).
    AddMonths(-1).ToString("yyyy-MM-01") -EndDate (Get-Date).
    ToString("yyyy-MM-01") -ResourceGroupName $department.
    ResourceGroup   $totalCost = ($costs | Measure-Object -Property
    PreTaxCost -Sum).Sum

    # Generate chargeback report
  New-Object PSObject -Property @{
        Department = $department.Name
        Cost = $totalCost
        Month = (Get-Date).AddMonths(-1).ToString("yyyy-MM")
    }
}
```

- **Cost optimization and governance:** Governance frameworks were established to enforce cost optimization practices, such as rightsizing resources, eliminating idle resources, and optimizing storage. Regular audits and reviews were conducted to ensure compliance with cost management policies. The governance framework included policies for regular review cycles and automated alerts for cost anomalies.

  The following PowerShell script automates this process by identifying resources that have not been used for over a month and then decommissioning them. By removing these idle resources, you can free up capacity and ensure that your cloud environment is operating efficiently. Below is the script that performs this task:

```powershell
# PowerShell script to identify and decommission idle resources
$idleResources = Get-AzResource | Where-Object { $_.LastUsed -lt (Get-
Date).AddMonths(-1) }
foreach ($resource in $idleResources) {
    Remove-AzResource -ResourceId $resource.Id -Force
}
```

The following are the steps to implement the governance framework:

1. **Policy definition:** Define policies for tagging, resource allocation, and decommissioning idle resources.

2. **Policy enforcement:** Use Azure Policy and Azure Automation to enforce these policies automatically.

3. **Regular audits:** Schedule regular audits to review policy compliance and identify optimization opportunities.

4. **Training and awareness:** Conduct training sessions to ensure all stakeholders understand the policies and their importance.

The following Azure Policy definition is an example of how to enforce a tagging policy that ensures all resources are tagged with a department and owner. If a resource lacks the required tags, the policy automatically adds them, maintaining compliance across the environment. Following is the policy definition:

```
# Example of setting an Azure Policy for resource tagging compliance
$definition = New-AzPolicyDefinition -Name "TaggingPolicy" -DisplayName
"Ensure resources are tagged with department and owner" -Policy '{
    "if": {
        "not": {
            "field": "tags.Department",
            "exists": true
        }
    },
    "then": {
        "effect": "modify",
        "details": {
            "roleDefinitionIds": [
             "/providers/Microsoft.Authorization/roleDefinitions/...",
              "/providers/Microsoft.Authorization/roleDefinitions/..."
            ],
            "operations": [
                {
                    "operation": "add",
                    "field": "tags.Department",
                    "value": "[parameters('Department')]"
                }
            ]
        }
    }
}'
```

- **Creating Azure workbooks for governance dashboards:** The team created Azure workbooks to support governance and provide a centralized view of resource utilization and cost metrics. These interactive dashboards offered customizable visualizations and reports, allowing stakeholders to monitor compliance, cost optimization, and resource utilization in real time.

The following are the steps to create Azure Workbooks:

1. **Define metrics and key performance indicators (KPIs)**: Identify KPIs and metrics to track, such as resource utilization, cost trends, and compliance with tagging policies.

2. **Create Queries**: Use KQL to write queries that fetch the required data from Azure resources and cost management data.

   The following Kusto Query Language (KQL) query is designed to be used in a Workbook to monitor tagging compliance across resources. It identifies resources that are missing essential tags, such as "Department" or "Owner," and provides a count of non-compliant resources by type. This query helps in quickly identifying areas where tagging policies may need to be enforced or corrected. Below is the KQL query:

```
// Example KQL query for Workbook to track tagging compliance
Resources
    | where isnull(tags['Department']) or isnull(tags['Owner'])
    | summarize count() by type
    | project ResourceType = type, NonCompliantCount = count_
```

3. **Design workbook**: Use the Azure Workbooks interface to design and configure the visualizations and reports based on the queries. Add interactive elements like dropdowns, filters, and time-range selectors to allow users to customize the view.

4. **Publish and share**: Save the workbook and share it with relevant stakeholders. Set up automated email reports or alerts for critical metrics to ensure timely awareness and action.

The following are the example workbook sections:

Tagging compliance: Track the compliance status of resources with the defined tagging policy.

This part of the query helps in identifying how many resource groups are tagged versus those that are not. This is crucial for ensuring that resource groups are properly categorized and managed.

```
//Tag Usage Overview
ResourceContainers
| where type =~ 'microsoft.resources/subscriptions/resourcegroups'
```

```
| extend TagBool = iff(tags != '' and tags != '[]', "Tagged","Untagged")
| summarize count() by TagBool
| project resourceGroup, tags
```

This query provides an overview of how many resources have tags applied and how many do not. Proper tagging is essential for cost management, governance, and resource organization.

```
//Tagged Resource Groups
Resources
| extend TagBool = iff(tags != '' and tags != '[]', "Tagged","Untagged")
| summarize count() by TagBool
```

This part of the script is used to determine the total number of untagged resources within the Azure environment. Knowing this helps in taking corrective actions to ensure all resources are properly tagged.

```
//Total Count of Untagged Resources
resources
| mvexpand tags
| where tags == '' or isempty(tags)
| project Name=id, subscriptionId
| summarize count()
```

This query helps in understanding the variety of tag keys being used across resources. This is useful for standardizing tagging practices and ensuring consistency in how resources are tagged.

```
//Unique Resource Tag Keys
resources
| mvexpand tags
| where tags != '' or isnotempty(tags)
| extend tagKey = tostring(bag_keys(tags)[0])
| extend tagValue = tostring(tags[tagKey])
| project tagKey, tagValue
| distinct tagKey
| summarize count()
```

Understanding the different tag values associated with keys provides insights into how resources are categorized and managed. This can help in refining tagging strategies to improve governance and reporting.

```
//Unique Resource Tags
```

```
resources
| mvexpand tags
| where tags != '' or isnotempty(tags)
| extend tagKey = tostring(bag_keys(tags)[0])
| extend tagValue = tostring(tags[tagKey])
| project tagKey, tagValue
| distinct tagKey, tagValue
```

This detailed listing of untagged resources allows for direct action to be taken to ensure that these resources are tagged appropriately. It provides a clear path for remediation.

```
//Untagged Resources
resources
| mvexpand tags
| where tags == '' or isempty(tags)
| extend tagKey = tostring(bag_keys(tags)[0])
| extend tagValue = tostring(tags[tagKey])
| project name, type, resourceGroup
```

By looking at both resource groups and their tags, this query helps to ensure that entire sections of your Azure environment are compliant with tagging policies. It helps identify any gaps in tagging at the resource group level.

```
//Untagged Resource Groups
ResourceContainers
| where type =~ 'Microsoft.Resources/subscriptions'
| extend SubscriptionName=name
| join ( ResourceContainers | where type =~ 'microsoft.resources/
  subscriptions/resourcegroups' | mvexpand tags | where tags == '' or
  isempty(tags)
| extend resourceGroupName=id, RGLocation=location) on subscriptionId
| project resourceGroupName, RGLocation, SubscriptionName
| summarize count()
```

The following Kusto Query Language (KQL) script is designed to identify and count the unique tag keys applied across all resource groups within an Azure subscription. This can help in auditing and enforcing tagging policies to ensure consistency and compliance in resource management.

```
//Unique Resource Group Tags Keys
ResourceContainers
```

```
| where type == "microsoft.resources/subscriptions/resourcegroups"
| mvexpand tags
| where tags != '' or isnotempty(tags)
| extend tagKey = tostring(bag_keys(tags)[0])
| extend tagValue = tostring(tags[tagKey])
| project tagKey, tagValue
| distinct tagKey
| summarize count()
```

This KQL script is designed to count the number of unique tag keys associated with resource groups within an Azure subscription. By analyzing the tag keys, this query helps you ensure that all resource groups are tagged consistently, which is crucial for resource management, governance, and cost optimization.

```
//Unique Resource Group Tags
ResourceContainers
| where type == "microsoft.resources/subscriptions/resourcegroups"
| mvexpand tags
| where tags != '' or isnotempty(tags)
| extend tagKey = tostring(bag_keys(tags)[0])
| extend tagValue = tostring(tags[tagKey])
| project tagKey, tagValue
| distinct tagKey, tagValue
```

The following KQL script is designed to identify and list all resource groups within an Azure subscription that do not have any tags applied. This can be particularly useful for identifying resources that may not be following your organization's tagging policies, which are crucial for proper resource management, cost allocation, and governance.

```
//Untagged Resource Groups List
ResourceContainers
| where type == "microsoft.resources/subscriptions/resourcegroups"
| mvexpand tags
| where tags == '' or isempty(tags)
| extend tagKey = tostring(bag_keys(tags)[0])
| extend tagValue = tostring(tags[tagKey])
| project name, subscriptionId
```

Benefits and impact of the solutions and remedies

The following are the benefits and impact of the solutions and remedies:

- **Benefits:**
  - **Improved cost visibility**: Detailed and accurate reporting of cloud costs by department and project provided greater transparency and control over expenditures. Custom dashboards assigned stakeholders, allowing them to monitor their usage and costs in real-time. This informed decision-making, making them feel more in control and responsible. The ability to visualize costs at granular levels helped identify and address cost drivers effectively.
  - **Accountability**: The chargeback mechanism held departments accountable for cloud usage, encouraging responsible consumption and cost awareness. Departments became more aware of their spending, leading to more efficient resource use. This accountability enabled a culture of financial responsibility and operational efficiency.
  - **Resource optimization**: Regular audits and automated cost optimization techniques improved resource utilization and efficiency. Identifying and decommissioning idle resources and enforcing rightsizing policies reduced waste and improved overall efficiency. Regular optimization reviews provided that resources were allocated based on actual needs rather than ideas.
  - **Budget control**: Predictable and controlled cloud spending reduced budget overruns and improved financial planning. The automated chargeback system ensured that each department stayed within its allocated budget, reducing the risk of unexpected costs. This predictability allowed for more accurate financial planning and resource allocation across the organization.
- **Impact:**
  - **Financial**: The enterprise achieved significant cost savings by eliminating waste and optimizing resource usage. The chargeback system enabled better budget management and financial accountability, leading to an overall improvement in the company's financial health. The cost savings were substantial enough to positively impact the enterprise's bottom line, freeing up funds for other strategic investments.
  - **Operational**: Streamlined operations with improved resource management and cost control. The automated chargeback system reduced manual effort and errors in cost allocation, freeing up valuable time for IT and finance teams to focus on strategic initiatives. The improved efficiency in resource management also translated to better service delivery and operational performance.

    o **Strategic**: Enabled strategic decision-making with accurate and timely cost data. The savings realized were reinvested into innovation and growth initiatives, driving business success, and maintaining a competitive edge in the market. The ability to allocate resources effectively and predict future costs provided a strategic advantage in planning and executing business objectives.

Case study 3: DevOps and FinOps collaboration

In modern enterprises, the collaboration between DevOps and FinOps teams appears powerful for achieving operational efficiency and financial accountability in cloud environments. DevOps enhances agility and deployment speed by facilitating development and operations processes. FinOps ensures fiscal sense by managing cloud costs and optimizing financial performance. When these two disciplines converge, organizations can unlock the possibility of their cloud investments by adjusting performance with cost efficiency.

The crossing of DevOps and FinOps brings an approach to cloud management. DevOps practices ensure that applications are delivered quickly using automation and **continuous integration/deployment** (**CI/CD**) pipelines. FinOps, on the other hand, provides the financial governance needed to monitor and control cloud spending, implementing policies and practices that ensure the cost-effective use of cloud resources.

This case study discusses the journey of a large enterprise that recognized the need for an environment between its DevOps and FinOps teams, Microsoft Azure. The enterprise identified that operations were leading to inefficiencies and missed opportunities for cost savings.

The case study details the solutions implemented and the actual benefits realized, showcasing the impact of effective collaboration between DevOps and FinOps. It shows how aligning technical and financial objectives can drive significant improvements in operational performance and cost management, ultimately supporting the enterprise's strategic goals.

The need

An enterprise with a complicated cloud infrastructure faced several challenges that necessitated collaboration between its DevOps and FinOps teams.

The primary issues included:

- **Rapidly increasing cloud costs**: As the organization scaled its cloud usage, costs increased rapidly without corresponding visibility and control mechanisms. This lack of transparency made it difficult to identify and address the root causes of cost spikes, leading to inefficient spending and finances. The enterprise needed tools and processes to achieve detailed insights into their cloud costs and manage them effectively.

- **Operational as team**: DevOps and FinOps teams operated, leading to inefficiencies and a need for more alignment between operational performance and financial objectives. This separation meant that DevOps focused on speed and reliability, often without considering cost drifts, while FinOps concentrated on financial control without understanding the operational needs. The lack of communication and collaboration resulted in inconsistent priorities and decision-making.

- **Resource over-provisioning**: Development and operations teams often over-provisioned resources to avoid performance issues, resulting in significant underutilization and wasted costs. Without tools to right size resources based on actual usage patterns, the enterprise frequently paid for more capacity than necessary. This over-provisioning was a marked contributor to escalating cloud costs.

- **Budget overruns**: Regular budget overruns occur due to unpredictable cloud spending and a lack of proactive cost management practices. Not having forecasting and budget tracking tools made predicting and controlling costs easier, leading to financial surprises and reactive cost-cutting measures. The enterprise needed a proactive approach to monitoring and managing cloud spending, ensuring it stayed within budget constraints.

The enterprise needed a strategy to integrate the DevOps and FinOps practices, ensuring that cloud operations were efficient and financially sustainable.

The solution

The enterprise's strategy to promote collaboration between DevOps and FinOps teams on Azure included several key components:

- **Shared goals and metrics:** Setting shared goals and **key performance indicators (KPIs)** that align with both teams' objectives. Metrics included cost per deployment, resource utilization efficiency, and budget adherence.

- **Collaborative planning:** Regular planning sessions involving DevOps and FinOps teams to set common goals and agree on metrics that matter to both sides. This ensured that financial considerations were integrated into the operational decision-making process.

- **Integrated dashboards and reporting:** Developing integrated dashboards using Azure Monitor, Azure Cost Management, and Azure DevOps to provide a suitable view of operational performance and cost metrics.

  This **Kusto Query Language (KQL)** script is designed to combine cost and performance metrics for Azure resources. By using a union operation, the query merges data related to both cost and CPU performance, allowing for a comprehensive analysis of resource usage in terms of both financial expenditure and computational efficiency.

```
// Example KQL query to combine cost and performance metrics
union (
    Usage
    | summarize Cost = sum(PreTaxCost) by ResourceGroup,
    bin(TimeGenerated, 1d)
    | project TimeGenerated, ResourceGroup, Cost
), (
    Perf
    | summarize AvgCPU = avg(CounterValue) by ResourceGroup,
    bin(TimeGenerated, 1d)
    | project TimeGenerated, ResourceGroup, AvgCPU
)
| join kind=inner (Usage | summarize sum(PreTaxCost) by bin(TimeGenerated,
1d)) on TimeGenerated
| project TimeGenerated, ResourceGroup, Cost, AvgCPU
```

- **Unified monitoring**: Creation of dashboards that allowed both teams to monitor key metrics in real time, enabling proactive management of both performance and costs. This integration helped ensure that operational decisions were informed by financial data.

- **Automated cost management:** Implementing automated cost management and optimization practices using Azure Automation and PowerShell scripts. These scripts were designed to enforce policies for resource provisioning, rightsizing, and shutting down idle resources.

The PowerShell script provided is designed to automate the process of rightsizing Azure Virtual Machines (VMs) based on their CPU usage. Rightsizing involves adjusting the resources allocated to a VM to better match its workload, which can help optimize performance and reduce costs.

```
# PowerShell script to automate rightsizing of resources
$vms = Get-AzVM
foreach ($vm in $vms) {
    $metrics = Get-AzMetric -ResourceId $vm.Id -MetricName
    "Percentage CPU" -TimeGrain "PT1H" -StartTime (Get-Date).
    AddDays(-7) -EndTime (Get-Date)
    $averageCPU = ($metrics.Data | Measure-Object -Property Average
    -Average).Average
```

```
if ($averageCPU -lt 20) {

    Resize-AzVM -ResourceGroupName $vm.ResourceGroupName -VMName
    $vm.Name -Size "Standard_DS1_v2"

}

}
```

- **Automated policies**: Implementation of scripts that automatically adjust resource allocations based on real-time usage data, ensuring that resources were neither over-provisioned nor underutilized. This automation reduced manual intervention and increased efficiency.

- **Collaborative governance framework:** Establishing a governance framework that involved both DevOps and FinOps teams in decision-making processes related to cloud resource management. Regular meetings and joint reviews were conducted to ensure alignment and continuous improvement.

This PowerShell script is an effective way to automate the rightsizing of Azure VMs based on their CPU usage. By regularly running this script, organizations can ensure that their VMs are appropriately sized for their workloads, helping to reduce costs and improve efficiency in the cloud environment.

```
# Example of setting up a governance policy for resource tagging

$definition = New-AzPolicyDefinition -Name "TaggingPolicy" -DisplayName
"Ensure resources are tagged with environment and cost center" -Policy
'{

    "if": {

        "not": {

            "field": "tags.Environment",

            "exists": true

        }

    },

    "then": {

        "effect": "modify",

        "details": {

            "roleDefinitionIds": [

             "/providers/Microsoft.Authorization/roleDefinitions/...",

              "/providers/Microsoft.Authorization/roleDefinitions/..."

            ],

            "operations": [

                {

                    "operation": "add",
```

```
                    "field": "tags.Environment",
                    "value": "[parameters('Environment')]"
                }
            ]
        }
    }
}'
```

- **Joint governance:** Both teams define and enforce governance policies, prioritizing operational efficiency and cost management. This collaboration helped align the goals of both teams and enabled better decision-making.

- **Training and culture building:** Conducting joint training sessions for DevOps and FinOps teams to build a shared understanding of each other's priorities and processes. This training highlighted the importance of cost management in operational decisions and the impact of operational efficiency on financial performance.

- **Cross-training programs**: Training programs were developed that educated both teams on each other's roles and the importance of their collaboration. This encouraged a culture of mutual respect and understanding, leading to more cohesive and effective teamwork.

- **Workshops and knowledge sharing**: Regular workshops and knowledge-sharing sessions to keep both teams informed about the latest tools, practices, and strategies for optimizing cloud operations and costs.

Benefits and impact of the solutions and remedies

The following are the benefits and impact of the solutions and remedies:

- **Benefits:**
  - **Improved cost visibility:** Integrated dashboards and reporting provided detailed, real-time insights into operational performance and cloud costs. This visibility enabled proactive management and timely adjustments to align with financial goals.
  - **Operational efficiency:** Collaboration led to more efficient use of cloud resources, with DevOps and FinOps teams jointly identifying and eliminating waste. Automated rightsizing and resource management ensured optimal utilization without manual intervention.
  - **Cost accountability:** Our shared metrics and goals were pivotal in promoting accountability for cloud spending across both teams. This accountability fostered more thoughtful provisioning and use of resources, aligning our operational decisions with our shared financial objectives.

    o **Budget control:** Enhanced budget control through predictive cost management and automated enforcement of cost-saving policies. The enterprise experienced fewer budget overruns and improved financial planning accuracy.

- **Impact:**

    o **Financial**: Optimizing resource utilization and eliminating unnecessary expenditures resulted in significant cost savings. The enterprise reduced cloud spending by 25%, translating to millions in annual savings.

    o **Operational**: Streamlined operations with enhanced collaboration and more efficient resource management. Reducing manual processes and improved team alignment led to faster deployments and better service delivery.

    o **Strategic**: Enabled strategic decision-making with accurate and comprehensive cost and performance data. Integrating DevOps and FinOps practices provided a holistic view of the cloud environment, facilitating better planning and execution of business strategies.

Conclusion

The integration of FinOps principles across various cloud management practices has shown benefits for large enterprises, as evidenced by the three case studies presented. These studies highlight the critical role of effective cost management, strategic collaboration, and robust governance in optimizing cloud expenditures while maintaining or enhancing operational efficiency.

Case study 1: FinOps cost optimization for a web application- The Implementing FinOps strategies for a web application hosted on Microsoft Azure showcased the importance of visibility, accountability, and proactive management. The enterprise achieved substantial cost savings and improved operational efficiency by addressing orphaned App Service Plans, idle App Services, and resource consolidation. This case underscored the need for continuous monitoring, automated optimization, and strategic planning to manage cloud costs effectively.

Case study 2: Cost allocation and chargeback in a large enterprise- Developing a comprehensive cost allocation and chargeback system demonstrated how detailed reporting, automated billing, and consistent governance can transform financial management in a cloud environment. By leveraging Azure's cost management tools and integrating automated chargeback mechanisms, the enterprise achieved better cost visibility, held departments accountable for their usage, and ensured budget adherence. This approach led to significant financial savings and more predictable budgeting, emphasizing the value of transparency and accountability in cloud financial management.

Case study 3: DevOps and FinOps collaboration: The collaboration between DevOps and FinOps teams highlighted the powerful impact of aligning technical and financial objectives. By integrating dashboards, automating cost management practices, and fostering a culture of shared goals and accountability, the enterprise streamlined operations and reduced cloud expenditures. The joint efforts of both teams led to optimized resource utilization, enhanced operational performance, and substantial cost savings. This case study illustrated the necessity of breaking down silos and promoting cross-functional collaboration to achieve holistic cloud management.

In the next chapter, readers will learn more about cloud cost management evolution by exploring different stages of evolution in terms of cloud financial management and how these modern approaches have been keeping us up with swift changes in technology patterns in public clouds. These include the Azure Well-Architected Framework and how it combines with FinOps to drive financial accountability across your organization, as well as maximize spending return in cloud cost optimization efforts. Next, the chapter will focus on AI and Machine Learning Workloads to specific strategies for Per-Azure: Cost Optimizations based around specialized optimization practices that are created in AI development focusing on tackling demanding high computation with fewer resource necessities, those all done without its overall performance and efficiency.

Join our book's Discord space

Join the book's Discord Workspace for Latest updates, Offers, Tech happenings around the world, New Release and Sessions with the Authors:

https://discord.bpbonline.com

## CHAPTER 11

Future Trends and Innovations in Azure FinOps

Introduction

As more organizations adopt cloud services, they aim for ways to make the most of their investments. Microsoft Azure offers tools and frameworks to help manage cloud finances effectively. This document looks at future trends in Azure FinOps, focusing on three key areas:

The concern now shifts to extracting more from what you invest and controlling the cost in optimal utilization of cloud services as most organizations tend towards will look forward for this way due to no infrastructure maintenance, eliminating high uptime and easier tracking. A business using Microsoft Azure can harness a broad set of tools and frameworks for managing the costs associated with cloud computing. One of the biggest keys to success is in adopting effective FinOps (financial operations) practice that helps you find a balance between innovation and fiscal responsibility, ensuring every dollar spent with your cloud provider broadly aligns back to high-value business goals.

This Azure FinOps landscape document covers important trends and practices that are changing the future of cloud financial management. First, it lays the groundwork for investing in cloud spending management best practices that not only rein in costs but also enable value creation. It should come as no surprise that the first best practice calls out integrating FinOps into your use of Azure Well-Architected Framework to maintain operational excellence and manage cost at a granular level.

With the increasing prevalence of **artificial intelligence (AI)** and machine learning workloads, it is crucial to have specialized cost optimization strategies. In this paper, we will examine how to manage the special requirements in workloads like AI and machine learning, protocols that allow an organization to leverage these technologies without running up a cost.

Running forward with these next-level strategies around FinOps, organizations can not only unlock improved financial agility but also maximize resource utilization while accelerating their competitiveness within the cloud arena.

Structure

In this chapter, we will go through the following topics:

- Cloud cost management evolution
- Azure well-architected framework and FinOps
- Azure cost optimization for AI and ML workloads

Objectives

This primary objective is to highlight the key motivations and benefits of using FinOps in a cloud-centric enterprise. Through three individual case studies, the paper aims to highlight common pain points that enterprises experience with cloud cost management and optimization — increased expenses, new reality, operational silos companionship, but not in a good fun way, and blown budgets are never nice. It shows real-world examples of ways to solve these problems through efficient FinOps practices, how resource optimization works, and how it helps reduce siloed technical and finance operations. The chapter also summarizes quantifiable FinOps-related gains seen in cost reduction, operational efficiency increases, and financial management improvement. The document highlights how the silos should be gotten rid of to have a successful approach in Performance vs. cost implementation by means of advertising cross-functional collaboration, especially among DevOps and FinOps teams. In addition, the post outlines a process for implementation that can act as a roadmap to FinOps and gives practical steps and execution strategies for other companies who are interested in fulfilling those principles. Enabling shared goals, leveraging cloud management tools, and conducting governance across the board. In the end, it helps organizations make those informed decisions while making their investments in the cloud align with long-term business goals.

The following writes up the points into a singular, coherent paragraph while staying true to its meaning and essence.

Cloud cost management evolution

Cloud cost management has developed significantly over the past decade, from basic monitoring and budgeting to comprehensive, data-driven strategies encompassing various practices and technologies. Here is an overview of the evolution of cloud cost management:

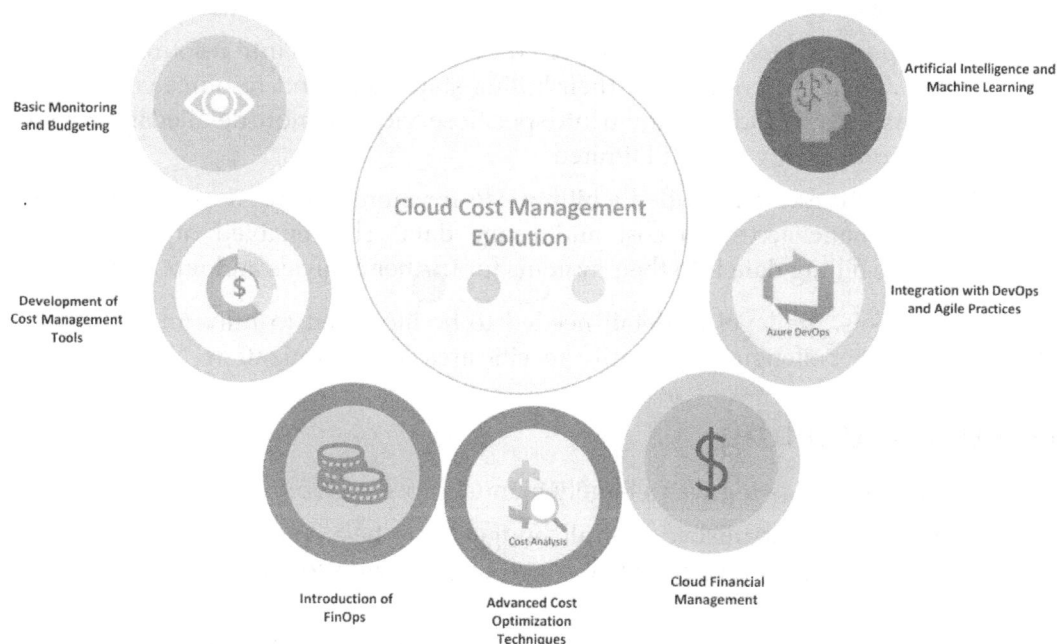

Figure 11.1: Cloud cost management evolution

Initial phase basic monitoring and budgeting in Azure

In the initial phase of cloud cost management, Azure users depended on essential tools provided by Microsoft to track their usage and costs. These tools were fundamental but offered crucial insights into resource consumption and expenditures. The primary focus was on essential monitoring, manual budgeting, and a reactive approach to cost management.

In the initial stages of Azure usage tracking and budgeting, organizations relied on basic tools and manual processes to manage their cloud expenses. These early efforts were crucial in laying the groundwork for more advanced cost management practices. Below are the key components and challenges associated with this phase.

Simple usage tracking

Azure offered basic dashboards and usage reports to help users track their resource usage. These tools included:

- **Azure Cost Management + Billing:** This feature delivered a high-level overview of usage and costs across various services. Users could see summaries of their spending on computing, storage, networking, and other resources.

- **Azure portal:** The Azure portal offered essential insights into resource usage and costs, allowing users to view their billing statements and resource consumption patterns. Users could drill down into specific services for more detailed information, but the granularity was still limited.

- **Billing API:** Azure provided a billing API for more advanced users that allowed programmatic access to cost and usage data. This enabled organizations to integrate billing data into their systems for further analysis and reporting.

Despite these tools, the level of detail needed to be increased to fully understand cost drivers, making it challenging to identify specific areas for optimization.

Manual budgeting

During this phase, budgeting was a largely manual process involving:

- Organizations established overall budgets for their Azure spending based on initial forecasts. These budgets were typically broad estimates rather than precise allocations.

- Users configured simple alerts to notify them when spending approached or exceeded predefined limits. For example, Azure allowed users to set up spending caps or alerts through the Azure portal or via email notifications.

- Organizations conduct periodic reviews of their Azure expenses at the end of each billing cycle. These reviews involved comparing actual spending against the established budgets and identifying discrepancies.

Reactive approach

The approach to managing Azure costs during this initial phase was predominantly reactive. Key characteristics of this approach included:

- Organizations primarily reviewed their Azure costs after they had been incurred. This post-spending analysis involved scrutinizing monthly billing statements and usage reports to identify cost spikes and anomalies.

- When unexpected cost spikes occur, organizations quickly investigate and address the causes of these spikes. This reactive approach often leads to temporary fixes rather than long-term solutions.

- Azure's essential tools needed advanced predictive capabilities, making it challenging for organizations to anticipate future spending patterns. With predictive analytics, users could optimize their resource usage proactively.

This reactive view often resulted in higher-than-expected cloud bills and inefficiencies in resource utilization. Organizations met challenges aligning their cloud spending with business objectives, highlighting the need for more cultivated cost management tools and practices.

Development of cost management tools

With the surge in cloud adoption, the demand for advanced cost management tools became apparent. In response, cloud providers stepped up, crafting comprehensive solutions tailored to empower organizations and IT professionals in managing and optimizing their cloud expenditures. This phase witnessed the introduction of provider-specific tools, detailed billing reports, and basic automation features, all of which significantly bolstered the ability to track, analyze, and control cloud costs.

Provider-specific tools

Cloud providers like Microsoft Azure began offering more advanced tools specifically designed for cost management. These tools provided greater visibility into cloud usage and costs, enabling organizations to make more educated decisions. Key advancements included:

- Azure presented this integrated key to help users monitor, allocate, and optimize their cloud spending. It proposed cost analysis, budgeting, and forecasting features, tracking costs across different services and departments. Users could access interactive dashboards to visualize spending patterns and identify cost-saving opportunities.
- Azure allows users to allocate costs to specific projects, departments, or teams using tagging and resource grouping. This granularity helps organizations understand which parts of their business are driving cloud costs and enables more exact budgeting and chargeback processes.
- Enhanced budgeting tools enabled users to set detailed budgets and forecasts based on historical spending patterns and projected usage. This allowed for more precise financial planning and proactive cost management.

Detailed billing reports

Introducing detailed billing reports was a significant advancement in cloud cost management. These reports provided a granular breakdown of cloud expenditures, offering more profound insights into spending patterns and cost drivers. Essential features of detailed billing reports include:

- Detailed reports provided a line-item breakdown of costs, showing expenditures by resource, service, and usage type. This level of detail allowed organizations to pinpoint specific areas contributing to high costs.

- Key to comprehensive historical billing data enabled users to analyze over time, compare month-to-month spending, and identify seasonal variations or anomalies in usage.

- Azure allows users to customize billing reports to suit their specific needs, such as filtering by resource type, department, or project. This flexibility made generating insights tailored to the organization's unique requirements easier.

Basic automation

Developing basic automation features marked a significant step forward in cloud cost management. Automation helped streamline cost management processes, reduce manual effort, and enhance the efficiency of cost control measures. Key automation features included:

- Azure introduced alerts that notified users when spending approached or exceeded predefined budgets. These alerts could be configured to begin at specific thresholds, enabling timely intervention to control cost.

- Azure began providing automated cost-saving recommendations based on usage patterns and best practices. For example, users received suggestions for rightsizing instances, purchasing reserved instances, or identifying underutilized resources.

- Basic automation tools like virtual machines allow users to schedule resources' start and stop times based on usage patterns. This helped optimize resource utilization and reduce costs by ensuring that resources ran only when needed.

Overview of financial operations

As enterprises began using cloud services, managing costs became necessary for their finances. This directed the creation of **Financial Operations (FinOps)** practices, which provided a more organized way to handle cloud expenses. FinOps includes tools and practices highlighting clear financial accountability when spending on cloud services.

The criticality grew as enterprises started to utilize cloud services, and there was a rising necessity to manage costs, which was bonded into the FinOps practices. FinOps provides a well-defined framework to manage cloud expenses with firm financial ownership.

FinOps adoption

FinOps, the practice of cloud financial governance, has defined with a set of cultural practices to see operations and is a logical follow-up to the rise of cloud cost optimization trends by providing a framework that includes principles, processes, and best practices that should help address the complexities of cloud finance and ultimately help cloud users better understand what they are spending and why. Some notable elements in FinOps adoption crystallized into core principles as follows: visibility, optimization, and Accountability, which are essential for controlling and optimizing costs and spending.

To effectively manage and optimize cloud financial operations, organizations often adopt structured approaches and create specialized teams. Key components of this strategy include:

- **Phases**: Inform, optimize, and operate, each of which speaks to a different view or aspect of controlling costs, from getting visibility of your spending to using and operating the resources and, finally, how to continually cost your use of these resources.
- **Dedicated FinOps teams**: Organizations created FinOps teams, which are made up of finance, engineering, and operations experts, to implement the practices and save on costs.

Cross-functional collaboration

Successful cloud cost management is a team effort that necessitates the participation of stakeholders from all corners of your organization:

- **Top caliber finance teams**: providing budget-to-actuals and working with engineering under an understanding of the business objectives to assure accountability for financial stewardship.
- **Engineering teams:** Collaborated with finance to gain a better understanding of costs, enabling them to optimize usage based on cost considerations.
- **Business teams**: Product managers and executives need visibility into cloud spending to make informed decisions and allocate budgets.

Shared accountability for cloud cost management is also conferred by this collaboration.

Data-driven decisions

The core principle of FinOps is to make informed decisions with data, a principle deeply connected to the very premise of cloud cost management:

- **Current insights**: with sophisticated monitoring and reporting tools, you get current updates on cloud costs.
- **Cost allocation and tagging**: Keep your spending granular and identify optimization opportunities.
- **Advanced analytics**: Machine learning and predictive analytics predict usage trends and opportunities for cost savings.
- **KPIs and benchmarks**: Organizations establish benchmarks and KPIs as part of cost management to gauge the success of the strategies and identify better ways of moving forward.

Integration with DevOps and Agile practices

Integrating cost management with DevOps and Agile practices became crucial as cloud computing developed. This integration ensured that cost optimization was implanted within the development and operational processes, leading to more efficient and cost-effective cloud usage. Key elements of this integration included cost-aware development, continuous cost optimization, and real-time monitoring.

Cost-aware development

Development teams began including cost considerations into their workflows, ensuring that financial implications were considered alongside technical and functional requirements. This shift towards cost-aware development involved:

- Developers started using tools and practices highlighting the cost implications of their design and architectural decisions. This included evaluating different infrastructure options, optimizing code for efficiency, and choosing cost-effective services and configurations.

- Organizations invested in training programs to educate developers on cloud cost management principles and best practices. This helped build a culture of cost consciousness within development teams, ensuring that cost optimization became a natural part of the development process.

- Development teams used cost estimation tools provided by cloud providers, such as the Azure Pricing Calculator, to forecast the costs of their applications and services. This enabled them to make informed decisions about resource allocation and budgeting.

Continuous cost optimization

Continuous integration and continuous delivery (CI/CD) pipelines began to include cost optimization checks and balances, ensuring that cost efficiency was maintained throughout the development lifecycle. Key practices in continuous cost optimization included:

- CI/CD pipelines were enhanced with automated cost checks that evaluated the cost impact of new code deployments and infrastructure changes. These checks helped identify potential cost issues early in the development process, allowing teams to address them before they reached production.

- CI/CD workflows incorporated performance and cost metrics to monitor the efficiency of applications and services. This included tracking resource utilization, response times, and cost per transaction, providing valuable insights for optimization.

- In cases where deployments resulted in unexpected cost spikes, CI/CD pipelines included rollback and remediation mechanisms. This allowed teams to quickly revert changes and implement cost-saving measures to minimize financial impact.

Real-time monitoring

Real-time monitoring and alerting systems became essential for maintaining cost efficiency in dynamic cloud environments. These systems provided immediate visibility into cloud usage and costs, enabling proactive management and optimization. Key aspects of real-time monitoring included:

- Organizations set up real-time alerts to notify stakeholders of significant cloud usage or cost changes. These alerts were triggered by predefined thresholds and anomalies, allowing teams to respond quickly to potential issues.

- Real-time dashboards and visualizations provided a comprehensive view of cloud spending and resource utilization. These tools helped teams monitor key metrics, identify trends, and make data-driven decisions to optimize costs.

- Advanced monitoring systems included anomaly detection capabilities that identified unusual patterns in cloud usage and costs. This helped detect potential inefficiencies, security incidents, or billing errors that could impact overall cloud expenses.

Cloud financial management

Cloud cost management involves financial control, governance, security, compliance, and sustainability. This strategy ensures that all parts of cloud usage are optimized for cost efficiency while utilizing organizational policies and environmental considerations.

Unified platforms

Unified cloud financial management platforms are critical for organizations combining various cost management elements. These platforms provide a centralized interface that combines financial data, governance, security, and compliance, offering a complete view of cloud operations. Key features of these platforms include:

- Unified platforms offer integrated dashboards that provide real-time insights into cloud spending, resource utilization, and compliance status. These dashboards help stakeholders monitor key metrics and make informed decisions.

- Many platforms support multiple cloud providers, allowing organizations to manage their costs across different environments from a single interface. This multi-cloud support facilitates cost management and ensures consistency in financial practices.

- Comprehensive platforms leverage advanced analytics to provide deep insights into cost drivers, usage patterns, and optimization opportunities. These analytics help organizations identify areas for improvement and implement cost-saving measures effectively.

Governance and policy enforcement

Effective cloud financial management requires governance and policy enforcement to ensure that cloud usage aligns with organizational standards and budgets. Automated policy enforcement mechanisms are crucial in maintaining compliance and controlling costs. Key aspects of governance and policy enforcement include:

- Organizations define policies for cloud usage, such as spending limits, resource allocation rules, and security requirements. Automated tools enforce these policies by monitoring cloud environments and taking corrective actions when violations occur.

- Continuous compliance monitoring ensures that cloud usage meets regulatory requirements and internal standards. This includes tracking compliance with data protection laws, industry standards, and corporate governance policies.

- Automated budget controls help prevent costs by enforcing spending limits and providing alerts when budgets are at risk of being exceeded. These controls enable proactive financial management and reduce the likelihood of unexpected expenses.

Sustainability considerations

As organizations become more environmentally aware, sustainability considerations are increasingly integrated into cloud cost management strategies. Optimizing for both cost and sustainability ensures that cloud operations are financially efficient and environmentally responsible. Key sustainability considerations include:

- Organizations consider the energy efficiency of their cloud resources and implement measures to reduce energy consumption. This includes rightsizing instances, using energy-efficient hardware, and optimizing workloads for minimal energy use.

- Tracking and minimizing the carbon footprint of cloud operations is a growing priority. Cloud providers often offer tools to measure and report the carbon emissions associated with resource usage, helping organizations make more sustainable choices.

- Implementing sustainable practices, such as using renewable energy sources, optimizing resource allocation to reduce waste, and promoting green cloud architectures, aligns financial management with environmental goals. These practices reduce costs and contribute to corporate social responsibility efforts.

Advanced cost optimization techniques

As organizations matured in cloud services, they adopted more developed techniques to optimize costs effectively. These techniques focused on maximizing efficiency, reducing waste, and ensuring that cloud spending was aligned with business objectives. Fundamental advanced cost optimization techniques included rightsizing and reservations, automated optimization, and cost allocation and chargeback methods.

Rightsizing and reservations

One of the techniques for cost optimization is rightsizing, which involves adjusting the size of cloud resources to match the actual demand. By rightsizing instances, organizations can avoid over-provisioning and ensure they are paying for something other than unused capacity. Key aspects of rightsizing and reservations include:

- Analyzing cloud resources' performance and usage patterns to determine the appropriate size for each instance. This ensures that resources are utilized effectively and effectively utilized, leading to cost savings.
- Purchasing reserved instances or savings plans for predictable workloads can reduce costs. These reservations typically offer discounts compared to on-demand pricing in exchange for committing to usage level over a period (e.g., one or three years).
- Implementing dynamic scaling policies that automatically adjust resource capacity based on real-time demand. This helps maintain optimal performance while minimizing costs during periods of low usage.

Automated optimization

Automation is important in advanced cost optimization, enabling organizations to manage cloud resources more efficiently and reduce manual intervention. Automated optimization tools and practices include:

- Using automation tools that continuously monitor cloud usage and make real-time adjustments to optimize resource allocation. These tools can automatically scale resources up or down based on demand, shut down unused resources, and apply cost-saving configurations.
- Defining policies that govern the provisioning, usage, and decommissioning of cloud resources. Automation tools can enforce these policies to ensure compliance and cost efficiency.
- Automating the scheduling of resource start and stop times based on usage patterns. For example, development environments can be automatically shut down outside working hours to save costs.

Cost allocation and chargeback

Cost allocation and chargeback methods enable organizations to track and manage cloud costs more precisely. These methods ensure that costs are accurately attributed to the appropriate departments, projects, or teams, facilitating better financial management and accountability.

Key aspects of cost allocation and chargeback include:

- Implementing a comprehensive tagging strategy to label cloud resources with metadata such as project names, departments, and cost centers. This allows for detailed tracking of resource usage and costs.

- Based on usage metrics, developing cost allocation models that distribute shared costs (for example, network bandwidth, storage) among various departments or projects. This ensures that each unit is charged fairly for its consumption.

- Implement chargeback mechanisms where departments are billed for cloud usage or show back mechanisms where usage and costs are reported without actual billing. These practices promote accountability and encourage cost-conscious behavior across the organization.

Creating financial dashboards that provide real-time visibility into cloud spending, split by department, project, or team. These dashboards help stakeholders understand their cloud costs and identify areas for optimization.

Artificial intelligence and machine learning

Artificial intelligence (**AI**) and **machine learning** (**ML**) managing cloud costs easier to expect, analyze, and optimize spending. These technologies help organizations make decisions, automate tasks, and improve cost efficiency. Using AI and ML in cloud cost management has improved predicting future costs, detecting unusual spending, and automating cost-saving measures. This gives decision-makers more control and confidence in managing their cloud expenses.

Predictive analytics

AI and ML algorithms are crucial in predicting future spending and finding cost-saving opportunities. Here is how they help:

- AI and ML can identify trends and predict future cloud resource needs by analyzing past usage data. This helps organizations forecast spending and set more accurate budgets.

- These predictive models estimate future resource requirements based on current usage and expected growth. This allows organizations to plan better and allocate resources efficiently, avoiding over-provisioning and underutilization.

- AI and ML analyze usage practices to suggest ways to save money, such as recommending the most cost-effective instance types, advising on reserved instance purchases, or highlighting underused resources that can be downsized or removed.

Anomaly detection

Advanced anomaly detection systems by AI and ML help spot unusual spending that may indicate inefficiencies or security issues. Here is how they work:

- AI-driven systems continuously monitor cloud usage and spending in real-time. They can spot variations from normal patterns, like sudden spikes in resource use or unexpected cost increases.

- When anomalies are detected, the system sends alerts and notifications, allowing teams to quickly investigate and resolve issues. This approach helps prevent cost and reduces the impact of security incidents or misconfigurations.

- AI and ML not only detect anomalies but also help identify their causes by analyzing related data and usage patterns. They can pinpoint issues such as inefficient resource use, unauthorized access, or billing errors.

Intelligent automation

Intelligent automation systems leverage AI and ML to automatically make cost-saving adjustments based on real-time data and predictive insights. Key features of intelligent automation include:

- Intelligent automation adjusts resource allocation in real time based on current demand and usage patterns. This ensures that resources are used efficiently, reducing waste and minimizing costs.

- AI-driven auto-scaling mechanisms dynamically scale resources up or down based on workload demands. This helps maintain optimal performance while avoiding unnecessary expenses during periods of low usage.

- Automation systems can enforce cost management policies by taking predefined actions when certain conditions are met. For example, they can automatically shut down unused resources, apply cost-saving configurations, or allocate resources to lower-cost regions.

Azure Well-Architected Framework and FinOps

Azure Well-Architected Framework is a standard that helps Azure workloads follow the six pillars to improve the quality of a workload, such that it helps a workload to:

- Azure WAF is hardened, available, and recoverable, ensuring robust security, continuous accessibility, and quick recovery during disruptions.

- Azure WAF provides customizable security settings, making it as secure as you want to meet your specific requirements.

- Optimized Azure WAF enhances security and generates a sufficient return on investment by reducing potential downtime and protecting against costly cyber threats.
- Azure WAF is built to promote sustainable development and operations, ensure long-term efficiency, reduce environmental impact, and maintain strong security.

These pillars are aligned with the goals of our Framework and the basis of it:

- Reliability
- Security
- Cost optimization
- Operational excellence
- Performance efficiency

Within each pillar, there are best practices, key risks/benefits, and tradeoffs. These design decisions must be balanced across all pillars, which cater to the needs of the business. The technical guidance available is generic enough to be used with any type of workload, and we have actual scenarios. This direct is more focused on Azure.

The architecture of a workload is not the same as its implementation. While the Well-Architected Framework can prepare you for success in the design phase, the implementation choices vary based on business requirements and the guidelines/restrictions your organization needs to adhere to.

The Well-Architected Framework is for teams that manage workloads and have cross-cutting concerns. For anyone involved in the life cycle of a Workload, this gives excellent visibility and guidance. Whether you are the architect who designs workloads, the developer who writes workloads, the operator who operates workloads, or even a business stakeholder who operates any ownership over a portion of workloads, you can use this framework.

Great advice, whether big or small. As an operator of a large or small enterprise or an ISV, you are one step closer to optimal design. The framework is suitable for different organizational structures and sizes, ensuring that users of workloads at any level can reap maximum benefits. This material may not be relevant if you seek advice to enable broader centralized controls for improving a portfolio of work on which you may deploy HTAP workloads.

We highly encourage using the Cloud Adoption Framework to help build the necessary context around this. If you are trying to design for something other than specific workloads on Azure, this is not for you.

Use Azure WAF assessments

The Azure **Well-Architected Framework (WAF)** is a set of principles that can be used to enhance the quality of a workload. For more information, see Azure Well-Architected Framework. Microsoft WAF Assessments are designed to take you to brief scenarios of questions, recommendations, and an actionable, informative guidance report. Grading gets time, but it is time nicely put in. Now, they extend this capability with Azure Advisor WAF Assessments to provide a comprehensive and interactive way to assess and identify gaps in your workloads over five pillars: reliability, cost, operational excellence, performance, and security via a set of questions relevant to your workload. Assessments are a scenario of several questions on your workloads, such that you need to provide recommendations that can be acted upon; they are insightful. We turned on two of these assessments for the preview release with Advisor.

Prerequisites

You can control access to Advisor WAF assessments using built-in roles. The permissions can vary by role.

Following table explain the roles and description about the role.

Name	Description
Reader	Check the assessments and recommendations for your subscription or workload.
Contributor	Perform assessments for a subscription or workload and prioritize the recommendations.

Table 11.1: WAF prerequisites

Azure Advisor assessments for your WAF

The following are the steps to create Azure Advisor assessments for your WAF:

1. Sign in to the Azure portal and select Advisor from any page. This will open the Advisor score dashboard.

2. Select **Assessments** from the left navigation menu. The Assessments page will open, displaying a list of completed or in-progress assessments

   This snapshot highlights the efficiency and thoroughness of the assessment process, emphasizing the completion of one assessment with no outstanding recommendations.

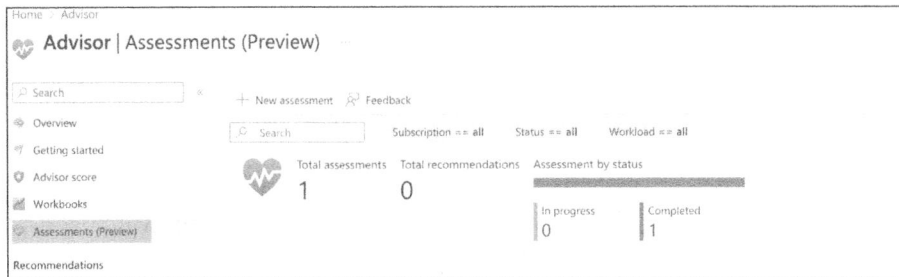

Figure 11.2: Azure Waf Advisor

Creating Azure Advisor WAF assessments

The following are the steps for creating Azure Advisor WAF assessments:

1. Select 'New Assessment.' An input area will open:

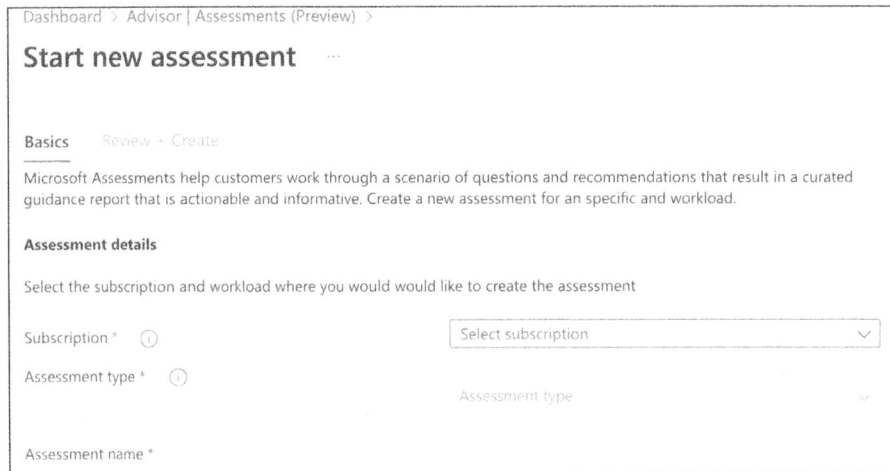

Figure 11.3: Azure WAF Assessment

1. Provide the input parameters:

    o **Select subscription:** From the dropdown list, select the available subscriptions. Please check: WAF Assessments preview is not available for all subscriptions. Once chosen, the system will seek out workloads with their subscription set to that.

    o **Workload (optional):** A list of any existing workloads for that subscription that you can configure and select.

    o **Assessment type:** In the initial preview release, two assessment types are available:

    - Azure well-architected review

    - Mission critical: well-architected review

- o **Name of the assessment:** Enter the evaluation's name. This will set the **Review + Create** option at the top of the page and the **Next** button at the bottom.

2. You can choose to:

- o View a completed recommendation and the recommendations that were generated.
- o Click on **Create Resume** to complete the assessment for which you initially started the evaluation. After that, if you click **Continue**, you will be redirected to the Learn platform to resume making the assessment.

  You cannot resume an in-progress assessment created by someone else. Finalize an evaluation that someone from your organization created and see the recommendations snapshots.

- o Create the new assessment. The latest assessment options form is reset to a page with tiles showing similar or existing assessments (when you arrow back a page to it or use the **Review and Create** tab). You can then proceed by selecting **Create** (at the bottom of the page), clicking here to start a new assessment (at the top of the page), or selecting **Previous**, which will take you back to Start new assessment (you will lose your workload type and assessment name choices).

This figure shows an overview of the Azure Well-Architected Review assessments in the Azure Advisor platform. Showing assessments in different progress states; completed, to be re-reviewed and incomplete. Users can see their own work (continue) or create a new one Every review is aimed at exploring significant areas from reliability, security to cost optimization and operational excellence delivering best practices that organizations can adopt in terms of improving their workloads performance and efficiency.

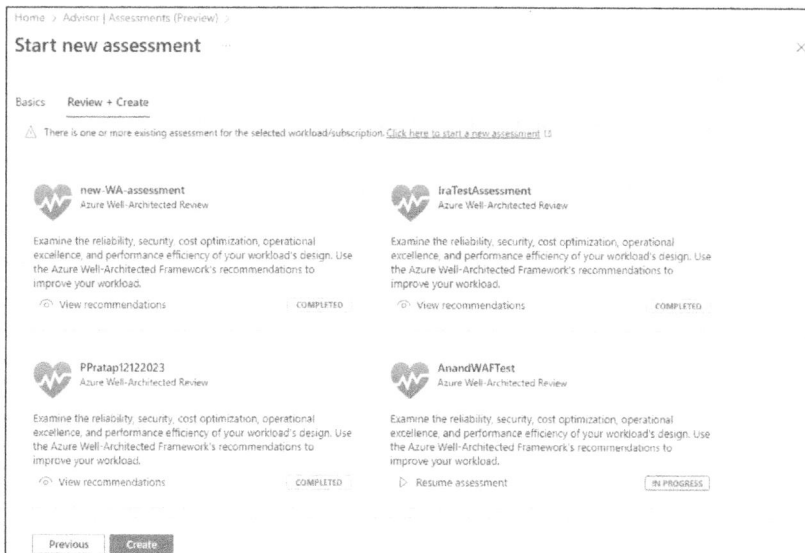

Figure 11.4: Azure Waf Assessment review

3. To begin the assessment creation process, select **Continue**. The assessment will start. The steps will vary depending on the chosen assessment type.

   The following figure depicts the assessment overview for an Azure Well-Architected Review, named `new-WA-assessment`. Tracks progress of the assessment, including key milestones and status of guidance results. This **Continue** button signals that you can go ahead and complete the assessment fully around reliability, security, cost optimization and operational excellence.

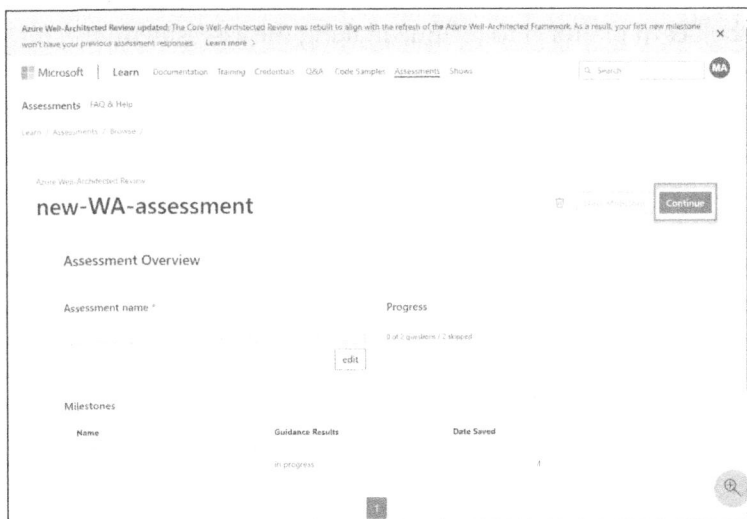

Figure 11.5: Azure Waf Assessment operation

4. The assessment begins, and the number of questions will vary based on the selected assessment type. The following screenshot is only an example:

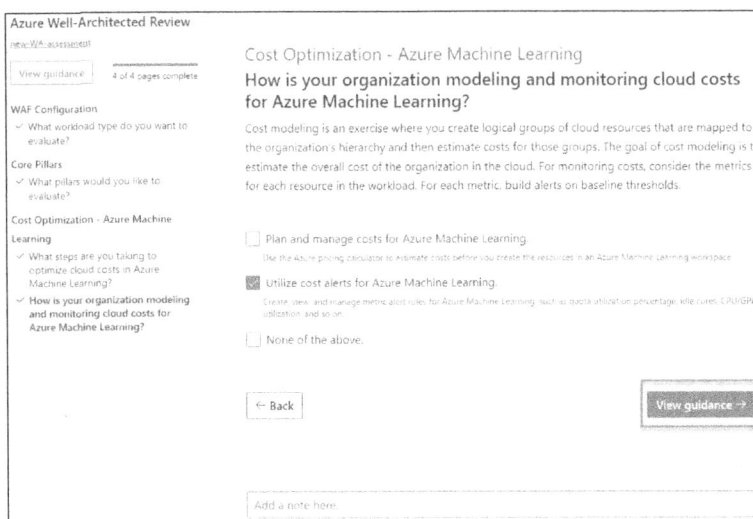

Figure 11.6: Azure Waf Assessment Guidance

Your answers to the questions are essential for the quality of the assessment recommendations. Respond to each question and click **Next** until you reach a page with **View Guidance**.

5. Select **View Guidance** to navigate the results page, as shown in the following screenshot:

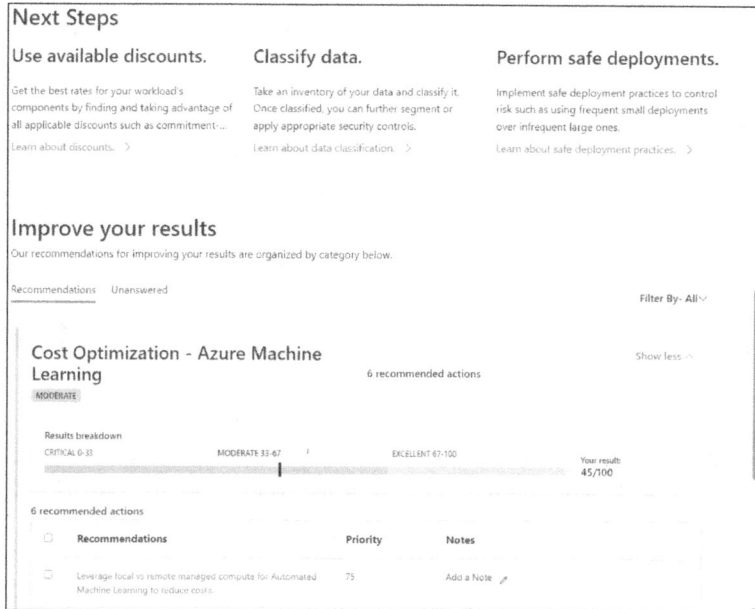

Figure 11.7: *Azure WAF Assessment recommendation report*

The assessment recommendations will be available in Azure Advisor within 8 hours of completion. You can also download them immediately.

Azure Cost Optimization for AI and ML workloads

We live in an age in which AI and ML are necessary to spark innovation and remain a serious player in the business arena. These enable companies to introduce new products/ services, automate specific processes, and make better decisions. Using AI/ML, companies can improve efficiencies, enhance consumer interactions, and tap into new avenues of growth. AI/ML tools have become essential for working with large datasets and gaining significant insight into them, all due to the exponential increase in data. It also provides insights into market trends and reading of customer behaviors and helps identify operational efficiencies that enable businesses to build data-driven strategies for better results. AI/ML can also automate mundane and complex jobs, eliminating human error and operational efficiency. This automation allows human resources to focus more on strategic activities and boost productivity.

In addition, AI/ML enables tailored customer experiences by evaluating each shopper's unique preferences and patterns, subsequently delivering increased customer satisfaction and loyalty. Benefits aside, AI/ML workloads are often computationally expensive and require sizable memory, storage, and data processing, leading to higher costs. These resources must be used wisely without spending money on books or exceeding the budgetary limits, for which cost control must be carried out effectively. Cost management is critical to ensure that AI/ML projects deliver real value to the organization and improve the ROI of these initiatives.

Cost control—Cost management ensures that AI/ML operations can safely scale sustainably for businesses without cost runaway or resource constraints. Cost managers must be underscored in managing costs for AI/ML polished projects, allowing for better resource allocation. A few projects may receive most of the financial and computational resources where they have the highest potential impact.

Track expenses and sense opportunities for savings

In today's cloud-driven world, effectively managing expenses and optimizing resources is crucial for organizations, especially when dealing with AI/ML workloads. By actively tracking expenses and identifying opportunities for savings, businesses can enhance their operational efficiency and reduce unnecessary costs.

Key strategies to achieve these objectives include:

- **Cost monitoring:**
  o Monitor spending on cloud computing, storage, and data processing for AI/ML workloads with analytics.
  o Discover overspending, the low-hanging fruit, increased visibility over costs, and more informed decisions on stage cost optimizations.

- **Resource optimization:**
  o Proper Scaling of AI/ML Resources according to the Working Load Reduces the number of unused resources.
  o You can choose a better type for yourself, such as Instances, or try to negotiate better cloud prices (this works, but only sometimes).

- **Savings opportunities:**
  o Monitor patterns of spending on AI/ML solutions.
  o Find ways to save costs, such as eliminating unused resources, enjoying reserved instance discounts, and using efficient data processing.

Plan and forecast AI/ML budgets

Effective financial management for AI/ML projects requires a comprehensive approach that includes strategic budget allocation, accurate forecasting, and continuous tracking and adjustment. By addressing each of these aspects, organizations can ensure that their AI/ML initiatives are not only financially sustainable but also aligned with business goals.

Key considerations for managing AI/ML project finances include:

- **Budget Allocation:**
  - Assign budgets for AI/ML projects based on specific resource requirements, expected timelines, and business impact.
  - Ensure budget aligns with strategic priorities and provides necessary resources for project success.
- **Forecasting:**
  - Analyzing historical spending, anticipated workload growth, and potential future resource needs can help develop accurate forecasts for AI/ML project costs.
  - Plan and allocate budgets effectively to avoid unexpected budget overruns.
- **Tracking and adjustment:**
  - Continuously monitor actual spending against forecasted budgets.
  - Make timely adjustments to ensure AI/ML investments stay within approved budget limits.

Gain visibility and accountability

To effectively manage and optimize the financial aspects of AI/ML projects, organizations must implement robust strategies for reporting, cost allocation, chargeback models, and automated policies. These strategies ensure transparency, accountability, and efficiency in managing AI/ML expenses, thereby fostering a culture of financial responsibility.

Key strategies include:

- **Detailed reporting:**
  - Create complete reports on AI/ML technology project cost, usage of resources, and cost factors.
  - Informed decisions by stakeholders and helped control overspending by teams.
- **Cost allocation:**
  - Readily attribute AI/ML costs to a project, department, or business unit to improve financial governance.

- **Chargeback model:**
  - o Use chargeback to put the onus on teams to pay for their AI/ML costs.
  - o Create a cost-conscious culture that promotes the judicious use of resources.
- **Automated policies:**
  - o Set policies to deploy cost control measures such as spending caps, resource quotas, and idle resource identification.

Scale AI/ML with cost efficiency

Optimizing AI/ML workloads in the cloud requires a strategic approach to resource management. By leveraging dynamic scaling, automated policies, continuous optimization, and flexible resourcing, organizations can achieve a balance between performance and cost-efficiency.

Key practices include:

- **Dynamic scaling:**
  - o Use auto-scaling capabilities to adjust AI/ML resources based on workload demands.
  - o Ensure payment is only for needed computing power when required.
- **Automated policies:**
  - o Manage the scaling of AI/ML resources based on utilization, cost thresholds, or business priorities.
  - o Ensure cost-efficient scaling without manual intervention.
- **Continuous optimization:**
  - o Regularly analyze AI/ML resource usage and costs.
  - o Adjust scaling policies to maintain optimal balance between performance and cost-efficiency.
- **Flexible resourcing:**
  - o Use a mix of on-demand, reserved instances, and spot pricing.
  - o Take advantage of cost-effective options while maintaining flexibility to scale up or down.

Achieve sustained cost savings

To effectively manage AI/ML projects and ensure financial efficiency, organizations need to focus on key aspects such as visibility, optimization, and accountability. These elements work together to provide a clear understanding of spending, improve resource management, and enforce responsible financial practices.

Key components include:

- Visibility:
  - o Gain comprehensive visibility into AI/ML spending through detailed reporting and analytics.
- Optimization:
  - o Use insights from cost monitoring to optimize AI/ML resources.
  - o Right-size resources, select cost-effective options, and automate scaling.
- Forecasting:
  - o Develop accurate budgets and forecasts to plan and allocate resources effectively.
  - o Avoid unexpected cost overruns.
- Accountability:
  - o Establish cost allocation and chargeback models to drive accountability and cost-consciousness among AI/ML teams.

Empower your AI/ML transformation

To achieve long-term success in AI/ML initiatives, it is essential to focus on optimizing costs, supporting scalable growth, gaining a competitive advantage, and ensuring sustainable success. These strategic priorities not only drive innovation but also position the organization for continued success in a rapidly evolving technological landscape.

Key strategic priorities include:

- **Cost-efficient innovation:**
  - o Optimize AI/ML costs to free up resources for innovative and impactful projects.
  - o Drive more excellent business value.
- **Scalable growth:**
  - o Support growing business demands with cost-efficient AI/ML scaling.
  - o Avoid budget overruns and resource constraints.
- **Competitive advantage:**
  - o Effective AI/ML cost management makes the organization more agile and responsive.
  - o Unlock new opportunities for growth and success.
- **Sustainable success:**
  - o Maintain cost-efficient AI/ML operations for long-term viability and sustainability.

AI/ML cost optimization

To optimize the financial efficiency of AI/ML projects, a structured approach is essential. This involves assessing current costs, identifying opportunities for savings, implementing strategic measures, and continuously monitoring these initiatives to ensure long-term cost-effectiveness.

Key steps in this approach include:

- **Assess current costs**: We conducted a detailed audit of cloud infrastructure for AI/ ML spending, bills, data storage, and model training.
- **Identify opportunities**: Investigate consumption behaviors, peak and low times, resource management, and tariffs to find ways to save money.
- **Implement strategies:** Create a process to save costs using AI/ML, employing techniques such as resizing resources and creating a cloud savings plan.
- **Monitor the Cost of AI/ML Efficiently:** Change strategies leading to cost-effective kept.

Conclusion

This chapter focuses on developing cloud cost management to keep up with the ever-increasing complexity and scale of cloud computing. That led to a deep dive into the Azure Well-Architected Framework and FinOps, two means to formalize practice and business operations to ensure you get the most out of your cloud usage in the most efficient, cost-effective manner. In closing, they will share some of our insights on cost optimization for AI and machine learning workloads in Azure and the savings strategies for projects using these high-demand resources to better enable innovation with responsible financial practices. Organizations that grasp and adhere to these principles can optimize returns on their cloud investments and ensure the longevity of operations while staying one step ahead in a rapidly changing technology world.

Join our book's Discord space

Join the book's Discord Workspace for Latest updates, Offers, Tech happenings around the world, New Release and Sessions with the Authors:

https://discord.bpbonline.com

## CHAPTER 12

Final Thoughts and Next Steps

Introduction

Cloud computing is an essential part of every business that wants to move faster, be more innovative, and be highly scalable in the rapidly evolving landscape of technology today. Given the rapidly increasing dependence on the cloud, managing and optimizing cloud costs have also become a core challenge. FinOps, a cultural and operational practice that combines financial management with cloud operations, fills this gap.

AZURE FinOps is the *process of bringing financial accountability to the cloud*; Azure FinOps focuses on organizations using Microsoft Azure Cloud Platform. FinOps integration can provide businesses with better visibility of cloud spending, informed financial decisions, and more optimal resource utilization. This guide covers the key fundamentals and best practices for unlocking Azure FinOps efficiency. In this series, they will walk you through end-to-end, from an introduction to the FinOps principles and benefits to Azure cost management services and tools.

The content covers setting up and working with Azure Cost Management and Billing, cost optimization strategies, and several surprises about monitoring, reporting, and governance to keep financial discipline on track. We will also discuss higher-end FinOps approaches and best practices with real-world examples and case studies, showing how these ideas can also work in practice.

Ultimately, we will cover what to expect for the future of Azure FinOps and what recent innovations are currently in the pipeline, ready to evolve the dynamics of the cloud that you have relied on to date. After this guide, you will be well-versed in Azure FinOps and the tools and techniques to help you manage your cloud costs and ultimately deliver more value and sustainability in your cloud investment.

Structure

In this chapter, we will go through the following topics:

- Recap of key concepts
- Final thoughts and next steps

Objectives

The objective of this section is to provide a comprehensive understanding of the key concepts of Azure FinOps, including its principles, benefits, and role in cloud cost management. By exploring these concepts, the goal is to equip readers with the knowledge necessary to effectively implement FinOps practices within their organizations, thereby enhancing decision-making, optimizing resource usage, and maximizing the financial return on cloud investments.

Recap of key concepts

In this section, we will go through the key concepts of our chapters:

- **Introduction to Azure FinOps:** With modern businesses quickly adopting the move towards innovation, efficiency, and scale, the cloud has become a cornerstone component in today's ever-evolving technological landscape. This has put a larger burden on the management and optimization of costs associated with cloud services though. FinOps — FinOps is a framework that combines systems, best practices, and culture medium. Concerning Azure - FinOps is the framework designed to improve the efficiency of cloud operation models, particularly with the financial expenses and economic aspects of the Azure cloud platform from Microsoft. With the power of FinOps, companies can better understand their Cloud accounting and leverage that understanding to make better financial decisions and optimize resource consumption.

  Implementing FinOps within an organization involves understanding its core principles and recognizing the value it brings to cloud cost management. By integrating financial operations with cloud strategies, organizations can optimize resource usage, enhance decision-making, and maximize returns on cloud investments.

  The key aspects of FinOps include:

  o **Understanding FinOps:** We discussed the principles that underpin FinOps, a cultural practice that aims to make charges transparent, inform and resist waste, and set costs optimally to enable distributed teams to make business trade-offs between speed, cost, and quality. It is important for organizations to understand some of the basic elements of FinOps for it to be effective and to be able to implement cloud cost management practices — correctly.

- o **Benefits of Azure FinOps** include better cost management, increased visibility, and more informed decision-making across teams. By adopting FinOps, organizations can ensure that cloud spending aligns with business objectives and maximize the return on their cloud investments.

- o **Role of Azure FinOps in cloud cost management**: We explored how FinOps integrates financial operations with cloud cost management to enhance efficiency and reduce waste. This integration helps businesses track real-time spending, identify cost-saving opportunities, and optimize resource usage.

- **Azure Fundamentals for FinOps**: Understanding the fundamentals of Azure is essential for implementing FinOps effectively. Azure provides a comprehensive suite of tools and services that support cost management and optimization, making it easier for organizations to control their cloud expenditures. These fundamentals include a broad overview of Azure services, effective use of resource groups and tagging, and leveraging Azure Cost Management and Billing tools.

To effectively implement FinOps practices and optimize cloud spending, it is crucial to utilize the right Azure services and tools. By organizing resources efficiently and leveraging advanced cost management solutions, organizations can gain better visibility into their expenditures, make informed decisions, and ultimately reduce costs.

The following strategies play a vital role in achieving these objectives:

- o **Azure Services Overview**: An overview of Azure services is necessary for executing FinOps practices; with hundreds of services in Azure — each with its own costs — understanding each and their different pricing models is crucial to controlling the cost. Compute services such as **Virtual Machines (VMs),** **Azure Kubernetes Service (AKS),** and serverless computing using Azure Functions offer a range of choices to meet your workload requirements at an optimal cost; Blob Storage — Disk Storage — File Storage — storage services with hot, cool, and archive tiers to fit access patterns and cost-efficiency needs. Virtual Networks, Load Balancers, and **Content Delivery Networks (CDNs)** are network services that manage settings to save on data transfer and pipe traffic better. Knowledge of these services helps organizations make the right tool and configuration choices, save costs, and use the resources effectively.

- o **Resource groups and tagging**: Organizing resources with resource groups and tagging is the basis for tracking and allocating costs correctly. Resource groups help to organize related resources based on projects, departments, or environments (for example, development, staging, and production). It allows for easier tracking and managing of costs and identifying and allocating expenses due partly to this standardized organizational structure. However, tagging assigns key-value pairs to resources and provides a flexible mechanism to categorize the resource. Resource tagging with useful details (for example, cost centers, project names, or owners) allows for accurate cost allocation and reporting. This makes it easier for you to perform cost analysis in detail, which means you can take better advantage of optimization opportunities and, in that way, better manage and visualize cloud expenditure.

o **Azure Cost Management and Billing**: Key to FinOps uses Azure Cost Management and Billing tools to monitor, analyze, and optimize cloud spending. The Cost Management Dashboard gives you a single place to monitor and analyze your cloud costs, showing you cost trends, forecasts, and budget tracking. And with visibility, businesses can narrow down where they spend money to find cost-reduction opportunities. Organizations can also set budgets and alerts to keep costs in check by proactively recognizing an existing or an upcoming problem. The cost analysis tool provides deep insight into your cloud costs by filtering and grouping your costs into various dimensions like resource type, location, and tags.

- **Setting up Azure Cost Management and Billing:** The next step is to set up the cost management tools in Azure—Azure Cost Management and Billing. Services used for all these, and similar things fall under one of the tools—cloud Cost management tools, which are designed to provide deep insights into cloud spending and help optimize these costs efficiently.

o **Azure Cost Management and Billing portal:** The Azure Cost Management and Billing portal is your centralized hub for managing your cloud expenditures. Businesses can use this portal to access a single console to track overall cloud spend across the organization. It shows detailed cost reports, spending trends, and projections on the portal, enabling organizations to monitor living expenses in real-time. This centralized view streamlines the monitoring and managing of costs, allowing businesses to detect and remedy any abnormalities or overruns more easily.

o **Enabling cost analysis and budgeting:** Configuration of cost center and budgeting is an important step to manage your cloud consumption cost in check. Organizations can create budgets for respective projects, departments, or resource groups in the Azure Cost Management and Billing portal. Above all, these budgets help clarify in what area your spending will be undertaken and under what condition you will act as your financial best friend. The portal's cost analysis tools provide deeper insights into spending patterns, helping businesses spot trends, identify anomalies, and gain visibility into potential cost optimization opportunities. With these, companies make the best assets on their financials and can scale back on their cloud budgets proactively.

o **Creating and managing azure subscriptions**: Azure often find themselves having to manage multiple Azure subscriptions. For years, this was one of the most wanted features in Azure, but when they finally introduced it, it was completely different from what we expected. Managing multiple subscriptions lets you organize resources, control access, and optimize costs. For e.g., you should always collect a set of shared resources grouped as that makes sense: from a project, department, or environment (whatever you are most likely to structure your subscription around) and apply proper segregation of duties for security and accountability. Better subscription management leads to more detailed cost visibility and accounting so businesses can keep a better pulse on the cloud's costs. In addition, organizing your subscriptions decently will help you identify orphaned resources for potential cost savings.

- o **Configuring billing alerts and notifications:** It also ensures we are better prepared for proactive cost management in the future by setting billing alerts and notifications within the Azure Cost Management and Billing portal. You can set alerts to notify stakeholders when spending is approaching or at budget thresholds. These notifications make it possible to intervene, prevent anyone from exceeding the limits imposed, and keep cloud costs within the limits you would like to set. Ensuring that the relevant team members are periodically notified of such spending patterns and potential budget breaches is a way to control the cloud finances and take appropriate actions whenever necessary.

- **Cost optimization strategies:** It really is a balancing act between utilizing the services as much as you need without overspending; this is where cost optimization comes into play with Azure. Cost optimization in Azure consists of tools and strategies that can be employed to ensure you are using resources as you should be being used and not spending more money on the resources. Some strategies are saving through opportunities such as right-sizing resources, reserved instances and savings plans, Azure Hybrid Benefit, spot instances, and low-priority VMs for non-critical workloads.

To achieve comprehensive and efficient cloud resource management, organizations can utilize advanced monitoring and analytics tools. These tools offer valuable insights into resource performance, cost management, and system optimization, enabling businesses to make informed decisions.

The following strategies are key to enhancing cloud operations:

- o **Right-sizing Azure Resources:** Sizing Azure Resources Sizing Azure Resources is defined as aligning the allocated resources with the actual requirement of the workload. Have you over-provisioned your infrastructure to avoid the unexpected surprises from under-provisioning your systems? Right-sizing requires a more in-depth examination of resource usage to update the capacity of VMs, storage, and other services to be appropriate for the volume used. Azure Advisor and Azure Monitor can help you identify underutilized resources and suggest potential changes. Matching resource capacity to workload means businesses can greatly cut down on costs and still maintain the required levels of performance.

o **Reserved instances and savings plans:** By utilizing reserved instances and savings plans, significant discounts of around 50-75% can be achieved by committing to long-term usage. With reserved instances, companies reserve virtual machines and other resources for one or three years at a discount over pay-as-you-go rates. A Savings Plan also allows you to pay a lower rate for compute services based on a commitment usage amount over time. Such plans offer sizeable discounts, a big way to save on cloud costs. Thanks to cost savings opportunities, businesses can review historical usage patterns to decide on the right commitment level.

o **Azure Hybrid Benefit:** Azure Hybrid Benefit allows businesses to utilize their on-premises licenses for Windows Server and SQL Server in Azure, so they could save a lot! The service will extend this benefit to virtual machines and SQL Server instances, and other services will not require customers to purchase new licenses. With the Azure Hybrid Benefit, organizations can fully utilize their investments and reduce overall cloud costs. This strategy is especially favorable for businesses with large on-premises infrastructure looking to move off-prem or to hybrid.

o **Spot instances and low-priority VMs**: Spot instances and low-priority VMs provide cost-effective capacity for non-critical workloads that can withstand interruptions. Spot instances are a feature that allows businesses to purchase Azure capacity at a fraction of the price of regular instances but are subject to deletion at short notice if the capacity is required elsewhere. Azure Batch also has low-priority VMs that offer the same cost savings via surplus capacity. These are great choices for batch processing, testing, and other workloads that can afford to be interrupted. Hence, organizations can benefit by using spot instances and low-priority VMs as part of their cloud strategy to reduce costs and effectively utilize Azure resources.

- **Monitoring and reporting**: There are a few key elements that will affect your cloud cost, one of which is effective monitoring and reporting. This method will allow businesses to monitor their performance, optimize costs, manage resources, and make financial-informed decisions. Azure comes with a set of tools built to give deep visibility into your resource and cost usage, enabling you to proactively manage and optimize costs.

To effectively manage cloud resources and optimize performance, organizations can leverage a variety of monitoring and analytical tools. These tools provide deeper insights into resource utilization, enable custom reporting, and support data-driven decision-making.

Key components of this approach include:

o **Azure Monitor and Metrics:** Azure Monitor is a very powerful monitoring tool that allows you to trace the performance and costs of your resources across your Azure environment. By giving organizations greater visibility into their cloud infrastructure, it offers a more granular view of how resources are being utilized and provides good insights into the efficiency of their cloud architecture. Metric Ref: Azure Monitor collects metrics from services such as your apps' health, availability, and performance. By examining these metrics, a company can find under-resourced areas and remove any staff or apps taking up unnecessary space, cutting back on spending.

o **Log analytics and Azure Monitor Workbooks:** Log Analytics is a feature of Azure Monitor that enables you to collect and analyze log data from various sources. It helps to observe trends, diagnose problems, and get better insight into the system's behavior. Log Analytics: Enables businesses to query log data to gain useful knowledge on optimizing resource usage, which would lead to higher performance. Log Analytics is further complemented by Azure Monitor Workbooks to provide a means of visualizing the data collected through the dashboards. Interactive and Shareable — Users can use these workbooks to design interactive and shareable reports to help share insights and KPIs tracking.

o **Creating and customizing dashboards:** Custom operating Dashboards provide real-time insights into spending and performance metrics for Azure. You can customize these dashboards to show the data that each stakeholder is most interested in so that all stakeholders have the required information. Custom dashboards help an organization better understand its cloud environments by visualizing the data in an intuitive and easily accessible format. A real-time view of spending trends, resource utilization, and performance allows users to act promptly on areas that need attention or an opportunity to be optimized.

o **Reporting and data visualization:** Detail reporting is especially important when communicating Cost Insight or making decisions with data. These reporting tools in Azure allow businesses to generate reports that provide a detailed overview of spending patterns, resource utilization, and opportunities for saving costs. These reports are customizable, so they can be tuned to highlight any part of the cloud spending ecosystem, no matter if the customer wants department-level or project-specific costs. These reports can be further enhanced by using data visualization features which can help present the information on them more easily and appealingly and help the stakeholders comprehend all the complex data effortlessly. With the right kind of reporting, businesses can keep a check on their financial accountability, align the numbers on cloud spending to the business objectives, and look for cost reduction and optimization opportunities.

• **Cost allocation and chargebacks:** Proper cost allocation and a flexible and efficient chargeback model are key to maintaining financial accountability within an organization. It conducts cost attribution processes, cost management automation, and responsible resource consumption.

Effective management of cloud resources in Azure requires the implementation of resource group tagging and cost allocation practices. These practices are essential for ensuring financial accountability and visibility within an organization.

o **Resource group tagging and cost allocation:** Azure Resource group tagging is the process of assigning tags to Azure resources; tags are key-value pairs for organizing and categorizing resources. It allows businesses to categorize resources based on projects, departments, or cost centers to allocate costs to the appropriate area. It ensures every team, or every department is responsible for their cloud spending, and then it helps to track the cost, where the cost is coming from, and how the resource is being utilized. You can map these tags to individual projects — giving cost visibility into those greatest areas of spend — and you may already be using these tags to help you refine alerts and directives.

o **Azure Cost Management APIs and Automation**: To automate cost-related tasks, Azure provides APIs for cost management. These APIs deliver accurate cost management standardization to reduce the need to manually manage costs while providing less potential for human mistakes through automation. These APIs automatically retrieve cost data, create reports, and enforce cost policies. You can create automated scripts that check for under-utilization and scale those resources down or shut them off seemingly automatically without constant user intervention.

o **Implementing show-back and chargeback models**: With this help, we distribute the cloud costs back to the departments or teams that used the resources using show-back and chargeback models. With show-back model, the responsible departments for the costs are informed about the costs they have caused but are not charged anything; the show-back is ideal for them to understand the use and agree that the cost will be charged. On the other hand, a chargeback model charges the departments or teams for cloud usage, bringing financial discipline on their part. Employing these models is good as it provokes teams to spend judiciously and makes them responsible.

o **Role-Based Access Control for Cost Management:** It guarantees the right people are using the right cost management tools and data. RBAC allows you to assign roles and permissions that reflect the user's role, helping your secure access to sensitive financial details and control who can perform specific cost-related actions in the account. Financial managers may, for example, be able to handle costs and manage budgets, while project managers only have access to the costs related to their projects. This controlled access reduces the potential threat of unauthorized access to cost control processes and ensures confidential information is available only to the correct people.

• **Governance and compliance:** In addition, governance and compliance are key to effective cost management and ensuring that all your practices comply with organizational and regulatory requirements. Azure provides policy enforcement tools integrating cost management, security data protection, and compliance based on regulations.

To ensure comprehensive cloud management and cost optimization, organizations must consider a range of policies, tools, and practices that not only reduce costs but also maintain compliance with industry standards and safeguard security.

Key strategies include:

o **Azure Policy and Cost Management:** Azure Policy is a service that allows organizations to create, assign, and manage policies to enforce different rules and effects over their resources — Case insensitive; used to ignore cases. Consider, for instance, the version control analogy; in version control, you typically want to mention whether it should be case-sensitive explicitly; Game over. By defining policies, businesses can ensure that each cloud usage adheres to their cost management practices and organization standards. For example, policies might include not creating spendy resource types in non-prod environments, or all resources should be tagged for cost tracking. Organizations can enforce these rules automatically using Azure Policy, which helps in managing costs and maintaining compliance with standards.

o **Azure Cost Management and Azure Security Center: -** Azure Security Center integration helps ensure cost optimization efforts do not introduce security risks and vice versa, as mentioned in a related Azure blog post. Azure Security Center is the solution to help us monitor and improve our cloud resources' security. By using these different tools together, businesses can make smart cost-saving decisions without compromising the security of their data and applications. For example, you can prevent reducing resources or modifying configurations for cost savings from opening security vulnerabilities within your environment.

o **Compliance and regulatory considerations:** Cost management best practices must also comply with regulatory standards to avoid penalties and legal troubles and maintain trust with customers and stakeholders. It is because different industries have different standards and practices that ensure that data is handled (and protected) appropriately. These rules are in place to ensure that businesses will not have to pay fines and suffer penalties. Azure also offers several tools and services to ensure that top standards of transparency and accountability are followed in compliance with SB 327. These include auditing features and compliance certifications. For example, Azure provides a plethora of industry-specific certifications, such as GDPR and HIPAA, to simplify business compliance.

o **Data protection and privacy:** Balancing controlling cloud costs while unlocking data protection and privacy is tricky. The safeguard of sensitive data is the darkest of them all, but they have to because It is all about information security and compliance with certain govt. Data protection in Azure includes encryption and access controls to secure your data. These capabilities guarantee that your data remains secure even as you are cost-optimizing. For example, if we secure data at rest and in transit using encryptions, data is not in readable format even if someone hacks and gets unauthorized access to stored data and stores it in their local machine.

- **Advanced Azure FinOps techniques**: This allows organizations to control and optimize their Azure cloud costs more efficiently by taking advantage of automation, **Infrastructure as Code (IaC)**, and integration with DevOps practices described previously in Advanced FinOps techniques. We use these methods to embed cost management in the heart of cloud operations, providing powerful financial governance at an optimal level of resource utilization.

In the pursuit of cloud cost efficiency, leveraging IaC and serverless computing can lead to significant savings while maintaining operational effectiveness. By automating resource management and optimizing workloads, organizations can reduce unnecessary expenses and improve the overall utilization of cloud resources.

Key strategies include:

- ○ **IaC for cost efficiency:** IaC route service provider streamlines and ensures that resources are deployed automatically and consistently to avoid misconfigurations that may result in additional charges. IaC allows organizations to build resource deployment templates that subscribe to best practices, thus saving the cost of going back and forth tuning the resources to them after deployment. For example, you can automate the provisioning of resources using IaC tools, such as ARM templates and Terraform, to provide cost-saving settings like selecting the right size for VMs or setting up auto-scaling policies. The result is a smoother systematic process that avoids over-provisioning and underutilizing the cloud so that overall cloud resources are better used.

- ○ **Azure Functions and Automation:** Azure Functions is an event-driven serverless compute- (functions-) solution that enables you to execute (code in response to an event that triggers the running of the code) without having to manage or provide any underlying regular self-hosted deadline infrastructure. Not only does Azure Functions cost significantly less than a set of VM instances and queues you would have otherwise needed, but you also only pay for what you use, so if your usage changes, the price does, too. With Azure Functions, organizations can automate all repetitive tasks like scaling resources, monitoring costs, remediation actions, etc. For instance, you can create a function that shuts down idle VMs at night or cleans up orphaned resources that are no longer required. These levels of automation allow for resources to be consumed only when necessary, helping to limit waste and the overall cost of the cloud.

- ○ **Serverless cost optimization:** Serverless computing provides a flexible way to build and deploy workloads without the need to manage infrastructure. Since you pay only for what you consume, it can be much more cost-effective than traditional hosting. Optimizing serverless workloads for cost-effectiveness involves monitoring usage and readjusting configurations as needed. On memory allocation and execution time of Azure Functions — similarly reducing costs by tuning(debugging), basically! Azure Logic Apps and Event Grid can create scalable, cost-effective, serverless workflows. Organizations can improve the overall value of their cloud spend by continuously optimizing serverless workloads.

o **Azure DevOps and FinOps integration**: Ensuring that cost management is ingrained with the development and deployment processes by integrating the DevOps practices with Finance. An environment in which development and finance can work together to optimize costs. Azure DevOps also offers a CI/CD suite of tools that can be combined with cost management checks at each stage of the deployment pipeline. For example, it is possible to let automated tests be set up to verify if the deployed resources meet cost-efficient standards, and alerts will fire if the costs exceed a certain predefined threshold. These principles allow organizations to control better what they spend in the cloud and start ensuring they treat cloud spending as a development concern by integrating the cost into their DevOps workflows.

• **Azure FinOps Best Practices**: Using the Azure FinOps best practices ensures that financial accountability is part of operations at every cloud level and that organizations can manage their cloud costs effectively. The main advantages of using cost optimization frameworks are creating a cost management culture, establishing collaboration and communication, continuous improvement, and iterative optimization.

Effective cloud cost management involves the implementation of structured frameworks, cultural shifts within the organization, and continuous collaboration. By focusing on these areas, organizations can optimize their cloud spending, encourage financial accountability, and drive ongoing improvements in cost efficiency.

Key approaches include:

o **Cost optimization frameworks**: Cost optimization frameworks offer a systematic way to locate and incorporate potential cost savings. These would be frameworks that provide guidance on evaluating, improving, and managing cloud spending with a series of steps. One such set of cost optimization principles is provided by the Azure Well-Architected Framework, which businesses can use to evaluate their current cloud environment to determine where they can improve and cut down costs. Organizations can methodically analyze cost optimization through a common framework to compile the larger scope of potential savings and act on them.

o **Building a FinOps culture**: Inculcating a FinOps culture in the organization is essential to sorting out cost management and laying the groundwork for financial accountability. These actions make up the notion of a FinOps culture, teaching teams how to think and talk about cost efficiency and empowering teams to make financially responsible decisions. One way to do this is to bake cost management principles into training programs by providing explicit goals around costs and recognizing/rewarding teams for their efforts to save costs. Shared cost management across an organization encourages a more proactive way to manage cloud expenses and creates a more responsible financial culture.

o **Collaboration and communication**: Good cost management requires good inter-team collaboration and communication. FinOps practices ensure that cost is an element of every part of the cloud operational lifecycle, requiring silhouette cooperation between the finance, operations, and development teams. This cross-team alignment is achieved through regular meetings, common dashboards, and joint planning sessions to keep everyone aware of what is being spent, what could be saved, and what changes are coming. When lines of communication are open, and teams collaborate, they can easily identify potential cost savings successfully, address concerns quickly, and optimize cost more effectively.

o **Continuous improvement and iterative optimization**: Cost management should be an ongoing and perfect process. The approaches to keeping costs under check also evolve as cloud usage and business requirements grow. All organizations must review their cost management practices regularly, understand what has worked and what else needs to be done, and always be prepared to change their approach as new learnings emerge and requirements evolve. Azure Cost Management and Azure Advisor are excellent tools in this regard, as they provide data and recommendations that can be used during continuous improvement. Businesses that are willing to commit to a continuous journey of monitoring, analyzing, and optimizing their costs will be able to make sure their cloud spending is as effective as possible and is perfectly aligned with their financial targets.

• **Case studies and real-world examples**: The following examples are borrowed from real-world usage and highlight how businesses have embarked upon Azure FinOps practices, benefiting from significant cost optimization, improved financial accountability, and team collaboration.

To illustrate the effectiveness of cloud cost optimization strategies, several case studies provide valuable insights into how different organizations have successfully managed their cloud expenditures while maintaining or enhancing performance. These case studies showcase practical applications of cost-saving measures, cost allocation, and collaborative approaches in cloud environments.

Key case studies include:

o **Case study 1: Cost optimization for a web application-** We discussed a case study of a medium-sized e-commerce company that had to save on their cloud costs for their high-traffic web app without compromising the high performance. The company implemented various cost optimization initiatives, such as right-sizing resources and using Azure Advisor to monitor VM utilization patterns and resize them accordingly. They used auto-scaling policies to scale resources up and down based on traffic demands and thus paid for only what they used. They also used one-year reserved instances for the VMs they knew they would always need the same size, delivering a 20-30% discount off pay-as-you-go pricing. In addition, using Azure Functions to move pieces of your application closer to serverless costs only the actual execution of functions. This led to a 30% monthly cost reduction with high performance and availability for their web application.

o **Case study 2: Cost allocation and chargeback in a large enterprise:** Cost Control at Scale for a Major Cloud-first Enterprise — As described in the customer business challenge study, a large enterprise with diverse departments and business units encountered challenges in controlling and managing cloud costs. They addressed this with a holistic cost allocation and chargeback model to drive better financial accountability. This involved standardizing their tagging practices across all departments and assigning tags for project names, cost centers, and department IDs to every resource. With Azure Cost Management and Billing, they create a budget for each department and are eligible for real-time dashboards for pricing strategies. Finance implemented a chargeback model so each department was charged for their real usage defects in the cloud as monthly bills (with itemized costs for computing, storage, networking, and so on.) based on tagging the resources that the respective data center resources would be migrated to. These automated monthly reports delivered an elaborate cost breakdown by department and the spending patterns that surfaced as potential areas ripe for some savings. As a result, this method encouraged more cost-effective behavior across departments, which led to a 20% cut in cloud spending overall as the departments themselves were responsible for using only what they consumed and started looking for ways to reduce costs.

o **Case study 3: DevOps and FinOps collaboration-** This case study showed a tech company combined DevOps and FinOps practices to gain better control over costs. The dev and finance teams worked together to operationalize cost controls in CI/CD pipelines. They put in place cost checks at every stage of the deployment process using Azure DevOps to automate and validate that resources could be provisioned in an effective and cost-efficient manner. Automated alerts to warn teams costs had gone over predefined thresholds, and for them to take immediate corrective actions. It built an ethos of financial responsibility and cost-control for developers, which meant cheaper code — cheaper dev and cheaper deployers. After combining DevOps with FinOps, the cloud expense was reduced considerably, and the cloud expenditure was additionally part of the work process, and it was more streamlined, which shows that cross-functional collaboration is one of the main factors for contemplating costing in a Cloud.

- **Future Trends and Innovations in Azure FinOps**: cloud adoption has forced cost management practices to rise to the occasion and evolve with new concepts and possibilities. As an emerging discipline, future Azure FinOps trends and innovations are only expected to further how businesses can manage and financially optimize their cloud consumption to be efficient, scalable, and financially accountable.

To effectively manage and optimize cloud resources, organizations can implement a variety of strategic measures. These measures not only help in reducing costs but also in enhancing operational efficiency.

The key strategies include:

- o **Cloud cost management evolution**: As cloud environments grow and become complex, the landscape of cloud cost management continues to change and evolve. Multi-cloud movements combined with a broader set of services deployed by the organization make traditional cost management strategies outdated. Cloud cost management has evolved significantly in recent years to use advanced analytics, machine learning, and automation to help organizations analyze spending trends and anticipate future costs. Today, we see AI-powered platforms helping businesses detect inefficiencies, forecast budget requirements, and automate the process of savings. To ensure that expenses are kept in check and to maximize your investment into the cloud-specific capabilities and advantages these advanced strategies will become essential due to increased dynamism in cloud environments.

- o **Azure well-architected framework and FinOps**: Bringing FinOps into the mix with the Azure Well-Architected is a big step in connecting cost management practices more closely to the governance practices that engender the best architecture. The Well-Architected Framework is a set of best practices that provide guidance on how companies should build and operate secure, high-performing, resilient, and efficient infrastructure for their applications in the cloud. Incorporating FinOps within this framework helps organizations build architectural decisions with financial accountability weaved inside them. This opens the door for businesses to evaluate their cloud resources in a structured way that allows for reducing and optimizing costs without compromising performance, security, or operational excellence. This 360-degree view can also help organizations balance the trade-off between saving money and implementing architectural best practices for better cloud operations over time.

- o **Azure Cost Optimization for AI and ML workloads**: Cost optimization for AI and ML workloads is challenging, both because of the high computational requirements of these workloads and because usage patterns can be sporadic and unpredictable. There exist concrete strategies to handle AI/ML expenses correctly. For these types of solutions, the evolution has also involved introducing tailored tools and services that offer fine-grain visibility into AI/ML resource consumption and costing. An example of this would be the cost management features you get with Azure Machine Learning that help track and control the spending on training and inference tasks. The question of tackling AI/ML costs can, of course, be limited by choice of cloud and region (which also changes over time). Still, more skilled management practices provide right-sizing compute resources, using spot instances for non-critical workloads, optimizing storage for large datasets, etc. Moreover, companies are leveraging modern scheduling and orchestration tools to efficiently plan and spread AI/ML workloads over time and space for resource-efficient and cost-effective utilization.

Final thoughts and next steps

In this section, we will go through the final thoughts and next steps:

- **Final thoughts**:
  - ○ FinOps in Azure is more than a way to reduce costs; it is about bringing those who spend and deliver products together into a unified culture of financial management and understanding the impact of decisions. Cloud management integrated with financial operations helps organizations gain insight into cloud expenditure and make well-informed decisions aligned with organizational goals. A holistic approach from Azure to manage cloud costs Cloud cost management evolution Getting Azure Well-Architected Framework support. The specific strategies to optimize for an AI and machine learning workload,
  - ○ Learning and adaption are key to Implementing Azure FinOps Practices. As cloud solutions, business processes, and demands evolve, the strategies and tools for cost control need to adapt. In cloud computing, industry leaders have embraced automation, leveraged advanced analytics, and worked across functions to stay ahead despite an ever-changing landscape.

- **Next steps**:

  Here are the steps you need to take to implement Azure FinOps within your organization effectively:

  1. **Snapshot of existing cloud expenditure:**
     a. Audit your current use and spending on cloud services.
     b. Find inefficiencies and opportunities for cost savings.
  2. **Adopt cost optimization frameworks**:
     a. Use structured frameworks like Well-Architected Framework to help when optimizing costs.
     b. The key is to keep on revisiting and updating your strategies to reflect the norms.

3. **Build a FinOps culture**:

    a. Train your employees in the significance of financial responsibility and cost control.

    b. Cultivate a low-overhead decision-making ethic throughout the org.

4. **Leverage Azure tools and services**:

    a. Utilize Azure Cost Management and Billing tools to gain insights into your cloud spending.

    b. Implement resource tagging, budget alerts, and automated cost management processes to streamline your efforts.

5. **Integrate FinOps with DevOps and security practices**:

    a. Ensure that cost management is embedded into your development and deployment workflows.

    b. Integrate cost considerations with security practices to balance cost efficiency and security.

6. **Focus on continuous improvement**:

    a. Regularly monitor and analyze your cloud spending.

    b. Iterate your cost management strategies based on new insights and changing business needs.

7. **Stay informed about future trends and innovations**:

    a. Keep up to date with the latest developments in Azure FinOps and cloud cost management.

    b. Be open to adopting new tools and practices to enhance your cost management capabilities.

This is how it helps drive better financial efficiency and smarter value from cloud investments and helps organizations implement Azure FinOps properly. FinOps adoption is a process that includes evolution, innovation, and collaboration but also helps in more reliable cloud operation analysis at reduced costs.

Join our book's Discord space

Join the book's Discord Workspace for Latest updates, Offers, Tech happenings around the world, New Release and Sessions with the Authors:

https://discord.bpbonline.com

Index

Made in the USA
Middletown, DE
20 February 2025